Goa &
Mumbai

Amelia Thomas
Amy Karafin

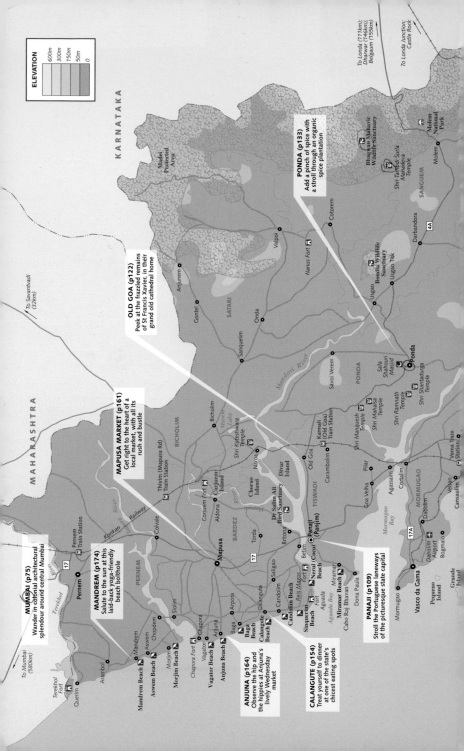

ELEVATION
- 600m
- 300m
- 150m
- 50m
- 0

MAHARASHTRA

KARNATAKA

MUMBAI (p75)
Wander in colonial architectural splendour around central Mumbai

MANDREM (p174)
Salute to the sun at this laid-back yoga-friendly beach bolthole

MAPUSA MARKET (p161)
Get right to the heart of a local market, with all its rush and bustle

OLD GOA (p122)
Peek at the frazzled remains of St Francis Xavier, in their grand old cathedral home

PONDA (p133)
Add a pinch of spice with a stroll through an organic spice plantation

ANJUNA (p164)
Observe the hip and the hippies at Anjuna's lively Wednesday market

CALANGUTE (p154)
Treat yourself to dinner at one of the state's chicest eating spots

PANAJI (p109)
Stroll the Portuguese laneways of the picturesque state capital

To Mumbai (580km)
To Savantvadi (32km)
To Londa (111km); Dharvar (146km); Belgaum (155km)
To Londa Junction; Castle Rock

Terekhol Fort
Querim
Arambol
Mandrem Beach
Aswem Beach
Morjim Beach
Vagator Beach
Anjuna Beach
Baga Beach
Calangute Beach
Candolim Beach
Singuerim Beach
Aguada Bay
Miramar Beach
Cabo Raj Bhavan
Dona Paula

Pernem
Chopdem
Morjim
Siolim
Vagator
Chapora Fort
Anjuna
Arpora
Baga
Saligao
Candolim
Reis Magos
Fort Aguada
Nerul (Coco) Beach
Betim
Panaji (Panjim)
Miramar

Pernem Train Station
Thivim (Mapusa Rd) Train Station
Mapusa
Torda
Britona
Aldona
Corjuem Fort
Corjuem Island
Moira
Chorao Island
Divar Island
Dr Salim Ali Bird Sanctuary

Terekhol River
Chapora River
Konkan Railway
Mandovi River

BARDEZ
PERNEM
BICHOLIM
SATARI
TISWADI
PONDA
SANGUEM
MORMUGAO

Colvale
Naroa
Bicholim
Shri Kafeshwara Temple
Moram Lake
Shri Mahalsa Temple
Shri Manguesh Temple
Karmali (Old Goa) Train Station
Old Goa
Carambolim
Pilar
Goa Velha
Agassaim
Cortalim
Verna Train Station
Velsao
Cansaulim

Sanquelim
Onda
Valpoi
Nanus Fort
Anjunem
Gontel
Cotorem
Savoi Verem
Safa Shahouri Masjid
Ponda
Shri Shantadurga Temple
Shri Ramnath Temple
Madei Protected Area
Bondla Wildlife Sanctuary
Ugao
Ugao Trik
Usgao
Darbandora
Shri Tambdi Surla Mahadeva Temple
Bhagwan Mahavir Wildlife Sanctuary
Molem
Molem National Park

Mormugao
Vasco da Gama
Dabolim Airport
Bogmalo
Pequeno Island
Grande Island

17
17A
4A

Mormugao Bay

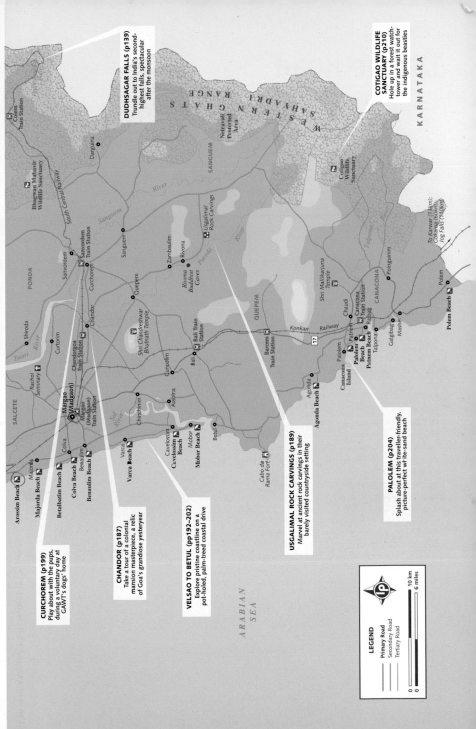

CURCHOREM (p199)
Play about with the pups, during a voluntary day at GAWT's dogs' home

CHANDOR (p187)
Take a tour of a colonial mansion masterpiece, a relic of Goa's grandiose yesteryear

VELSAO TO BETUL (pp192–202)
Explore pristine coastline on a pot-holed, palm-treed coastal drive

DUDHSAGAR FALLS (p139)
Trundle out to India's second-highest falls, spectacular after the monsoon

COTIGAO WILDLIFE SANCTUARY (p210)
Hole up in a forest watch-tower and wait it out for the indigenous beasties

USGALIMAL ROCK CARVINGS (p189)
Marvel at ancient rock carvings in their barely visited countryside setting

PALOLEM (p204)
Splash about at this traveller-friendly, picture-perfect white-sand beach

WESTERN GHATS SAHYADRI RANGE

KARNATAKA

ARABIAN SEA

LEGEND
Primary Road
Secondary Road
Tertiary Road

0 ___ 10 km
0 ___ 6 miles

On the Road

AMELIA THOMAS Coordinating Author

We're at Polem Beach (p187), the southernmost stretch of sand in the state, and it's almost lunch-time. Our four small children are having fun in their little local kindergarten further north; sea birds wheel overhead, occasionally plummeting in pursuit of an unfortunate fish. All's quiet. There's not another soul about. A thali beckons. A faint breeze blows. Just another perfect Goan day.

AMY KARAFIN My partner and I took his bike to Sanjay Gandhi National Park (p106), stopping here, at Aarey Milk Colony, on the way. Aarey is this huge spread of nature right in the city, with tons of palm trees and – true to Mumbai form – a Ferris wheel and couples hiding in bushes. We kept tripping over them while looking for (equally well-hidden) birds.

Traveller Highlights

Every traveller has their own impression of Goa: idyllic beaches, languid palm trees, Portuguese colonial-era architecture, buzzing bazaars, tropical wildlife, spicy curries, and the bustle and colour of subcontinental life (but at a leisurely tropical pace). We asked Lonely Planet authors, staff and travellers to tell us about their favourite Goan sights and experiences.

ANDREW LUBRAN

1 DREAMY PALOLEM

A beautiful palm-fringed curve of sand set between rocky headlands and lined with beachfront restaurants and beach huts. Palolem (p204) strikes the perfect balance between remoteness and comforts providing you with all you need and more on a beach holiday as well as great seafood and cocktails, but without any hotels. You'll need a week plus.

Karen Burrows, Traveller, New Zealand

PAUL BEINSSEN

A GOAN HOME

Nothing beats being invited to a Goan home to bask in the hospitality of the locals. They will buy the freshest fish and vegetables and put together a meal that just goes so well together. It will leave you feeling totally *susegad* (content).

Karishma Pais, Traveller, India

3

2

PANAJI (PANJIM)

Kick back in a centuries-old Portuguese merchant's house in Panaji's historic Fontainhas district (p112), then wander the colourful back lanes before stopping in for a Goan fish curry.

Trent Paton, Lonely Planet Staff

4

WALK DOWN MARINE DRIVE IN MUMBAI

Come on, you *have to have to* do this, preferably in the evening. The lights of the city come on, the 'Queen's Necklace' lights up, the sea takes on a romantic hue and the scene will not fail to dazzle you.

Maheshwari Godse, Traveller, India

ANJUNA FLEA MARKET

Anjuna flea market (p168) is one of those fantastic travel clichés. While its existence would be under threat without the constant arrival of coachloads of package-holiday day-trippers, its charm is undeniable. Sacred cows, sadhus, snake charmers, satchels, silks and spices attack the senses and vie for your business. A must-see.

Dan Green, Lonely Planet Staff

GREG ELMS

5

TRAVEL BY TRAIN

We made the journey from Mumbai to Goa on the Konkan Railway (p240), passing some of the most beautiful scenery in India.

Gayatri Ganesh, Traveller

ANDERS BLOMQVIST

6

MICHAEL COYNE

7 MUMBAI TALENT SCOUTS

If you're a foreigner and you're wandering along the Causeway in Colaba (p81), you might be approached to be an extra in a Bollywood film. They won't pay you what they promised, you'll be dressed in hideous costumes, they won't feed you and it'll take 10 times as long as they say. But it's the best 'tell-your-grandkids' story!

Stephanie Wheeler, Traveller, Australia

GREG ELMS

8 SPICE FARMS

Take a fragrant tour of a spice farm around Ponda (p134). You may even encounter a friendly elephant.

Amelia Thomas, Lonely Planet Author

MAPUSA MARKET

Mapusa market (p162) serves up hot fritters and *bhaji-pau*. And if you're looking for locally made *chouriço* (the Goan version of a Portuguese sausage) this is the best place to pick it up. It's fresh and tasty.

Karishma Pais, Traveller, India

9

GREG ELMS

CHILLED ARAMBOL (HARMAL)

Waking up in Arambol (p175) to the sound of lapping waves and looking past your feet to see the length of the beach, the ocean calling you – is priceless. Walk north to the next bay for a sandier and even more beautiful beach, shared with only one or two others. And chill…

Karen Burrows, Traveller, New Zealand

10

MICHAEL TAYLOR

ANDREW LUBRAN

11 BEACH CYCLING

The best way to spend a few hours in South Goa is, when the tide is out, to rent a bike in Colva (p194) and cycle south along the beach to the estuary by the Leela hotel. A long stretch of this beautiful beach is completely unspoilt with not a beach bar in sight.

Chantal Havard, Lonely Planet Staff

NOBORU KOMINE

12 OLD GOA

As you approach Old Goa (p122), glimpses of bell towers and churches appear through the trees. Once you're there you'll find the extraordinary remains of a city that once rivalled Lisbon in terms of wealth and power, awaiting your exploration.

Clifton Wilkinson, Lonely Planet Staff

LIFE ON THE BACKROADS

Snaking into the lush Goan countryside, the dusty roads out of Anjuna take in a vista of daily Indian life a world away from the backpacker throng so quickly left behind: dilapidated dwellings; kids playing cricket in sun-bleached fields; sari-clad women walking barefoot with baskets on their heads; and ancient wizened banyan trees.

Trish Pinto, Traveller, Australia

GREG ELMS

NEIL SETCHFIELD

14 SLEEP IS OVERRATED

The entire town of Anjuna (p164) buzzes with an unmistakeably psychedelic energy. Beautiful, aloof, bohemian types glide around town during the day, then gather on beaches and hilltops for 12 hours plus of dancing to trance pumped out by world-renowned DJs. If you get the chance to attend a full-moon party you won't be disappointed.

Rachel Hunter, Traveller, USA

PETER PTSCHELINZEW

15 HEADING NORTH FROM ANJUNA

We hired motorbikes in Anjuna and headed north along the coast, stopping at Chapora Fort (p170) for its expansive coastal views before zooming past the local fishermen in Siolim (p173). Last stop was Mandrem Beach (p174), where a beer and a fish curry gave us the courage to get back on the bikes and head south.

Jessica Crouch, Lonely Planet Staff

LIQUID LIGHT/ALAMY

16 TAXI RIDE FROM CHAPORA TO ARAMBOL

A beautiful journey from Vagator and Chapora (p168) through the back roads of Goa to Arambol (p175). Perhaps the most memorable thing about the journey was listening to the driver's repeated playing of the Hindi version of the macarena.

Tom Arr-Jones, Traveller

Contents

On the Road	4

Goa & Mumbai Highlights	5

Destination Goa	15

Getting Started	17

Events Calendar	22

Itineraries	25

History	29

The Culture	42

Food & Drink	52

Environment	62

Activities	70

Mumbai (Bombay)	75
History	76
Orientation	77
Information	77
Sights	81
Activities	88
Walking Tour	89
Courses	90
Mumbai for Children	91
Tours	91
Sleeping	92
Eating	96
Drinking	99
Entertainment	100
Shopping	101
Getting There & Away	103
Getting Around	104
GREATER MUMBAI	**106**
Elephanta Island	106
Sanjay Gandhi National Park	106

Central Goa	107
Panaji	109
West of Panaji	120
Panaji to Old Goa	122
Old Goa	122
Divar Island	130
Goa Velha	131
Talaulim	132
Pilar	132
Ponda	133
Around Ponda	134
Bondla Wildlife Sanctuary	137
Molem & Around	138
Tambdi Surla	139

North Goa	141
Along the Mandovi River	143
Candolim, Sinquerim & Fort Aguada	147
Calangute & Baga	154
Mapusa	161
Anjuna	164
Vagator & Chapora	168
Siolim	173
Morjim	174
Aswem	174
Mandrem	174
Arambol (Harmal)	175
North of Arambol	178

South Goa	179
Margao	181
Around Margao	184
Vasco da Gama	189
Around Vasco da Gama	190
Bogmalo to Betalbatim	190
Colva	194
Benaulim	197
Varca, Cavelossim & Mobor	198
Assolna to Agonda	201
Chaudi	204
Palolem	204
South of Palolem	208
Cotigao Wildlife Sanctuary	210
Galgibag	210
Polem	211

specifically for the spiritual: yoga, ayurveda and reiki, along with shiatsu, t'ai chi and every other imaginable alternative therapy, are on offer here in constantly changing permutations. And still, this isn't all. Travellers, both luxury or shoestring, are drawn to Goa's beach huts or boutique hotels, depending on their state of mind and bank balance, while wildlife-lovers flock here in search of creatures of the marine, mountainous, furry, flying and feathered kind. Those more interested in the anthropological than the ornithological are intrigued by Goa's riot of religions (luckily, rarely literally) and their attendant festivals that often cross religious boundaries to be celebrated with aplomb by all.

But that's not to say that, despite its myriad charms, Goa's a perfect paradise. A sorely stressed environment is one of its major troubles, along with poverty, prostitution, a shady drugs trade, violent crime and police corruption. Goa's environment has been heavily burdened by an onslaught of tourism over the last 40 years, but equally by the effects of industry, logging, iron-ore mining, uncontrolled industrial growth and some destructive local customs. Rare turtle eggs have traditionally been considered a delicacy; plastic bottles lie in vast glaciers as unreceding as the real kind are the reverse; and vagrant cows feast on refuse from unfragrant rubbish bins. Meanwhile, animal shelters overflow with unwanted domestic creatures and children's homes struggle to provide shelter, safety and education for the state's shockingly large population of at-risk and orphaned children. A number of charities – both locally run and foreigner-helmed – address some of these issues, though, as they'll attest, their level best is seldom enough.

Despite its manifold problems, whether you choose to ply the state squeezed sardine-like into a faithful chugging bus or opt to buzz its byways by scooter or on a roaring Royal Enfield motorbike, the more you explore, the more you'll love this little haven amid the maelstrom that is India. Wander its riotous markets, experience a blazingly colourful Muslim, Hindu or Catholic festival, then lie back and relax with a sunset cocktail or an ayurvedic massage on its glorious beaches, where coconut palms murmur gently overhead and crabs scuttle silently in the shallows. However you choose to travel – and whether you're here to find yourself, find a quiet stretch of sand, or find an arboreal puff-throated babbler – Goa will likely leave you as hooked as one of the evening's sumptuous seafood specials.

Getting Started

The breadth of foreign visitors to Goa, from two-week package tourists to long-term travellers and young families with toddlers in tow, is a testament to its many and varied charms, and to the sheer ease of travelling here compared to some other Indian states. The state's diminutive size makes it easy to navigate, either by bus, taxi, motorbike or hire car, allowing you to hop easily from place to place, or pick your perfect base and head out on day trips to explore the rest.

Travel in Goa is generally more expensive than the rest of the country, but its vast range of facilities – from the most basic of beach shacks to five-stars exuding opulence – means that you can travel hassle-free here on any budget, although over Christmas and New Year the crowds descend and prices tend to skyrocket accordingly.

As with any holiday destination, there are health and safety elements to be considered and the sea should be treated with particular respect (drownings are sorrowfully commonplace each season), but the laid-back attitude of locals, along with the sunny charms of the state itself, mean that Goa couldn't be an easier place to visit.

WHEN TO GO

The best, and most popular, time to visit Goa is during the cooler months of November to March, when the weather is wonderful, rain is a distant memory, and the seas are calm and clear. Arriving in October, at the very start of the tourist season, you'll find beaches luxuriously empty, but many facilities, such as shops, restaurants, beach shacks and beach-hut operations, aren't yet up and running. As March stretches into April and May, the weather grows hot and humid, and swimming becomes trickier due to rougher seas. Beaches slowly empty of tourists but, much like October, this means that facilities aren't as extensive, businesses slowly shutting up shop to await the return of tourists the following November.

See Climate Charts (p226) for more information.

Many Goans, however, feel that the monsoon, which douses Goa between June and the end of September, is when the state is at its very best. Parties and celebrations are held to welcome the rains, and the countryside turns lush and green almost overnight. Swimming in the sea generally is off-limits during monsoon, since tides are strong, and most tourist facilities are closed, meaning that if you visit at this time you'll have the place to yourself for bargain-basement prices.

Without doubt the peak season for visitors to Goa is over the short Christmas and New Year period, when prices are hiked phenomenally and many places are booked solid a year in advance. Yet this is a great time to be

---

DON'T LEAVE HOME WITHOUT...

- A few extra luggage items for a local charity
- A reliable padlock, for securing belongings while staying in palm-thatched beach huts
- A torch to navigate poorly lit streets and negotiate frequent power cuts
- Your driving licence (and copies) for hiring a scooter, motorbike or car
- Your bank card for withdrawing cash: Goa's now well equipped with ATMs statewide
- Something long-sleeved to throw on when visiting churches, temples and mosques

in Goa: the weather is glorious, the atmosphere is suitably festive, the tinsel is liberally festooned, and fireworks grace the evening sky. Though Goa's frenetic party scene of years gone by has now slowed to a trickle, this is when all the best parties are held, and music festivals grace the northern coast's clubs and beaches. Don't expect peace and quiet, but for gleeful Christmas spirit under the tropical sun it surely can't be beaten.

COSTS & MONEY

Something likely to strike you repeatedly as strange while you're in Goa is the wildly varying differences in prices. A fill-you-up thali meal at a local lunch joint, for example, might cost Rs50, while dinner at a cool Calangute restaurant can easily set you back Rs5000. A night's stay in a simple Arambol beach hut might go for Rs150, while a five-star suite further down the coast will cost Rs150,000. The price of a coffee at a frothy countrywide chain will be more than many Goans make in a whole working week.

If you're travelling on a budget it's possible to survive on Rs400 (US$10) per day, getting about by local bus, staying in rock-bottom beach huts and eating exclusively in local-orientated restaurants. Outside the November to March high season, accommodation costs are substantially reduced but, on the other hand, many of the budget beach huts have been carefully packed away for the monsoon. At the other end of the scale, staying at boutique hotels or five-star resorts, eating at top-end options, buying cool local handicrafts, enjoying a few daily sunset cocktails and day-tripping by taxi can easily see you spending US$250 a day or more.

It's equally easy to steer a comfortable middle course. Opting for simple yet atmospheric accommodation, dining at a combination of beach shacks and local lunch joints, hiring a scooter to get about and allowing for a bit of nightlife, you should be able to get by on around US$25 per day. Top that up with an occasional bit of fine dining, a yoga class several times per week, a massage now and then and a night or two of luxury in a cool Goan getaway, and US$50 per day will do the trick nicely.

TRAVELLING RESPONSIBLY

Responsible travel in Goa takes into account two key factors: first, the state's sorely taxed environment, and second, cultural sensitivity toward the local population. Consideration of both can help to minimise your impact while holidaying here, and help make a positive difference to some of Goa's biggest problems.

In the last two decades, tourism has overtaken mining as Goa's most significant industry, and the annual influx of holidaymakers now outnumbers the state's entire permanent population. Strains on the environment seem inevitable with so many people passing through a small and delicate area, a problem compounded by a local government keen to encourage midrange and top-end travel, rather than the more ecoconscious hippies of yesteryear.

Five-star hotels, with lush, landscaped grounds, put increasing pressure on the water resources available for locals, and at some times of the year villagers survive with just a trickle of water while tourists frolic nearby in the pool. Massive amounts of refuse are generated by tourists (think how many mineral-water bottles a single visitor gets through in a fortnight), and there are few facilities for recycling or responsible disposal of waste. Moreover, irresponsible hotel construction has blighted once beautiful beaches – head to Bogmalo (p191) if you need proof – and high-paying hotel kitchens push the price of simple market ingredients such as rice, eggs and vegetables to ever-increasing heights. Thus, while budget travellers have traditionally posed

HOW MUCH?

Bhaji-pau breakfast Rs8

Lunchtime thali Rs50

One-hour bus ride Rs8

Professional shave Rs50

Happy hour cocktail Rs100

See also Lonely Planet Index, inside front cover

TOP TIPS FOR RESPONSIBLE TRAVEL

- Support those who support the environment – choose accommodation that implements an ecofriendly approach to waste management.

- Spread the wealth: eat at local restaurants as well as tourist-orientated get ups, and don't stick solely to this guidebook's recommendations.

- Consider buying souvenirs from cooperatives or charity concerns.

- Read up on local charities (p73) and try to help out in any way you can, however small – even if only by saving your old holiday newspapers for the cages of the local dog shelter.

- Refill water bottles with filtered water (some restaurants and hotels offer this for free) or buy the larger-sized 5L and 20L Bisleri bottles, which come with a refundable deposit.

- Use bath and shower water sparingly – water shortages for local villagers usually occur at the end of the tourist season.

- If you're travelling with tinies, opt for reusable nappies over disposable ones – local laundry costs are negligible and will return your terry-towels fresh and fragrant.

- Be culturally sensitive away from the beaches: cover the bikini and hide the Speedos while shopping in the centre of town.

- Think carefully about your attitude to beggars and beach hawkers, and remember that, even if they're annoying, there's a reason they're plying the beaches for very little cash.

social challenges to local Goans through nudity, partying and drug use, it's undeniable that bamboo and palm-thatch beach huts can be dismantled at the end of a season, and that local restaurants have frequently benefited from shoestring travellers' custom.

Culturally, too, Goa faces challenges as a result of tourism. Many impoverished Indians arrive in the state hoping to make money from tourists by begging, which in turn begs the crucial question: 'to give or not to give?' The hardline school says 'don't', arguing that it's impossible to know whether the money you give will be used in a positive way, and that begging often supports an evil, pimp-controlled industry whose victims are the beggars themselves. More moderate members of this camp argue that money is better given to charitable organisations; cynics might counter that this proclamation is all very well, but question how many people actually end up doing so. In contrast are those who simply take each individual situation at face value, and acknowledge that sometimes a beggar is simply a person in genuine need of help. Local Indians (even those who are obviously not wealthy) also often give something, and there's always the option of offering food if you're uncomfortable giving money. Ultimately the choice is a personal one, but either way it's not a decision to be taken lightly.

Finally, in terms of responsible cultural travel, comes the question of dress. Though Goans are used to seeing tourists in skimpy swimwear along the beach, it's still considered highly culturally insensitive for women to swim or sunbathe topless, or for anyone to sunbathe nude. Away from the beach, it's good manners to cover the shoulders and upper legs; refraining from heading into town in your bikini top and shorts is simply a polite way of respecting locals' own propensity for modesty, and will be quietly appreciated.

On visits to churches, shrines, temples and mosques, it's likewise appropriate to cover up, and it is customary to take off your shoes before entering a Hindu temple or a local home. Don't shout or smoke at

Mapusa's Other India Bookstore (p162) is a great place to look for books on all things green and responsible in Goa. Titles are also available online at www.other indiabookstore.com.

religious sites; never touch a carving or statue of a temple deity, and Hindu etiquette advises against touching anyone on the head, or directing the soles of your feet at a person or religious image.

TRAVEL LITERATURE

There's surprisingly little travel literature available about Goa, considering its perennial popularity as a destination. Titles that are widely available are truly tried and tested traveller favourites, though no less worth picking up for that.

TOP PICKS

BEST HIDDEN BEACHES

Believe it or not, you can still fulfil those castaway longings on Goa's golden sands, though with the advantage that you'll never be *too* far from a nice, icy drink.

- **Agonda** (p202) Brisk surf, nesting turtles, broad sands and serenity: a nature-lover's dream.
- **Mandrem** (p174) Salute to the sun on a picture-perfect, spiritually slanted beach.
- **Polem** (p211) Ignore the tales of unfriendly smugglers, and head off to explore Goa's southernmost sands.
- **Butterfly Beach** (p206) Pay the ferryman in Palolem to take you north to this tiny lepidopterous cove.
- **Querim** (p178) Scoot up from Arambol to find more elbow-room along the northern sands.

BEST ECOCONSCIOUS STAYS

If you're up for luxury without paying the environmental price, these cool concerns are attempting to minimise their environmental impact.

- **Yoga Magic, Anjuna** (p167)
- **Elsewhere, Mandrem** (p175)
- **Casa Susegad, Loutolim** (p186)
- **Backwoods Camp, Matkan** (p140)
- **Bhakti Kutir, Palolem** (p207)

BEST WILDLIFE WATCHING

Go wild for all things furry and feathered, with a trip to one of the following clean, green escapes.

- **Cotigao Wildlife Sanctuary** (p210) Position yourself all along the watchtower and wait for the creatures to emerge.
- **Dr Salim Ali Bird Sanctuary** (p122) Goa's glorious birdlife is resplendent on this riverine island sanctuary, easily explored by dugout canoe.
- **Bondla Wildlife Sanctuary** (p137) Remote and wildlife-filled; you'll find few hikers to share your forest trails here.
- **Bhagwan Mahavir Wildlife Sanctuary** (p138) Sleep over in tented luxury then venture into this vast park, to spy India's second-highest waterfalls.
- **Netravali Protected Area** (p210) Drive up into the heart of the Western Ghats, and wander unmarked forest paths to spot the shy and retiring species who make their homes here.

The indisputable classic is Richard Burton's *Goa and the Blue Mountains or Six Months of Sick Leave,* originally published in 1851. This irreverent account of his journey through Goa southwards to Ootacamund makes grand Victorian reading, despite all its characteristic condescension, and can be picked up in paperback at bookshops statewide.

A perfect partner to Burton, and a wildly contrasting historic account of Goa, can be found in Gita Mehta's *Karma Cola,* set this time in the state's infamous 1970s 'freak scene', with searing, enduring insights into the excesses that accompany some travellers' quests for spiritual enlightenment in India.

For something a little more varied, worth dipping into is *Reflected in Water: Writings on Goa,* edited by Jerry Pinto. Here literary luminaries like Graham Greene and William Dalrymple offer their impressions of the sunny state, along with writings from prominent Goans and fascinating historical titbits.

Delving back still further into history, and perfect for those keen on Goa's opulent heritage, seek out the vivid *Voyage to the East Indies, the Maldives, the Moluccas and Brazil,* by 17th-century traveller François Pyrard, who journeyed through the state in its glory days, after being shipwrecked nearby in 1608.

More contemporary is Alexander Frater's *Chasing the Monsoon* (1991), which chronicles the writer's journey following the onset of the monsoon as it moves north through India. Frater passes through a grey and rainy Goa, painting a vivid puddled portrait of a season that few travellers ever see in person.

A growing number of elderly Goans are these days publishing memoirs and biographies with small local publishing houses. These can prove unpolished gems for really getting beneath the state's skin, but print runs can be short and titles difficult to obtain once the first batch sells out. Head to the Golden Heart Emporium in Margao (p182), and browse its excellent selection of local writings on Goa, to find the latest available titles.

> Pick up the Goa Foundation's sourcebook *Fish, Curry and Rice* (Rs400), available statewide, to get to grips with Goa's tourism, environmental and social issues.

INTERNET RESOURCES

Goa Tourism (www.goa-tourism.com) The state tourism body, the Goa Tourism Development Corporation (GTDC), offers online information on its hotels, range of day trips and multiday tours, and tourism-related news. Also see p235.

Goa World (www.goa-world.com) This site offers lots of general information on Goa, and a link to a Konkani music radio station, to get you into the heady Goan mood before you arrive.

Goacom (www.goacom.com) A good all-rounder with news clips, up to date 'What's On' listings, and dozens of 'how to' video recipes for creating Goan and Indian classics.

Herald (www.oherald.com) Check out the online edition of Goa's *Herald* newspaper to keep up-to-date on local news.

Lonely Planet (www.lonelyplanet.com) Start your internet explorations here with succinct travel summaries, hotel reviews and Thorn Tree traveller forum.

Navhind Times (www.navhindtimes.com) Competing with the *Herald* for the top news spot, the *Navhind Times* offers daily Goan news and features.

Events Calendar

When it comes to festivals, Goans and Mumbaikers alike enjoy any excuse to party and barely a week goes by without a *festa* illuminating the calendar, ranging from dignified deity-inspired ceremonies to huge and raucous street parades. Many festival dates shift annually; check online at www.goa-tourism.com for up-to-date information.

JANUARY

BANGANGA FESTIVAL
A classical music festival held early in the month at the Banganga Tank in Mumbai (Bombay).

MUMBAI FESTIVAL
Based at several stages around the city, it showcases the food, dance and culture of Mumbai. See www.mumbaifestival.ind for more details.

REIS MAGOS FESTIVAL   6 Jan
Held at Reis Magos, Chandor and Cansaulim, this festival sees a re-enactment of the journey of the Three Wise Men to Bethlehem, with young boys playing the Magi and white horses providing their transport.

SHANTADURGA
Also known as the 'Procession of the Umbrellas', this is one of the most attended of Goa's festivals, wherein a solid silver statue of Hindu goddess Shantadurga is carried from Fatorpa to Cuncolim, fronted by 12 umbrella-carrying young men.

FESTA DAS BANDEIRAS
Migrant working men return home to Divar Island in mid-January, to celebrate their local saint's day by waving the flags of the countries in which they're currently working and, more bizarrely, firing dozens of peashooters at each other.

REPUBLIC DAY   26 Jan
Though Goa only became part of India in 1961, India's celebration of its 1950 establishment as a republic is nevertheless celebrated here with gusto.

FEBRUARY

ELEPHANTA FESTIVAL
Classical music and dance celebrated on Elephanta Island (p106) on the outskirts of Mumbai.

KHALA GHODA FESTIVAL
Getting bigger and more sophisticated each year, this two-week-long offering in Mumbai has a packed program of arts performances and exhibitions. Check out www.khalaghodaassociation.com for more specifics.

SHIGMOTSAV (SHIGMO)   full moon period
Goa's take on the Hindu festival of Holi marks the onset of spring with statewide parades, processions, and revellers flinging huge quantities of water and coloured tikka powder with wild abandon.

CARNIVAL   3 days before Lent
Three days of mirth and mayhem characterise Panaji's annual Carnival, held on the three days prior to the onset of the Catholic calendar's Lent. Festivities come to a head on Sabado Gordo (Fat Saturday), when you'll see a procession of floats through the city's packed streets. See p118 for more details.

HANUMAN FESTIVAL
Ten days in February see the Hindu monkey god Hanuman celebrated at Panaji's Maruti Temple, with huge statues of the deity paraded about, and a street fair up and running throughout the surrounding neighbourhood.

SHIVRATI
To celebrate the traditional anniversary of the God Shiva's wedding day, large-scale religious celebrations are held at the many Shiva temples across Goa.

MARCH–APRIL

PROCESSION OF   5th Mon during Lent
ALL SAINTS
Held in Goa Velha, this is the only procession of its sort outside Rome, where dozens of huge statues of the saints are paraded throughout the village, and people from all over Goa are drawn to the accompanying festivities.

EASTER
Churches fill up statewide over the Christian festival of Easter, with plenty of High Masses and family feasting thrown in for good measure.

FEAST OF OUR LADY OF MIRACLES

16 days after Easter

Held in Mapusa, this cheerful festival – also known as a *tamasha* – is famously celebrated by both Hindus and Christians at Mapusa's Church of Our Lady of Miracles.

MAY

IGITUN CHALNE

One of the most distinctive festivals in Goa, this is specific to the temple in Sirigao (near Corjuem Fort in Bicholim taluka). *Igitun chalne* literally means 'fire-walking', and the high point of the festival comes when devotees of the goddess Lairaya walk across a pit of burning coals to prove their devotion.

JUNE

FEAST OF ST ANTHONY

13 Jun

This feast in honour of Portugal's patron saint takes on particular significance if the monsoon is late in appearing, in which case each Goan family must lower a statue of the saint into its family well to hasten the onset of the rains in hope of ensuring bountiful crops.

SANJUAN

24 Jun

The Feast of St John (or *Sanjuan*, in the local Konkani dialect) sees young men diving dangerously into wells to celebrate the monsoon's arrival, and torching straw dummies of the saint himself, to represent John's baptism and, consequently, the death of sin.

SANGODD

29 Jun

The annual Feast of St Peter and St Paul marks another monsoonal celebration, and is particularly ebullient in Candolim, where boats are tied together to form floating stages and costumed actors play out *tiatrs* (Konkani dramas) to vast crowds.

AUGUST

NARIYAL POORNIMA

Festivals in the tourist hub of Colaba in Mumbai kick off with this celebration of the start of the fishing season after the monsoon.

INDEPENDENCE DAY

15 Aug

India's 1947 independence from Britain is celebrated with an annual public holiday.

FEAST OF THE CHAPEL

15 Aug

Coastal Cabo Raj Bhavan draws scores of visitors each 15 August, on India's Independence Day, to a special church service in honour of its 500-year-old chapel's feast day.

BONDERAM

4th Sat in Aug

Celebrated on sleepy Divar Island, processions and mock battles commemorate historical disputes that took place over island property.

SEPTEMBER

GANESH CHATURTHI

Mumbai's biggest annual festival – a 10- to 11-day event in celebration of the elephant-headed Ganesh – sweeps up the whole city and is also celebrated in numerous other towns in the region: the 10th day, which sees millions descend on Mumbai's Chowpatty Beach to submerge the largest statues, is particularly ecstatic.

OCTOBER–NOVEMBER

MAHATMA GANDHI'S BIRTHDAY

2 Oct

A national holiday and Remembrance Day in memory of India's legendary leader.

FEAST OF THE MENINO JESUS

2nd Sun in Oct

Coastal Colva's village church sees its small and allegedly miracle-working statue of the Infant Jesus dressed up and paraded before scores of devoted pilgrims at this important village festival.

DUSSHERA

This nine-day Hindu festival celebrates the god Rama's victory over Ravana in the Hindu epic Ramayana, and the goddess Durga's victory over Mahishasura. It is celebrated throughout the region with bonfires – burning effigies of the baddies – and schoolchildren's performances of scenes from the life of Rama.

DIWALI

A five-day Hindu 'festival of lights', this beautifully illuminated festival celebrates the victory of good over evil with the lighting of oil and butter lamps around the home, lots of gentle familial celebration and plenty of less peaceful firecrackers.

COLABA FESTIVAL

A small arts festival held in Colaba (Mumbai) that sometimes overlaps with Diwali festivities.

FEAST OF OUR LADY OF LIVRAMENT

Each mid-November sees a cheerful street fair set up in Panaji, outside the tiny Chapel of St Sebastian, in the Goan capital's atmospheric old Fontainhas district.

INTERNATIONAL FILM FESTIVAL OF INDIA

This annual film festival (www.iffi.gov.in) – the country's largest – graces Panaji's big screens with a gaggle of Bollywood's finest glitterati jetting in for premieres, parties, ceremonies and screenings.

PRITHVI THEATRE FESTIVAL

A showcase in Mumbai of what's going on in contemporary Indian theatre; also includes performances by international troupes of artists. See www.prithvitheatre.org for details of the festival's events.

VIJAYA UTSAV FESTIVAL

An arts festival held every November in Hampi Bazaar.

DECEMBER

FEAST OF ST FRANCIS XAVIER   3 Dec

Thousands upon thousands of pilgrims file past the remains of St Francis Xavier in this weeklong festival and fair, complete with large-scale open-air Masses.

FEAST OF OUR LADY OF THE IMMACULATE CONCEPTION   8 Dec

Panaji's wedding-cake Church of the Immaculate Conception plays host to this feast and large, joyful fair.

LIBERATION DAY   17 Dec

This unusually sober celebration marks Goa's 'liberation' from Portugal by India in 1961 with military and air force parades.

CHRISTMAS   24 & 25 Dec

Midnight Masses abound in Goa on 24 December, traditionally known as Misa de Galo ('Cock's Crow') since they often stretch on far into the wee hours, while Christmas Day on the 25th is celebrated with feasting, fireworks and festivities by locals and tourists alike.

SUNBURN FESTIVAL   Christmas period

For the last couple of years, 'Asia's biggest music festival' (www.sunburn-festival.com) has set up camp in Candolim over Christmas and New Year. Check the website for details, and if it continues to run to form, you'll find a four-day dance music extravaganza filled with international DJs and all-day partying.

SIOLIM ZAGOR   1st Sun after Christmas

Siolim's unusual, multifaith Zagor involves night-long festivities, with a candlelit procession culminating in folk plays, music and celebrations throughout the northern village streets.

Itineraries
CLASSIC ROUTES

NORTHERN NAMES   Two Weeks / Terekhol Fort to Fort Aguada

Start your northern odyssey with a stay at fascinating **Terekhol Fort** (p178), the perfect antidote to the task of getting to Goa. From here, hop on a ferry south for a solitary sunbathe in **Querim** (p178), then head to **Arambol** (p175) for some beach-hut living and a firmly festival vibe. Continue south to mellow **Mandrem** (p174) for some serious serenity and a yoga lesson or two, then move on to **Aswem** (p174), perhaps for lunch in its renowned French-inspired beach shack, and to **Morjim** (p174) for a walk along the pretty estuary banks.

Next, head inland via Siolim to get to **Chapora** (p168) and **Vagator** (p168) to experience the final dregs of the Goa Trance scene, and watch the hippies brandishing their *charas* and chillums. Then set off to spend time in **Anjuna** (p164), coinciding with its legendary Wednesday flea market to sniff out a bargain, then continue your shopping spree at workaday **Mapusa** (p161), its own, locally flavoured market, best experienced on a Friday morning.

Backtrack to **Baga** (p154) and **Calangute** (p154) to pick up the pace, hit the clubs and dine on fine foodstuffs, then head south to **Candolim** (p147) for a jaunt up the hill to impressive **Fort Aguada** (p148), ending your journey, as it began, in the shadow of Portugal's once-mighty colonial conquests.

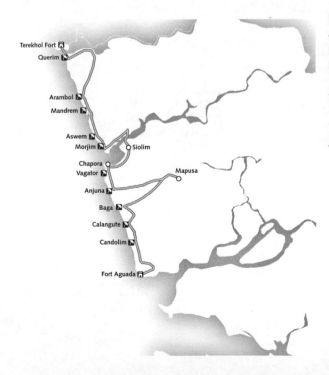

From Portuguese forts to hippie hang-outs made infamous in the 1960s when the first beach bums blazed their heady trail, this 50km journey – possible by bus, taxi or under your own steam – takes you through the dizzyingly diverse worlds of North Goa's beaches.

SOUTHERN SUN   Two Weeks / Margao to Polem

Stock up on supplies for your journey in relaxed, workaday **Margao** (p181), then head briefly northwest, to begin your sandy sojourn on the sands of **Velsao** (p192). From Velsao, head slowly down the coast, stopping off at the beaches of **Arossim** (p192), **Utorda** (p192), **Majorda** (p193) and **Betalbatim** (p194) along the way, perhaps with a swanky night or delicious dinner at one of this stretch's five-stars thrown in.

Stop in at **Colva** (p194) or **Benaulim** (p197) to replenish your supply of essentials or spend the night, then continue on down along the lazy sands of **Varca** (p198) and on to **Cavelossim** (p199) for an evening of live music at its cool jazz club. From here, detour to **Mobor** (p201) to get a feel for pristine estuarine life, then double back to Cavelossim to jump on a ferry to **Assolna** (p201), and begin your exploration of Goa's southernmost stretch.

Follow the coastal road through bucolic **Betul** (p202) all the way to **Agonda** (p202) where you can relax in barefoot splendour, and get stuck into those books you've brought along for the ride. Next, head down to **Palolem** (p204) where the pace is a little less lazy, and try to track down one of its locally famous 'Silent Parties'. Base yourself in Palolem, or in nearby **Patnem** (p208), to explore the south's **hidden coves** (p206), or to take a day trip down to **Galgibag** (p210) or **Polem** (p211), two of the state's quietest beaches, gracing the coast along the slow road down to Karnataka.

Become a beach baby in the extreme, with this 50km route along the south coast's stunning stretches of sand and quiet coastal villages. Hire a motorbike or scooter for the best beachside idling, allowing you to hop off, and dip in, as often as your heart desires.

ROADS LESS TRAVELLED

AN INLAND ADVENTURE   Two Weeks / Panaji to Palolem

Begin in **Panaji** (p109), the languid state capital, perfect for shopping, eating, drinking and roaming around its lazy Latin-flavoured streets. Next, head east along the Ribandar Causeway to World Heritage–listed **Old Goa** (p122), where the ghosts of Goan history await. Backtrack to **Ribandar** (p122) to catch a ferry to **Chorao Island** (p122), home of the **Dr Salim Ali Bird Sanctuary** (p122), then ferry-hop to **Divar Island** (p130) for its sleepy island life, and take a third ferry to **Naroa** (p143), to the tiny, ancient **Shri Saptakoteshwara Temple** (p143) and quiet **Mayem Lake** (p144).

Head west across to **Corjuem Island** (p144), stopping in at **Aldona** (p144), **Pomburpa** (p145), and sleepy **Britona** (p145) on the banks of the Mandovi River. Turn south, skirting Panaji, via **Goa Velha** (p131) and **Agassim** (p132), on the road to sleepy, ancestral **Loutolim** (p185). Rest up here, before pressing east to the temples and spice farms of **Ponda** (p133). Head further east to explore one of Goa's two wildlife sanctuaries: bird-filled **Bondla** (p137) or **Bhagwan Mahavir** (p138), with its giddy waterfall. Detour to the ancient **Tambdi Surla Mahadeva temple** (p139), then head south to **Chandor** (p187). Here, explore Goa's grandest mansions, or root out the traces of its long-gone empires, then head through small, busy **Quepem** (p188) to the **Rivona Buddhist caves** (p188) and **Usgalimal rock carvings** (p189), continuing on to the mysterious **Netravali Bubble Lake** (p210). Then make one final inland excursion to beautiful **Cotigao Wildlife Sanctuary** (p210) to top it all off, then head to picture-perfect **Palolem** (p204) to rest up.

Remind yourself that there's far more to Goa than beaches with a stunningly diverse 200km adventure exploring historic forts, temples, mansions and churches. Trek into wildlife-rich national parks and explore far-flung tracts of country-side, with the occasional dose of luxury thrown in for good measure.

TAILORED TRIPS

GOA WITH CHILDREN

Strolling Goa's sands today, you'll see more visiting children cavorting here than ever before. Goans love children, and your little ones will be greeted with smiles, sweets and treats in abundance.

First and foremost, hit the beach, with paddling opportunities and rock pools galore (though it's important to heed advice on swimming safety). For a traveller-type vibe, try southern **Palolem** (p204) or northern **Arambol** (p175) – both increasingly popular with families – while the coastal strip between **Velsao** (p192) and **Mobor** (p201) has lots of five-star resorts catering to small travellers, with kids' clubs on-site and shallow swimming pools.

Even fussy eaters in Goa will have no trouble satisfying small appetites, but head to **Panaji** (p117), **Calangute** (p159) or **Baga** (p159) for the widest choice of dining; even the fanciest places are decidedly child-friendly. In

Panaji and **Margao** (p181) you'll also find lots of toy shops and bookshops catering to smaller travellers, while Panaji offers sunset **river trips** (p115) and a comfortable multiplex **INOX cinema** (p119) for when the heat gets too much. Small astronomers might also be keen to head up to its night-time **public observatory** (p115).

Kids will delight in a visit inland to a **spice plantation** (p134) with an opportunity to ride an elephant, and older children will love the trek to **Dudhsagar Falls** (p139). Weary parents might also be pleased to know that **Arambol** (p175), **Anjuna** (p164) and **Palolem** (p204) all have kindergartens that run seasonally: seek out in-the-know parents when you arrive.

TO MARKET, TO MARKET

Leave room in your luggage and prepare to fill up on Goan goodies, on a stellar shopping spree or two. Start in Panaji with a wander around its atmospheric **municipal market** (p119) to drink chai amid the blur of bargaining. Step it up a notch with some upmarket shopping at the boutique shops of 18th June Rd and the lifestyle stores and bookshops scattered about town.

In North Goa, drop in to **Calangute** (p154) and **Baga** (p154) for a whole host of shopping options, from street stalls to air-conditioned mini-malls, with a few unique boutiques sandwiched in between.

On any given Wednesday, take a deep breath and launch yourself into the chaos of the **Anjuna flea market** (p168), where the hippie days of old collide with everything that typifies Goa today. Wait for Friday to hit manic local **Mapusa market** (p162), the biggest market-day event in the whole stay, and try to drop in on picturesque **Siolim** (p173), where crustaceans are sold along the Chapora River each morning and St Anthony's Chapel bursts to life every Wednesday morning as fresh-produce vendors pour in.

Down in South Goa, where life still operates at a laid-back pace, take in the atmosphere of the covered **MC New Market** (p183) in Margao.

History

A quick 100,000-year skip through the history of little, lush Goa offers you a keen insight into some of the region's most mysterious and alluring archaeological and historic remains, and into the Goan psyche itself. The state's story is – quite understandably – one of conflicts and conquests, with suitors throughout history vying for her delicate hand.

The greatest lasting influence you'll notice is the mark of her most recent conqueror, the Portuguese, who ruled Goa from 1512 to 1961, yet they weren't the first to arrive here. Archaeologists now believe even Goa's earliest inhabitants were settlers from elsewhere, arriving to tame this brilliant patch of emerald and aquamarine from the opposite side of the Western Ghats. Thus it's not hard to see why Goans are generally so welcoming to successive waves of foreign visitors, having started out as visitors – albeit in pre-history – themselves.

PREHISTORIC BEGINNINGS

A trip out into the Goan hinterland, to the extraordinary riverside rock carvings of Usgalimal (p189), will provide you with pictorial evidence of the people considered Goa's earlier hunter-gatherers, believed to have inhabited the Goan hinterland some time during the Upper Palaeolithic era, which stretched from 100,000 BC to 10,000 BC. No one really knows where these tribes originally came from; some believe they arrived as migrants from Africa, others that they were from eastern Asia, or were a northern tribe forced southwards by instability in their homeland.

As the lifestyle of these early Goans became more settled, formal agriculture developed and villages sprang up, and the tribes began to look beyond the confines of their coastal territory, establishing links with the other peoples of southern India. Around 2400 BC society was likely profoundly altered by the arrival of Aryan migrants from the north, who brought with them Goa's earliest strands of Hinduism, along with improved farming techniques. A second wave of Aryans migrated southwards in around 700 BC, which may have included important groups such as the Bhojas, Chediyas and Saraswat Brahmins, who would come to precedence over the coming centuries.

EARLY WRANGLINGS

Goa's history becomes less of a mystery around the 3rd century BC, when it's known to have become part of the mighty Mauryan empire, which expanded southwards through India following the decline of Alexander the Great's northwest Indian empire. Goa became part of an administrative area

According to legend, Goa's name came from Lord Krishna, who was so enchanted by the land that he named it after the cows ('Go' in Sanskrit) belonging to the charming milkmaids he encountered – for whom Krishna had quite a predilection.

TIMELINE

100,000–10,000 BC	2400–700 BC	CIRCA 300 BC
Hunter-gatherer tribes inhabit the Goan interior, evident in the rock carvings at Usgalimal and stone implements discovered at the Zuari River, near Dudhsagar Falls.	Goa experiences at least two waves of Aryan immigration, bringing with them improved farming techniques and the first elements of what would become Hinduism.	Goa comes under the control of the Mauryan empire, with the great emperor Ashoka sending the first Buddhist missionary to Goa to try to convert the population. With Ashoka's death, this initial attempt fails.

LET THERE BE GOA

According to Hindu legend, Goa and the Konkan coastline were created by the god Parasurama, the sixth incarnation of Vishnu, one of the three most important Hindu gods. After many years of fighting to avenge the murder of his father, Parasurama finally came to the Sahyadri Ranges (Western Ghats), which now form the border between Goa and Karnataka. In search of a completely pure piece of land upon which his Brahmin caste could live in peace, Parasurama stood atop the Western Ghats and shot an arrow towards the Arabian Sea, commanding the tide to retreat to the point where the arrow landed. It's said the arrow fell where Benaulim stands today (*baan* meaning 'arrow', *ali* meaning 'village'), and the virgin stretch of coastline that was revealed as the waves receded became the coastal plain of Goa. Parasurama promptly performed his first fire sacrifice in the north of the country (modern-day Pernem), and then peopled his new land with 96 Brahmin families.

known as Kuntala, and the entire area became known to the Mauryans as Aparanta Desh, meaning 'beyond the end'. Ashoka, probably the greatest of the Mauryan emperors, soon sent a Buddhist missionary to convert the locals; the monk set up shop in a rock-cut cave near modern day Zambaulim, preaching nonviolence and urging the tribes to give up their nasty habit of blood sacrifice. Though he had some success, introducing the plough and spreading literacy, his liturgy fell largely on deaf ears, and following the rapid demise of the Mauryans after the death of Emperor Ashoka in 232 BC, Goa soon reverted to Hinduism, commingled with tribal practices.

The next seven centuries saw Goa ruled from afar by a series of powerful Hindu dynasties, including the Pallavas, Rashtrakutas and Chalukyas, who installed their own governors and increased international trade and prosperity throughout the region; records show that Goan goods and spices regularly made their way to Africa, and across to the Middle East and Rome. However, continued wrangling between dynasties offered the opportunity for a homespun dynasty to quietly emerge, and in AD 420 the Kadambas declared independence from the Pallavas, and consolidated their control of the region by forming strong military bonds with their neighbours and creating their very own ruling 'royal family'.

THE GOLDEN AGE OF THE KADAMBAS

Finally, Goa had some stability. By the late 6th century, the Kadambas had seized control of the previous rulers' base camp, Chandrapur (at modern-day Chandor), and developed it into a large and beautiful city, known to Medieval Arab map-makers as Zindabar. This became the Kadamba capital until around 1054, when they upped sticks to a new base, blessed with a deep, wide harbour for all-important trade purposes, at the mouth of the Zuari River. The new capital was christened

AD 420	1054	1352
Goa's home-grown Hindu rulers, the Kadambas, rise to power over their distant overlords, and install their own royal family, ushering in a period of religious tolerance, prosperity and innovation.	The capital shifts from Chandrapur (modern-day Chandor) to Govepuri (now Goa Velha). Wealth and trade skyrocket, with locals building vast homes and places of worship with the profits of the spice trade.	After suffering three centuries of Muslim raids, Goa comes under rule of Muslim Bahmanis and almost all trace of the Kadambas' Hindu legacy is quickly destroyed, except for the Tambdi Surla Mahadeva temple.

Govepuri by its Kadamba king, Jayakeshi I, and is today the sleepy village of Goa Velha.

You'd never guess today, wandering the sleepy villages of Chandor or Goa Velha, that just 1000 years ago both were mighty cities, serving such crucial roles in the region's history. Chandrapur was sacked in the 14th century by Muslim warlord Ghiyas-ud-din Tughluq, and Govepuri would also eventually be ransacked and abandoned. Yet at the time, Govepuri, in particular, was grand and highly international, with merchants regularly arriving from as far afield as Malabar, Bengal and Sumatra.

In contrast with what was to come, the Kadamba rule was a period of tolerance. Muslim merchants from Arabia and East Africa were encouraged to settle, Hindu temples were constructed statewide and prestigious academic institutions were inaugurated. Yet, like all good things, it was not to last. The success of the Kadambas signalled their own downfall, with Muslim raiders keen on getting their own piece of the Kadamba wealth pouring into Goa from the 10th century onwards. Today, the sole Kadamba structure to survive the troubled years to follow is the melancholy Tambdi Surla Mahadeva temple (p139), saved from a grisly fate solely due to its remote jungle location.

> The Kadambas, whose name has become synonymous with main bus stations throughout Goa, were originally local feudatories of the Hoysala kingdom; the roaring lion of their dynastic crest is now the state bus company logo.

THE RISE AND FALL OF THE BAHMANIS

Though the first Muslim raids on Goa began in the 10th century, the Kadambas' peace was finally shattered at the beginning of the 14th century. In 1312 Govepuri, and much else along with it, was destroyed (though rapidly rebuilt) under Ala ud-din Khilji, the sultan of Delhi. Fifteen years later the Muslims returned under Mohammed Tughlaq and the old capital of Chandrapur was levelled. Raids continued unabated until finally, in 1352, Goa came under the permanent Muslim rule of the Bahmanis and the region's years of religious tolerance were brought to an abrupt and painful end.

The Bahmanis immediately set about a harsh regime of Hindu persecution, destroying the grand Kadamba temples (with the exception of Tambdi Surla) and killing their priests. Many Hindus fled south, as the Bahmanis themselves encountered conflict in the form of the mighty Vijayanagar Empire, which had its capital at Hampi (see p216) and controlled much of southern India. In 1378 the Vijayanagar army finally succeeded in taking Goa from the Bahmanis, massacring many Muslims in revenge for the killings of their fellow Hindu Kadambas.

With the Vijayanagar dynasty at the helm, a century of peace followed, accompanied by excellent trade, with spices flowing freely from Goan plantations to the Arab lands and beyond.

In the 15th century the ousted Bahmanis grew determined to win back their old territory, finally wresting Goa back into the hands of the Bahmani kingdom in 1472. As if in revenge for the effort they had expended, the Bahmanis wreaked havoc on the capital Govepuri, whose decline was already

1378	**1472**	**1498**
Goa is wrestled from the repressive Bahmani regime by the Hindu Vijayanagar dynasty. Almost 100 years of prosperity follow, with Govepuri serving as an entry point for Arab horses for the Vijayanagar cavalry.	The Bahmanis make their comeback, launching a massive land-and-sea invasion to recapture Goa. Finding the capital Govepuri in decline, they found Ela (now Old Goa), a new capital on the banks of the Mandovi River.	Portuguese captain Vasco da Gama arrives in Goa, making him the first European to reach India via the Cape of Good Hope. The Portuguese hope this will allow them to dominate Eastern trade routes.

Goa for the next 250 years, and are now known as the Velhas Conquistas (Old Conquests).

In 1565 trouble reared its head once more, when a coalition of Muslim rulers crushed the Hindu Vijayanagar army at the Battle of Talikota, culminating in the sacking of Hampi, its glorious inland capital. With the Muslim kingdoms in alliance and rid of their greatest enemy, it was inevitable that the Portuguese would once again make the firing line, and in 1570 the combined forces of Bijapur, Ahmednagar and Calicut besieged Goa. Despite their overwhelming superiority in numbers, they failed to break the defence, and after a year-long siege, plagued by malaria and sickness, the attackers gave up and withdrew.

THE INQUISITION ARRIVES

Although a handful of priests arrived armed with missionary zeal in Goa with Albuquerque's fleet, missionary work was relatively low-key in Goa for Portugal's first 30 years on the subcontinent. Initially, Albuquerque's approach was enlightened: Hindus were considered friends against the Muslim foe, and 'conversion' was largely confined to allowing Portuguese soldiers to marry local women, so that their children would be raised Christian.

In 1532 Goa's first Vicar General arrived, and the age of tolerance was over. In 1541, following the arrival of a handful of zealots, laws were passed ordering the destruction of all Hindu temples, along with the introduction of strict laws forbidding the observance of Hindu rituals, and other regulations stating that only those who were baptised could retain the rights to their land. This was followed in 1545 with the banning of collective idol worship, and the exile of all Brahmin priests, then, in 1559, idols were also banned from private homes. But this was only the beginning. Some half-century earlier, in the late 15th century, Spain and Portugal's fearsome Medieval Tribunal of the Holy Office, better known as the Inquisition, had been re-established in Spain and Portugal against a background of rumours that many new Christians, including those who had been converted from Judaism, were secretly still observing their old faith. Many escaped the oppression in Portugal by relocating to the colonies. It wasn't long before accusations followed them, and missionaries became scandalised at the lax and louche behaviour of both the new Christians and the other Portuguese settlers. In 1560 the Tribunal of the Holy Office – or Goan Inquisition – arrived to set things straight.

Establishing itself at the sultan's old palace in Ela (Old Goa), the tribunal soon began flexing its ecclesiastical muscles. Hindus were forbidden to practise their faith, and even the Christian population lived in fear of being accused of defying the Catholic Church. Following initial interrogation, the more fortunate victims were stripped of their possessions; those who

A taluka is a Goan district, of which there are 11. Salcete derives from the Sanskrit *sassast*, meaning '66', after the 66 Brahmin families who first settled there; Tiswadi (from *tis* meaning '30') is named for its original 30 families.

During his time in Goa, Afonso de Albuquerque banned the Hindu practice of *sati*, the self-immolation of women on their husband's funeral pyre.

1664	1683	1737
The Hindu Marathas, under the leadership of legendary, fearsome warrior Shivaji, temporarily take parts of Goa, alerting the Portuguese to the dangers lurking in eastern, as well as western, powers.	The Marathas, led by Sambhaji (Shivaji's son), come dangerously close to Old Goa; the Portuguese viceroy prays to the long-dead body of Francis Xavier for deliverance, and miraculously – and temporarily – it arrives.	The Marathas finally capture the talukas (districts) of Bardez and Salcete – except for the well-fortified forts at Reis Magos, Aguada, Mormugao and Rachol.

were less lucky were detained indefinitely in the dungeons beneath what now became the Palace of the Inquisition.

Next, those who were judged guilty underwent the notorious autos-da-fé (trials of faith), a terrifying public ceremony conducted in the square outside the Sé Cathedral accompanied by the tolling of the great cathedral bell. Those who refused to recant their heresy would usually be burned at the stake; those willing to admit to it were strangled before the pyre was lit.

Though Portugal's fearsome Inquisition reigned with religious terrorism for more than two centuries, astonishingly it still failed to eradicate Hinduism entirely from Goa. Many Hindus fled across the Mandovi River, into the region around modern-day Ponda, smuggling their religious statuaries to safety and secretly building temples to house them. Thousands of others died at the whim of interrogators who sat around the dreaded 'Inquisition table', now housed at the Goa State Museum in Panaji; see p47 for more on their dark and dreaded deeds.

> If you're fluent in written French, seek out 17th-century French traveller Charles Dellon's first-hand account of the Goan Inquisition, *L'Inquisition de Goa*, which captures the full, abject horror of the era.

'GOA DOURADA'

Although the Roman Catholic church usherred in an era of misery, not all of the religious orders came tarred with the same cruel and zealous brush. By the mid-16th century, Franciscan, Dominican and Augustinian missionaries, along with the Jesuits and others, were present in Goa, establishing hospitals and schools, and teaching alternative methods of farming and forestry.

> The first printing press in India was established in Old Goa in 1556 by the Jesuits.

Meanwhile, when they weren't busy converting the masses, they were masterminding much of Goa Dourada's (Golden Goa's) glorious ecclesiastical building boom. Levies from the lucrative international spice and horse trades financed work on the Sé Cathedral, commenced in 1562, and on the Basilica of Bom Jesus, built between 1594 and 1605. Soon Old Goa's population stood at 300,000, larger than London or Lisbon itself, and though life was perilous – many would-be emigrants perished at sea en route, or soon succumbed to the frequent attacks of malaria, typhoid and cholera that swept the city – life in Goa seemed truly golden.

Though the Inquisition continued to terrorise the population, everyday life remained scandalously decadent, with contemporary visitors providing shocking accounts of the prostitution and adultery rife in the outwardly ecclesiastical city. Even the Jesuits, including a young Francis Xavier (later to be canonised; see the box, p36), sent by Portugal's King Dom Joao III, seemed unable to stem the debauched flow, and private lives were gloriously lax for those safe from the Inquisitors' table.

> On encountering Francis Xavier's 'incrupt body' in 1634, a Portuguese noblewoman named Dona Isabel de Caron was allegedly so anxious to obtain a relic that she bit off his little toe – and it gushed fresh blood into her mouth.

PORTUGAL FADES & THE MARATHAS ATTACK

Just as 'Goa Dourada' and its magnificent Old Goa edifices were in their ascendancy, Portugal's own fortunes were beginning to wane.

1739	**1781–88**	**1787**
The Portuguese sign a treaty with the Marathas, handing over large tracts of their northern territory near Mumbai in exchange for full Maratha withdrawal from Goa.	The Novas Conquistas (New Conquests) sees Portugal add the talukas of Pernem, Bicholim and Satari to its territory, delineating, by 1788, the confines of the Goan state as we see it today.	The first serious local attempt to overthrow the Portuguese, the Pinto Revolt, is attempted; it's unsuccessful and its leaders are either tortured and executed, or shipped to Portugal.

THE 'INCORRUPT' BODY OF ST FRANCIS XAVIER

Goa's patron saint, Francis Xavier, was born into a wealthy and aristocratic family in Navarre, Spain, on 7 April 1506. He studied at Paris University, where he met Ignatius Loyola and thus came to the early turning point in his life. Together with five others, they formed the Society of Jesus (the Jesuits) in 1534 and almost immediately hatched plans to travel to the Holy Land, where they hoped to convert the Muslim masses. Though their plans fell through, there was plenty to be done in other areas, and when missionaries were requested for the eastern empire, it seemed an ideal opportunity.

In April 1541, Xavier sailed for Goa, arriving in May 1542, from which he commenced his missionary voyages to Ceylon, Malacca and Japan. In February 1552 he persuaded the viceroy to allow him to plan an embassy to China, but died en route on the island of Sancian, off the Chinese coast, on 2 December 1552.

After his death (so the story goes) his servant emptied several sackfuls of quicklime into his coffin to consume the missionary's flesh in preparation for the return of the mortal remains to Goa. Yet, two months later, when the body was transferred to Malacca, it remained in perfect condition – 'incorrupt' despite all that quicklime. The following year, Francis Xavier's body was returned to Goa, where its preservation was declared a miracle.

The church was somewhat slower to acknowledge the feat, requiring a medical examination to establish that the body had not been embalmed. This was performed in 1554 by the viceroy's

---

In 1580, bankrupted by a disastrous campaign in North Africa, Portugal was annexed by Spain, and it wasn't until 1640 that the Portuguese regained independence. Though this inevitably dealt a great blow to the colonies, a far greater threat lurked in the emergence of European rivals in the eastern oceans. In 1612 a Portuguese fleet was defeated off the coast of Surat, in western Gujarat, by the ships of the British East India Company, instantly making the British a force to be reckoned with in the Arabian Sea. Only by allowing the British to trade freely in all of Portugal's eastern ports, an agreement reached by the Convention of Goa in 1635, did their threat subside.

By the early 1660s the Portuguese were also facing a threat from the east. Shivaji, the great leader of the Hindu Maratha dynasty, whose homeland lay in the Western Ghats, temporarily succeeded in taking the neighbouring territories of Bicholim and Pernem in 1664, signalling a Maratha problem that would cause grief for the Portuguese for the next almost 80 years. In 1683 the Maratha army, commanded by Shivaji's son, Sambhaji, came so close to Old Goa that defeat seemed inevitable. Miraculously, the Marathas withdrew at the last minute, threatened by Muslim Mughal forces to their rear, but returned again in 1737 to take the whole of Bardez, except for the heavily fortified forts at Aguada and Reis Magos, and the whole of Salcete, apart from the forts at Mormugao and Rachol. Finally, a May 1739 treaty forced the Portuguese to hand over large tracts of their

1787	1835	1835
Portugal struggles silently against a small-scale British occupation at two of Goa's forts, evidence of which still remains in the form of a small British military cemetery.	Goa's senate moves from Old Goa to a healthier capital at Panjim (today's Panaji). Goa's viceroy, Dom Manuel de Portugal e Castro, levels the dunes and drains the swamps to make it a habitable alternative.	On 4 May, a bloody but ultimately doomed military coup sees a battalion of soldiers destroy the fort of Gaspar Dias and murder the regiment inside it, signifying a growing mistrust of the Portuguese government.

physician, who declared that all the internal organs were still intact and that no preservative agents had been used. Noticing a small wound in Xavier's chest and demanded that two attendant Jesuits insert their fingers. 'When they withdrew them,' he noted, 'they were covered with the blood which I smelt and found to be absolutely untainted.'

Finally, in 1622, Francis Xavier was canonised. By then, holy relic hunters had corrupted the incorruptible: in 1614 Xavier's right arm had been removed and divided between Jesuits in Japan and Rome (where it could allegedly still sign its name), and by 1636 parts of one shoulder blade and internal organs had been scattered throughout Southeast Asia. Even his diamond-encrusted fingernail was removed, and is now squirreled away at the Pereira-Braganza house in Chandor (p188).

At last, by the end of the 17th century, the body reached an advanced state of desiccation and the miracle appeared over. The Jesuits decided to enclose the corpse in a glass coffin out of view, and it wasn't until the mid-19th century that it was wheeled back out to please gaping visitors.

Nowadays, once every decade on Xavier's feast day, 3 December, the glass coffin containing the body is paraded through Old Goa for closer examination by the masses. The next grisly airing will take place in 2014.

northern territory, near Mumbai (Bombay), in exchange for a full Maratha withdrawal from Goa.

EXPANSION & DECLINE

The latter half of the 18th century saw both the expansion of the colony and the acceleration of its decline. In 1764 the local Raja of Sonda, beset by an enemy, asked the Portuguese to occupy his lands in order to protect them. Although he intended the occupation to be temporary, the Portuguese obligingly moved into what today are the talukas of Ponda, Sanguem, Quepem and Canacona, and the acquisition of the Novas Conquistas (New Conquests) became permanent. The final pieces of the Goan puzzle were completed between 1781 and 1788, when the Portuguese added the northern talukas of Pernem, Bicholim and Satari to the colony.

At the same time the character of the colony was changing. The old licentiousness of Old Goa was on the wane, partly due to the long-running effects of the Inquisition (which finally ground to a halt in the early 19th century) and partly since Old Goa, once a thriving city of gorging and godliness, continued to succumb to plague after horrific plague. Though hangers-on clung grimly to Old Goa for another few decades, by 1822 Old Goa's monuments had become lost in a tangle of jungle. The senate was formally moved to Panjim (present-day Panaji) in 1835, and eight years later the city officially became Goa's capital.

1843	**1850**	**1926**
Panjim becomes Goa's new official capital, and Old Goa is left almost uninhabited, except for a handful of hardy monks and nuns.	British adventurer Richard Burton describes Old Goa, in his travelogue *Goa and the Blue Mountains*, as a place of 'utter devastation', with a hanging-on population 'as sepulchral-looking as the devastation around them'.	Portugal declares itself a republic, and right-wing dictator Dr Antonio de Oliveira Salazar takes the helm, refusing to relinquish control over the country's colonies despite Portugal's own grievous economic woes.

Meanwhile, Portugal continued to struggle with troublemakers within and without. In 1787 the short-lived Pinto Revolt, whose conspirators were largely Goan clerics, sought to overturn their overlords' rule. The revolt was discovered while it was still in the planning, and several of the leaders were tortured and put to death, while others were imprisoned or shipped off to Portugal (see p147). Outside, Portugal struggled against the British who, during the Napoleonic Wars, thought it prudent to protect Goa from potential French invasion, and ended up occupying Fort Aguada and Cabo Raj Bhavan for the best part of a decade. Portugal, realising its power couldn't match that of the new empire, quietly acquiesced.

> Though the British never made a formal attempt to annex Goa, in 1839 the British government offered to buy Goa from the Portuguese for £500,000.

END OF AN EMPIRE

The 19th century in Goa saw increasing calls for freedom from the restraints of Lisbon rule. In 1834 the Portuguese government, having suffered its own civil war, gave governorship of Goa to Bernardo Peres da Silva, a nationalist Goan, in an attempt to quell the calls, an attempt that failed due to Portugal's fears that da Silva would cave in to local demands, above those of the Portuguese government. In 1835 a bloody military coup, resulting in the 'massacre of Gaspar Dias', whereby one rebel soldier band massacred a regiment stationed at Gaspar Dias, confirmed that tensions were already running high.

Further manifestations of the desire to shake free from Portugal came in a series of uprisings by a clan called the Ranes, hailing from Satari taluka in the northeast. For more than 50 years such sporadic violence was handled by Portuguese viceroys with a mixture of military suppression and concessions until in 1912, after 14 rebellions, the Ranes were finally crushed by military force. Meanwhile, across Europe, politicians publicised Goa's plight, highlighting the continuing second-class status of its Hindu population, whose members were denied governmental posts despite making up the majority of Goa's most successful businessmen.

> Goa's first newspaper, O Heraldo, was launched in 1900. It's now the top-selling daily Herald (www.oheraldo.in).

Independence grew no more likely following Portugal's declaration as a republic in 1926, and by the 1940s the Goan leaders were taking their example from the Independence movement across the border in British India, with prominent, wealthy figures such as Luis de Menezes Braganza championing the cause.

> Panaji's 18th June Rd is so-called to commemorate the 1946 actions of Dr Ram Manohar Lohia, and his contribution to Goa's eventual freedom from colonialism.

On 18 June 1946 a demonstration in Margao led to the public arrest of a prominent independence activist, Dr Ram Manohar Lohia, after he had been threatened at gunpoint to prevent him from addressing the crowd. The event provided the incentive needed to motivate the people, and large-scale demonstrations were soon held. In the aftermath, many activists were arrested, and an estimated total 1500 people were incarcerated. In response,

1940s	1953	1954
In line with India's own struggle for independence, Goa's independence movement slowly gains ground.	Diplomatic relations between Portugal and newly independent India collapse following the Portuguese government's failure to show interest in discussing Goa's independence.	Dr T B Cunha (dubbed the 'Father of Goan Nationalism') forms the Goa Action Committee, following Gandhi's tenet of satyagraha (nonviolent protest).

a militant wing of the Independence movement was formed, called Azad Gomantak Dal (AGD), which carried out raids on police stations and public industries. Nevertheless, on 10 June 1947 the Portuguese Minister of Colonies, Captain Teofilo Duarte, warned that the 'Portuguese flag will not fall down in India without some thousands of Portuguese, white and coloured, shedding their blood in its defence'.

THE MARCH TO INDEPENDENCE

When overtures by the newly independent Indian government were made to the Portuguese in 1953, the lack of any formal response made it apparent that the Portuguese had no intention of withdrawing. Consequently, on 11 June 1953 diplomatic relations between the two countries were broken off.

A year later, a satyagraha (nonviolent protest) against the Portuguese establishment was called by Goans themselves, and many of its participants beaten, imprisoned or exiled. Exactly a year later, as a mark of indignation at the treatment of the first Goan satyagrahis (nonviolent protesters), a second protest was organised, this time to be conducted by Indians from outside Goa. On the morning of the rally more than 3000 protesters, including women and children, entered Goa at various points along the border with India. In response to this openly peaceful protest, Portuguese security forces charged at protesters with batons and opened fire. Some of the protesters were killed and hundreds more were injured.

During this period India manoeuvred for international support, attempting to exert pressure on more established members of the UN to persuade the Portuguese to leave peacefully. India's Prime Minister, Jawaharlal Nehru, was opposed to taking Goa by force, fearing this would jeopardise the entire ethos of achieving political change by peaceful means. He also recognised it possible that Goans might not vote for independence if they were given a free choice.

In an attempt to allay Goan fears, Nehru addressed the issue publicly:

Goa has a distinct personality, and we have recognised it. It will be a pity to destroy that individuality, and we have decided to maintain it. With the influx of time, a change may come. But it will be gradual and will be made by the Goans themselves. We have decided to preserve the separate identity of Goa in the Union of India and we hold to it firmly. No agitation against it will be to any purpose.

Finally, Nehru found himself pushed to the brink when, in November 1961, Portuguese troops stationed 10km south of Goa opened fire on Indian fishing boats. Thus, on the night of 17 December 1961 Operation Vijay finally saw Indian troops crossing the border. They were met with little resistance and by evening of the following day the troops reached Panaji.

Portugal's dictator Dr Antonio de Oliveira Salazar attempted to lobby world leaders into condemning India's claims over Goa: he even managed to persuade John F Kennedy to write to Nehru, advising him against the use of force on the issue.

1955	1961	1962
On 15 August a huge satyagraha is called. Portuguese troops open fire on protestors; many are arrested, beaten, imprisoned and exiled to Africa.	On 17 December, Indian troops cross the border into Goa; by 19 December, an Indian flag flies atop Panaji's Secretariat Building.	Under the provisions of the Constitution 12th Amendment Act of 1962, the former Portuguese colonies of Goa, Daman and Diu are integrated with the Indian Union, effective from the first day of 'liberation' in 1961.

The Culture

GOAN IDENTITY

With the constant comings and goings of the sultans, kings, governors and colonising cultures of the last several thousand years, Goans have grown adept at clinging tight to their indigenous traditions, while blending in the most appealing elements of each successive visitation. Goans today take substantial pride in their Portuguese heritage – evident in their names, music, food and architecture – combining this seamlessly with Hindu festivals, Konkani chatter, Christmas parties, a keen interest in the English football leagues and, with the recent influx of Russian travellers to Goa's shores, an uncanny ability to rustle up a good bowl of borscht.

Modern Goa, moreover, is a place where some of those visitors have set down roots and decided to stay, where the hippies of the '60s have gone native, and where children of a whole host of cultures, alongside centuries-old Goan families, now deem themselves part of the cultural landscape. Here 'local' can mean a hole-in-the-wall *feni* (palm liquor) joint where patrons chat in Konkani and gaze at Bollywood music videos, or a chic boutique hotel whose patrons are simultaneously British and fourth-generation inhabitants of India, from a old-fashioned dynasty brewing up one of the country's most popular beers. Local can also mean a gleeful beach party with young Goans dancing the night away with international travellers, or a whitewashed Catholic church rubbing shoulders with a Hindu shrine, where Christian wakes are held by candlelight in honour of Hindu deities.

But whether Catholic Goan, Hindu Goan, Muslim Goan or 'new' Goan, some things unite everyone native to the eclectic state. Everyone has a strong opinion about the constantly changing faces of Goa, and of what it means, in essence, to be Goan. Everyone possesses a set of nostalgic memories of 'the way things used to be', whether this means the opulent landowning days of Portuguese dependence, the trippy free-love '60s, or the calm before the package-holiday storm. And above all, Goans across the state are eager to ensure, each in their own individual way, that Goa doesn't lose its alluring, endearing, ever-evolving distinctiveness in the centuries to come.

LIFESTYLE

Compared to the rest of the country, Goa is blessed with a relatively high standard of living, with healthcare, schooling, wages and literacy levels all far exceeding the national average. Its population of somewhere around 1.5 million is divided almost exactly down the middle between rural and

Unlike Hindi, the Konkani language doesn't have its own script, but is mostly written in the Roman alphabet. Like elsewhere in India, English is widespread in Goa, but these days Portuguese is mostly confined to wealthier, aristocratic Goan families, and to the older residents of Panaji's Latin Quarter.

For tips on culturally responsible travel, see Travelling Responsibly (p18)

SUSEGAD

You won't get far in Goa without spotting references to *susegad*, a *joie de vivre* attitude summed up along the lines of 'relax and enjoy life while you can'. Originating from the Portuguese word *sossegado* (literally meaning 'quiet'), it's a philosophy of afternoon naps, long, lazy evenings filled with *feni* (palm liquor) and song, and generally living life with a smile. On the 25th anniversary of Goan Independence, even Prime Minister Rajiv Gandhi described how 'an inherent nonacquisitiveness and contentment with what one has, described by that uniquely Goan word *sossegado*, has been an enduring strength of Goan character.'

In essence, it's *susegad* that makes a visit to Goa so special, with people ready to smile and say hello, to let you onto a crowded bus or simply sit and chat the warm tropical hours away.

urban populations, and many people continue to make their living from
tilling the land or raising livestock.

However, there are still those who fall desperately far below the poverty
line. You'll notice slums surrounding the heavy industry installations as you
drive south on the national highway from Dabolim Airport. Many migrant
workers, attracted to Goa by the hopes of benefiting from its tourist trade,
end up begging on its beaches, and hundreds of homeless children from
surrounding states are supported by local and international charities (see
p72 for more details).

Another acute local problem, linked both to poverty and Goa's liberal
attitude to drinking, is alcoholism. There are tens of thousands of registered
alcoholics in the state, and many more unregistered sufferers; you're sure to
witness the fallout of too many *fenis* in those stumbling about outside local
bars at some time during your visit.

Robert S Newman's *Of Umbrellas, Goddesses & Dreams* is a series of essays on Goan culture and the changes of the past two decades by an American writer and regular visitor to Goa.

Traditional Culture

Though many cultural traditions, particularly within Goa's Christian and
Hindu communities, overlap and mingle, you'll find some traditional practices
still going strong in Goa.

MARRIAGE

Though 'love marriages' are increasingly in vogue in Goa, in Christian and
Hindu circles alike, both communities still frequently use a matchmaker or
local contacts to procure a suitable partner for a son or daughter. If all else
fails, you'll find scores of ads listed in the newspaper classifieds, emphasising
the professional qualifications, physical attributes and 'wheatish' complexion
of the young, eligible individual.

Generally, following Hindu marriages, the young wife will leave her family
home to live with her husband's family. However, this is not always the case,
and many young couples today are choosing to branch off to begin their
own family home. Dowries are usually still required by the groom's family
in both Christian and Hindu weddings, either helping facilitate a match or
hindering it; a mixed-caste marriage will become much more acceptable if
there's a good dowry, but a high-caste girl from a poor family can find it
very difficult to secure a partner of a similar 'status'.

Teresa Albuquerque's *Anjuna: Profile of a Village in Goa* offers an in-depth portrait of a particularly prominent Goan village across the years, delving deep into its history, architecture, folklore and traditions.

Hindu weddings in Goa are lengthy, gleeful and colourful, while Christian
wedding ceremonies are more sombre (though the party afterwards usually
kicks up a storm) and similar to those in the West, with some elements, such
as the ritual bathing of the bride, borrowed from Hinduism. *Chudas*, green
bracelets traditionally worn by married women, are donned by both Hindu
and Christian brides, and tradition dictates that, should her husband die
before her, the widow must break the bangles on his coffin.

DEATH

Death, as everywhere, is big business in Goa, and you'll spot plenty of coffin makers, headstone carvers and hearse services on your travels. In the
Christian community, personal items are placed with the deceased in the
grave, including (depending on the habits of the deceased) cigarettes and a
bottle of *feni,* while most Hindus are cremated. Annual memorials, wakes
and services for the dead are honoured by Christians and Hindus alike.

There are numerous superstitions in the Hindu and Christian communities about restless spirits – particularly of those who committed suicide or died before being given last rites – and a number of measures are
undertaken at the funeral to discourage the spirit from returning. The
clothing and funeral shroud are cut, and a needle and thread are placed

in the coffin. The spirit of the deceased who wishes to come back must first repair its torn clothing, a task that takes until daylight, at which time departure from the grave is impossible.

Goa's tribal Gauda people take wedding nerves to the extreme: the day before the big day itself, the Gauda groom ritually runs away before being captured and returned by his friends.

Contemporary Issues

WOMEN IN GOAN SOCIETY

Generally, the position of women in Goa is better than that elsewhere in India, with women possessing property rights, education options and career prospects not shared by their sisters in other states. The result of Goa's progressive policies today is that women are far better represented than elsewhere in professions and positions of influence. While men undoubtedly still predominate, and many women still choose to fulfil traditional household roles, around 15% of the state's workforce are women, many of whom fill roles as doctors, dentists, teachers, solicitors and university lecturers, and 30% of panchayat (local government council) seats are reserved for women.

FEMALE FOETICIDE

Throughout India, baby boys frequently remain favoured over baby girls, particularly among the poor, and largely for what are seen as practical reasons. Girls require dowries when they get married, and then generally leave home to support their husband and his family. Conversely, boys, so the logic goes, will stay close to home, supporting their parents through old age.

In a bid to counter the practice of aborting female foetuses, the determination of sex of the unborn child has been made illegal under India's Prohibition of Sex Selection Act. But despite the law, the number of girls born continues to fall significantly short of the number of boys, and although Goan girls don't suffer ill-treatment to the same extent as girls in other regions of India, Goan organisations remain committed to actively promoting equality, and you'll pass plenty of posters cheerfully declaring 'Girl or Boy, Small Family is Joy'.

ECONOMY

Goa's economy, thriving on a combination of tourism and iron-ore mining, has given rise to a healthy Gross Domestic Product, annually coming in at around US$3 billion, about 2½ times higher than the national average. Around 12% of all tourists to India arrive annually in Goa, with the tourist figures now far exceeding the permanent population.

In 2008 and 2009 tourism to Goa fell dramatically, due to a combination of the global economic downturn and fears of terrorism spawned by a spate of bombings and the 2008 Mumbai (Bombay) attacks. Locals held on, in the hope that next season's trade would pick up, but it remains to be seen whether Goa's tourist-driven economy will recover quickly.

POPULATION

At the last national census, conducted in 2001, Goa's population was put at around 1.34 million, confirming that the state's population had doubled in size in just 40 years; it's now thought to hover at the 2 million mark. Alongside the permanent population and some 2 million annual tourists, Goa also supports a vast seasonal swell of migrant workers, functioning as labourers, beach hawkers, hotel workers, waiters, cooks, market sellers and, sadly, beggars on Goa's busy beaches.

RELIGION
Goa's Religious Diversity

Though Christianity, through centuries of Portuguese rule, has long appeared to hold sway in Goa, only around 30% of Goa's population is, in fact, Christian. The vast majority of Goans, around 65%, is Hindu, while the remaining 5% is mostly Muslim.

Statistical data doesn't reveal the true religious diversity that typifies the state. During the fierce imposition of Christianity by the Portuguese, particularly through vicious Inquisition-led repression, many Hindus fled to safety in parts of the state still considered safe, while others converted to the new faith and remained in Portuguese territory. Thus, for many generations, many Goan families have contained both Catholic and Hindu members.

The distinction was further blurred by the ways in which Christianity was adapted to appeal to the local population. As early as 1616 the Bible was translated into Konkani, while in 1623 Pope Gregory extended permission for Brahmin families converting to Catholicism to retain their high-caste status, and for a number of local festivals and traditions to continue to be observed.

Even today, this fusion of these religions is evident. The countless white-washed churches around the state demonstrate the splendid adaptation of Christianity; Christ and the Virgin Mary are often adorned with Hindu flower garlands, and Mass is said in Konkani. Christians and Hindus frequently pay respects to festivals of the others' faith, with both Christmas and Diwali frequently each being a source of celebration and *mithai*-giving (sweet-giving) for all.

That's not to say that Goa is free from religious tensions. In 2006 anti-Muslim riots, initially caused by the destruction of a makeshift village mosque in Sanvordem, shook Goa's religiously tolerant to the core. Moreover, a spate of robberies of relics from churches and Hindu temples has sparked public debate on religious tolerance, ultimately, and happily, reinvigorating the fervour with which the majority respect different faiths.

Throughout Goa, you'll find reference to Our Lady of Health Vailankali, whose church lies in Tamil Nadu, several days' bus ride away. Goan Christians in need of health-related divine intervention often head off to this shrine, established in the 17th century after a series of apparent miracles and apparitions.

GOA'S CASTE SYSTEM: HINDU & CHRISTIAN ALIKE

Every Hindu is born into an unchangeable social class, a caste or varna. Though its origins are hazy, the system seems to have been developed by the Brahmins (the highest, priest class) in order to maintain superiority over India's indigenous Dravidians. Eventually, the caste system became formalised into four distinct classes, each with its own rules of conduct and behaviour.

These four castes, in hierarchical order, are the Brahmins (Bamons in Konkani; priests and teachers), Kshatriyas (Chardos in Konkani; warriors and rulers), Vaisyas (merchants and farmers) and Sudras (peasants and menial workers). Beneath the four main castes is a fifth group, the Untouchables (Chamars in Konkani; formerly known as 'Harijan', but now officially 'Dalits' or 'Scheduled Castes'). These people traditionally performed 'polluting' jobs, including undertaking, street sweeping and leather working; though discrimination against them is now a criminal offence in India, it's nevertheless still an unfortunate part of life.

While the caste system doesn't play as crucial a part in life in Goa as elsewhere in India, it's nevertheless still recognised and treated in a uniquely Goan way, and wealthy landowners and holders of public office remain largely of the Bamon or Chardo castes.

The Christian community also quietly adheres to the caste system, a situation that can be traced back to Portuguese rule since, as an incentive to convert to Catholicism, high-caste Goan families were able to keep their caste privileges, money and land. Even today, in village churches, high-caste Christians tend to dominate the front pews and the lower caste the back of the congregation, and both Hindus and Christians carefully consider questions of caste when selecting candidates for a suitable marriage match.

Hinduism

Though Hinduism encompasses a huge range of personal beliefs, the essential Hindu belief is in Brahman, an infinite being, or supreme spirit, from which everything derives and to which everything will return. Hindus believe that life is cyclical and subject to reincarnations (avatars), eventually leading to moksha spiritual release. An individual's progression towards that point is governed by the law of karma (cause and effect); good karma (through positive actions such as charity and worship) may result in being reborn into a higher caste and better circumstances, and bad karma (accumulated through bad deeds) may result in reincarnation in animal form. It's only as a human that one can finally acquire sufficient self-knowledge to achieve liberation from the cycle of reincarnation.

For easy-to-read depictions of the Hindu holy texts, look out for Amar Chitra Katha's colourful comic-book-style versions of the Ramayana and the Mahabharata.

HINDU WORSHIP

Hindu homes often have a dedicated worship area, and you'll likely find even the most simple dwelling has a corner shrine, complete with images, incense, candles and garlands. Beyond the household hearth, temples (mandirs or *devuls* in Konkani) are the focal point of religious life, containing a deity *(devta)* that is worshipped as an embodiment of a god or goddess themselves, with the deities ranging from simple symbolic stones to superbly crafted statues.

Hindu *puja* (worship) ranges from silent prayer to elaborate ceremonies, and usually culminates in *darshan,* the ritual viewing of this deity. Devotees leave the temple with a handful of *prasad* (temple-blessed food, usually in the form of a sweet), having bowed before the deity, and presented an offering to the temple priest *(pujari).* Other forms of worship include *aarti* (auspicious lighting of lamps) and bhajans (devotional songs), while temple priests spend their days chanting Sanskrit verses, dressing the *devta,* and anointing the foreheads of the faithful with vermillion paste *(tilak).*

Aside from gods, goddesses and *devtas* themselves, Hindus have long worshipped animals, particularly snakes and cows, for their symbolism. The cow represents fertility and nurturing, while snakes are associated with fertility and welfare. Cows take full advantage of their special status in Goa, lazing in the middle of even chaotic highways, seemingly without a care in this mortal coil.

Goan Hindu homes are identifiable by the multicoloured *vrindavan* (ornamental container) that stands outside the front of the house. Growing inside it is the twiggy tulsi plant, sacred to Hindus since in mythology the tulsi is identified as one of the god Vishnu's lovers, who his consort, Lashmet, turned into a shrub in a fit of jealousy.

Christianity

Christianity has been present in Goa since the arrival of the Portuguese in the 16th century, who enforced their faith on Goa's Muslim and Hindu population by way of the Goan Inquisition (see the box, opposite, and p34). By the time Hindus and Muslims were once again able to practise freely, Catholicism had taken root and was here to stay.

Though whitewashed churches grace the centre of every Goan village, and are attended with smart clothes and enthusiasm each Sunday, Goa's most impressive Christian edifices are without doubt at Unesco World Heritage–rated Old Goa, which are open daily for you to check out. Even outside Old Goa, you'll be welcomed into any Goan church, provided you dress with respect, though in smaller villages you might have to hunt around to find someone with a key.

For the last 30 years or so, a second form of Christianity – known as 'Charismatic Christianity' – has being gaining ground in Goa. Worship of this nature is far less staid than the traditional old Catholic Mass, involving lots of dancing, singing and sometimes 'speaking in tongues', with readings from the New Testament allegedly used to harness the power of the holy spirit, heal the sick and banish evil forces. Unlike mainstream Catholicism, Charismatic Christianity's services are usually in the open air, and its priests

THE HORRORS OF THE INQUISITION

Of all Portugal's alleged abuses of its Goan subjects, the terrors to which the population was subjected under the iron rule of the Inquisition – also known as the Holy Office or Santo Officio – were undoubtedly the worst.

The Holy Inquisition was dispatched to Goa in 1560 on royal command, originally conceived to target 'New Christians' (Cristianos Nuevos), the forcibly converted Jews and Muslims of Portugal who had fled to the country's colonies and 'lapsed' back to their original faiths. By the time the Inquisition arrived life was already becoming increasingly difficult for the region's Hindus, who for some years had been enduring a slowly eroding official tolerance to their faith. Idols had been banned, temples closed and priests banished. Now, with the arrival of the Inquisitors, matters went from bad to worse: refusing to eat pork was now an imprisonable crime, as was possession of turmeric, incense and other items used in traditional Hindu worship.

Though the genuinely louche and licentious Portuguese gentry went generally above the law, the lower, indigenous classes soon found themselves at risk of imprisonment in the fearsome dungeons of the Palace of the Inquisition, the *Orlem Ghor* (big house), of Old Goa, with tortures such as the rack, flesh-eroding quicklime, burning sulphur and thumbscrews awaiting them until they confessed to heresy.

Once a confession had been extracted, the despairing prisoner then languished in a window-less cell, awaiting one of the Inquisition's famous autos-da-fé (trials of faith). During the morbidly theatrical 'trials', dozens of prisoners, dressed in tall mitres and robes emblazoned with macabre images of human beings engulfed in flames, would be marched across the city of Old Goa, from the Palace of the Inquisition to the Church of St Francis of Assisi, amid crowds of onlookers and to the solemn tolling of the Sé Cathedral bell.

Inside the church, following a lengthy sermon, the judgments were read to the accused. The lucky ones were to endure slavery abroad; the less lucky would be burned alive at the stake. In the period between 1560 and 1774 (after which records become sketchy) a total of 16,176 people were arrested by the Inquisition, mostly Hindus, though more than two-thirds of those burned alive were Jews who had been forcibly converted as Cristianos Nuevos. In 1814 the Inquisition was finally repealed, as part of an Anglo-Portuguese treaty, and most of its later records destroyed.

It's hard today to imagine the full horror of the Inquisition, but stroll Old Goa with its tales in mind and you'll likely shiver despite the tropical heat. The table at which the Inquisitors came to their evil decisions is preserved at the State Museum in Panaji (p114), while a crucifix that stared down from behind them at their victims remains nearby, in the Chapel of St Sebastian (p112).

reject all notions of caste. Understandably, this makes the movement particularly popular among Goa's lower castes, who are frequently relegated to the back seats at more conventional church services.

Islam

Brought to Goa in the 11th century by wealthy Arab merchants, who were encouraged by local rulers to settle here for reasons of commerce, Islamic rule predominated in the region for large chunks of medieval Goan history.

With the arrival of the Portuguese, Islam all but disappeared in Goa, and now remains in only small communities. Most Goan Muslims today live in Goa's green heartland, around Ponda, in the vicinity of the state's biggest mosque, the Safa Masjid.

Goan villages are divided into *waddos* (wards); traditionally, all the members of one caste lived in a single *waddo*, meaning that each *waddo* became associated with a particular profession.

ARTS
Music & Dance

Listen carefully beyond the Bob Marley, lounge and techno jumble of the beach shacks, and you'll hear Goa's own melodies, which, like most other things in the state, are a heady concoction of East and West.

occasionally, recent refurbishment, while a visit to Calizz is a wonderful way to bring yourself up to speed with Goa's architectural heritage.

Churches also bear the hallmarks of Portuguese influence, many of them cruciform design and constructed from local laterite stone, whitewashed and plain since laterite is too coarse to support fine carving. In contrast, even the humblest of village churches usually sports a sumptuous interior, with an elaborate gilt reredos (ornamental screen), lots of carving, painting, chandeliers, and other embellishment adorning the altar before it and chancel in front of that. Peek into any village church you come across to be dazzled by light, gilt and colour, and don't miss a stop off at Panaji's Church of Our Lady of the Immaculate Conception (p113), or at Old Goa for even statelier examples of Goa's Catholic architectural heritage.

Goan temples are yet another form of architectural hybrid, enfolding both Muslim and Christian elements into traditional Hindu designs. Domed roofs, for example, are a Muslim trait, while balustraded facades and octagonal towers are borrowed from Portuguese church architecture.

Many architectural features in Goa are standard to temples countrywide. The pillared pavilion is known as the *mandapa*, and the inner sanctum, where the deity or *devta* resides, is called the *garbhagriha*. The area in between the two is known as the *antaralya*, on either side of which are smaller shrines to other deities worshipped at the temple. The most unusual and distinctive features, however, of Goan temples are the unique-to-the-region 'light towers', known as *deepastambhas*, which look a little like Chinese pagodas and are atmospherically decorated with oil lamps during festival periods. For more on Goan temple architecture, check out the boxed text, p136.

Before the availability of glass, windows were filled with translucent oyster shells. The 7cm- to 10cm-diameter discs were set in wooden frames and allowed a gentle, cool light to filter into the rooms.

Painting

Although there's no style that is particularly distinctive to Goa, some of the state's most historic artistic output can be seen in the murals at Rachol Seminary (p185), in the ornately decorated churches across Goa, and adorning the portraiture-heavy walls of Goa's grand mansion homes. Today, Goa's budding artists are nurtured at the College of Art in Panaji, after which most opt to travel out of the state to study art at a higher level elsewhere.

Out and about in Goa, the two artists you're most likely to come across are Dr Subodh Kerkar, whose work fills the Kerkar Art Complex in Calangute (p157), and artist and illustrator Mario Miranda, whose distinctive style adorns everything from books to billboards to the walls of Café Mondegar (p100) in Mumbai.

Cinema

The Indian film industry is the largest on the planet, with around 800 movies produced annually, most of them elaborate, formulaic melodramatic Bollywood montages that celebrate romance, violence and music, with saccharine lip-synched duets and fantastic dance routines, all performed by Indian megastars who are worshipped like deities countrywide. It's absolutely imperative, during any stay in Goa, to see at least one of these incredible creations of high camp, and Panaji's the place to do so, with the comfortable INOX Cinema (p119) and the far more gritty and atmospheric Cine Nacional (p119) the best cinematic destinations.

The INOX also plays host to Goa's grand and glittering annual International Film Festival of India (IFFI; www.iffi.gov.in), the country's largest festival, which sees Bollywood's greatest and most glorious jetting in for preening and partying all along the red carpet.

GOA SUPREME

Fans of the enigmatic Jason Bourne might recognise a small road bridge, spanning the Nerul River north of Candolim, from which Bourne's girlfriend plunged to a watery grave following a high-octane *Bourne Supremacy* (2004) car chase.

This scene was one of several filmed in Goa, which hops from Palolem to Panaji and on to Candolim. But if you really want to tread in Bourne's footsteps, check in – as did his alter ego, Matt Damon – to the nearby Fort Aguada Beach Resort (p152) to see how the amnesiac assassin kicked back after a long, hot day of filming.

Theatre

Goa's theatre scene is dominated by the unique local street plays known as *tiatr* and *khell tiatr* (a longer form of *tiatr* performed only during festivals such as Carnival and Easter). The *tiatrs*, almost all of which are in Konkani, provide a platform for satire on politics, current affairs and day-to-day domestic issues. Each comprises seven acts of 15 or so minutes each, with song and dance interspersed merrily in between.

The first ever *tiatr*, called *Italian Boy*, was created by Lucasinho Ribeiro, a Goan living in Mumbai who brought the art form back to Goa with him in 1894. Since 1974 Panaji's Kala Academy (p119) has held an annual festival (all performed in Konkani) each November, showcasing the work of well-known *tiatr* writers.

SPORT

Just about everyone knows how seriously Indians take the pursuit of cricket, but it may come as a surprise to learn that Goa's top sport is in fact football (soccer), another legacy left over from the days of Portuguese rule. Every village has at least one football team, and sometimes several – one team for each small ward of the village – and league games are fiercely contested.

The result of this keen village following has been the creation of several teams that regularly perform at National Football League (NFL) level, and these days there are even Goan players in the national football squad. The main Goan teams to watch are Salgaonkar SC from Vasco da Gama, Dempo SC from Panaji, and Churchill Brothers SC from Margao, and matches are played out at the Jawaharlal Nehru Stadium, near the Margao bus station, regularly attracting up to 35,000 fans. The official soccer season runs from January to May; tickets to the matches generally cost less than Rs30 and can be bought at the ticket kiosks on match days.

Goans are also keen cricketers and you'll see plenty of dusty playing fields being used for local matches. Volleyball, too, is a firm local favourite, with regular matches played at sunset on beaches and on almost every village green.

A good source of all things cultural for travellers to Goa is the online 'lifestyle magazine' *Goa Groove*, www.goagroove.com.

Food & Drink

Goan cuisine, with its seemingly infinite combinations of coconut, chillies, vinegar, rice and spice, is one of the world's original fusion foods, rich in Portuguese and South Indian heritage and distinctly different from the culinary inclinations of the rest of India. '*Prodham bhookt, magi mookt,*' say the locals in Konkani; 'You can't think until you've eaten well,' and Goans take the sating of their appetites extremely seriously.

Though vegetarian Indian food is in no short supply throughout the state, many Goans, unlike most other Indians, are hearty meat-eaters and, with an equally prolific stock of fresh seafood at their disposal, typically Goan dishes come with a meaty or fishy accent. The very best of Goan cuisine isn't all that easy to come by outside local homes and speciality restaurants, and the most delicious dishes are set aside for the feast days, saints' days, birthdays, weddings and religious holidays that Goans are so very fond of celebrating. Hunt about in local haunts, however, and your search will be rewarded with mouth-watering Goan curries galore, such as *xacutis, vindalhos, cafrials* and *balchãos.*

You'll also find that neither sweet stuff nor alcohol is neglected in Goa. Alcohol doesn't carry the stigma here of elsewhere in the country, and beer, brandy, local firewater *feni* and, increasingly, Indian and Portuguese wines (all in various states of drinkability) are imbibed and enjoyed by locals and visitors alike. In the sweet department, creations are cooked up in combinations of sugar, cardamom, coconut and jaggery (dark palm sugar): they might not be bikini-conducive, but they sure do taste divine.

> Dig into *Savour the Flavour of India*, an authentic collection of Goan and Indian recipes by Edna Fernandes.

STAPLES & SPECIALITIES

Given Goa's seaside location and its proliferation of rivers, streams, lakes and canals, it's little wonder that fish is the traditional local staple, with over a hundred varieties of freshwater and saltwater fish and seafood on the regular Goan menu. Almost every Goan eats a simple staple lunch of *fish-curry-rice,* a piece of crisp fried mackerel steeped in a thin coconut, tamarind and red chilli sauce and served with a heaped mound of rice; you'll find it on any 'nonveg' restaurant's menu, and it's a cheap and tasty way to fill up at midday.

Aside from all things aquatic, chicken and pork are the meats of favour (you'll see the live versions gadding about in every Goan farmyard), and the latter makes for another local lunchtime favourite, served up in the form of a piled plate of Goan *chouriços.* These air-dried spicy red pork sausages (similar to chorizo from Spain) are flavoured with *feni* (palm liquor), toddy (palm sap) vinegar and chillies, and strung in desiccated garlands from streetside stalls, to be rehydrated, fried up and served with fresh *pau,* fluffy white bread rolls that are part of Portugal's lasting legacy to the state.

> According to linguists, there's no such thing as an Indian 'curry' – the word, an anglicised derivative of the Tamil word *kari* (black pepper), was used by the British as a term for any dish including spices.

Goans also have an insatiably sweet tooth, specialising in a vast range of elaborate puddings and cakes. Look out for local sticky specialities, made of combinations of sugar, eggs and coconut, alongside the more standard variety of Indian sweets piled high in confectioners' windows.

Spices

Head to one of Goa's heavenly scented spice farms and you'll find evidence of the much sought-after spices that kept conquerors coming back to Goa for centuries. South India still produces the very best of the world's black pepper crop, an essential ingredient in savoury dishes worldwide, while locally produced turmeric, coriander and cumin seeds form the basis of many an Indian curry.

Goan cooking involves liberal use of these and other spices, pounded together to make mouth-watering masalas (spice mixtures), with plenty of fiery fresh chilli and pungent garlic thrown into the mix, while tamarind and *kokum* (a dried fruit used as a spice) are both widely used in the makings of Goan cuisine. With these few simple spices as a base, Goan cooks are able to conjure a wealth of subtly different flavours.

Rice

Rice is by far the most important staple in India, providing most meals for most people throughout most of their lives, and Goa is no exception. Long-grain white rice is the most common, served piping hot with just about any cooked meat or vegetable dish, and ladled up in mountains with each lunchtime thali (traditional all-you-can-eat meal). In its more sophisticated guises, rice is cooked up to make *pulao* (pilau; aromatic rice casserole), or as a Muslim biryani, with a layer of vegetable, chicken or mutton curry hiding under a ricey surface. Both these dishes are prevalent on Indian menus throughout the state, and make a great change whenever you're thoroughly tired of the plain white variety.

Dhal

Vegetarian or omnivorous, Christian, Hindu or Muslim, India is united in its love for dhal (lentils or pulses), the style of which differs depending on what part of the region you're in.

Most commonly in Goa, you'll find three types of dhal gracing the menu: thin, spicy *sambar*, served with many breakfast dishes; 'dhal fry', which is yellow, mild and has the comforting consistency of a thick soup; and 'dhal makhani', richer and darker, spiked *rajma* (kidney beans), cream and onions and another handful or two of some of the 60 types of pulses grown in the country. Various other forms of pulses, including *kabuli chana* (chickpeas)

Rice is used to symbolise purity and fertility in Hindu wedding ceremonies and is often used as *puja* (offering) in temples.

GOAN NUTS

Swaying coconut palms comprise the very essence of the Goan landscape, but they're far more than just a photogenic sunset sight. Goans alone get through something approaching 40 million coconuts every year, and the simple coconut is responsible for the livelihoods of around 18% of the state's population.

Coconut flesh, known as copra, gives flavour and substance to almost every Goan speciality dish, both savoury and sweet, as well as providing oil for use in other sorts of cooking, soap manufacture, hair oil and cosmetics. The hairy outer shell of the coconut is spun into water-resistant coir rope, and used by Goan fishermen to secure their boats.

But the humble coconut's usefulness doesn't stop there. Its sap, known as toddy, is collected by toddy tappers, who shinny up their swaying trees two or three times daily. It's then fermented and made into that killer liquor, *feni*, which is drunk widely; often a little too widely by the toddy tappers themselves. Coconut wood is used for timber, and its leaves provide roofing for many a lean-to shelter and simple traveller beach hut.

Out and about on the Goan beach, you're bound to be approached by coconut vendors keen to cut open a fresh fruit, so that you can sip on the vitamin-rich milk. It makes a refreshing change from an everyday soft drink, and offers up a true, unadulterated taste of Goa. Just don't, whatever you do, set up your sleeping bag beneath a coconut palm: a few victims a year meet their maker by way of fruit that go bump in the night.

THE MOST IMPORTANT MEAL OF THE DAY

Keen breakfasters will delight in the range of options on offer in Goa, from the 'banana-honey-porridge' of the beach shacks to the South Indian treats of the Goan breakfast table.

Don't miss the classic *bhaji-pau*, a white bread roll *(pau)* served ready to dunk into a spicy side curry (bhaji). Washed down with a glass of hot chai, it's simply one of the world's best and simplest breakfasts, and will set you back a mere Rs15 or so. Each establishment has its own take on the bhaji that makes up *bhaji-pau*: some are potato-based, others include black-eyed beans, chickpeas and caramelised onions. And in some more adventurous establishments, you'll get further options: try a cashew nut bhaji, and swap your *pau* for *paratha* (a griddle-fried, pancakelike bread).

Mouth-watering *masala dosas* (thin pancakes of rice and lentil batter, fried and folded, and often served with masala-spiced potato filling) are also served up for breakfast, as are the other southern specialities of *idli* (round steamed rice cakes often eaten with *sambar* and chutney) and *vada* (also spelt 'wada'; potato and/or lentil savoury doughnut, deep-fried and served with *sambar* and chutney). Whatever combination you choose, cornflakes will never seem the same again.

---

and *lobhia* (black-eyed beans), also turn up regularly in that delicious Goan breakfast staple, *bhaji-pau*.

Meat

While India likely has more vegetarians than the rest of the world combined, Goa's specialities are distinctly carnivorous, and though religious taboos make beef forbidden to Hindus, and pork to Muslims, you'll find more than a few members of those faiths who keep strictly to the rule only on religious holidays.

Get Goan recipes, from *fish-curry-rice* to *bebinca* (rich Goan dessert made from coconut and egg yolk), online at www.indianfoodforever .com/goan/.

Alongside the lunchtime *chouriço* sausages, look out for *xacuti*, a spicy sauce – pronounced sha-*coo*-tee – originally used to create vegetarian dishes (*sha* means 'vegetable', and *cootee* means 'finely chopped', in Konkani) but also now found in meaty incarnations, usually combining coconut milk, freshly ground spices and red chillies.

Chicken and seafood are frequently served for dinner basted with *rechead,* a spicy marinating paste, which sees its host fried, grilled or baked in a tandoori oven. Dry-fried chicken might otherwise be served spicy *cafrial* style – marinated in a green masala paste and sprinkled with toddy vinegar. Meanwhile, the original *vindalho* – far from being the sole preserve of something-to-prove British vindaloo-loving curry house lads – is a uniquely Goan derivative of Portuguese pork stew that traditionally combines *vinho* (wine vinegar) with *ahlo* (garlic) and spices.

Seafood

Portugal's culinary influence on Goan cuisine is especially evident in its approach to all things of the sea, with dishes such as *recheiado* (stuffed fish) and *caldeirada* (stewed fish) reflecting the state's colonial heritage. The true Goan seafood staple, however, remains simple, cheap and spicy *fish-curry-rice*.

For the sake of tourist tastebuds, many places present fish and seafood – primarily kingfish, pomfret, shark and tuna – altogether unspiced, and instead opt for fish grilled or cooked in a light garlic sauce. Traditional Goan cooking usually involves seasoning the seafood in one masala or another, and the results are usually very spicy.

Among the most famous Goan fish dishes is *ambot tik,* a slightly sour curry that can be prepared with either fish or meat, but most often with the former. *Caldeirada,* meanwhile, is a mildly flavoured dish in which fish or prawns are cooked into a kind of stew with vegetables, flavoured with wine. *Recheiado* is a delicious preparation in which a whole fish, usually a mackerel or pomfret, is slit down the centre and stuffed with a spicy red sauce, after which it's fried up in hot oil. A final regular on Goan menus is *balchão*, a deliciously rich and tangy dark red tomato and chilli sauce, often used to cook tiger prawns or fish, and gobbled up with liberal quantities of fresh bread.

Pickles, Chutneys & Relishes

No Indian meal is complete without one, if not all, of the above, and a relish can be anything from a roughly chopped onion to a delicately crafted fusion of fruit, nuts and spices. The best known is raita (mildly spiced yoghurt, often containing shredded or diced cucumber, carrot, tomato or pineapple; served chilled), while *chatnis*, as chutneys are locally known, can come in any number of varieties (such as sweet and salty) and can be made from many different vegetables, fruits, herbs and spices. But proceed with caution before polishing off that pickled speck of lime on one side of your thali; it'll quite possibly be the hottest thing on the whole plate.

> The *bhut jolokia*, grown in the northeast of India, is the world's spiciest chilli according to the *Guinness Book of Records*. It's also known as the 'ghost chilli', since those who eat it, according to locals, are in danger of ending up as one.

Dairy products

Milk and milk products make an enormous contribution to Indian cuisine, and Goa's cooking relies on them: a small pot of glistening white *dahi* (curd) is served with most meals, most traditionally in an unfired clay pot, and is wonderful for taming fiery masalas; Indian paneer cheese is a godsend for the vegetarian majority; popular lassi (yoghurt drink) is just one in a host of nourishing sweet and savoury drinks; ghee (clarified butter) is the traditional and pure cooking medium; and the best local sweets are made with milk.

Recently, Goa has seen a rise in the number of European-style cheeses on offer in its shops and restaurants. Maia Cheese, based in Palolem, was founded by a Russian expat, who used her expertise to turn local buffalo milk into tasty mozzarella, and also creates a host of other delicious soft cheeses and sour creams. Kodaicanal and Auroville dairies, both in nearby states, have also branched out into cheese making, creating fetas, cheddars and even blue cheese in generally tasty varieties. Most can be bought at grocery shops statewide, and are to be found gracing many a beachside Italian restaurant's pizza.

> Each year more than 13 tonnes of pure silver are converted into the edible foil that's added to Indian sweets for decoration.

Sweets

Look out for *bebinca*, the most famous of Goan sweets, a rich and delicious 16-layer coconut pancake-type cake, which is whipped up with sugar, nutmeg, cardamom and egg yolks. Also be sure to sample *batica*, a squidgy coconut cake best served piping hot from the oven; *doce* made with chickpeas and coconut; and *dodol*, a gorgeous, gooey fudgelike treat, made from litres of fresh coconut milk, mixed with rice flour and jaggery and boiled gently for hours on end, a time-consuming speciality generally reserved for the most special of occasions.

DRINKS
Nonalcoholic Drinks

There's nothing more refreshing on a hot, tropical day than a steaming glass of chai (tea), boiled for hours with milk, sugar and masala spices, and served piping hot, sweet and frothy. You'll find chai on sale at every tiny stall and lunch stand, and the general rule is that the simpler the place, the better it will taste. Try as you might, you'll never quite get it to taste the same back home, without the dust, grime and decades-old teapot.

Coffee is less widely consumed by local Goans, but you'll have no problem finding the instant kind; 'milk coffee', as it's sold in beach shacks, is usually

> Legend says that Buddha, after falling asleep during meditation, decided to cut off his eyelids in an act of penance. The lids grew into the tea plant, which, when brewed, banished sleep.

a boiling hot cup of steamed milk, with a spoonful of Nescafé sprinkled on top. Goa is increasingly finding its way into the speciality coffee market, and fragrant loose beans for home grinding can be bought at local markets, while high-end coffee stands – selling the full line of macchiato through to Americano – are popping up in many tourist hot spots.

Aside from the long line of sweet and fizzy drinks, there are several less tooth-eroding options. 'Lime-soda' is a standard (soda water mixed with freshly squeezed lime juice); ask for it 'plain' if you don't want sugar or salt added. Lassis are a great, healthy breakfast drink; again, these can be made sweet or salty, but are especially delicious in the banana or mango varieties. Freshly squeezed fruit and vegetable juices are also generally available at most beach shacks; the best are seasonal, and watermelon or pineapple are two sure-fire hits.

If you're in the mood for a wee dram, take note that Bagpiper Whisky is India's best-selling whisky, and the 4th-biggest seller worldwide.

Alcoholic Drinks

Goans love to drink – a fact sadly attested to by the state's high level of alcoholism – and alcohol is widely available and extremely cheap (with the exception of wine) across the state.

Aside from *feni*, the local moonshine (see the box, opposite), Goa's tipple of choice is beer, and Kingfisher and Kings are the two local favourites. Increasingly, foreign labels are available in Goa, some imported, and others – such as San Miguel – brewed domestically under licence.

Hard liquor, known in India as IMFL – Indian-made foreign liquors – is largely cheap, and palatable if mixed with something soft, sweet and bubbly. You'll have fun choosing from the names on offer; opt for a Honeybee or an Old Monk depending on your inclination.

Wine, though not India's strong point, is slowly growing in popularity in Goa, but you'll pay dearly for choosing the grape over the grain: bought at a liquor store, even a mediocre bottle of local or Portuguese wine costs in the region of Rs500. Unless you're a fan of all things sickly sweet, avoid Madeira in its red, white and rosé varieties – though drunk cold on ice, it tastes a bit like dessert wine – and local port wines are almost all on the supersweet side. Domestic wines, such as Sula, Chateau Indage and Grover, are all at the high end of what the Indian wine world has on offer, while expat-haven supermarkets such as those in Candolim and Anjuna stock a huge range of international wines for those desperately seeking sauvignon.

A portal to websites about Indian wine, www .indianwine.com, has notes on manufacturers, information on growing regions and more.

CELEBRATIONS

Goans need only the flimsiest excuse to celebrate and almost every month has a festival that requires feasting. Weddings are occasions to indulge gastronomic fantasies. Receptions begin with toasts, the cutting of an elaborate cake and ballroom dancing. The meal features roast suckling pig and other pork dishes such as *sorpotel,* one of Goa's most famous meat dishes, prepared with a combination of the meat and organs (kidneys, liver, heart and blood). These are diced and cooked in a thick and very spicy sauce flavoured with *feni* to give it an added kick. Seafood also features on the menu at such feasts, tables groaning under the weight of dishes such as fish aspic (set in gelatine), oyster pie, stuffed and grilled *surmai* (mackerel) and curried or fried prawns. Desserts might include *bebinca,* crème caramel and *leitria* (an elaborate sweet made with coconut covered by a lacy filigree of egg yolks and sugar syrup).

Although Hindu festivals have sometimes solemn, sometimes technicolour sheens of religious reverence, they're also occasions for feasting and each festival has its own special dishes. Sweets are considered the most luxurious of foods and almost every occasion is celebrated with a staggering range. *Karanjis,* crescent-shaped flour parcels stuffed with sweet *khoya* (milk solids) and nuts, are synonymous with Holi, the most boisterous Hindu festival, and it wouldn't be the same without *malpuas* (wheat pancakes dipped in syrup), *barfis* (fudgelike sweets) and *pedas* (multicoloured pieces of *khoya* and sugar). Pongal (Tamil for 'overflowing') is the major harvest festival of the south and is most closely associated with the dish of the same name, made with the season's first rice along with jaggery, nuts, raisins and spices. Diwali, the festival of lights, is the most widely celebrated national festival, and some regions have specific Diwali sweets. If you're in Mumbai (Bombay), don't miss the delicious *anarsa* (rice-flour cookies).

While the majority of the state marks its religious fervour by frenzied feasting, the most significant month for the other 5% is Ramadan, the Islamic month of fasting, when Muslims abstain from eating, smoking or drinking even water between sunrise and sunset. Each day's fast is often broken with dates – the most auspicious food in Islam – followed by fruit and fruit juices, then followed up with a huge meal after sunset. On the final day of Ramadan, Eid al-Fitr, an extravagant feast, celebrates the final end to the fast, with especially succulent biryanis and yet another huge proliferation of sugary sweets.

> To watch online videos of Goan recipes in the making, go to www.ifood.tv/network /goan_/recipes.

WHERE TO EAT & DRINK

Goa's eating-out options are almost equally divided into the 'local' and 'nonlocal' varieties: the local serving up Indian cuisine of one sort or another, and the nonlocal encompassing everything from beach shacks to Tibetan kitchens to authentic French fine dining.

The simplest local restaurants, widely known as 'hotels' – though they have no rooms on offer – are generally divided into the 'veg' and 'nonveg'

FENI

It's as clear as water, it tastes like aromatic gasoline and it really packs a punch – Goa's most famous spirit is the double-distilled and fearfully potent *feni*. There are two types of *feni*, both of which are made from local ingredients.

Coconut or palm *feni* is made from the sap drawn from the severed shoots on a coconut tree. In Goa this is known as toddy, collected year-round by toddy tappers, so palm *feni* is in plentiful supply at all times.

Caju (cashew) *feni*, whose taste is slightly more refined and tequila-like, can only be made during the cashew season in late March and early April. The cashew apple, when ripe, turns a yellow-orange colour and the nut ripens below it. When the fruit is harvested, the nuts are dried in the sun and the apples are trampled to collect the juice. Both palm toddy and *caju* juice can be drunk fresh immediately – the juice only begins to ferment after it's been left in the sun for a few hours.

After the fermentation process, the juice is placed in a large terracotta pot over a wood fire; the vapour exits through a tube that typically passes through an oil drum filled with water, below which the distillate is collected. The result is *uraq*, a medium-strength spirit (10% to 15% proof), some of which is kept and sold. The majority though, is distilled again to make *feni*. By the time it comes out of the second distillation, Goa's signature drink has an alcoholic strength of around 30% to 35% proof.

Feni first-timers might decide to mix it with a soft drink, or just close their eyes and take their medicine. Goans are keen to offer advice to foreigners: don't drink it on an empty stomach; don't mix it with other spirits; and certainly don't swim after a couple of *fenis*. They're right, since you generally don't feel its effects until you stand up and try to walk a straight line.

A shot of *feni* in any bar or restaurant costs from Rs20 to Rs40. You can also buy colourful decorative bottles from wine stores (between Rs100 and Rs400), a good gift for friends you want to incapacitate.

varieties, and are the very best destinations for a good, cheap breakfast or a filling thali lunch. The same goes for *dhabas*, wayside eateries which were originally the domain of North India, but nowadays are also on the highways and byways throughout Goa. The rough-and-ready but extremely tasty food served in these ramshackle shacks has become a genre of its own known as '*dhaba* food'.

Midrange Indian restaurants meanwhile generally serve one of two basic genres of Indian food: South Indian (which means the vegetarian food of Tamil Nadu and Karnataka) and North Indian (which comprises richer, and often meatier, Punjabi-Mughlai food). Panaji, in particular, has a wonderful array of midrange local restaurants, where you'll enjoy tandoori specialities. The final (and rarest) type of local restaurant are those serving Goan cuisine itself. You'll likely have quite a search, though, to locate them, as they're not at all as common as you might think or hope.

India has more than 500 varieties of mango, and supplies 60% of the world with what is regarded as the 'king of fruit'.

Away from the beach shacks and chic lounges of Calangute and Baga, the best place for a tipple or two is a hole-in-the-wall local bar. Dingy walls, plastic chairs and an ever-playing TV are all prerequisites for the places locals come to sip a cold beer or superstrength *feni*, and are a crucial component of any 'authentic' Goan experience. Many close for a siesta after lunch, reopening around sunset, but make up for the loss in drinking time by staying open well on into the wee hours.

Street Food

Whatever the time of day, people are boiling, frying, roasting, peeling, juicing, simmering or baking food in streetside stalls to lure passers-by. Deep-fried fare is largely the staple of the streets, and you'll encounter samosas (deep-fried pyramid-shaped pastries filled with spiced vegetables and sometimes meat), *aloo tikka* (mashed potato patties) and *bhajia* (vegetable fritters) in varying degrees of spiciness, along with *puri* (also spelt 'poori'; thin puffed-up deep fried breads).

In general, don't be frightened to tuck into street food. *Bhelpuri*, a Mumbai fried-noodle snack food that takes on a totally regional twist in Goa, roasted sweet-corn cobs and other tasty titbits are all on offer. A good rule of thumb is that if locals are eating at a streetside stand, it's a pretty safe bet that you can too, so follow your nose and the evening buzz to street food tasty as any gourmet's offerings, but instead sold for peanuts.

VEGETARIANS & VEGANS

Tens of millions of Indian vegetarians can't be wrong – and India has the world's best breadth of choice for those who abstain from fish, flesh and fowl. You might experience some challenges if you're vegan, since

---

VEGETARIAN STAPLES

Here are a few old faithfuls you'll see gracing most menus, perfect for tucking into a conscience-free dinner.

Aloo Gobi Potato and cauliflower in a thick masala sauce

Dhal Makhani Black lentils and red kidney beans cooked up in a rich creamy sauce

Vegetable Korma Vegetables cooked in a mild coconut sauce, usually far less heavy than the kind at the curry house back home

Malai Kofta Vegetable dumplings steeped in a rich, sweet sauce

Tandoori Paneer Tikka Indian cheese coated in hot and sour paste, and oven-baked with accompanying vegetables

Channa Masala Chickpeas marinated in a spicy, tomatoey sauce

it's sometimes hard to work out whether food has been cooked in oil or ghee (clarified butter) but a quick peek into the kitchen will usually clear things up. And take note: the sauces of meaty Goan specialities almost always contain no meat or fish, so it's worth asking your waiter whether it's possible to whip up a vegie version. A simply stunning *xacuti* and *vindalho* can be made with mixed vegetables, chickpeas, or in a satisfying potato-and-cauliflower combination.

You'll find vegetarian restaurants usually well labelled (look for the sign saying 'Veg Restaurant') and almost everywhere; vegetarian joints serving up South Indian cuisine are often locally known as *udupis*.

HABITS & CUSTOMS

Goans eat three main meals per day, with frequent snack stops in between. Breakfast is southern-style: a plate of *idlis* (round steamed rice cakes) with sambar, a *masala dosa* (thin pancake filled with vegies, such as spiced potatoes) or *bhaji-pau,* washed down with a plain lassi or chai. Lunch is also quite simple: most people eat *fish-curry-rice,* or an all-you-can-eat thali, consisting of several small curries, a dhal, curd, a tiny salad, a couple of pappadams, pickle and a large portion of rice to mix it all together with.

Dinner is the largest meal of the day, rarely eaten late since power cuts are frequent outside the big towns and people – except those heading off to late-night bars – tend to retire to bed early. Most beach shacks and restaurants stop serving food towards 11pm, though you'll find street stalls and some restaurants, in the biggest resorts, open throughout the night for postclubbing sustenance.

Food & Religion

Food, in India at large, is integral to spiritual advancement and, regardless of creed, Indians share the belief that food is just as important for fine-tuning the spirit as it is for sustaining the body. However, the rules seem to be less stringent in easygoing Goa, and many otherwise observant religious Goans are more flexible than others on what's on- and off-limits culinarily.

Broadly speaking, Hindus avoid foods that are thought to inhibit physical and spiritual development, although there are few hard-and-fast rules, except for the taboo of eating beef. Devout Hindus avoid alcohol and foods such as garlic and onions, which are thought to heat the blood and arouse passions, and the great majority are vegetarian. Some foods, such as dairy products, are considered innately pure and are eaten to cleanse the body, mind and spirit. Ayurveda, the ancient science of life, health and longevity, also heavily influences food customs (see p74). Goa's Muslims, like Muslims everywhere, shun pork and pork products, while its Christian population has no particular food taboos.

Food Etiquette

When out and about in non-Western restaurants, try to eat only with your right hand; the left is considered unclean and for the purposes of ablution only. If you are invited to dine with a family, always take off your shoes and wash your hands before sitting down to your meal.

COOKING COURSES

Despite Goa's unique cuisine, there aren't, as yet, many organised cooking classes on offer. Keep an eye out, though, for notices on informal courses held by locals, especially in Palolem, Arambol and Anjuna.

The one exception is provided courtesy of the UK-based company **India on the Menu** (www.indiaonthemenu.com), which runs all-vegetarian cooking courses

Great Goan Cooking: 100 Easy Recipes by Maria Teresa Menezes is a great source of recipes all gorgeously Goan.

from its purpose-built kitchen near Panaji. Choose from a single Saturday Curry Morning to a full week's cooking course, with culinary day trips to markets and other local attractions for foodies.

EAT YOUR WORDS

If you want to be able to say it before you eat it, turn to the Language chapter (p252) for help with pronunciation.

Useful Phrases

Do you accept credit cards?	kyaa aap kredit kaard lete/letee haing? (m/f)
What would you recommend?	aap ke kyaal meng kyaa achchaa hogaa?
Please show me the menu.	tumcho aaije meno kithe aasa
I'm (a) vegetarian.	maing shaakaahaaree hoong
I'd like the..., please.	muje... chaahiye
The bill, please.	bill aad

Please bring a...	... laaiye
fork	kaangtaa
glass	glaas
glass of wine	sharaab kee kaa glaas
knife	chaakoo
mineral water	minral vaatar
plate	plet
spoon	chammach

I don't eat...	maing... naheeng kaataa/kaatee (m/f)
Could you prepare a meal	kyaa aap... ke binaa kaanaa taiyaar kar sakte/saktee
without...?	haing? (m/f)
beef	gaay ke gosht
fish	machlee
meat stock	gosht ke staak
pork	suar ke gosht
poultry	murgee
red meat (goat)	bakree

I'm allergic to...	muje... kee elarjee hai
nuts	meve
seafood	machlee
shellfish	shelfish

Food Glossary

ambot tik	sour curry dish made with meat or fish and flavoured with tamarind
balchão	fish or prawns cooked in a rich, spicy tomato sauce; balchão de peixe is made with fish, balchão de porco is made with pork
bebinca	richly layered, pancake-like Goan dessert made from egg yolk and coconut
cafrial	method of preparation in which meat, usually chicken, is marinated in a sauce of chillies, garlic and ginger and then dry-fried
caldeirada	a mild curry of fish or prawns layered in a vegetable stew
caldin	mild meat or vegetable dish cooked in spices and coconut milk
chai	tea
chouriço	spicy air-dried pork sausages, fried up and served for lunch
dhaba	basic restaurant or snack bar
doce	sweet made with chickpeas and coconut

dodol	traditional fudgey Christmas sweet made with rice flour, coconut milk and jaggery
dosa	paper-thin lentil-flour pancake, eaten for breakfast
feni	Goa's most famous drink, a liquor distilled from coconut-palm toddy or juice of cashew apples
fish-curry-rice	Goa's staple dish, a simple concoction of mackerel in spicy, soupy curry served with rice
kofi	coffee
kokum	dried fruit used as a spice
sanna	steamed rolls or cakes made with rice flour, ground coconut and toddy
sorpotel	pork liver, heart or kidney cooked in thick, slightly sour, spicy sauce and flavoured with *feni*
thali	a selection of curries, salad, pickle and rice, served on a metal platter, making for a cheap and filling lunch option
udupi	vegetarian cafe or canteen, selling South Indian–style snacks and thalis; also known as an udipi
uttapam	griddle-fried rice flour pancake
vindalho	hot and sour curry, usually using pork, spiced with chillies, vinegar and garlic; completely unlike the Western curry-house killer, vindaloo
xacuti	spicy sauce made with coconut milk, lemon juice and plenty of red chilli

Environment

For the four decades since Goa's Portuguese overlords finally left its shores, Goa has experienced phenomenal, and often flawed, growth in tourism, industry and population, taxing sometimes to the limit its stunning, diverse, yet fragile environment. The strains of overfishing, deforestation, mining and pollution have all taken their toll and, though environmental activists do what they can, the somewhat bleak picture painted by the current environmental situation still obscures Goa's incredibly beautiful and unique landscape.

THE LAND

Goa occupies a narrow strip of the western Indian coastline, approximately 105km long and 65km wide, with a total area of just 3701 sq km, but within this relatively tiny area is an incredibly diverse mixture of landscapes, flora and fauna. This landscape divides down into three basic sections: the rich, lush Western Ghats Ranges, the laterite-stone midland section, and the low coastal plain, all three threaded through with wide, lazy rivers and scores of smaller streams.

The state is also chopped into two administrative districts – North and South Goa – their major towns being Panaji (formerly Panjim, the state capital) and Margao (formerly Madgaon) respectively. Beyond this simple subdivision Goa is further divided into 11 talukas (districts): Pernem, Bicholim, Satari, Bardez, Tiswadi and Ponda in North Goa, and Mormugao, Salcete, Sanguem, Quepem and Canacona in the south. It shares state borders to the north and northeast with Maharashtra, and to the south and southeast with Karnataka.

Goa – A View from the Heavens, by Gopal Bodhe, is a beautifully photographed book dedicated to Goa's environment and heritage.

Western Ghats

In the east of the state lie the foothills and peaks of the gorgeous green Western Ghats, whose name derives from the Sanskrit for 'sacred steps'. The mountain range runs along the entire west coast of India, separating the Deccan plateau to the east from the lower-lying coastal areas. In Goa the Western Ghats are made up of the local Sahyadri Range, and comprise around one-sixth the total area of the state. The ghats also provide the source of all seven of Goa's main rivers, the longest of which, the Mandovi, meanders for 77km to the Arabian Sea.

This lush deciduous region, responsible for channelling much-needed water down onto the plains, is in definite danger. Deforestation, due to logging, threatens its forests along with the some 3500 species of flowering plants (representing an incredible one-third of India's total variety) and diverse bird, animal and insect life that call the ghats home. Soil erosion, as a result of deforestation, represents a danger to the midland beyond, potentially creating flooding and destroying long-established irrigation channels; see p68 for more information.

Midland Region

Goa's grassy hinterland lies between the ghats and the coast, a huge area mostly made up of laterite plateaus of between 30m and 100m in elevation, with thin soil covering rich sources of iron and manganese ore. The midland has thus become the scene of large-scale open-cast mining, evident in the red gashes in the Goan hillside, and the relentless lines of iron ore trucks chugging to and fro like determined colonies of worker ants.

In areas not blighted by mining, fragrant spice, fruit, cashew (Goa's principal cash crop) and areca nut plantations predominate, particularly in the valley areas where the soil is richer. Terraced orchards here make efficient use of limited water sources, supporting coconut palms along with jackfruit, pineapple and mango groves.

Coastal Plain

Though just a fraction of the total area of the state, the coastal region is Goa's main claim to fame and supports the overwhelming majority of its population Here, mangroves line tidal rivers, providing a unique habitat for birds, marine animals and even crocodiles, while vivid green paddy fields, coconut groves and sea- and river-fishing provide the majority of the population's food.

These fields and groves, inland from Goa's brilliant beaches, stand on estuarine flood plains, known locally as *khazans,* made up of land reclaimed from the sea many centuries ago by the building of *bunds* (embankments), whose slim canals, sluices and floodgates allow controlled use of land.

Most such land is irrigated with fresh water, though many of its small canals are filled at least partially with salt water for use in fish farming. Other areas are purposely flooded with salt water, which is then left to evaporate for the collection of salt.

These 180 sq km of coastal lands are probably the most threatened of all Goa's habitats. The beaches, and sea waters beyond them, have already been severely damaged by unfettered and irresponsible tourist development, untreated sewage, pollution from sea tankers and iron ore mining, poor local land management, and the creation of several eyesore power stations and chemical plants; see p67 for more.

> The areca nut is the main source of betel, which in turn creates *paan,* that mildly addictive chewable *digestif* substance consumed, and spat out in great red liquid streams, daily by millions of Indians.

WILDLIFE

Despite Goa's diminutive size, the state's unique topographical and environmental variation allows for an amazing array of fauna, though some of the most impressive mammalian species now occur in only very small numbers and most are incredibly shy and hard to spot. The forested areas of the Western Ghats have traditionally provided habitat for some extremely rare animals but, unless you're prepared to spend several days camped out in a wildlife sanctuary, you're unlikely to see many mammals beyond the most common Goa has on offer – though these still make fascinating viewing.

Bird enthusiasts will likely find Goa twitchers' heaven. With incredible, iridescent avian life even flitting casually past your beach-hut window, Goa's the place for both the amateur and serious birdwatcher, so pack your guidebook and binoculars and prepare yourself for a spectacular feathery show.

> The myth of the creation of Goa (see Let There Be Goa, p30) is thought to have derived from the land reclamation that was first undertaken here by colonisers around 1500 BC.

Animals
MAMMALS

Though Goa remains home to more than 50 kinds of wild mammals, the more impressive species such as wild elephants and leopards (known in India as panthers) are today few and far between, having fallen victim to hunting or fled to the most inaccessible areas of the Western Ghats.

More common, however, is the 'mini-leopard' or leopard cat (known as the *vagati* in Konkani), a greyish fluffy-tailed creature about the size of the domestic variety, and the Indian civet, slightly larger with a striped tail and long pointed snout. Among the dog family, jackals, striped hyenas and wild dogs are all occasionally sighted in the Goan hinterlands.

Of the state's mischievous monkey life, Goa has two common and frequently spotted kinds: smallish, scavenging bonnet macaques; and larger, black-faced, long-limbed Hanuman langurs. Far less common is the

> The destruction of *bunds* (embankments) is thought to be to blame for a resurgence in the deadly Japanese Encephalitis disease in Goa, since polluted, flooded land is the ideal breeding ground for the disease's carrier, the *culex vishnui* mosquito.

nocturnal, bulgy-eyed slender loris (a distant relation of the lemur), only occasionally found in the dense forests of Molem and Canacona, though sometimes captured and kept as pets by its village people. There are also very occasional sightings of shaggy, lumbering woodland sloth bears, which can grow up to 1.5m long and feed largely on bees, ants and termites.

Less reclusive inhabitants of Goa's countryside include common mongooses, which are found near settlements, and have a predilection for snakes and scorpions. Common otters and smooth Indian otters, both fond of quiet stretches of Goan riverbank, are also frequently seen. The Western Ghats are also home to Indian giant squirrels, which are found in the forests of Molem, Valpoi and Canacona. They're double the size of their European counterparts and can leap distances of 20m from branch to branch. Their relatives in Goa include three-striped palm squirrels and five-striped palm squirrels.

Among the animals found at ground level are common, snuffling Indian porcupines and wild boar, both of which are notorious for damaging crops. In Goa's wildlife sanctuaries, you'll hopefully come across gaur (Indian bison) ,charismatic and primeval-looking creatures with smooth black hide and knee-high white 'socks'. You may also spot sambars (buff-coloured deer), chitals (spotted deer) and barking deer. One of the rarer animals to inhabit Goa's forests is the nocturnal pangolin, otherwise known as the scaly anteater.

Common dolphins are found off the coastline and can often be seen on 'dolphin spotting' boat tours, while bats come out in force as the Goan sun goes down. Along with fruit bats and Malay fox vampires (which, true to their title, feed off the blood of live cattle), huge flying foxes are the easiest to spot, flying out in noisy communities and boasting a wingspan of more than a metre.

REPTILES, SNAKES & AMPHIBIANS

The best place to spot reptiles and amphibians – aside from the common house geckos you'll see roaming beach hut walls at night in search of insects – is in the paddy fields and villages of rural Goa.

Snakes are common in Goa, though largely reclusive, with 23 species in all, eight of which are venomous. The Indian and King cobra comprise two of the latter, whose venom is lethal if not treated quickly. Only outdoing them in the poison stakes is the krait, a grey-blue creature with faint white markings, whose bite – even from a baby – is deadly. If you're planning on spending plenty of time hiking, or in very rural areas, it pays to do some extra research into snake types, and be mindful of the location of the nearest clinic equipped with antivenenes, just in case. However, it's more likely that any encounters you have with snakes will be with those of the nonpoisonous

When's best for wildlife watching? As soon after the monsoon as possible. October is perfect, when tourist numbers and temperatures are low, and animals are attracted to still verdant watering holes.

Brush up on your Kipling for an encounter with a charismatic mongoose: the tale of Rikitiki-tavi is a great one for getting your kids geared up for a wildlife-spotting expedition.

ECOFRIENDLY PIG OUT

Goa's farmyards are teeming with creatures, most of which are destined, at some point, for the plate. But aside from spicy *chouriços* (Goan sausages), there's another traditional reason for the prevalence of pigs next to Goan village homes.

Though you may never encounter one during your stay in Goa, the old-fashioned (and slightly disconcerting) Goan toilet is a squat-style affair whose pipe runs out of the cubicle and directly into the pigsty behind it, making the sound of contented snuffling an unusual accompaniment to a normally solitary activity.

However strange it may seem to Western eyes and ears, the pig toilet is the ultimate ecofriendly lavatorial solution, dealing with issues of sewage disposal and pig food in one environmental go, and arguably – for faint-hearted travellers, at least – doing its bit to promote vegetarianism too.

THE TURTLE WIND

Each November, a strong breeze known as the 'turtle wind' heralds the arrival of olive ridley marine turtles to lay eggs on a clutch of Goan beaches. It's believed that these females – who live for over a century – return to the beach of their birth to lay eggs, courtesy of an incredible in-built 'homing device', often travelling thousands of kilometres to do so.

One such beach is Morjim in North Goa (see p174), but turtle numbers over the last century have slowly dwindled to dangerous levels due to poaching. On investigation, locals were digging up the eggs and selling them as delicacies at market, and any turtle found out of the water was generally killed for its meat and shell. Increased tourism to Goa has also taken its toll; eggs were, for years, trampled unwittingly at rave parties, while sea and light pollution continue to threaten the survival of those that manage, against the odds, to hatch.

In 1996 the Goa Foundation, on the urging of several concerned local residents, finally stepped in and enlisted the help of the Goa Forest Department to patrol the beach and instigate a turtle conservation program. Locals who once profited from selling the eggs are now paid to guard them at the several turtle protection sites (at Morjim, Agonda and Galgibag beaches) established for this very purpose. Drop into one of its information huts, or go to www.goaforest.com, to learn more.

variety; green whip snakes, golden tree snakes, rat snakes, cat snakes, wolf snakes and Russel sand boas are just some of these species.

Kusadas (sea snakes) are common along the coastline, but are most often seen dead on the beach; they generally live in deep waters, far off the coast, and since they're unable to move on land they die if they become stranded. *Kusadas* are deadly poisonous, but luckily are also extremely timid, with fangs located so far back in their mouths that they rarely get enough grip to give a proper bite.

Goa is also home to a small population of other creatures, including chameleons, monitor lizards, turtles and two species of crocodile. Flap-shell turtles and black-pond turtles are both freshwater species and are plentiful during the monsoon, while a third species, the olive ridley sea turtle, is in grave danger of extinction (see The Turtle Wind, above). Though crocs are also threatened with extinction, they're still pretty easy to spot, especially the saltwater variety (known locally as 'salties'), which inhabit stretches of the Mandovi and Zuari estuaries, and the Cambarjua Canal near Old Goa.

The second type, known as 'Mandovi Muggers', are less aggressive towards humans than salties, despite their title, and mostly inhabit Mandovi River waters around Divar and Chorao Islands, though they sometimes make it up as far as the Cambarjua Canal. The name in fact stems from their Konkani name, *magars*, rather than a propensity for human flesh, but are still said to have been introduced to the area by former ruler of Goa, the Bijapuri Yusuf Adil Shah, to guard against surprise attackers and to deal with would-be escapee slaves. The Portuguese, taking lessons from the earlier Bijapuris, also employed muggers to dispose of troublesome Muslim prisoners-of-war. Several Goan day-tripping companies today advertise 'crocodile-spotting' trips along the likeliest stretches, to observe the muggers and salties from a far less intimate distance.

S Prater's *The Book of Indian Animals* and Romulus Whitaker's *Common Indian Snakes* are two reliable guides to the nonhuman residents of Goa.

In the Goan village of Dhurbat, crocodiles on the canal are worshipped as the guardian spirits of the community.

BIRDS

Keen birdwatchers will be in seventh heaven in Goa, and even those with little previous experience in all things avian will have a great time gazing at them, and getting to know the species of the region. See p71 for details of how and where to spot them.

Out of Town

On the outskirts of town and in open spaces, a flash of colour may turn out to be an Indian roller, easily identified by its brilliant blue flight feathers. Drongos are also quite common; shiny black birds with distinctive forked tails that typically perch on a post or obliging cow. Pipits and wagtails strut in large flocks among the harvest stubble; wagtails, unsurprisingly, can be recognised by their habit of wagging their tail.

Common hoopoes, with their orange-brown bodies and black-and-white wings, tails and black-tipped crests, are often seen (or their distinctive 'hoo-po-po' bird call heard) in open country, around cultivated fields and villages, while birds of prey such as harriers and buzzards soar overhead seeking out unwary birds and small mammals. Kites and vultures can wheel on thermals for hours on end; ospreys, another species of large hawk, patrol reservoirs and waterways, to feed on fish seized with hooked talons.

Waterways

Stalking on long legs at the shallow edge of tanks and ponds are various species of egret, graceful white tapers of birds with long necks and dagger-like bills. Their elegant poise belies the deadly speed with which they spear frogs and fish. Cattle egrets wander among livestock, looking for large insects stirred up by their namesake.

Indian pond herons, also known as paddy birds, are small and well camouflaged in greys and browns. They are almost invisible until they take off, showing their pure white wings.

Colourful kingfishers, Goa's unofficial mascot made famous by its cold and frothy namesake beverage, wait patiently on overhanging branches before diving down for their prey. Several species are to be seen in the area, including black-and-white pied kingfishers; tiny, colourful common kingfishers (also known as river kingfishers); and the striking stork-billed kingfishers, sporting massive red bills. The water's edge is also home to smaller species, such as the plovers, water hens and coots that feed and nest among the dense vegetation.

Forests

Patches of forest support a rich variety of feathered species, some of which specialise in picking grubs off the forest floor, while others forage among the branches and leaves.

Among those more often heard than seen are woodpeckers, whose characteristic drumming sound is made as they chisel grubs from under the bark of trees. Its colourful relatives include the barbets, which sit on the topmost branches of trees and call incessantly in the early morning, and Indian koels, whose loud, piercing cry can be unrelenting in spring.

Fruiting trees are a magnet for many of the region's bird species, including green pigeons and imperial pigeons; noisy flocks of colourful parrots; minivets with their splendid red-and-black or orange-and-black plumage; and various cuckoo-shrikes and mynahs, including hill mynahs, an all-black bird with a distinctive yellow 'wattle' about the face. Sadly, hill mynahs are sought after as cage birds, since they can be tamed and taught how to talk.

The jewel in Goa's avian crown are three magnificent species of hornbill, which, with their massive down-curved bills, resemble the toucans of South America. At the other end of the spectrum in size, the iridescent, nectar-feeding purple sunbirds are equally brilliant, if not as keenly sought. A host of smaller birds, such as flycatchers, warblers, babblers and little tailorbirds (so-called because they make a neat little 'purse' of woven grass as a nest), forage for insects in every layer of tree-filled vegetation.

Birds of Southern India by Richard Grimmet and Tim Inskipp is a comprehensive birdwatching field guide, considered by many as the 'must have' guide to the region. Also comprehensive is *A Field Guide to the Birds of the Indian Subcontinent* by Krys Kazmierczak and Ber van Perlo.

Plants

A bumper crop of flowering plants, grasses, brackens and ferns all play their part in Goa's ecology, with most diversity apparent in the thick green of the Western Ghats, comprising some of Asia's densest rainforest. On their lower slopes, thinner, drier soil supports lateritic semi-evergreen forest; in other places (such as Cotigao Wildlife Sanctuary) the arid landscape leads to savannah-like vegetation. In wetter patches of the lower slopes, timbers such as teak are grown.

In the folds between the hills where shade and springs are found, the small valleys are often extremely fertile. Centuries-old methods are still followed in the cultivation of spices and fruits: coconut palms are cultivated not only for the nuts and toddy, but also to give shade to less hardy trees. Beneath the canopy of coconut palms and mango trees, the tall, slender areca nut palms are grown. These, in turn, shelter an incredible variety of fruit trees and spice plants, including pineapples, bananas, pepper and cinnamon.

The coastal region has a similarly wide range of flora, with saline conditions supporting a substantial area of mangrove swamps. Banyan and peepul trees, both revered by Hindus and the former by Buddhists too, provide shade for the shrines that often pop up beneath them, and peepuls are often planted in temple courtyards, to be decorated with lucky strips of red cloth. Banyans can reach staggering ages and heights, and are distinctive for the rootlike shoots they send out, for propagation purposes, from their lower branches.

> Aside from flora indigenous to Goa, many types of trees and plants were introduced by the Portuguese, including rubber trees, pineapples and chilli plants.

WILDLIFE SANCTUARIES

Roughly 12%, or 455 sq km, of Goa's total area is given over to wildlife sanctuaries and reserves. Add to this the forestry-department–protected beaches and large areas of untouched forest along the southern coast, and Goa remains – despite its environmental woes – an optimistically green place.

Its three main wildlife sanctuaries were created in the late 1960s: Bondla (p137), which also contains Molem National Park; Bhagwan Mahavir (p138); and Cotigao (p210). All are well worth exploring. There's also tiny Dr Salim Ali Bird Sanctuary on Chorao Island (p122), a haven for beautiful bird species. In 1999 two new wildlife reserves – Madei (208 sq km) in Satari taluka and Netravali (211 sq km; p210) in Sanguem taluka – were declared protected areas, but so far these fledgling reserves lack infrastructure, and consequently are seldom visited. However, the creation of these protected areas links the sanctuaries running along the Western Ghats, providing a crucial corridor for Goa's still abundant wildlife.

See individual listings for details on the sanctuaries and reserves, and how to visit, and p71 for more information.

ENVIRONMENTAL ISSUES
Conservation

In addition to Goa's wildlife sanctuaries, reserves and turtle conservation efforts, various other environmentally minded activities are under way, though the state would benefit from more effort in this area. The **World Wildlife Fund** (www.wwfindia.org) has become increasingly active in Goa in recent years, while the **Save Goa Campaign** (www.savegoa.com) is helping find solutions to Goa's environmental woes.

Goa's **Green Cross** (www.greencrossgoa.org) conducts environmental awareness campaigns alongside taking practical conservation action, while **Green Goa Works** (www.greengoaworks.com) is a nonprofit company chaired by Goan fashion designer Wendell Rodrigues, which is working to promote the use of effective microorganisms (EM) in hotels, households and markets to reduce

FADING FISHERIES

Somewhere in the region of 50,000 Goans are dependent on fishing for their family income, but Goa's once-abundant waters are today facing a serious threat from overfishing, and locals now reminisce about their younger days when *ramponkars* (fishermen), in their simple wooden outriggers, would give away 60cm-long kingfish because they had so many to spare. These days it's difficult to buy fish direct from boats, and even local markets offer slim pickings because much of the best fish is sold directly to upmarket hotels, exported, or shipped to interstate markets where the best prices are fetched. Naturally this has driven up the price of seafood, not only for tourists, but for Goans who rely on their staple *fish-curry-rice*.

Overfishing has become a phenomenon since modern motorised trawlers, owned and operated by wealthy businessmen, started to eclipse the simple traditional fishing methods of the *ramponkars* in the 1970s. Despite a law limiting trawlers to beyond a 5km shoreline 'exclusion zone', trawlers stay relatively close to the shore, adversely affecting the *ramponkars'* catch, while their use of tightly knit nets, which don't allow juvenile fish to escape (these are either thrown away or used for fertiliser) has further dwindled fish stocks. Although the *ramponkars* continue to press for change, Goan state legislature seems helpless in the face of powerful trawler owners, while the seas slowly empty and irreversible damage is done to maintaining this precious resource.

environmentally hazardous waste. Goa's **Peaceful Society** (www.peacefulsociety.org) has also been running conservation projects for the last 25 years.

In 1964 the **Archaeological Survey of India** (asi.nic.in) assumed responsibility for conservation of the state's monuments, including buildings of Old Goa, with facilities and finances for maintenance and restoration work. The **Goa Forestry Department** (www.goaforest.com) is responsible for the condition of the state's forests, national parks and turtle protection programs.

The **Goa Foundation** (www.goacom.com/goafoundation) is the state's leading environmental group. It works to maintain and protect Goa's environment by campaigning (often successfully) against mass developments, and runs a series of educational programs to inform people as to how they can minimise their impact on the environment.

The nonprofit organisation **United Planet** (www.unitedplanet.org) runs various volunteer projects in Goa, including a sea turtle conservation initiative. Check its website for details.

Deforestation

Over-cutting of the forested Western Ghats began at the beginning of the 20th century, and by the time the Portuguese departed considerable damage had been done. Shortly after Independence, licences were granted for further large-scale felling. In some cases the cleared land was replanted with imported crops such as eucalyptus and rubber plants which, in themselves, can be destructive to the natural ecosystem. In many cases deforestation was permanent, with land being used for roads, open-cut mining and other development.

Meanwhile, the construction of reservoirs in the hills near the Maharashtra border has proved particularly damaging, with whole valleys submerged under the new reservoirs, and neighbouring areas deforested to rehouse the families made homeless by the flooding.

Environmental groups now estimate that more than 500 hectares of Goa's forests are disappearing every year, and that a mere 8% to 12% of the state now consists of dense forest.

The damage caused by deforestation is far-reaching. The habitats of many of Goa's native animals are disappearing, as are the homelands of several of the minority peoples of the state. The tribal Dhangars, Kunbis and Velips, whose way of life revolves around agriculture and animal husbandry, have been forced into smaller and smaller pockets of land.

In an effort to curb the damage, the government has stepped up its efforts to protect Goa's forests: felling fees now apply and licences must be issued. In addition, it claims that since 1984 it has planted several thousand hectares of land under its Social Forestry scheme.

Mining

Nearly half the iron ore exported annually from India comes from Goa. Goa's mines produce ore exclusively for export (mostly to China), and for eight months of the year huge barges ferry the ore along the Zuari and Mandovi Rivers to waiting ships, representing, in total, around 10% of Goa's GDP.

Such large-scale extraction of ore has had a destructive effect on the Goan hinterland and the coastal region. Because no stipulation for environmental reconstruction was made when mining concessions were issued, many mines have simply been abandoned once extraction was complete.

Out of the 80 million tonnes of rock and soil extracted annually, only 13 million tonnes are saleable ore. Surplus is dumped on the spoil tips and a huge quantity of soil is washed away, smothering both river and marine life. Other side effects of mining have been the destruction of the local water table and the pollution of air and drinking water, causing respiratory problems in residents close to iron ore mines and water shortages throughout the dry season.

Tourism

While bringing countless jobs and raising standards of living for many in Goa, tourism has also had a considerable environmental impact on Goa. Count up the plastic mineral water bottles you use during your visit, then multiply this figure by three million; this alone, combined with unchecked hotel building, inadequate sewage facilities, water-guzzling swimming pools and landscaped lawns, combines to create quite a problem.

However, there are some simple ways to minimise your negative impact on Goa's environment. See p18 for a few important tips.

Since it was first conceived, the Konkan Railway has been the source of much outrage by environmentalists, who are concerned about its interference with heritage sites in Goa, and its disturbance of irrigation channels.

Activities

Goa has become Activities Central of late, with a whole host of options available for travellers, such as water sports, volunteering, alternative therapies and yoga. There's no shortage of noticeboards and keen individuals on hand to bring you up to speed on what's around, whether you're keen to perfect your posture, dive the depths, play with puppies or spy on diffident deer. Also be on the lookout for seasonally changing courses of other varieties: you'll find meditation, philosophy, Indian cookery, dance and music classes and courses appearing on the scene with increasing regularity. Keep a close eye on flyers and posters adorning beach resort walls, cafes and lamp posts to get the best possible picture of what's on offer.

OUTDOOR ACTIVITIES

DIVING

Although Goa is not internationally renowned as a diving destination, its waters are regarded as the third-best spot for diving in India (after the Andaman and Lakshadweep Islands).

The shallow waters off the coast are ideal for less-experienced divers; typical dives are at depths of 10m to 12m, with abundant marine life to be seen. The only problem is that visibility is unpredictable; on some days it's 30m, on others it's closer to 2m. The dive season runs from November to April, and costs for an introductory dive plus four further guided excursions come in at around Rs14,000.

Marine life you're likely to encounter while deep beneath the sea includes angelfish, parrotfish, wrasses, lionfish, sharks (reef tip and shovel-nosed among others), stingrays, gropers, snapper, damselfish, barracuda, sea cucumbers and turtles. The highlights of diving in Goa are the wreck dives – there are literally hundreds of wrecks along Goa's coastline, including Portuguese and Spanish galleons and more recent wrecks of merchant and naval ships.

Goa's shipwreck history dates back to the 2nd century BC, though the wrecks you'll encounter beneath its waters are not quite so antique. It's said that vast quantities of treasure still lie on its ocean beds, remnants from the wrecks carrying wealthy Portuguese traders.

There are some basic ecofriendly points to consider, to help preserve the ecology and beauty of Goa's reefs and seas while you're exploring. First, avoid touching or standing on living marine organisms or dragging equipment across the reef. Polyps can be damaged by even the gentlest contact. If you must hold on to the reef, only touch exposed rock or dead coral. Next, be conscious of your fins. Even without contact, the surge from fin strokes near the reef can damage delicate organisms. Take care not to kick up clouds of sand, which can smother organisms. Third, practise and maintain proper buoyancy control. Major damage can be done by divers descending too fast and colliding with the reef.

Equally, it's important to take great care in underwater caves. Spend as little time inside them as possible as your air bubbles may be caught within the roof and thereby leave organisms high and dry. Take turns to inspect the interior of a small cave. Meanwhile, resist the temptation to collect or buy corals or shells or to loot shipwrecks, and ensure that you take home all your rubbish and any litter you may find as well. Plastics in particular are a serious threat to marine life. Finally, do not feed fish, and never interact with turtles, should you be lucky enough to encounter them. Keep a respectful distance and remember – they're endangered!

SAFETY GUIDELINES FOR DIVING

Before embarking on a scuba-diving, skin-diving or snorkelling trip, carefully consider the following points to ensure a safe and enjoyable experience:

■ Possess a current diving certification card from a recognised scuba-diving instructional agency (if scuba-diving).

■ Be sure you are healthy and feel comfortable diving.

■ Obtain reliable information about physical and environmental conditions at the dive site (eg from a reputable local dive operation).

■ Ask about the environmental characteristics that can affect your diving and how locally trained divers deal with these considerations.

■ Be aware of local laws, regulations and etiquette about marine life and the environment.

■ Dive only at sites within your realm of experience; if available, engage the services of a competent, professionally trained dive instructor or dive master.

■ Be aware that underwater conditions vary significantly from one region, or even site, to another. Seasonal changes can significantly alter any site and dive conditions. These differences influence the way divers dress for a dive and what diving techniques they use.

Popular dive sites include Grande Island and St George's Island, while south of Goa, Devbagh Island (near Karwar) and Pigeon Island off the Karnataka coast are also frequently used. Professional Association of Dive Instructors (PADI) accredited operations in Goa are the environmentally conscious **Barracuda Diving** (see p156), and the long established **Goa Diving** (see p191).

WATER SPORTS

Though most water sports outfits are run on a rather seasonal, itinerant basis, there's an annually growing range of varieties on offer, the most popular being jet skiing, parasailing, kayaking and, on windier days, surfing. The beaches of Colva (p194), Benaulim (p197), Baga (p154), Sinquerim (p147) and Calangute (p154) are particularly heavy on all these options, and it's important to haggle for the best price among sometimes stiff competition. Palolem (p204) usually has a few kayaks on offer too, while nearly all the five-star resorts in South Goa offer a range of water sports, albeit at higher prices than their independent competitors.

For something slightly more unusual (and better established), head to Patnem, where **Goa Sailing** (p208) offers courses aboard its 15ft catamarans, a wonderful way to experience the life on the ocean waves.

WILDLIFE WATCHING

All creatures great and small are out in all their glory in Goa, from the blazing kingfishers that fleck the coastal strip's luminescent paddy fields, to the temple and spice-farm elephants that bestow blessings and elephant rides upon paying visitors.

There's little in life as restful as finding your deserted stretch of beach and then settling in to observe the crabs, gulls, sea eagles and the occasional cavorting dolphin that are so much part of Goa's seaside landscape, or watching the wary tree frog that appears croaking on your balcony each evening as the sun sets.

Goa's wilder expanses host little-seen wonders, such as gaurs (Indian bison), porcupines, wild boar, and the occasional pangolin (scaly anteater) or leopard. A loud rustle in the leaves overhead often signals the

For Mumbai's (Bombay's) own version of water sports, see p89 for details of the rafting, canoeing, jet skiing and boating activities available out of the heart of the big city.

arrival of a troupe of mischievous langur monkeys, who appear in family groups to steal unattended food from backyards, and generally cause mirth and mayhem.

Taking a riverine trip inland, you might be rewarded with a spotting of wild crocodiles, otters, and yet more birdlife, whose names alone make the trip worthwhile: just try spotting a Ceylon frogmouth or a fairy bluebird without at least the hint of a satisfied smile.

Goa's not the only place for good birdwatching; see Birdwatching in Mumbai (pp88-9) for an account of Mumbai's own feathered friends.

Head to **Cotigao Wildlife Sanctuary** (p210), the more remote **Bondla Wildlife Sanctuary** (p137) or **Bhagwan Mahavir Wildlife Sanctuary** (p138) to scout out birds and beasts alike, or to one of the **spice plantations** (p134) near Ponda, where birdlife is particularly diverse. If butterflies or dragonflies are your thing, consider a tour courtesy of **Canopy Ecotours** (p206), or maybe a stay at the restful **Backwoods Camp** (p140) if you're itching for some twitching. For more avian enjoyment, a trip to the **Dr Salim Ali Bird Sanctuary** (p122) on Chorao Island is recommended. Other sites of interest to birdwatchers are the wetlands at Carambolim (12km east of Panaji) and Shiroda (40km southeast of Panaji), and even the marshland south of the Baga River.

If you're looking for some organisation behind your nature exploration, **Day Tripper** (p157) in Calangute offers various nature-related tours, while **John's Boat Tours** (p150) in Candolim, and **Betty's Boat Tours** (p200) in Cavelossim both offer birdwatching boat trips, along with sea-based dolphin tours and crocodile-spotting trips up the Mandovi River. At almost any beach, though, you'll be sure to find someone with a boat and a strong desire to show you (on a no-show, no-pay basis) those adorable grey mammals of the waves.

DAY TRIPS & TOURS

A great way to see more of Goa, if you're on a tight time schedule, is to sign up for a day trip or two. Almost every beach resort has its own slew of tour operators, offering visits out to the hard-to-get-to sights that would otherwise be tricky without your own transport.

It's a good idea to look around a bit before plumping for the ideal tour – many of which can be undertaken on the water instead of on wheels, cruising Goa's coast or serene inland waterways. The state tourism group, the **GTDC** (see p235) offers a surprisingly good range of bus-based day trips, taking in a quite astonishing number of sights in just one day. Though it's not the most restful or thorough way to travel, the tours are good value for money, and the drivers are usually more careful than most.

A good book to accompany you on your travels around Goa is Inside Goa by Manohar Malgonkar, beautifully illustrated by famous local cartoonist Mario de Miranda.

Check individual chapter listings for particularly recommended day-tripping outfits, such as **Day Tripper** (p157) in Calangute, and **John's Boat Tours** (p150), based in Candolim. Don't forget about the local fishermen lingering around almost every beach, willing to take you out on the waves for a dolphin-watching expedition, or allowing you to accompany them on a fishing expedition, to see how a number of locals make their hard-earned living.

VOLUNTEERING

More and more visitors to Goa are keen to put something back into this beautiful, alluring but sometimes vulnerable state. One great way to do this is to spend part of your stay volunteering: whether it's a few hours, days or weeks spent doing good for some of Goa's residents, you'll likely gain a unique and rewarding insight into your destination, and come away feeling that incredible high that can be obtained by helping others.

Also see p67 for conservation groups who sometimes have volunteer posts on offer.

PLANNING

Many of Goa's volunteering options require a little advance planning, and it pays to be in touch with organisations well before you depart home, in order to make sure they know you're on your way. Moreover, working with children requires criminal record background checks, so takes a few months to organise. Some animal-related concerns, such as the Goa Animal Welfare Trust and International Animal Rescue, along with the **Goa SPCA** (www.goaspca.org), are happy to receive casual help: just turn up and they'll find you something useful to do.

GETTING INVOLVED

'Never work with children or animals,' so the old thespian adage goes, but for those with the opportunity to volunteer some of their time while in the sunny state, many opportunities exist for helping small creatures with two or four – and sometimes even three – legs who need help most.

El Shaddai (☎ 6513286, 6513287; El Shaddai House, Socol Vaddo, Assagao) is a British-founded charity that aids impoverished and homeless children throughout Goa and beyond, running a number of day and night shelters, an open school and children's homes throughout the state. Volunteers (who undergo a rigorous vetting process) able to commit to more than four weeks' work with El Shaddai are encouraged to contact James d'Souza (☎ 9225901266). This is an undertaking to arrange in advance, since it can take up to six months to complete the vetting process. You can also sponsor a child: contact El Shaddai in Assagao for details.

Children Walking Tall (☎ 09822124802; www.childrenwalkingtall.com; 'The Mango House', near Vrundavan Hospital, Karaswada, Mapusa, Goa) was founded in 2004, and helps Goa's street and slum children, with its day-care centre, medical, educational, nutritional and all sorts of other, essential aid. Volunteers can fill a variety of roles, as teachers, childcare assistants and outreach workers, while there are also positions available for qualified doctors and nurses. Check Children Walking Tall's website for complete details.

International Animal Rescue (IAR; ☎ 2268328/272; www.iar.org.uk/india/goa; Animal Tracks, Mandungo Vaddo, Assagao) is an internationally active charity, helping Goa's furry and feathery sick, unwanted and strays. It runs its Animal Tracks rescue facility in Assagao, near Mapusa, in North Goa. Visitors and volunteers (both short and long term) are always welcome, and IAR's website includes a 'Needs List' of things you might be able to fit into your backpack and bring from home, including antiseptic ointment, flea powder and puppy toys. You'll also find a downloadable PDF of info for willing volunteers. If you find an animal in distress in Goa, call the shelter for help.

Goa Animal Welfare Trust (GAWT; ☎ 2653677; www.gawt.org; Old Police Station, Curchorem) is based in South Goa, and operates an animal shelter at Curchorem (situated in the Old Police Station on the main road), helping sick, stray and injured dogs, cats and even a calf or two, and is open daily from 9am to 5pm for visits. GAWT, like IAT, undertakes extensive dog sterilisation projects throughout Goa, offers low-cost veterinary care, deals with animal cruelty cases and finds homes for stray puppies. Volunteers are welcome, if only for a few spare hours, and GAWT also operates a shop and information centre in Colva (see also p199).

Mumbai has its own huge range of innovative day trips on offer; choose from heritage and 'reality' walks through the city's slums, to a quick sail on the super-luxurious Taj yacht. See p91 for more details.

YOGA & ALTERNATIVE THERAPIES

From ashtanga through to Zen, every imaginable form of yoga, along with ayurvedic massage and a multitude of other spiritually orientated health regimes, is practised, taught and relished in Goa. Palolem and Patnem in the south of the state, and Arambol, Mandrem and Anjuna in the north, are particularly great places to take courses in reiki and manifold forms of yoga, t'ai chi and healing, and many also host retreat centres for longer meditation and yoga courses. Teachers and practitioners are mostly an ever-changing parade of foreigners who set up shop as soon as the monsoon subsides, and offer their services to the scores who come seeking enlightenment, illumination or any spark of spiritual something.

But Goa's commitment to its visitors' wellbeing doesn't stop there. Take a Vipassana retreat (an intensive, silent, inward-looking form of meditation; see p177), lay your hands on a spot of reiki (healing through the laying-on of hands), or seek out t'ai chi, Zen Buddhism, belly dancing, sacred drumming circles, tarot, palmistry or healing colour therapies. It's all here in balmy – and sometimes barmy – Goa.

AYURVEDA

By far the most popular of all the myriad regimes on offer in Goa is ayurveda, the ancient science of plant-based medicine, whose Sanskrit name comes from a combination of *ayu* (life) and *veda* (knowledge). Illness, in the doctrine of ayurveda, comes from a loss of internal balance, which can be restored through a combination of massage and *panchakarama* (internal purification).

The first part of the regime comprises an hour-long massage with warm medicated oils, followed by a cleansing steam bath. This sort of massage is available almost anywhere in Goa, though it's best to go by local recommendation to seek out the very best ayurvedic hands on offer.

The second part, an internal purification, takes rather more than an hour, and most people opt for a fortnight's course of treatment in order to feel the advantages. In this case, your cure will comprise a carefully tailored diet, exercise regime and a series of treatments to supplement your massages. For most of us, intent on finding our balance aboard a sun bed, the hour-long treatment inevitably wins out as most appealing. Ayurvedic clinics and massage parlours can be found at every beach destination. If you're thinking of going a little upmarket, South Goa's the place to do it, with its five-star palaces dotting the coast between Velsao and Mobor offering swanky spas, where traditional practices are given a new, superluxury spin.

YOGA

Second only to ayurveda in Goa is yoga, in all its various guises. Try your hand at ashtanga (fluid and challenging, the basis for 'power yoga') or hatha (gentler and slower paced), iyengar (slow and steady, often using blocks and straps) or vinyasa (built around a 'sun salutations' sequence), to find the pose and poise that suits you best. You'll find everything in Goa, from a one-hour drop-in class to a six-month intensive teachers' course, and look out for children's yoga classes, which crop up seasonally, and will help even tiny tots improve their posture, concentration and general elasticity.

Ancient ayurveda resources described 2000 species of plants, of which at least 550 are still in use today.

For a comprehensive introduction to yoga, pick up the highly respected *Light On Yoga: The Bible of Modern Yoga* by BKS Iyengar, the inventor of the iyengar yoga method himself.

Mumbai (Bombay)

Mumbai is big. It's full of dreamers and hard-labourers, actors and gangsters, stray dogs and exotic birds, artists and servants and fisherfolk and *crorepatis* (millionaires) and lots and lots of other people. It has the most prolific film industry, one of Asia's biggest slums and the largest tropical forest in an urban zone. It's India's financial powerhouse, fashion capital and a pulse point of religious tension. It's evolved its own language, Bambaiyya Hindi, which is a mix of…everything. It has some of the world's most expensive real estate and a knack for creating land from water using only determination and garbage.

But wait. Mumbai is not frantic, it's not *overwhelming*. Or at least, it doesn't have to be. Contrary to what you might think, you may not have almost just died in that taxi or been rushed by that station crowd or run over by that guy with the funny outfit and the monkey. The city just has its own rhythm, which takes a little while to hear: it's a complex but playful raga, a gliding, light-footed dance that all of Mumbai seems to know.

So give yourself some time to learn it and appreciate the city's lilting cadences, its harmonies of excess and restraint. The stately and fantastical architecture, the history hanging in the air of the markets, the scent of jasmine in the ladies' car of the train, the gardens and street vendors and balloon-wallahs and intellectuals in old libraries – it will all take you in if you let it. So sit back, develop your equanimity, and let yourself become part of the song.

HIGHLIGHTS

■ Eat in one of India's best **restaurants** (p96), then watch – or be one of – the beautiful people at a posh **bar, lounge** (p99) or **club** (p100)

■ Stock up on odd and exquisite things at Mumbai's ancient **bazaars** (p103) and outsource your wardrobe to its **boutiques** (p102)

■ Admire the grandiose frilliness of Mumbai's colonial-era architecture: **Chhatrapati Shivaji Terminus** (p85), **University of Mumbai** (p84) and **High Court** (p83)

■ Resist the urge to bow down before the commanding triple-headed Shiva sculpture at **Elephanta Island** (p106)

■ Feel the city's sea breeze among playing kids, big balloons and a hot-pink sunset at **Chowpatty Beach** (p86)

Chowpatty Beach ★
Chor Bazaar ★
Mangaldas Market
★★ Crawford Market
★ Chhatrapati Shivaji Terminus
High Court ★
University of Mumbai ★
Elephanta Island ★

GREATER MUMBAI

0 ——— 5 km
0 ——— 3 miles

Esselworld & Water Kingdom
Borivali
To Ahmedabad (415km)
Gorai Ferry
Sanjay Gandhi National Park
Gorai Island
Manori Creek
Kandivali
Kanheri Caves
Marve Jetty
Malad
To Nasik (160km)
Tulsi Lake
Malad Creek
Goregaon
Aarey Milk Colony
Vihar Lake
Jogeshwari
Powai Lake
Western Express Hwy
Andheri
Juhu
Domestic Terminal
International Terminal
Thane Creek
ARABIAN SEA
Vile Parle
Eastern Express Hwy
Santa Cruz
Lokmanya Tilak (Kurla)
To Pune (140km)
Khar *Khar Rd*
Kurla
Bandra
Dharavi
Mahim
Chembur
To Karjat (81km)
See Central Suburbs Map (p94)
Matunga Rd Train Station
Thane Creek
Dadar *Wadala*
Worli *Sewri*
Lower Parel
Mumbai Central Train Station
Butcher Island
Chhatrapati Shivaji Terminus (Victoria Terminus)
Elephanta Island
Churchgate Train Station
Fort
Gateway of India
Colaba
Mumbai Harbour
See Mumbai (Bombay) Map (p78–9)
To Mandwa (20km)
Uran

FAST FACTS

Population 16.4 million
Area 440 sq km
Telephone code ☎ 022
Languages Marathi, Hindi, Gujarati
When to go October to February

HISTORY

Koli fisherfolk have inhabited the seven is-lands that form Mumbai as far back as the 2nd century BC. Amazingly, remnants of this cul-ture remain huddled along the city shoreline today. A succession of Hindu dynasties held sway over the islands from the 6th century AD until the Muslim Sultans of Gujarat annexed the area in the 14th century, eventually ceding it to Portugal in 1534. The only memorable contribution the Portuguese made to the area was christening it Bom Bahai, before throwing the islands in with the dowry of Catherine of Braganza when she married England's Charles II in 1661. The British government took pos-session of the islands in 1665, but leased them three years later to the East India Company for the paltry annual rent of UK£10.

Then called Bombay, the area flourished as a trading port. So much so that within 20 years the presidency of the East India Company was transferred to Bombay from Surat. Bombay's fort was completed in the 1720s, and a cen-tury later ambitious land reclamation projects joined the islands into today's single landmass. Although Bombay grew steadily during the 18th century, it remained isolated from its hin-terland until the British defeated the Marathas (the central Indian people who controlled much of India at various times) and annexed substantial portions of western India in 1818.

The fort walls were dismantled in 1864 and massive building works transformed the city in grand colonial style. When Bombay took over as the principal supplier of cotton to Britain during the American Civil War, the population soared and trade boomed as money flooded into the city.

A major player in the Independence move-ment, Bombay hosted the first Indian National Congress in 1885, and the Quit India campaign was launched here in 1942 by frequent visitor Mahatma Gandhi. The city became capital of the Bombay presidency after Independence, but in 1960 Maharashtra and Gujarat were divided along linguistic lines – and Bombay became the capital of Maharashtra.

The rise of the pro-Maratha regionalist movement, spearheaded by the Shiv Sena (Hindu Party; literally 'Shivaji's Army'), shattered the city's multicultural mould by actively discriminating against Muslims and non-Maharashtrans. The Shiv Sena won power in the city's municipal elections in 1985. Communalist tensions increased and the city's cosmopolitan self-image took a bat-tering when nearly 800 people died in riots following the destruction of the Babri Masjid in Ayodhya in December 1992.

The riots were followed by a dozen bomb-ings on 12 March 1993, which killed more than 300 people and damaged the Bombay Stock Exchange and Air India Building. The more recent train bombings of July 2006, which killed more than 200 people, and November 2008's coordinated attacks on 10 of the city's landmarks, which lasted three days and killed 173 people, are reminders that tensions are never far from the surface.

In 1996 the city's name was officially changed to Mumbai, the original Marathi name derived from the goddess Mumba, who was worshipped by the early Koli residents. The Shiv Sena's influence has since seen the names of many streets and public buildings changed from their colonial names. The airport, Victoria Terminus and Prince of Wales Museum have all been renamed after Chhatrapati Shivaji, the great Maratha leader, although the British names of these and most streets are still in popular local use.

ORIENTATION

Mumbai, the capital of Maharashtra, is an island connected by bridges to the mainland. The island's eastern seaboard is dominated by the city's (off-limits) naval docks. The city's commercial and cultural centre is at the southern, claw-shaped end of the island known as South Mumbai. The southernmost peninsula is Colaba, traditionally the travellers' nerve-centre ,with most of the major attractions, and directly north of Colaba is the busy commercial area known as Fort, where the old British fort once stood. It's bordered on the west by a series of interconnected, fenced grassy areas known as maidans (pronounced may-*dahns*).

Though just as essential a part of the city as South Mumbai, the area north of here is collectively known as 'the suburbs'. The airport (p103) and many of Mumbai's best restaurants, shopping and night spots are here, particularly in the upmarket suburbs of Bandra and Juhu.

Maps

Eicher City Map Mumbai (Rs250) is an excellent street atlas, worth picking up if you'll be spending some time here.

INFORMATION
Bookshops

Vendors lining the footpaths around Flora Fountain, the maidans and Mahatma Gandhi (MG) Rd sell new and secondhand books.
Crossword (Map pp78–9; ☎ 23842001; Mohammedbhai Mansion, NS Patkar Marg, Kemp's Corner; ☯ 11am–8.30pm) Enormous.

Oxford Bookstore (Map p84; ☎ 66364477/88; www .oxfordbookstore.com; Apeejay House, 3 Dinsha Wachha Marg, Churchgate; ☯ 10am-10pm) Modern, with a tea bar.
Search Word (Map p83; ☎ 22852521; Metro House, Colaba Causeway, Colaba; ☯ 10.30am-8.30pm) Small and tidy, with a choice selection of books and magazines.
Strand Book Stall (Map p84; ☎ 22661719; www .strandbookstall.com; Cowasji Patel Rd; ☯ 10am-8pm Mon-Sat) Old-school and smart, with good discounts.

Internet Access

Portasia (Map p84; ☎ 22032022; Kitab Mahal, Dr Dadabhai Naoroji Rd, Fort; per hr Rs20; ☯ 9am-9pm Mon-Sat) Entrance is down a little alley; look for the 'cybercafe' sign hanging from a tree.
Sify iWay (per 3hr Rs125) Churchgate (Map p84; Prem Ct, J Tata Rd; ☯ 9am-11pm); Colaba (Map p83; Colaba Causeway; ☯ 8am-11.30pm) The Colaba branch entrance is on JA Allana Marg.

Libraries & Cultural Centres

Alliance Française (Map p84; ☎ 22035993; 40 New Marine Lines; annual membership Rs1000; ☯ 9.30am-5.30pm Mon-Fri, to 1pm Sat)
American Information Resource Center (Map p84, ☎ 22624590; http://mumbai.usconsulate.gov/airc.html; 4 New Marine Lines, Churchgate; annual membership Rs400; ☯ library 10am-6pm Mon-Fri)
British Council Library (Map pp78–9; ☎ 22790101; www.britishcouncilonline.org; 1st fl, Mittal Tower A Wing, Barrister Rajni Patel Marg, Nariman Point; monthly membership Rs250; ☯ 10am-6pm Tue-Sat)
David Sassoon Library & Reading Room (Map p84; ☎ 22843703; www.davidsassoonlibrary.com; MG Rd, Kala Ghoda; 45-day/annual membership Rs500/2200; ☯ 8am-9pm)
Max Mueller Bhavan (Goethe Institut; Map p84; ☎ 22027542; www.goethe.de/mumbai; K Dubash Marg, Fort; ☯ library 11am-6pm Mon-Fri)

Media

To find out what's going on in Mumbai, check out the free **City Info**, available in hotels and restaurants, the *Hindustan Times*' **Café** insert or the hippest option, **Time Out Mumbai** (www.timeout mumbai.net; Rs30), published every two weeks.

Medical Services

Bombay Hospital (Map p84; ☎ 22067676, ambulance 22067309; www.bombayhospital.com; 12 New Marine Lines)
Breach Candy Hospital (Map pp78–9; ☎ 23672888; www.breachcandyhospital.org; 60 Bhulabhai Desai Rd, Breach Candy) Best in Mumbai, if not India.

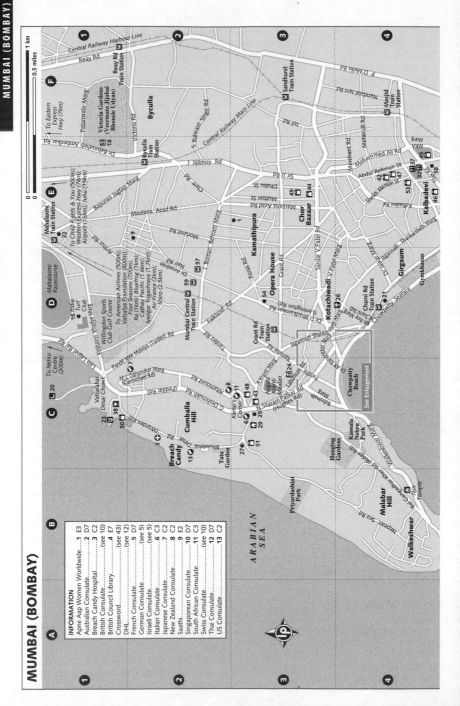

MUMBAI (BOMBAY)

INFORMATION

Apne Aap Women Worldwide......1	E3
Australian Consulate...................2	D7
Breach Candy Hospital................3	C2
British Consulate...................(see 10)	
British Council Library................4	E7
Crossword..........................(see 43)	
DHL.................................(see 12)	
French Consulate.......................5	D7
German Consulate...................(see 5)	
Israeli Consulate....................(see 5)	
Italian Consulate........................6	C3
Japanese Consulate.....................7	C2
New Zealand Consulate.................8	C2
Saathi................................9	E2
Singaporean Consulate................10	D7
South African Consulate...............11	C3
Swiss Consulate....................(see 10)	
Thai Consulate........................12	D7
US Consulate...........................13	C2

ARABIAN SEA

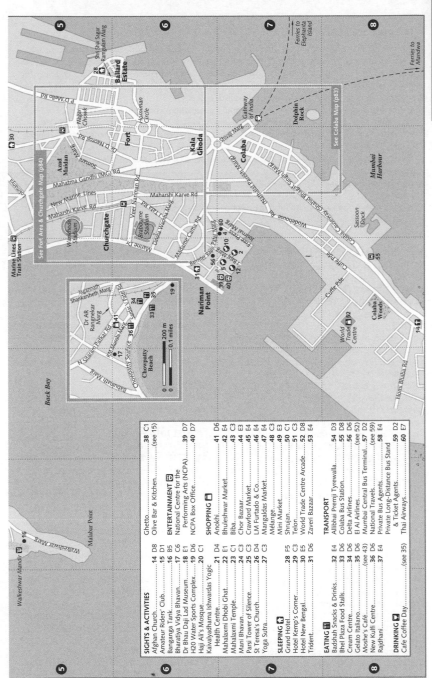

SIGHTS & ACTIVITIES
Afghan Church...........................14 D8
Amateur Riders' Club....................15 D1
Banganga Tank..........................16 B5
Bharatiya Vidya Bhavan.................17 C6
Dr Bhau Daji Lad Museum...............18 E1
H2O Water Sports Complex..............19 D6
Haji Ali's Mosque.......................20 C1
Kaivalyadhama Ishwardas Yogic
  Health Centre.........................21 D4
Mahalaxmi Dhobi Ghat..................22 E1
Mahalaxmi Temple......................23 C1
Mani Bhavan...........................24 C3
Parsi Tower of Silence..................25 C3
St Teresa's Church......................26 D4
Yoga Sutra............................27 C3

SLEEPING
Grand Hotel...........................28 F5
Hotel Kemp's Corner...................29 C3
Hotel New Bengal......................30 E5
Trident...............................31 D6

EATING
Badshah Snacks & Drinks...............32 E4
Bhel Plaza Food Stalls..................33 D6
Cream Centre.........................34 D6
Gelato Italiano.........................35 D6
Moshe's Café..........................(see 43)
New Kulfi Centre......................36 D6
Rajdhani..............................37 E4

DRINKING
Cafe Coffee Day.......................(see 35)

Ghetto................................38 C1
Olive Bar & Kitchen...................(see 15)

ENTERTAINMENT
National Centre for the
  Performing Arts (NCPA).............39 D7
NCPA Box Office.......................40 D7

SHOPPING
Anokhi...............................41 D6
Bhuleshwar Market....................42 E4
Biba.................................43 C3
Chor Bazaar..........................44 E3
Crawford Market......................45 E4
LM Furtado & Co......................46 E4
Mangaldas Market.....................47 E4
Mélange..............................48 C3
Mini Market..........................49 E3
Shrujan..............................50 C1
Telon................................51 C3
World Trade Centre Arcade.............52 E4
Zaveri Bazaar.........................53 E4

TRANSPORT
Allibhai Premji Tyrewalla...............54 D3
Colaba Bus Station....................55 D8
Delta Airlines.........................56 D6
El Al Airlines.........................(see 52)
Mumbai Central Bus Terminal..........57 D2
National Travels......................(see 59)
Private Bus Agents....................58 E4
Private Long-Distance Bus Stand
  & Ticket Agents.....................59 D2
Thai Airways.........................60 E7

READING MUMBAI

Containing all the beauty and ugliness of the human condition, it's little wonder that Mumbai has inspired some of the subcontinent's best writers as well as international scribes like VS Naipaul and Pico Iyer. Leading the field are Booker Prize–winner Salman Rushdie (*Midnight's Children, The Moor's Last Sigh* and *The Ground Beneath Her Feet*) and Rohinton Mistry (*A Fine Balance* and *Family Matters*), who have both set many novels in the city.

The list of other good reads is, like Mumbai's population, endlessly multiplying.

Maximum City: Bombay Lost and Found Equal parts memoir, travelogue and journalism, Suketu Mehta's epic covers Mumbai's riots, gang warfare, Bollywood, bar dancers and everything in between. The ultimate chronicle of the city's underbelly.

Shantaram Gregory David Roberts' factional saga about an Australian prison escapee's life on the run in Mumbai's slums and jails.

Rediscovering Dharavi Kalpana Sharma's sensitive and engrossing history of Dharavi's people, culture and industry.

Bombay, Meri Jaan A heady anthology of politics, pop culture, literature and history edited by Jerry Pinto and Naresh Fernandes.

Royal Chemists (Map p84; ☎ 22004041-3; 89A Maharshi Karve Rd, Churchgate; ⏰ 8.30am-8.30pm Mon-Sat)

Sahakari Bhandar Chemist (Map p83; ☎ 22022399; Colaba Causeway, Colaba; ⏰ 10am-8.30pm)

Money

You'll never be far from an ATM in Mumbai, and foreign-exchange offices changing cash and travellers cheques are also plentiful. Nominal service charges are common.

Akbar Travels (Map p84; ☎ 22633434; 4th fl, 167/169 Dr Dadabhai Naoroji Rd; ⏰ 10am-7pm Mon-Sat)

Kanji Forex (Map p84; ☎ 22040206; 40 Veer Nariman Rd, Fort; ⏰ 9.30am-6pm Mon-Fri, 9.30am-4pm Sat)

Thomas Cook (⏰ 9.30am-6pm Mon-Sat); Fort (Map p84; ☎ 22048556-8; 324 Dr Dadabhai Naoroji Rd); Colaba (Map p83; ☎ 22882517-20; Colaba Causeway)

Photography

Standard Supply Co (Map p84; ☎ 22612468; Image House, Walchand Hirachand Marg, Fort; ⏰ 10am-7pm Mon-Sat) Everything you could possibly need for digital and film photography.

Post

The **main post office** (Map p84; ☎ 22620956; ⏰ 9am-8pm Mon-Sat, 10am-5.30pm Sun) is an imposing building behind Chhatrapati Shivaji Terminus (CST; Victoria Terminus). **Poste restante** (⏰ 9am-8pm Mon-Sat) is at Counter 1. Letters should be addressed c/o Poste Restante, Mumbai GPO, Mumbai 400 001. Bring your passport to collect mail. The **EMS Speedpost parcel counter** (⏰ 9am-10pm Mon-Sat, 10am-4.30pm Sun) is across from the stamp counters. Regular parcels can be sent from the parcel office behind the main building. Opposite the post office, under the tree, are parcel-wallahs who will stitch up your parcel for Rs40. The **Colaba post office** (Map p83; Henry Rd) is convenient.

Private express-mail companies:

Blue Dart (Map p84; ☎ 22822495; www.bluedart.com; Khetan Bhavan, J Tata Rd; ⏰ 10am-8pm Mon-Sat)

DHL (Map pp78-9; ☎ 22837187; www.dhl.co.in; Embassy Centre, Nariman Point; ⏰ 9am-8.30pm Mon-Sat).

Telephone

Justdial (☎ 69999999; www.justdial.com) and ☎ 197 provide Mumbai phone numbers.

Tourist Information

Government of India tourist office (Map p84; ☎ 22074333; www.incredibleindia.com; 123 Maharshi Karve Rd; ⏰ 9am-6pm Mon-Fri, to 2pm Sat) Provides information for the entire country.

Government of India tourist office airport booths domestic (☎ 26156920; ⏰ 7am-9pm); international (☎ 26829248; ⏰ 24hr)

Maharashtra Tourism Development Corporation booth (MTDC; Map p83; ☎ 22841877; Apollo Bunder; ⏰ 8.30am-3.30pm Tue-Sun & 5.30-8pm Sat-Sun) For city bus tours (p91).

MTDC reservation office (Map p84; ☎ 22845678; www.maharashtratourism.gov.in; Madame Cama Rd, opposite LIC Bldg, Nariman Point; ⏰ 9.30am-5.30pm Mon-Sat) Information on Maharashtra and bookings for MTDC hotels and the *Deccan Odyssey* train package.

Travel Agencies

Akbar Travels (Map p84; ☎ 22633434; Terminus View, Dr Dadabhai Naoroji Rd, Fort; ⏰ 10am-7pm Mon-Sat)

Magnum International Travel & Tours (Map p83; ☎ 22838628; 10 Henry Rd, Colaba; ⏰ 10am-5.30pm Mon-Fri, to 3.30pm Sat)
Thomas Cook (Map p84; ☎ 22048556-8; 324 Dr Dadabhai Naoroji Rd, Fort; ⏰ 9.30am-6pm Mon-Sat)

Visa Extensions
Foreigners' Regional Registration Office (FRRO; Map p84; ☎ 22620446; Annexe Bldg No 2, CID, Badaruddin Tyabji Rd) Near Special Branch. Does not officially issue extensions on tourist visas; even in emergencies they will direct you to Delhi. However, some travellers have managed to procure an emergency extension here after much waiting and persuasion.

SIGHTS
Colaba
For mapped locations of all the following sights, see p83.

Sprawling down the city's southernmost peninsula, Colaba is a bustling district packed with street stalls, markets, bars and budget-to-midrange lodgings. **Colaba Causeway** (Shahid Bhagat Singh Marg) dissects the promontory and Colaba's jumble of side streets and gently crumbling mansions.

Sassoon Dock is a scene of intense and pungent activity at dawn (around 5am) when colourfully clad Koli fisherfolk sort the catch unloaded from fishing boats at the quay. The fish drying in the sun are *bombil*, the fish used in the dish Bombay duck. Photography at the dock is forbidden.

While you're here, pop into the 1847 Church of St John the Evangelist, known as the **Afghan Church** (Map pp78-9), dedicated to British forces killed in the bloody 1838–43 First Afghan War.

During the more reasonable hours of the day, nearby **Colaba Market** (Lala Nigam St) is lined with jewellery shops and fruit-and-veg stalls.

GATEWAY OF INDIA
This bold basalt arch of colonial triumph faces out to Mumbai Harbour from the tip of Apollo Bunder. Derived from the Islamic styles of 16th-century Gujarat, it was built to commemorate the 1911 royal visit of King George V. It was completed in 1924. Ironically, the gateway's British architects used it just 24 years later to parade off their last British regiment as India marched towards Independence.

These days, the gateway is a favourite gathering spot for locals and a top spot for people-watching. Giant-balloon sellers, photographers, beggars and touts rub shoulders with Indian and foreign tourists, creating all the hubbub of a bazaar. Boats depart from the gateway's wharfs for Elephanta Island and Mandwa.

The **horse-drawn gilded carriages** that ply their trade along Apollo Bunder are known as Victorias. A whirl around the Oval Maidan at night, when you can admire the illuminated buildings, should cost (after bargaining) around Rs150/250 for 15/30 minutes.

TAJ MAHAL PALACE & TOWER
This sumptuous hotel (p95) is a fairy-tale blend of Islamic and Renaissance styles jostling for prime position among Mumbai's famous landmarks. Facing the harbour, it was built in 1903 by the Parsi industrialist JN Tata, supposedly after he was refused entry to one of the European hotels on account of being 'a native'. The Palace side has a magnificent grand stairway that's well worth a quick peek, even if you can't afford to stay or enjoy a drink or meal at one of its restaurants and bars.

Kala Ghoda
'Black Horse', the area between Colaba and Fort, contains most of Mumbai's main galleries and museums alongside a wealth of colonial-era buildings. The best way to see these buildings is on a guided (p91) or self-guided (p89) walking tour.

MUMBAI BY NUMBERS

- Number of black taxis: about 40,000
- Population density: 29,000 people per square kilometre
- Average annual income: Rs48,900 (US$1000, or three times the national average)
- Number of public toilets for every 1 million people: 17
- Number of people passing through Chhatrapati Shivaji Terminus (Victoria Terminus) daily: 2.5 million
- Number of people in an 1800-person-capacity train at rush hour: 7000
- Proportion of Mumbai built on reclaimed land: 60%
- Number of Bollywood movies made since 1931: 68,500

MUMBAI IN...

Two Days

Start at the granddaddy of Mumbai's colonial-era giants, the old Victoria Terminus, **Chhatrapati Shivaji Terminus** (CST; p85) and stroll up to **Crawford Market** (p103) and the maze of bazaars here. Lunch at **Rajdhani** (p98), with a juice shake from **Badshah Snacks & Drinks** (p97).

Spend the afternoon at the **Oval Maidan** (p83), checking out the cricket and the grand edifices of the **High Court** (p83) and the **University of Mumbai** (p84). Walk down to the **Gateway of India** (p81) and **Taj Mahal Palace & Tower** (p81) and, after the sun sets, eat streetside at **Bade Miya** (p96). Swap tall tales with fellow travellers at **Leopold's Café** (p99).

The next day, soak in the serenity of Malabar Hill's **Banganga Tank** (p87) and head to Kemp's Corner for lunch at **Moshe's Cafe** (p97) and some shopping. Make your way down to **Mani Bhavan** (p86), the museum dedicated to Gandhi, and finish the day with a **Chowpatty Beach** (p86) sunset and *bhelpuri* (crisp fried thin rounds of dough mixed with puffed rice, lentils, lemon juice, onions, herbs and chutney).

Four Days

See **Elephanta Island** (p106) and spend the afternoon visiting the museums and galleries of **Kala Ghoda** (p81). In the evening, head to Bandra for a candle-lit dinner at **Sheesha** (p99), followed by some seriously hip bar action at **Zenzi** (p100).

Another day could be spent visiting the **Dhobi Ghat** (p87) and the nearby **Mahalaxmi Temple** and **Haji Ali's Mosque** (p87). Lunch at **Olive Bar & Kitchen** (p100) at Mahalaxmi Racecourse and then spend the afternoon wandering the tiny lanes of **Kotachiwadi** (p86) and finish in style downtown at **Indigo** (p97).

CHHATRAPATI SHIVAJI MAHARAJ VASTU SANGRAHALAYA (PRINCE OF WALES MUSEUM)

Mumbai's biggest and best **museum** (Map p84; ☎ 22844484; www.bombaymuseum.org; K Dubash Marg; Indian/foreigner Rs15/300, camera/video Rs200/1000; ⊗ 10.15am-6pm Tue-Sun), this domed behemoth is an intriguing hodgepodge of Islamic, Hindu and British architecture displaying a mix of dusty exhibits from all over India. Opened in 1923 to commemorate King George V's first visit to India (back in 1905, while he was still Prince of Wales), its flamboyant Indo-Saracenic style was designed by George Wittet – who also did the Gateway of India.

The vast collection inside includes impressive Hindu and Buddhist sculpture, terracotta figurines from the Indus Valley, miniature paintings, porcelain and some particularly vicious weaponry. There's also a natural-history section with suitably stuffed animals. Take advantage of the free, multilanguage audioguides as not everything is labelled.

Students with a valid International Student Identity Card (ISIC) can get in for a bargain Rs10.

GALLERIES

The **National Gallery of Modern Art** (Map p83; ☎ 22881969/70; MG Rd; Indian/foreigner Rs10/150; ⊗ 11am-6pm Tue-Sun) has a bright, spacious and modern exhibition space showcasing changing exhibitions by Indian and international artists. **Jehangir Art Gallery** (Map p84; ☎ 22843989; 161B MG Rd; admission free; ⊗ 11am-7pm) hosts interesting shows by local artists; most works are for sale. Rows of hopeful artists often display their work on the pavement outside. Nearby, the museum's contemporary-art annexe, **Museum Gallery** (Map p84; ☎ 22844484; K Dubash Marg; ⊗ 11am-7pm) has rotating exhibitions in a beautiful space.

KENESETH ELIYAHOO SYNAGOGUE

Built in 1884, this impossibly sky-blue **synagogue** (Map p84; ☎ 22831502; Dr VB Gandhi Marg) still functions and is tenderly maintained by the city's dwindling Jewish community. One of two built in the city by the Sassoon family (the other is in Byculla), the interior is wonderfully adorned with colourful pillars, chandeliers and stained-glass windows – best viewed in the afternoons when rainbows of light shaft through.

Fort

For mapped locations of the following sights see p84.

Lined up in a row and vying for your attention with aristocratic pomp, many of

COLABA

0 —————— 200 m
0 —————— 0.1 miles

INFORMATION
Colaba Post Office.........................1 B3
Magnum International Travel &
   Tours...2 B3
MTDC Booth.................................3 C2
Sahakari Bhandar Chemist..........4 B1
Search Word.................................5 B2
Sify iWay.......................................6 B3
Thomas Cook.........................(see 33)

SIGHTS & ACTIVITIES
Colaba Market.........................(see 25)
Gateway of India..........................7 C2
Horse-drawn Gilded Carriages....8 C2
National Gallery of Modern Art....9 B1
Reality Tours & Travel.................10 B2
Taj Mahal Palace & Tower.........11 B2

SLEEPING
Ascot Hotel.................................12 A3
Bentley's Hotel...........................13 A3
Hotel Moti...................................14 B2
Hotel Suba Palace......................15 B1
India Guest House..................(see 19)
Regent Hotel...............................16 B2
Salvation Army Red Shield
   House......................................17 B3
Sea Palace Hotel........................18 B3
Sea Shore Hotel..........................19 B4
Taj Mahal Palace & Tower........20 B2
YWCA...21 B1

EATING
Bade Miya...................................22 B2
Bagdadi......................................23 B2
Basilico.......................................24 A4
Colaba Market............................25 A4
Delhi Darbar...............................26 B2
Falafel's......................................27 B1
Indigo...28 B2
Indigo Delicatessen....................29 B2
Kailash Parbat.............................30 A4
Ming Palace................................31 B2
New Laxmi Villas........................32 B2
Saharkari Bhandar Supermarket..(see 4)
Theobroma.................................33 A3

DRINKING
Barista..34 A4
Barista..35 B1
Busaba.......................................36 B1
Café Mondegar...........................37 B1
Henry Tham's..............................38 C1
Kamat Sweets & Snacks.............39 B2
Leopold's Cafe............................40 B2

ENTERTAINMENT
Cooperage Football Ground.......41 A1
Polly Esther's..............................42 B2
Regal..43 B1
Voodoo Pub................................44 B4

SHOPPING
Antique & Curio Shops...............45 B2
Central Cottage Industries
   Emporium...............................46 B1
Cottonworld Corp......................47 B2
Courtyard....................................48 A4
Inshaallah Mashaallah................49 B2
Phillips..50 B1

TRANSPORT
BEST Bus Depot..........................51 A2
BEST Bus Stand...........................52 B1
BEST Bus Stand...........................53 B1
Boats to Elephanta Island &
   Mandwa.................................54 C2
Jet Airways.................................55 A1
Maldar Catamarans Ticket
   Office................................(see 3)
PNP Ticket Office...................(see 3)

Mumbai's majestic Victorian buildings pose on the edge of **Oval Maidan**. This land, and the **Cross** and **Azad Maidans** immediately to the north, was on the oceanfront in those days, and this series of grandiose structures faced west directly out to the Arabian Sea. The reclaimed land along the western edge of the maidans is now lined with a remark-able collection of art deco apartment blocks. Spend some time in the Oval Maidan admiring these structures and enjoying the casual cricket matches.

HIGH COURT

A hive of daily activity, packed with judges, barristers and other cogs in the Indian justice system, the **High Court** (Eldon Rd) is an elegant 1848 neo-Gothic building. The design was inspired by a German castle and was obviously intended to dispel any doubts about the authority of the justice dispensed inside, though local stone carvers presumably saw things differently: they carved a one-eyed monkey fiddling with the scales of justice on one pillar. You are permitted (and it is highly recommended) to walk around inside the building and check out the pandemonium and pageantry of public cases that are in progress.

UNIVERSITY OF MUMBAI (BOMBAY UNIVERSITY)

Looking like a 15th-century French-Gothic masterpiece plopped incongruously among Mumbai's palm trees, this university on Bhaurao Patil Marg was designed by Gilbert Scott of London's St Pancras Station fame. You can go inside both the exquisite **University Library** and **Convocation Hall**, but the 80m-high **Rajabai Clock Tower**, decorated with detailed carvings, is off-limits.

ST THOMAS' CATHEDRAL

Recently restored to its former glory, this charming **cathedral** (Veer Nariman Rd; ⏰ 6.30am-6pm) is the oldest English building standing in Mumbai (construction began in 1672, though it remained unfinished until 1718). The cathedral is an interracial marriage of Byzantine and colonial-era architecture, and its airy, whitewashed interior is full of exhi-

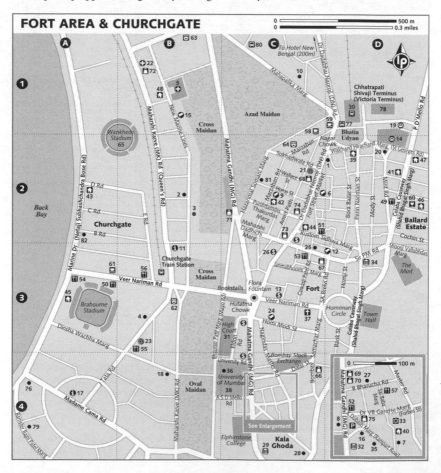

bitionist colonial memorials. A look at some of the gravestones reveals many colonists died young of malaria.

CHHATRAPATI SHIVAJI TERMINUS (VICTORIA TERMINUS)

Imposing, exuberant and overflowing with people, this is the city's most extravagant Gothic building, the beating heart of its railway network, and an aphorism for colonial India. As historian Christopher London put it, 'the Victoria Terminus is to the British Raj what the Taj Mahal is to the Mughal empire'. It's a meringue of Victorian, Hindu and Islamic styles whipped into an imposing, Daliesque structure of buttresses, domes, turrets, spires and stained-glass windows. Be sure to get close to the jungle-themed facade, particularly around the reservation office: it's adorned with peacocks, gargoyles, cheeky monkeys and lions.

Designed by Frederick Stevens, it was completed in 1887, 34 years after the first train in India left this site. Today it's the busiest train station in Asia. Officially renamed Chhatrapati Shivaji Terminus (CST) in 1998, it's still better known locally as VT. It was added to the Unesco World Heritage list in 2004.

MONETARY MUSEUM

While you're in the area, pop into this tiny and thoughtfully presented **museum** (☎ 22614043; www.rbi.org.in; Amar Bldg, Sir PM Rd; admission Rs10; ⓧ 10.45am-5.15pm), run by the Reserve Bank of India. It's an engrossing historical tour of India through coinage: from early concepts of cash to the first coins of 600 BC, through Indo-European influences, right up to today's Gandhi-covered notes. Also on display is the world's smallest coin, probably found in the crack of an ancient couch.

INFORMATION
Akbar Travels...........................**1** D2
Alliance Française...................**2** B2
American Information Resource
  Centre................................**3** B2
Blue Dart...............................**4** B3
Bombay Hospital.....................**5** B1
Canadian Consulate................**6** C2
Concern India Foundation.........**7** D4
David Sassoon Library &
  Reading Room.......................**8** D4
Dutch Consulate.....................**9** C2
Foreigners' Regional Registration
  Office (FRRO).....................**10** C1
Government of India Tourist
  Office................................**11** B3
Irish Consulate......................**12** D3
Kanji Forex...........................**13** C3
Main Post Office....................**14** D2
Maldives Consulate................**15** B1
Max Mueller Bhavan..............**16** D4
MTDC Reservation Office........**17** A4
Oxford Bookstore..................**18** B4
Parcel Office (Main Post Office).**19** D1
Parcel-wallahs......................**20** D2
Police Quarters..................(see 10)
Portasia..............................**21** C2
Royal Chemists....................**22** B1
Sify iWay............................**23** B3
Sri Lankan Consulate.............**24** C3
Standard Supply Co..........(see 39)
Strand Book Stall..................**25** C3
Thomas Cook.......................**26** C3
Welfare of Stray Dogs............**27** D4

SIGHTS & ACTIVITIES
Bombay Natural History
  Society..............................**28** C4
Chhatrapati Shivaji Maharaj
  Vastu Sangrahalaya (Prince
  of Wales Museum)..............**29** C4

Chhatrapati Shivaji Terminus
  (Victoria Terminus)............**30** D1
High Court............................**31** C3
Jehangir Art Gallery................**32** D4
Keneseth Eliyahoo Synagogue..**33** D4
Monetary Museum..................**34** D3
Museum Gallery.....................**35** D4
Rajabai Clock Tower...............**36** C4
St Thomas' Cathedral.............**37** C3
University of Mumbai..............**38** C4

SLEEPING
Hotel City Palace...................**39** D2
Hotel Lawrence.....................**40** D4
Hotel Oasis...........................**41** D2
Hotel Outram........................**42** C2
Intercontinental....................**43** A2
Residency Hotel.....................**44** C2
Sea Green Hotel....................**45** A3
Sea Green South Hotel.......(see 45)
Traveller's Inn.......................**46** D2
Welcome Hotel......................**47** D2
West End Hotel.....................**48** B1

EATING
210°C.............................(see 55)
Anubhav...............................**49** D2
Gaylord................................**50** A3
Ideal Corner.........................**51** C2
Khyber.................................**52** D4
Mahesh Lunch Home..............**53** C3
Moshe's Café....................(see 70)
Pizzeria................................**54** A3
Relish..............................(see 55)
Samrat.................................**55** B3
Shivala.............................(see 39)
Suryodaya............................**56** B3
Trishna................................**57** D4

DRINKING
Barista.................................**58** C1

Café Coffee Day.....................**59** D1
Café Universal.......................**60** D2
Cha Bar...........................(see 18)
Dome.............................(see 43)
Mocha Bar............................**61** A3
Samovar Café....................(see 32)

ENTERTAINMENT
Eros....................................**62** B3
Metro Big.............................**63** B1
Not Just Jazz By The Bay......(see 54)
Sterling................................**64** C2
Wankhede
  Stadium.............................**65** B2

SHOPPING
Bombay Paperie....................**66** C4
Bombay Store.......................**67** C3
Chimanlals............................**68** C2
Cotton Cottage.....................**69** D4
Fabindia...............................**70** D4
Fashion Street.......................**71** C2
Kala Niketan.........................**72** B1
Khadi & Village Industries
  Emporium...........................**73** C2
Planet M...............................**74** C2
Rhythm House.......................**75** D4

TRANSPORT
Air India...............................**76** A4
Bus Stand.............................**77** D1
Central Railways Reservation
  Centre...............................**78** D1
Indian Airlines..................(see 76)
Kingfisher.............................**79** A4
Private Buses to Goa & Bus
  Agents...............................**80** C1
Qantas.................................**81** C2
Virgin Atlantic.......................**82** A2
Western Railways Reservation
  Centre...........................(see 11)

BOLLYWOOD DREAMS

Mumbai is the glittering epicentre of India's gargantuan Hindi-language film industry. From silent beginnings with a cast of all-male actors (some in drag) in the 1913 epic *Raja Harishchandra*, to the first talkie, in 1931, *Lama Ara*, today the industry churns out more than 900 films a year – more than any other industry (yes, Hollywood included). Not surprising considering it has one-sixth of the world's population as a captive audience, as well as a sizable Non-Resident Indian (NRI) following.

Every part of India has its regional film industry, but Bollywood continues to entrance the nation with its winning escapist formula of masala entertainment – where all-singing, all-dancing lovers fight and conquer the forces keeping them apart. These days, Hollywood-inspired thrillers and action extravaganzas vie for moviegoers' attention alongside the more family-oriented saccharine formulas.

Bollywood stars can attain near godlike status in India. Their faces appear in advertisements around the country, and Bollywood star-spotting is a favourite pastime in Mumbai's posher establishments.

Extra, Extra!

Studios often look for extras for background scenes and sometimes want Westerners to add a whiff of international flair (or provocative dress, which locals often won't wear) to a film. It's become so common, in fact, that in 2008, 100,000 junior actors nearly went on strike to protest, among other things, losing jobs to foreigners, who will work for less and come with no strings attached.

If you're still game, just hang around Colaba. Scouts, sent by the studios to conscript travellers for the following day's shooting, will usually find you. You receive Rs500 for a day's work, but it can be a long, hot day standing around on the set without promised food and water; others have described the behind-the-scenes peek as a fascinating experience. Before agreeing to anything, always ask for the scout's identification.

Chowpatty Area

For mapped locations of the following sights see pp78-9.

MARINE DRIVE & CHOWPATTY BEACH

Built on land reclaimed from Back Bay in 1920, **Marine Drive** (Netaji Subhashchandra Bose Rd) arcs along the shore of the Arabian Sea from Nariman Point past Chowpatty Beach (where it's known as Chowpatty Seaface) and continues to the foot of Malabar Hill. Lined with flaking art deco apartments, it's one of Mumbai's most popular promenades and sunset-watching spots. Its twinkling night-time lights earned it the nickname 'the Queen's Necklace'.

Chowpatty Beach (Girgaon Chowpatty) remains a favourite evening spot for courting couples, families, political rallies and anyone out to enjoy what passes for fresh air. Eating an evening time *bhelpuri* (crisp fried thin rounds of dough mixed with puffed rice, lentils, lemon juice, onions, herbs and chutney) at the throng of stalls found here is an essential part of the Mumbai experience. Forget about taking a dip: the water is toxic.

MANI BHAVAN

As poignant as it is tiny, this **museum** (☎ 23805864; www.gandhi-manibhavan.org; 19 Laburnum Rd; admission free; ⊙ 9.30am-5.30pm) is in the building where Mahatma Gandhi stayed during visits to Bombay from 1917 to 1934. The museum showcases the room where the leader formulated his philosophy of satyagraha (nonviolent protest popularised by Gandhi) and launched the 1932 Civil Disobedience campaign that led to the end of British rule. Exhibitions include a photographic record of his life, along with dioramas and original documents, such as letters he wrote to Adolf Hitler and Franklin D Roosevelt. Nearby, August Kranti Maidan is where the campaign to persuade the British to 'Quit India' was launched in 1942.

Kotachiwadi

For mapped locations of the following sights see pp78-9.

This *wadi* (hamlet) is a bastion clinging onto Mumbai life as it was before high-rises. A Christian enclave of elegant, two-storey wooden mansions, it's 500m northeast of Chowpatty, lying amid Mumbai's predominantly Hindu and Muslim neighbourhoods.

These winding laneways allow a wonderful glimpse into a quiet life free of rickshaws and taxis. To find it, aim for **St Teresa's Church** on the corner of Jagannath Shankarsheth Marg and RR Roy Marg (Charni Rd), then duck into the warren of streets directly opposite.

Malabar Hill

For mapped locations of the following sights see pp78–9.

Mumbai's most exclusive neighbourhood of sky-scratchers and private palaces, **Malabar Hill** is at the northern promontory of Back Bay and signifies the top rung for the city's social and economic climbers.

Surprisingly, one of Mumbai's most sacred and tranquil oases lies concealed among apartment blocks at its southern tip. **Banganga Tank** is a precinct of serene temples, bathing pilgrims, meandering, traffic-free streets and picturesque old *dharamsalas* (pilgrims' rest houses). The wooden pole in the centre of the tank is the centre of the earth: according to legend, Lord Ram created the tank by piercing the earth with his arrow.

The lush and well-tended **Hanging Gardens** (Pherozeshah Mehta Gardens) on top of the hill are a pleasant but often crowded place for a stroll. For some of the best views of Chowpatty and the graceful arc of Marine Drive, visit the smaller **Kamala Nehru Park**, opposite. It's popular with couples, and there's a two-storey 'boot house' and colourful animal decorations that the kiddies like.

Mahalaxmi to Worli

For mapped locations of the following sights see pp78–9.

MAHALAXMI DHOBI GHAT

If you've had washing done in Mumbai, chances are your clothes have already visited this 140-year-old **dhobi ghat** (place where clothes are washed). The whole hamlet is Mumbai's oldest and biggest human-powered washing machine: every day hundreds of people beat the dirt out of thousands of kilograms of soiled Mumbai clothes and linen in 1026 open-air troughs. The best view, and photo opportunity, is from the bridge across the railway tracks near Mahalaxmi train station.

MAHALAXMI TEMPLE

It is only fitting that in money-mad Mumbai one of the busiest and most colourful temples is dedicated to Mahalaxmi, the goddess of wealth. Perched on a headland, it is the focus for Mumbai's **Navratri** (Festival of Nine Nights) celebrations in September/October. After paying your respects to the goddess, climb down the steps, making your way towards the shore, and snack on tasty *gota bhaji* (fried lentil balls) at the cliffside Laxmi Bhajiya House.

HAJI ALI'S MOSQUE

Floating like a sacred mirage off the coast, this mosque is one of Mumbai's most striking shrines. Built in the 19th century on the site

---

THE PARSI CONNECTION

Mumbai has a strong – but diminishing – Parsi community. Descendants of Persian Zoroastrians who fled persecution by Muslims in the 7th century, the Parsis settled in Bombay in the 17th and 18th centuries. They proved astute businesspeople, enjoyed a privileged relationship with the British colonial powers, and became a powerful community in their own right while remaining aloof from politics.

With the departure of the British, the Parsi influence waned in Mumbai, although they continued to own land and established trusts and estates built around their temples, where many of the city's 60,000-plus Parsis still live.

Perhaps the most famous aspect of the Zoroastrian religion is its funerary methods. Parsis hold fire, earth and water sacred and do not cremate or bury their dead. Instead, the corpses are laid out within towers – known as Towers of Silence – to be picked clean by vultures. In Mumbai the **Parsi Tower of Silence** (Map pp78-9) is on Malabar Hill (although it's strictly off-limits to sightseers).

The Parsi population has been declining steadily for decades; in 1940–41, the census counted 115,000 in India, Pakistan and Bangladesh, but the 2001 census recorded only 70,000 in India. (According to one survey, only 99 Parsis were born in 2007.) Their numbers are projected to fall to 23,000 by 2020, at which point they will be counted, officially, as a tribe.

of a 15th-century structure, it contains the tomb of the Muslim saint Haji – legend has it that Haji Ali died while on a pilgrimage to Mecca and his casket miraculously floated back to this spot. A long causeway reaches into the Arabian Sea, providing access to the mosque. Thousands of pilgrims, especially on Thursdays and Fridays, cross it to make their visit, many donating to the beggars who line the way; but at high tide, water covers the causeway and the mosque becomes an island.

Erosion has taken its toll on the concrete structure and, at press time, demolition of the building, along with construction of a new mosque in white Rajasthani marble, was under way. The dargah will remain open, but access may be limited.

NEHRU CENTRE

This **cultural complex** (off Map pp78-9; ☎ 24964676; www.nehru-centre.org; Dr Annie Besant Rd, Worli) includes a decent **planetarium** (☎ 24920510; adult/child Rs50/25; ☺ English show 3pm Tue-Sun), theatre, **gallery** (☎ 24963426; ☺ 11am-7pm) and the serpentine but interesting history exhibition **Discovery of India** (admission free; ☺ 11am-5pm). The architecture is striking: the tower looks like a giant cylindrical pineapple, and the planetarium resembles a UFO.

ACTIVITIES
Birdwatching

Mumbai has surprisingly good birdwatching opportunities (see the boxed text below). Sanjay Gandhi National Park (p106) is popular for woodland birds, while the marshlands of industrial Sewri (pronounced *shev*-ree) swarm with birds in winter. Contact the **Bombay Natural History Society** (BNHS; Map p84; ☎ 22821811; www.bnhs.org; Hornbill House, Dr Salim Ali Chowk, Shaheed Bhagat Singh Rd, Kala Ghoda) or Sunjoy Monga at **Yuhina Eco-Media** (☎ 26341531) for information on upcoming trips.

To visit Sewri on your own, check tide timings and arrive three to four hours before, or two hours after, high tide. Take the Harbour Line train from CST to Sewri, get off on the east side and take an autorickshaw or walk 1km to the Colgate factory. Then turn right for Sewri Bunder. Bring binoculars.

BIRDWATCHING IN MUMBAI

Sunjoy Monga has been watching and listening to Mumbai's birds for 40 years.

When did you start birdwatching? My family first stayed downtown, in a congested area full of pigeons, and I would watch them. But then we shifted in 1968 to Kandivali in northwestern Mumbai, where at the time it was all groves, almost a forest and a little river. We could see a lot of birds from my home, and it just took off from there.

I'm surprised that birds still like it here. It's so polluted. Actually, in urban areas, there's a featherfolk phenomenon happening. While some species lose out, the concentration of certain birds in the urban context – the numbers, and also the variety – is actually rising in many parts of the world, and especially the tropics.

Why? Well, the warmth of the urban world and the variety of stuff available in a limited area – the amount of garbage, all that filth, as well as, often, a wealth of introduced flowering and fruiting plants. At landfills, you have huge numbers of birds, thousands. Waders, wagtails, raptors… Certain bird species are even expanding. The cattle egret is worldwide now, I think, except for Antarctica. They're common in South Mumbai around railway tracks.

What's the deal with the pink flamingos at the Colgate factory? At Sewri, the huge numbers of birds could actually be related to the industrialisation – the warm water and food, like algae, that arise from the pollution. The pink flamingos started to be observed in the early 1990s.

What other birds visit Sewri? Waders, gulls, terns, a lot of egrets, herons… The mangroves themselves attract birds, so wherever mangroves are surviving, you'll find a good number of birds. Most of Mumbai's mangroves are along Thane Creek. But probably as much as half of the mangroves across the Mumbai region have disappeared over the last few decades, I would say – especially in northwest Mumbai, in Manori Creek, Malad Creek, in all the small creeks around Mumbai. They're not designated protected areas.

What about the national park? We have approximately 300 species of birds there, the bulk of them woodland birds, but also many aquatic birds because of the freshwater lakes there. It has

Horse Riding

The **Amateur Riders' Club** (Map pp78-9; ☎ 65005204/5; www.arcmumbai.com; Mahalaxmi Racecourse; ☎ office 9am-5.30pm Mon-Fri, 9am-1pm Sat) has horse rides for those who know how to ride for Rs1000 per 30 minutes; escorts cost Rs250 to Rs500 extra. If you don't, 10-day camps, with a half-hour lesson daily, cost Rs4500. Both require advance booking at the office.

Water Sports

At Chowpatty Beach, **H2O Water Sports Complex** (Map pp78-9; ☎ 23677546/84; www.drishtigroup.com; Marine Dr, Mafatlal Beach; ☺ 10am-10pm Oct-May) rents out jet skis (per 10 minutes Rs950), kayaks (per half-hour Rs150) and speed boats (per person per 'round' – about five minutes – Rs100) – all weather permitting (it often doesn't). It also operates cruises (p91)

Outbound Adventure (☎ 9820195115, www.out boundadventure.com) runs one-day rafting trips on the Ulhas River near Karjat, 88km southeast of Mumbai, from July to early September (Rs1500 per person). After a good rain, rapids can get up to Grade III+, though usually the rafting is much calmer, with lots of twists and zigzags. OA also organises camping and canoeing trips.

WALKING TOUR

Mumbai's distinctive mix of colonial-era and art deco architecture is one of its defining features. Look for the hard-to-find guidebook *Fort Walks* at local bookshops to learn more.

Starting from the **Gateway of India** (**1**; p81) walk up Chhatrapati Shivaji Marg past the members-only colonial relic **Royal Bombay Yacht Club (2)** on one side and the art deco residential-commercial complex **Dhunraj Mahal (3)** on the other towards **Regal Circle (4**; SP Mukherji Chowk). Dodge the traffic to reach the car park in the middle of the circle for the best view of the surrounding buildings, including the old **Sailors Home (5)**, which dates from 1876 and is now the Maharashtra Police Headquarters, the art deco cinema **Regal (6;** p101) and the old **Majestic Hotel (7)**, now the Sahakari Bhandar cooperative store.

Continue up MG Rd, past the beautifully restored facade of the **National Gallery of Modern Art (8**; p82). Opposite is the **Chhatrapati Shivaji**

---

some amazing birds; we've sighted rarities like the great and malabar pied hornbills, and the malabar trogon, among others.

What are some of your favourites? My favourite would have to be the greater racket-tailed drongo. That's an absolute exhibitionist of a bird, a real flamboyant character. In the city, my favourite is the house crow.

Ugh. Really? It's a very colourful character. It's immensely adaptable, good at finding solutions to problems. The nesting material it uses is astounding, from sticks to metal wires, spectacle frames, all kinds of paraphernalia. I've got crow nests made of plastic bags, shells, dice. And we found a nest made completely – completely – of sanitary napkins.

Brilliant! Absolutely! Hugely adaptable! It's a great bird. I love it.

What are some other good birdwatching places? Thane Creek and Sewri, even the other creeks on a good day. Aarey Milk Colony, a 3000-plus–acre grassy wilderness near the park, the Powai Lake area. And little parks and gardens, especially in South Mumbai, are wintering grounds, little stopovers. Elephanta Island has a mix of waders and woodland birds, some raptors also. Overall in Mumbai, almost 400 species of birds have been recorded, just under a third of India's total count.

Wow. What is it about the city? Mumbai is wonderfully cocooned by nature on all sides. On the eastern side is forest, the Sahyadri Hills, the Western Ghats. In the central area, Mumbai lies in the fertile Konkan. Then there are the creeks, the sandy coast and also grass and scrub. Add to that the gardens and parks and all the conditions created by people.

What's your favourite place? I do a lot of good birdwatching just by the roadside. My ears and eyes are really well attuned, I'd say, so I can pick up sounds among traffic and commotion. I'll hear a little snatch of a song and I can find the bird. But the crow remains my favourite. It will always be my favourite.

Sunjoy Monga is the author of Birds of Mumbai, The Mumbai Nature Guide *and* City Forest, Mumbai's National Park.

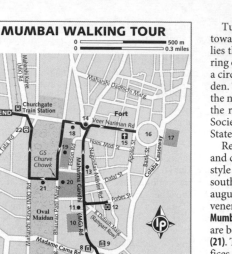

MUMBAI WALKING TOUR

Start	Gateway of India
Finish	Churchgate train station
Distance	2.5km
Duration	3 hours minimum

Maharaj Vastu Sangrahalaya (9; Prince of Wales Museum; p82); step into the front gardens to admire this grand building. Back across the road is the 'Romanesque Transitional' **Elphinstone College (10)** and the **David Sassoon Library & Reading Room (11**; p77), where members escape the afternoon heat lazing on planters' chairs on the upper balcony.

Cross back over to Forbes St to visit the **Keneseth Eliyahoo Synagogue (12**; p82) before returning to MG Rd and continuing north along the left-hand side to admire the vertical art deco stylings of the **New India Assurance Company Building (13)**. In a traffic island ahead lies the pretty **Flora Fountain (14)**, named after the Roman goddess of abundance, and erected in 1869 in honour of Sir Bartle Frere, the Bombay governor responsible for dismantling the fort.

Turn east down Veer Nariman Rd, walking towards **St Thomas' Cathedral (15**; p84). Ahead lies the stately **Horniman Circle (16)**, an arcaded ring of buildings laid out in the 1860s around a circular and beautifully kept botanical garden. The circle is overlooked from the east by the neoclassical **Town Hall (17)**, which contains the regally decorated members-only Asiatic Society of Bombay Library and Mumbai's State Central Library.

Retrace your steps back to Flora Fountain and continue west past the Venetian Gothic–style **State Public Works Department (18)**. Turn south on to Bhaurao Patil Marg to see the august **High Court (19**; p83) and the equally venerable and ornately decorated **University of Mumbai (20**; p84). The facades of both buildings are best observed from within the **Oval Maidan (21)**. Turn around to compare the colonial edifices with the row of art deco beauties lining Maharshi Karve (MK) Rd, culminating in the wedding-cake tower of the **Eros Cinema (22)**. End your walk at Churchgate train station.

COURSES
Yoga
Several yoga classes are held daily at the **Kaivalyadhama Ishwardas Yogic Health Centre** (Map pp78–9; ☎ 22818417; www.kdham.com; 43 Marine Dr, Chowpatty; ☺ 6.30-10am & 3.30-7pm Mon-Sat). Fees include a Rs500 (students/seniors Rs400/300) monthly membership fee and a Rs300 admission fee.

The **Yoga Institute** (Map p94; ☎ 26122185; www .theyogainstitute.org; Shri Yogendra Marg, Prabhat Colony, Santa Cruz East; per 1st/2nd month Rs400/300), near Santa Cruz station, has daily classes as well as weekend and weeklong programs.

Iyengar Yogashraya (off Map pp78–9; ☎ 24948416; www.bksiyengar.com; Elmac House, 126 Senapati Bapat Marg, Lower Parel; per class Rs276) has classes in iyengar yoga, including some for the developmentally disabled. There is a Rs276 admission fee.

Language
Professor Shukla is based at **Bharatiya Vidya Bhavan** (Map pp78-9; ☎ 23871860; cnr KM Munshi Marg & Ramabai Rd, Girgaon) and offers private Hindi, Marathi and Sanskrit classes (Rs500 per hour). Contact this worldly octogenarian directly to arrange a syllabus and class schedule to suit your needs.

Crafts
The **Khatwara Institute** (Shri Khatwari Darbar; Map p94; ☎ 26042670, cnr Linking Rd & Khar Station Rd, Khar West)

offers dozens of courses, lasting from three days to one month, for women only (sorry guys!) in Arabic *mehndi* (decorative henna tattoos), 'basic' *mehndi*, block printing, embroidery, sewing and cooking, among other things. Call Vanita for details.

MUMBAI FOR CHILDREN

Rina Mehta's www.mustformums.com has the Mumbai Mums' Guide, with info on crèches, health care and even kids' salsa classes in the city. *Time Out Mumbai* (Rs30) often lists fun things to do with kids.

Little tykes with energy to burn will love the Gorai Island amusement parks, **Esselworld** (Map p76; ☎ 28452222; www.esselworld.com; adult/child Rs480/350; ☉ 11am-7pm) and **Water Kingdom** (Map p76; ☎ 28452310; adult/child Rs480/350; ☉ 11am-7pm). Both are well maintained and have lots of rides, slides and shade. Combined tickets are Rs680/550 (adult/child). Off-season weekday ticket prices are lower. It's a Rs35 ferry ride from Borivali jetty.

Several museums have kid-friendly exhibits, including the **Prince of Wales Museum** (p82), with lots of stuffed animals, and **Mani Bhavan** (p86), with fascinating dioramas of Gandhi's life.

Nature trips for kids are often conducted by BNHS (p88) and Yuhina Eco-Media (p88),

while **Yoga Sutra** (Map pp78-9; ☎ 32107067; www .yogasutra.co.in; Chinoy Mansions, Bhulabhai Desai Rd, Cumballa Hill; drop-in classes Rs250-500) has kids' yoga classes, taught in English.

TOURS

Fiona Fernandez's *Ten Heritage Walks of Mumbai* (Rs395) contains excellent walking tours in the city, with fascinating historical background.

Bombay Heritage Walks (☎ 23690992; www.bom bayheritagewalks.com), run by two enthusiastic architects, has the best city tours. Private guided tours are Rs1500 for up to three people, Rs500 for each additional person. Email enquiries and bookings are best.

Transway International (☎ 26146854; transway tours@hathway.com; per 1-/2-/3-person tour Rs2250/ 3100/4050) runs five-hour day or night tours of South Mumbai's sights. Prices include pick-up and drop-off.

MTDC (p80) runs one-hour open-deck **bus tours** (Rs120, weekends 7pm & 8.15pm) of illuminated heritage buildings. They depart from and can be booked near the Apollo Bunder office. **H2O** (p89) arranges 45-minute day (Rs200 per person, minimum four people) and night (Rs280, 7pm to 11pm) cruises.

Cruises (☎ 22026364; ☉ 9am-8.30pm) on Mumbai Harbour are a good way to escape the city and

---

DHARAVI SLUM

Mumbaikers had mixed feelings about the stereotypes in 2008's runaway hit, *Slumdog Millionaire* (released in Hindi as *Slumdog Crorepati*). But slums are very much a part of – some would say the foundation of – Mumbai city life. An astonishing 60% of Mumbai's population live in shantytowns and slums, and the largest slum in Mumbai is Dharavi. Originally inhabited by fisherfolk when the area was still creeks, swamps and islands, it became attractive to migrant workers, from South Mumbai and beyond, when the swamp began to fill in as a result of natural and artificial causes. It now incorporates 1.75 sq km sandwiched between Mumbai's two major railway lines and is home to more than one million people.

While it may look a bit shambolic from the outside, the maze of dusty alleys and sewer-lined streets of this city-within-a-city are actually a collection of abutting settlements. Some parts of Dharavi are mixed population, but in others, inhabitants from different parts of India, and with different trades, have set up homes and tiny factories. Potters from Saurashtra live in one area, Muslim tanners in another, embroidery workers from Uttar Pradesh work alongside metalsmiths, while other workers recycle plastics as women dry pappadams in the searing sun. Some of these thriving industries export their wares, and the annual turnover of business from Dharavi is thought to top US$650 million.

Up close, life in the slums is strikingly normal. Residents pay rent, most houses have kitchens and electricity, and building materials range from flimsy corrugated-iron shacks to permanent, multistorey concrete structures. Many families have been here for generations, and some of the younger Dharavi residents even work in white-collar jobs. They often choose to stay, though, in the neighbourhood they grew up in.

offer the chance to see the Gateway of India as it was intended. Ferry rides (Rs50, 30 minutes) depart from the Gateway of India.

For the luxury version, hire the **Taj Yacht** (up to 10 people per 2hr Rs48,000); contact the Taj Mahal Palace & Tower (p95) for details.

The Government of India tourist office (p80) can arrange **multilingual guides** (per half/full day Rs600/750). Guides using a foreign language other than English will charge at least Rs200 extra.

Whether or not to visit a slum area on a tour is a delicate question. **Reality Tours & Travel** (Map p83; ☎ 9820822253; www.realitytoursandtravel.com; Unique Business Centre, 1st fl, Nawroji F Rd, Colaba; short/long tours Rs400/800) runs guided tours of Dharavi (see boxed text p91) and tries to do it right. Photography is strictly forbidden and 80% of post-tax profits go to Dharavi-based NGOs.

SLEEPING

You'll need to recalibrate your budget here: Mumbai has the most expensive accommodation in India. Book ahead at Christmas and in Diwali season.

Colaba is compact, has the liveliest foreigner scene and many of the budget and midrange options. Fort is more spread out and convenient to sights and the main train stations (CST and Churchgate). Most of the top-end places are dotted around the suburbs; hotels in Juhu are convenient for the trendy Bandra district.

To stay with a local family, contact the Government of India tourist office (p80) for a list of homes participating in Mumbai's **paying-guest scheme** (r Rs250-2000; ⌘).

Budget
COLABA
For mapped locations of the following venues see p83.

Salvation Army Red Shield House (☎ 22841824; 30 Mereweather Rd; dm incl breakfast Rs195, d/tr/q incl full board & without bathroom Rs600/897/1116, d with AC & full board without bathroom Rs891; ⌘ ⌨) Salvy's is a Mumbai institution popular with travellers counting every rupee. The large, ascetic dorms are clean, though bed bugs make the odd cameo appearance (they seem to like the women's dorm). Rooms can be reserved in advance, but for dorm beds come just after the 9am kick-out to ensure a spot, as they can't be booked ahead.

Sea Shore Hotel (☎ 22874237; 4th fl, Kamal Mansion, Arthur Bunder Rd; s/d without bathroom Rs400/550) In a building housing several budget guest houses, the Sea Shore has a clean and friendly atmosphere that makes up for the shoebox-sized rooms and plywood walls. It's worth paying extra for a window and harbour views. On the floor below, India Guest House (☎ 22833769; singles/doubles without bathroom Rs350/450) is a less clean but passable backup, with even shoddier walls.

YWCA (☎ 22025053; www.ywcaic.info; 18 Madame Cama Rd; dm/s from Rs787/896; s/d with AC from Rs1035/1655; ⌘ ⌨) The vibe here is very clean and monastic. The frosty-cold lobby has an internet and ISD booth and an overwhelming feeling of orderliness. Renovated rooms, meanwhile, including spacious three- and four-bed dorms, have geysers and immaculate bathrooms. Rooms facing the front can be noisy and/or smelly, but the flip side is that they have pretty balconies. Rates include tax, breakfast, dinner and 'bed tea', and the guest house takes men and women.

Hotel Moti (☎ 22025714; hotelmotiinternational @yahoo.co.in; 10 Best Marg; s/d/tr with AC Rs1500/2000/3000; ⌘) Occupying the ground floor of a gracefully crumbling, beautiful colonial-era building, rooms are nothing special, really, but they have ghosts of charm and some nice surprises, like ornate stucco ceilings. Some are huge and all have fridges filled with soda and bottled water which is charged at cost – one of the many signs of the pragmatic and friendly management.

FORT
For mapped locations of the following venues see p84, unless otherwise stated.

Hotel New Bengal (Map pp78-9; ☎ 23401951-6; www .hotelnewbengal.com; Sitaram Bldg, Dr Dadabhai Naoroji Rd; s/d incl breakfast from Rs1000/1150, without bathroom Rs495/695; ⌘) This well-organised Bengali-run hotel occupies a rambling, mazelike building perennially buzzing with Indian businessmen. They know a good thing when they see it: tidy rooms are an excellent deal. Look at a few, as some have lots of natural light while others flirt with pokiness.

Hotel Lawrence (☎ 22843618; 3rd fl, ITTS House, 33 Sai Baba Marg; s/d/tr without bathroom incl breakfast & tax Rs500/600/800) Modestly tucked away in a little side lane, Lawrence is a pleasant place with basic, clean rooms and affable management (ask them about their meditation practice!). The foyer has fun, original '70s styling and the location can't be beat.

Hotel Outram (☎ 22094937; Marzaban Rd; d with AC Rs1550, s/d without bathroom Rs670/830; ❄) This plain but superfriendly place is in a quiet spot between CST and the maidans. It's definitely rundown and a little dark, with unexciting shared bathrooms, but it has a tiny bit of character, some old-fashioned architectural details and peaceful, green surrounds.

Traveller's Inn (☎ 22644685; 26 Adi Marzban Rd, Ballard Estate; r from Rs780; ❄) On a quiet, tree-lined street, the tiny Traveller's Inn has well-kept rooms and professional, friendly staff. Rooms have new tiles and geysers and are small but don't feel cramped. Deluxe rooms have kooky decor, eg crown molding, funky colours and a metal locker like from gym class! There are also singles with shared bathroom (Rs364) that are usually unavailable.

Hotel City Palace (☎ 22666666; www.hotelcitypalace.net; 121 City Tce, Walchand Hirachand Marg; s/d with AC from Rs1250/1900, with AC & without bathroom from Rs850/1350; ❄) City Palace is organised, clean and quiet, despite its location across from CST; the downside is the tininess of the rooms, which seem to increase in height only in higher price brackets. (Standard rooms have oddly low ceilings that are conducive to claustrophobia.) Doable if you're only in Mumbai for a night or two.

Hotel Oasis (☎ 22697887/8, fax 22697889; 276 Colaba Causeway; r Rs980, s/d with AC Rs930/1340; ❄) Rooms are incredibly small and they need some paint, but they're spick and span and a stone's throw from CST. The kooky pastel design scheme makes you feel like you're inside an ice-cream cone. In a good way.

our pick **Welcome Hotel** (☎ 66314488-90; welcome _hotel@vsnl.com; 257 Colaba Causeway; s/d from Rs2530/2980, without bathroom from Rs1270/1450; ❄) You've never seen anything so clean in your life. Even rooms without bathrooms are fabulous, with segregated shared bathrooms that are positively spotless. Reception and room staff are cheerful, while the common areas' grey carpeting, grey stone walls and gleaming black-granite stairs are unintentionally high-fashion. Top-floor rooms are very bright and have awesome views of CST. Rates include breakfast and evening tea.

CST has superexcellent, always full **retiring rooms** (dm from Rs300, s/d with AC from Rs700/1400; ❄) for those on their way in or out. Rooms have high ceilings and tall, old wooden windows and doors set with crazed glass. Check in at the office of the Deputy Station Manager (Commercial), near platform 8/9. They don't take reservations, but you may be able to book one day in advance if you're sweet.

THE SUBURBS
Hotel Kemp's Corner (Map pp78-9; ☎ 23634646; 131 August Kranti Marg; s/d from Rs1500/2000; ❄) With the old-school price and the great spot close to the Kemp's Corner fashion bonanza, you might forgive the occasional carpet bald spot of this old-fashioned place. It's worth forking out a bit more for the deluxe double rooms, but all rooms have tree views and a bit of old-timey character, eg white-painted furniture.

Midrange
COLABA
For mapped locations of the following venues see p83.

Bentley's Hotel (☎ 22841474; www.bentleyshotel.com; 17 Oliver Rd; s/d incl breakfast & tax from Rs1620/2010; ❄) Bentley's definitely has the most charm of any hotel around, with old-school floor tiles and colonial wooden furniture in some rooms. The hotel is spread out over several buildings on Oliver St and nearby Henry Rd, and all rooms are spotless and come with TV and optional AC (around Rs275 extra). But the welcome is a bit harsh and the service can be indifferent – definitely a weak spot. Rooms come in dozens of sizes and flavours: rooms 31 and 21 have balconies overlooking a garden (you'll have to book months in advance), while the cheaper ones on Henry Rd are a bit noisier.

Sea Palace Hotel (☎ 22854404/10; www.seapalacehotel.com; 26 PJ Ramchandani Marg; s/d with AC from Rs3500/4000; ❄) The standard doubles here are small and the whole place is done in slighly nauseating colour schemes (eg lime yellow), but the gorgeous sea views from the pricier rooms (doubles Rs6250) redeem it. Sort of. The best part is the patio restaurant downstairs, just across from the sea.

Hotel Suba Palace (☎ 22020636; www.hotelsubapalace.com; Battery St; r with AC incl breakfast Rs3700; ❄ 💻) Soothing neutral tones permeate the newly renovated Suba Palace, from the tiny taupe shower tiles in the contemporary bathrooms to the creamy crown molding and beige quilted headboards in the tastefully remodelled rooms. Comfy, quiet and central.

Regent Hotel (☎ 22871853/4; www.regenthotelcolaba.com; 8 Best Marg; s/d/tr with AC incl breakfast

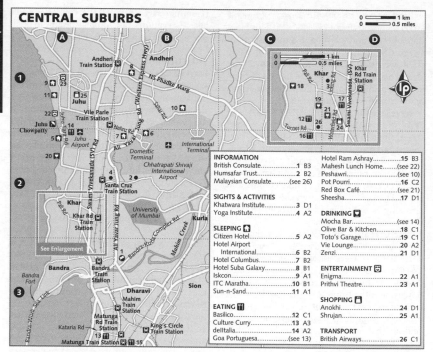

CENTRAL SUBURBS

INFORMATION	
British Consulate..................1 B3	
Humsafar Trust....................2 B2	
Malaysian Consulate..........(see 26)	

SIGHTS & ACTIVITIES	
Khatwara Institute...............3 D1	
Yoga Institute.....................4 A2	

SLEEPING	
Citizen Hotel.......................5 A2	
Hotel Airport	
International.....................6 B2	
Hotel Columbus..................7 B2	
Hotel Suba Galaxy..............8 B1	
Iskcon................................9 A1	
ITC Maratha.....................10 B1	
Sun-n-Sand......................11 A1	

EATING	
Basilico............................12 C1	
Culture Curry...................13 A3	
delItalia...........................14 A2	
Goa Portuguesa..............(see 13)	

Hotel Ram Ashray.............15 B3	
Mahesh Lunch Home.......(see 22)	
Peshawri..........................(see 10)	
Pot Pourri........................16 C2	
Red Box Café...................(see 21)	
Sheesha..........................17 D1	

DRINKING	
Mocha Bar.......................(see 14)	
Olive Bar & Kitchen..........18 C1	
Toto's Garage...................19 C1	
Vie Lounge......................20 A2	
Zenzi...............................21 D1	

ENTERTAINMENT	
Enigma............................22 A1	
Prithvi Theatre.................23 A1	

SHOPPING	
Anokhi............................24 D1	
Shrujan...........................25 A1	

TRANSPORT	
British Airways.................26 C1	

Rs3700/3900/4200;) This stylish, Arabian-flavoured hotel has marble surfaces and soft pastels aplenty. Comfortable, freshly painted rooms all have fridge, an enclosed balcony, and a prayer mat (just in case!).

Ascot Hotel (66385566; www.ascothotel.com; 38 Garden Rd; d with AC incl breakfast from Rs5500;) From the decadent marble bathrooms with bathtubs and soft lighting to the warm beiges and creams in the huge, uncluttered rooms, the Ascot is all class. Rooms have internet connection and DVD players, and front rooms get lots of natural light and tree views. The service seems a bit disorganised, though, for the price.

FORT, CHURCHGATE & MARINE DRIVE
Residency Hotel (Map p84; 22625525-9; resi dencyhotel@vsnl.com; 26 Rustom Sidhwa Marg, Fort; s/d from Rs2000/2200;) We love how the Residency bucks the trend and doesn't double its rates every other year. It has good vibes like that. Rooms are very small but tasteful and come with fridges, flat-screen TVs and flip-flops (see what we mean?). The lobby and hallways have lots of marble and plants all around and

a skylit atrium. There's wi-fi available and free internet access.

West End Hotel (Map p84; 22039121; www .westendhotelmumbai.com; 45 New Marine Lines; s/d with AC from Rs3200/3600;) You'd half expect Austin Powers to be swinging in this hotel's grey velour–lined bar, Chez Nous. The hotel has a funky, unintentionally retro feel, and the old-fashioned rooms are plain but roomy, with soft beds. The catch is a 20% tax charged on rooms. Wi-fi available.

Grand Hotel (Map pp78-9; 66580500; www.grand hotelbombay.com; 17 Shri Shiv Sagar Ramgulam Marg, Ballard Estate; s/d/tr incl breakfast Rs3500/4000/5000;) The Grand is a good deal, with spunk – note the plaques labelling everything in the 1960s-era lobby. The place is superquiet – you can hear a pin drop in the placid, robin's egg–blue hallways – and rooms are well kept and extremely clean. The furniture is so dated that it's coming back around to brilliant. Wi-fi and computer use are free.

Sea Green Hotel (Map p84; 66336525; www.sea greenhotel.com; 145 Marine Dr; s/d Rs2400/2950;) and **Sea Green South Hotel** (Map p84; 22821613; www .seagreensouth.com; 145A Marine Dr; s/d Rs2400/2950;)

are identical art deco hotels with spacious but spartan AC rooms, originally built in the 1940s to house British soldiers. Ask for one of the sea-view rooms as they're the same price. Both places are great value – even with the 10% service charge.

THE SUBURBS

There are several midrange hotels on Nehru Rd Extension in Vile Parle East near the domestic airport, but rooms are overpriced and only useful for early or late flights. Juhu is convenient for Juhu Beach and for the restaurants, shops and clubs in Bandra.

For mapped locations of the following venues, see opposite.

Iskcon (☎ 26206860; guesthouse.mumbai@pamho .net; Hare Krishna Lane, Juhu; s/d incl tax Rs2095/2495, with AC incl tax Rs2395/2995; 🅿) Part of Juhu's lively Hare Krishna complex, this very efficiently managed guest house is spread out across two buildings – one of which is flamingo pink. Rooms are big and spick and span – those in the original building have balconies – but don't have TV or fridge. A good vegetarian buffet restaurant, Govinda's, is on site.

Hotel Suba Galaxy (☎ 26821188; www.hotelsuba galaxy.com; NS Phadke Marg, Saiwadi, Andheri East; s/d with AC incl breakfast from Rs2800/5000; 🅿) Clean lines, oversized windows and mirrors, and lots of darkwood laminate and bright white makes for good-looking rooms in this newish tower 4km from the international airport. The standard single is a box, but even that has all the mod cons – flat-screen TV, broadband, etc. Oh, and lots of fluffy pillows.

Hotel Columbus (☎ 26182029; hotel_columbus@rediff mail.com; 344 Nanda Patkar Rd, Vile Parle East; s/d with AC from Rs3000/3500; 🅿 🖳) One of the few decent midrange hotels in the domestic airport area, the Columbus is on a cute, tree-lined street off Nehru Rd (opposite the BP petrol pump), away from the airport chaos. The gussied-up deluxe rooms (Rs4000) have stylised woodgrain accents and flat-screen TVs and aspire to high design.

Hotel Airport International (☎ 26182222; www .hotelairportinternational.com; Nehru Rd, Vile Parle East; s/d with AC incl breakfast from Rs5000/6500; 🅿) This is the pick of the Nehru Rd hotels, it's so close to the domestic airport you can see the runway from some rooms. Just renovated, rooms are impeccably clean, compact and tastefully done; superdeluxe rooms have bathtubs and fridges. Wi-fi available.

Citizen Hotel (☎ 66932525; www.citizenhotelmum bai.com; Juhu Tara Rd, Juhu; s/d with AC from Rs7000/7500; 🅿 🖳) The Citizen's location, right on the beach, is what you're paying for here, but rooms are also well maintained, with marble floors and marble-top furniture, flat-screen TVs, wi-fi access, fridges – and, of course, excellent views. The place also has an AC restaurant and a patio cafe, both overlooking the sea.

Sun-n-Sand (☎ 66938888; www.sunnsandhotel.com; 39 Juhu Beach, Juhu; r with AC from Rs10,500; 🅿 🖳 🏊) The Sun-n-Sand has been offering up beachfront hospitality for decades. The best rooms here are the sea-facing ones (Rs12,000): lots of silk and shades of tangerine complement the pool, palm-tree and ocean views from the huge window. It's off Juhu Rd, near the old Holiday Inn.

Top End

Trident (Oberoi Hotel; Map pp78-9; ☎ 66324343; www .tridenthotels.com; Marine Dr, Nariman Point; s/d from Rs17,250/18,500; 🅿 🖳 🏊) The Trident is, along with the Oberoi, part of the Oberoi Hotel complex. But the Trident wins out both on price and on the spiffy, streamlined design of its restaurants, bars and pool area. Plus, it reopened like a champion less than a month after 2008's three-day terrorist occupation.

InterContinental (Map p84; ☎ 39879999; www.in tercontinental.com; 135 Marine Dr, Churchgate; r incl breakfast from Rs18,500; 🅿 🖳 🏊) You'll want to pay a little extra for the splendid sea views at this sophisticated boutique-style hotel. Room decor is cosy but understated, with clean lines and warm tones. The stunning Dome bar and restaurant (p100) elegantly crowns the rooftop and overlooks the sea.

Taj Mahal Palace & Tower (Map p83; ☎ 66653366; www.tajhotels.com; Apollo Bunder, Colaba; tower rooms s/d from Rs18,250/19,750, palace rooms from Rs25,250/26,750; 🅿 🖳 🏊) We already loved it, but when it got back on its feet just three weeks after the November 2008 terrorist attacks (following massive construction work and blessings from leaders of seven religions), we were floored. A Mumbai landmark since 1903, this distinguished hotel, with its sweeping arches, staircases and domes, is unstoppably exquisite. Palace rooms are peaceful, heritage and plush, with separate foyer and soothing white-marble bathroom, plasma TV with internet hookup and a separate breakfast nook (some with Gateway views). Tower rooms are gorgeous but not as special. Even if you don't stay here, have a drink or meal in one of its many excellent bars and restaurants.

Fabulous digs in the suburbs:

Four Seasons Hotel (off Map pp78-9; ☎ 24818000; www.fourseasons.com; Dr E Moses Rd, Worli; r from Rs17,650; ✄ ⌨ ☏) Great sea views and elegance. The service is exceptional, the staff practically psychic.

ITC Maratha (Map p94; ☎ 28303030; www.itcwelcom group.in; Sahar Rd, Andheri East; s/d incl breakfast & tax from Rs22,000/23,500; ✄ ⌨ ☏) The five-star with the most luxurious Indian character, from the Jaipur-style lattice windows around the atrium to the silk pillows on the beds.

EATING

Food options in the metropolis are as diverse as the squillion inhabitants – go on a cultural history tour by sampling Parsi *dhansak* (meat with curried lentils and rice), Gujarati or Keralan thalis ('all-you-can-eat' meals) and everything from Mughlai kebabs and Goan *vindalho* (vindaloo) to Mangalorean seafood. If you find Bombay duck on a menu, remember it's actually *bombil* fish dried in the sun and deep-fried.

Don't miss Mumbai's famous *bhelpuri*, readily available at Chowpatty Beach (p86). During the Islamic holy month of Ramadan, fantastic night food markets line Mohammed Ali and Merchant Rds in Kalbadevi. Street stalls offering rice plates, samosas, *pav bhaji* (spiced vegetables and bread) and *vada pav* (deep-fried spiced-lentil-ball sandwich) for Rs5 to Rs15 do a brisk trade around the city.

For self-caterers, the **Colaba market** (Map p83; Lala Nigam St) has fresh fruit and vegetables. **Saharkari Bhandar Supermarket** (Map p83; ☎ 22022248; cnr Colaba Causeway & Wodehouse Rd; ✄ 10am-8.30pm) and, even better, **Suryodaya** (Map p84; ☎ 22040979; Veer Nariman Rd; ✄ 7.30am-8.30pm) are well-stocked supermarkets.

Colaba

For mapped locations of the following venues see p83.

Theobroma (Colaba Causeway; confections Rs20-100; ✄ 8.30am-midnight) Theobroma calls its creations 'food of the gods' – and they are. Dozens of perfectly executed cakes, tarts and chocolates, as well as sandwiches and breads, go well with the coffee here. The solo hazelnut mousse cake (Rs80) or the genius pistachio-and-green-cardamom truffle (Rs25) will take you to the next plane.

Bagdadi (11 Tulloch Rd; mains Rs20-70; ✄ 7am-12.30am) Bagdadi is full of everyday guys who come for the traditional Mughlai food and no-nonsense service. There's lots and lots of fish, prawns and meat (including beef brain fry; Rs40) on the menu, cooked up in biryanis and daily-changing specials. The best-deal rotis in town are enormous and cost Rs7. But alas, 'food will not be served to drunken person'.

New Laxmi Vilas (19A Ram Mansion, Nawroji F Rd; light meals Rs18-55, mains Rs40-85) A budget eatery that serves great southern specialities in comfortable, modern, AC surrounds. Dosas are the speciality; one reader even wrote in to say 'we still dream of the meals we ate there'. The thalis (Rs43) are also high calibre.

Kailash Parbat (5 Sheela Mahal, First Pasta Lane; mains Rs40-78) Nothing fancy, but a Mumbai legend nonetheless thanks to its inexpensive Sindhi-influenced vegetarian snacks, mouth-watering sweets and extra-spicy masala chai. Kailash Parbat Hindu Hotel across the street is its also good, more playful, cousin.

Bade Miya (Tulloch Rd; meals Rs50-80; ✄ 7pm-3am) As Mumbai as traffic jams, this street-stall-on-steroids buzzes nightly with punters from all walks of Mumbai life lining up for spicy, fresh grilled treats. Grab a chicken tikka roll to go, or sample the *boti kebab* (lamb kebab) or *paneer masala* (unfermented-cheese and tomato curry) on the footpath.

Falafel's (Wodehouse Rd; sandwiches & salads Rs55-125; ✄ 11am-midnight) It's verymuch like a chain restaurant and a bit too marketing-savvy for our tastes, but there's no denying that the falafel, hummus and Greek salads are delish.

Basilico (☎ 66345670; Sentinel House, Arthur Bunder Rd; mains Rs210-375; ✄ 7.30am-midnight) A *très* sleek, Euro-style bistro, Basilico whips up creative fresh pastas, salads and couscous that will make you melt. Vegies will flat out die – from either the wholesome green salad (mixed lettuce, corn, asparagus and sprouts with feta, lime and olive-oil dressing; Rs225) or the homemade mushroom and goat-cheese canelloni (Rs340). The *coup de grâce*? It's also a bakery. The Bandra branch (Map p94, ☎ 67039999, open noon to midnight) is on St John Rd, next to HDFC, Pali Naka.

Indigo Delicatessen (Pheroze Bldg, Chhatrapati Shivaji Marg; mains Rs245-495; ✄ 9am-midnight) Indigo's less expensive sister is just as elegant as the original, with good jazz on, warm but sleek decor and massive wooden tables. It has breakfast

---

DABBA-WALLAHS

A small miracle of logistics, Mumbai's 5000 *dabba* (food container)-wallahs (also called tiffin-wallahs) work tirelessly to deliver hot lunches to office workers throughout the city.

Lunch boxes are picked up each day from restaurants, homes, mothers and wives and carried on heads, bicycles and trains, and taken to a centralised sorting station. A sophisticated system of numbers and colours (many wallahs are illiterate) is then used to determine where every lunch must end up. More than 200,000 meals are delivered in Mumbai in this way – always on time, come (monsoon) rain or (searing) shine.

This same intricate supply-chain system has been used for centuries, and dabba-wallahs are known to take immense pride in their work. Considering that on average only about one mistake is made every six million deliveries, they've certainly earned it.

---

any time (Rs145 to Rs265), casual meals and desserts, teas, wines (Rs360 to Rs710 per glass) and a selection of breads and imported cheeses.

Indigo (☎ 66368980; 4 Mandlik Marg; mains Rs485-985; 🕑 noon-4pm & 7-11pm) Colaba's finest eating option, Indigo has inventive European cuisine, a long wine list, sleek ambience and an absolutely gorgeous roof deck lit with fairy lights. Daily specials come with wine recommendations. Favourites include the soft basil-crusted Norwegian salmon, with asparagus, beetroot couscous and lemon and orange-caper butter (Rs985); or lemon ricotta tortellini with fennel spinach sauce, porcini mushrooms and walnuts (Rs585). Bookings are essential.

Also recommended:

Delhi Darbar (Holland House, Colaba Causeway; mains Rs85-175; 🕑 11.30am-12.30am) Excellent Mughlai, tandoori and Middle Eastern.

Ming Palace (Colaba Causeway; mains Rs160-680; 🕑 11.30am-3.15pm & 6.45-11.30pm) Quality Chinese with gargantuan portions.

Kala Ghoda & Fort

Badshah Snacks & Drinks (Map pp78-9; opposite Crawford market; snacks Rs20-95; 🕑 7am-12.30am) Badshah been serving snacks, fruit juices and its famous *falooda* (rose-flavoured drink made with milk, cream, nuts and vermicelli) to hungry bargain-hunters for more than 100 years.

Anubhav (Map p84; 292 Shahid Bhagat Singh Marg; mains Rs40-75; 🕑 8am-9.45pm Mon-Sat) This local veg joint, aka the Veg Delite, has good South Indian food, as well as a smattering of Punjabi standbys. There are six – count 'em, six – kinds of vegetarian biryani, and a tasty lunch thali, known simply as 'lunch' (Rs45).

Ideal Corner (Map p84; Gunbow St, Fort; mains Rs40-90; 🕑 9am-4.30pm Mon-Fri) This classic Parsi cafe

has the style to match its odd little spot in the crook of a funky, rounded building, with a royal-blue and mango colour scheme and wooden stairs leading to a loft space. But the most artful thing here is the fresh, homemade dishes on the daily-changing menu. Even a simple *khichdi masoor pappad* (lightly spiced rice and lentils; Thursday) is memorable.

Shivala (Map p84; Walchand Hirachand Marg; mains Rs50-110) Shivala is a working-fellas' joint with excellent North Indian food (and the requisite South Indian and Chinese offerings). The AC room upstairs is way contemporary, with lots of glass, pebbles and blue light, but also views: Shivala is just across from Bhatia Udyan, the pocket of green in front of CST.

Moshe's Cafe (Map p84; Fabindia, 1st fl, Jeroo Bldg, MG Rd, Kala Ghoda; light meals Rs60-135; 🕑 10am-7.45pm) After shopping downstairs, refuel with Moshe's excellent salads, sandwiches, baked goods, coffees and smoothies. The marinated garlic, mushroom, leek and bell-pepper open-faced sandwich with melted mozzarella on brown bread will make you collapse with pleasure on your bag of new block-printed kurtas (shirts). There's also a Moshe's in Kemp's Corner (Map pp78-9, open 11am to 8.30pm).

Mahesh Lunch Home (Map p84; ☎ 22023965; 8B Cowasji Patel St, Fort; mains Rs120-400; 🕑 11.30am-3.30pm & 6-11.30pm) A great place to try Mangalorean seafood in Mumbai. It's renowned for its ladyfish, pomfret, lobster and crabs, and its *rawas tikka* (marinated white salmon) and tandoori pomfret are outstanding. There's also a branch on Juhu Tara Rd (Map p94; ☎ 26108848).

Trishna (Map p84; ☎ 22703213-5; Sai Baba Marg, Kala Ghoda; mains Rs160-490; 🕑 noon-3.30pm & 6.30pm-midnight) This might just be the best seafood in town. One reader wrote in to describe how a dish here sent her into deliciousness shock ('This was the best fish I have EVER had!'). It specialises in Mangalorean preparations, and the crab with butter, pepper and garlic and various shrimp dishes – all brought to your table for inspection – are outstanding.

Rajdhani (Map pp78-9; 361 Sheikh Memon St, Kalbadevi; thali Rs225; ☺ noon-4pm & 7-10.30pm) Opposite Mangaldaas Market, Rajdhani is famous for its Gujarati and Rajasthani thalis. It's a great spot to refuel while shopping in the markets. On Sundays, dinner isn't served and lunch prices are slightly higher.

Khyber (Map p84; ☺ 40396666; 145 MG Rd, Fort; mains Rs275-475; ☺ 12.30-4pm & 7.30pm-midnight) Khyber serves up Punjabi and other North Indian dishes in moody, burnt-orange, Afghan-inspired interiors to a who's who of Mumbai's elite. The food is some of the city's best, with the meat-centric menu wandering from kebabs and biryanis to its *pièce de résistance*, *raan* (a whole leg of slow-cooked lamb).

Churchgate

For mapped locations of the following venues, see p84.

Pizzeria (Soona Mahal, 143 Marine Dr; pizza & pasta Rs145-350; ☺ noon-midnight) Serves up pizzas and pasta dishes along with Indian wines, but the ocean views are the real draw.

Samrat (☎ 42135401; Prem Ct, J Tata Rd; lunch/dinner thalis Rs190/220; ☺ noon-4pm & 7-10.45pm) A busy traditional Indian pure-veg restaurant, Saurat is part of a family restaurant at the same location. Relish (mains Rs150 to Rs250, open noon to midnight) is the funkier cousin, with dishes ranging from Lebanese platters to Mexican, while 210°C is an outdoor cafe and bakery (coffees and pastries Rs20 to Rs80; open noon to 11pm).

Gaylord (☎ 22821259; Veer Nariman Rd; meals Rs190-650; ☺ 12.30-3.30pm & 7.30-11.30pm) Great North Indian dishes served with over-the-top, Raj era–style dining complete with tuxedo-wearing waiters hanging on your every gesture. It also serves domestic and imported wines (Rs175 to Rs600 per glass).

Chowpatty

For mapped locations of the following venues see pp78-9.

The evening stalls at Bhel Plaza on Chowpatty Beach are the most atmospheric spots to snack on *bhelpuri* (Rs20) or *panipuri*

(small, crisp puffs of dough filled with spicy tamarind water and sprouted gram; Rs15). Mobile chai-wallahs do the rounds.

New Kulfi Centre (cnr Chowpatty Seaface & Sardar V Patel Rd; kulfi per 100gm Rs18-38; ☺ 9am-1.30am) Serves the best *kulfi* (firm-textured ice cream flavoured, often with pistachio) you'll have anywhere, which means it's the best-tasting thing in the entire world. When you order, the *kulfi* is placed on a betel-nut leaf and then weighed on an ancient scale – which makes it even better.

In fact, there's a lot of serious ice-cream action going on here:

Cream Centre (Chowpatty Seaface; mains Rs100-195; ☺ noon-midnight) An excellent ice-cream parlour in a bright, slick interior. Oh, and real food, too: a pure-veg hodgepodge of Indian, Mexican and Middle Eastern.

Gelato Italiano (Chowpatty Seaface; scoops Rs30-70; ☺ 11am-12.30am) Flavours like custard-apple sorbetto or limoncello – yum.

The Suburbs

North Mumbai's trendy dining joints centre on Bandra West and Juhu, while *bhelpuri*, *panipuri*, et al are served at Juhu Chowpatty. For mapped locations of the following venues see p94.

our pick **Hotel Ram Ashray** (Bhandarkar Rd, Matunga East; light meals Rs12-38; ☺ 5.30am-9.30pm) We wouldn't send you to Matunga – on the Central line, no less – if this weren't something special. Tucked away in a Tamil enclave near King's Circle (a stone's throw from the station's east exit), Ram Ashray is popular with southern families for its spectacular dosas, *idli* (round steamed rice cakes) and *upma* (semolina cooked with onions, spices and coconut). You won't taste a better coconut chutney anywhere (sorry, Chennai).

Culture Curry (Kataria Rd, Matunga West; mains Rs129-459; ☺ noon-3.30pm & 7pm-12.30am) As the Culture Curry folks rightly point out, there's a lot more to southern food than *idli* and dosas. Exquisite dishes from all over the South, ranging from Andhra and Coorg to Kerala, are the specialty here. Vegies are particularly well served: the Kooru Curry (kidney and green beans in coconut gravy; Rs179) is extraordinary. The same owners run Diva Maharashtracha, down the street, and Goa Portuguesa, next door, specialising in fiery Goan dishes. Guitar-strumming musicians and singers wander between the two connected spaces.

Pot Pourri (Carlton Ct, cnr of Turner & Pali Rds, Bandra West; mains Rs150-285; noon-midnight Mon-Sat, 9am-midnight Sun) In a good spot for watching Bandra streetlife, Pot Pourri serves up sandwiches and Western- and Eastern-style cuisine. It excels with the Asian stuff: the Thai papaya salad (Rs115) and veg or meat *khau suey* (Burmese noodles with a coconut broth; Rs265) are superb.

Sheesha (66770555; 7th flr, Shoppers Stop, Linking Rd, Bandra West; mains Rs170-250; 11.30am-1.30am) With maybe the most beautiful ambience in town, Sheesha's alfresco rooftop lair has glass lanterns hanging from wooden beams, comfy couches and coloured-glass lamps high above the city and shopping madness below. You almost forget about the food – good Indian fare (Goan fish curry; Rs245) nestling alongside 386 varieties of kebab (Rs130 to Rs220). Reserve on weekends.

Red Box Cafe (155 Waterfield Rd, Bandra West; mains Rs190-375; noon-1.30am) Where Bandra's beautiful people go when they want something 'simple'. Red Box does good sandwiches, salads, pizza, fondue and espresso. There's Wham! playing in the background, picture windows and outdoor tables, and a red-and-black goth-meets-McDonald's design scheme. It works, though, on some weird level.

delltalia (26284040; Juhu Tara Rd, opposite Juhu Beach; mains Rs280-410; 11.30am-3pm & 7.30pm-12.30am) The Italian villa decor here – the semi-alfresco terrace with hanging plants, the faux terracotta walls, the wooden pantry on the 1st floor – is a little theme-y but lovely even so, especially at night. Some of the Italian food here (ahem, pizza) is so-so, but most is sublime, for example, the artichoke and bocconcini salad with sundried tomato. Bottles of Italian wine start at Rs1500.

Peshawri (28303030; ITC Maratha, Sahar Rd; mains Rs500-1250; 12.30-2.45pm & 7-11.45pm) Make this Indian north-west frontier restaurant, just outside the international airport, your first or last stop in Mumbai. You won't regret forking out for the leg of spring lamb and amazing dhal Bukhara (a thick black dhal cooked for a day!). The ITC is also home to Dakshin (open 7.30pm to 11.45pm) – better for vegetarians – serving some of Mumbai's finest southern food.

DRINKING

Mumbai's lax attitude to alcohol means that there are loads of places to drink – from hole-in-the-wall beer bars and chichi lounges to brash, multilevel superclubs. You'll pay around Rs80 to Rs130 for a bottle of Kingfisher in a bar or restaurant, a lot more in a club or fashionable watering hole.

If it's the caffeine buzz you're after, espresso is ubiquitous.

Cafes

Kamat Sweets & Snacks (Map p83; 24 Colaba Causeway; teas & coffees Rs7-38) It's just tea, sweets and snacks and it's small and cramped, but we just can't resist the retro vibe – or the cold coffee with ice cream (Rs38).

Mocha Bar (coffees Rs30-175, light meals Rs95-175; 10am-1:30am) Churchgate (Map p84; 82 Veer Nariman Rd); Juhu (Map p94; 67 Juhu Tara Rd) This atmospheric, Arabian-styled cafe is often filled to the brim with bohemians and students deep in esoteric conversation, or just gossip. Cosy, low-cushioned seating, hookah pipes, exotic coffee varieties and world music add up to longer stays than you expected.

Samovar Café (Map p84; Jehangir Art Gallery, 161B MG Rd, Kala Ghoda; 11am-7.30pm Mon-Sat) This intimate place inside the art gallery overlooks the gardens of the Prince of Wales Museum and is a great spot to chill out over a beer, mango lassi or light meal.

Cha Bar (Map p84; 66364477; Oxford Bookstore, Apeejay House, 3 Dinsha Wachha Marg, Churchgate; 10am-9.30pm) An inspiring range of teas and tasty snacks amid lots of books.

Meanwhile, Barista and Café Coffee Day are still trying to out-Starbucks each other: **Barista** (coffees Rs38-85; 9am-1am) Colaba (Map p83; Colaba Causeway); Colaba (Map p83; Arthur Bunder Rd); CST (Map p84; Marzaban Rd) **Café Coffee Day** (coffees Rs34-90; 8am-midnight) Chowpatty (Map pp78-9; Chowpatty Seaface); CST (Map p84; Marzaban Rd)

Bars

SOUTH MUMBAI

For mapped locations of the following venues see p83, unless otherwise indicated.

Leopold's Café (cnr Colaba Causeway & Nawroji F Rd; 7.30am-midnight) Love it or hate it, most tourists end up at this Mumbai travellers' institution at one time or another. Around since 1871, Leopold's has wobbly ceiling fans, open-plan seating and a rambunctious atmosphere conducive to swapping tales with random strangers. Although there's a huge menu, the lazy evening beers are the real draw.

Café Universal (Map p84; 299 Colaba Causeway; 10am-11pm Mon-Sat, 7-11pm Sun) A little bit of France near CST. The Universal has an art nouveau look to it, with butterscotch-colour walls, a wood-beam ceiling and lots of windows, and is a comfy, pretty place for happy hour.

Busaba (22043779; 4 Mandlik Marg; noon-3.30pm & 6pm-1am) Red walls and contemporary art of Buddhas give this loungey restaurant-bar a nouveau Tao. It's next to Indigo so gets the same trendy crowd but serves cheaper, more potent cocktails. The upstairs restaurant serves pan-Asian (mains Rs300 to Rs750); its back room feels like a posh treehouse. Reserve ahead.

Café Mondegar (22020591; Metro House, 5A Colaba Causeway; 8am-12.30am) Like Leopold's, Café Mondegar is usually filled entirely with for-eigners, but some readers find it less over-whelmingly foreign somehow. It also has more character. 'Purple Haze' seems to be always playing on the CD jukebox.

Henry Tham's (22023186; Apollo Bunder; 12.30-3pm & 7.30pm-1.30am) This superswanky bar-cum-restaurant features towering ceil-ings, gratuitous use of space and strategically placed minimalist decor. It's a darling of the Mumbai jet set and therefore *the* place to see and be seen. The real star here, though, is the Chinese food.

Dome (Map p84; 39879999, ext 8872; Hotel InterContinental, 135 Marine Dr, Churchgate; 6pm-1.30am) This white-on-white rooftop lounge has awe-some views of Mumbai's curving seafront. Cocktails beckon to the hip young things of Mumbai nightly – get out your Bollywood star-spotting logbook.

THE SUBURBS

Ghetto (Map pp78-9; 23538418; 30B Bhulabhai Desai Marg, Mahalaxmi; 7pm-1.30am) This graffiti-covered rocker's hang-out blares rock nightly to a dedicated set of regulars.

Shiro (off Map pp78-9; 66155980; Bombay Dyeing Mills Compound, Worli; 7pm-1.30am) No lounge anywhere has ambience as soothing as Shiro's. Water pours from the hands of towering Balinese stone goddesses into lotus ponds, which reflect shimmering light on the walls. Lighting is soft and dramatic, with lots of candles (and good Japanese food).

Toto's Garage (Map p94; 26005494; 30 Lourdes Heaven, Pali Naka, Bandra West; 6pm-1am) Forget the beautiful people. Toto's is a local joint where you can go in your dirty clothes, drink

beer and listen to '80s music with the locals. Get there early or you won't get a seat.

Vie Lounge (Map p94; 26603003; Juhu Tara Rd, Juhu; 4.30pm-1.30am) Right on Juhu Beach is this glamorous party spot (opposite Little Italy restaurant). The drinks menu is 18 pages long and includes aged imported whiskies. It's also a nice place for an early-evening coffee and snack. Call before coming to check there isn't a private Bollywood bash on.

Zenzi (Map p94; 66430670-2; 183 Waterfield Rd, Bandra West; 7pm-1am) This stylish hang-out pad is a favourite among the well-heeled. Comfy lounges are sheltered by fairy lights and a tree growing out of one wall, and the burnt-orange decor is bathed in soft light. It's at its best when the canopy is open to the stars.

Olive Bar & Kitchen (Map p94; 26058228; Pali Hill Tourist Hotel, 14 Union Park, Khar West; 7.30pm-1.30am) Hip, gorgeous and snooty, this Mediterranean-style restaurant and bar has light and delicious food, soothing DJ sounds and pure Ibiza decor. Thursday and weekends are packed. The open-ing of a new branch at Mahalaxmi Racecourse (open for lunch and dinner, till 1.30am), next to the Turf Club, made South Mumbai's rich and famous very happy.

ENTERTAINMENT

The daily English-language tabloid *Mid-Day* incorporates the *List*, a guide to Mumbai enter-tainment. Newspapers and *Time Out Mumbai* (p77) list events and film screenings, while www.gigpad.com has live-music listings.

Nightclubs

The big nights in clubs are Wednesday, Friday and Saturday, when there's usually a cover charge. Dress codes apply so don't rock up in shorts and sandals.

Enigma (Map p94; 66933288; JW Marriott, Juhu Tara Rd, Juhu; 9.30pm-3am Wed-Sun) For Bollywood star-spotting, Enigma is the place. It doesn't get going till after midnight, but then it *really* gets going. The couples cover is Rs1000.

Ra (off Map pp78-9; 66614343; Phoenix Mills, Senapati Bapat Marg, Lower Parel; 9pm-1.30am Wed-Sat) Where the city's beautiful people come to shake their money-makers. Ra's glass roof opens wide to the stars, and your wallet will open even wider to pay for its top-notch cocktails. Cover for couples is Rs1000, but you may be able to call ahead and get on the guest list.

Polly Esther's (Map p83; 22871122; Gordon House Hotel, Battery St, Colaba; cover per couple Rs800-1500; 9pm-

2.45am Tue-Sun) Wallowing in a cheesy time-warp of retro pop, rock and disco, this mirror-plated, groovy nightclub still manages to pull a crowd. It comes complete with a *Saturday Night Fever* illuminated dance floor and waiters in Afro wigs. Wednesday is free for the gals.

Voodoo Pub (Map p83; ☎ 22841959; Kamal Mansion, Arthur Bunder Rd, Colaba; cover Rs250; ⊗ 8.30pm-1.30am) Hosting Mumbai's only regular gay night (Saturday; cover Rs300), this dark and sweaty bar has little going for it on other nights of the week.

Cinema

It would be a crime not to see a movie in India's film capital. Unfortunately, Hindi films aren't shown with English subtitles. The following all show English-language movies, along with some Bollywood numbers.

Eros (Map p84; ☎ 22822335; MK Rd, Churchgate; tickets Rs60-100)

Metro Big (Map p84; ☎ 39844060; MG Rd, New Marine Lines, Fort; tickets Rs250-750) This grand dame of Bombay talkies was just renovated into a multiplex.

Regal (Map p83; ☎ 22021017; Colaba Causeway, Colaba; tickets Rs100-150) Check out the art deco architecture.

Sterling (Map p84; ☎ 66220016; Marzaban Rd, Fort; tickets Rs120-150)

The lesbian and gay organisation **Bombay Dost** (http://bombay-dost.pbwiki.com) organises 'Sunday High', a twice-monthly screening of queer-interest films, usually in the suburbs.

Music, Dance & Theatre

Bluefrog (off Map pp78-9; ☎ 40332300; www.bluefrog .co.in; D/2 Mathuradas Mills Compound, NM Joshi Marg, Lower Parel; admission after 9pm Sun & Tue-Thu Rs300, Fri & Sat Rs500; ⊗ 7pm-1am Tue-Sun) The most exciting thing to happen to Mumbai's music scene in a long time, Bluefrog is a concert space, production studio, restaurant and one of Mumbai's most happening spaces. It hosts exceptional local and international acts, and has cool booth seating.

Not Just Jazz by the Bay (Map p84; ☎ 22851876; 143 Marine Dr; admission weekdays/weekends Rs150/200; ⊗ noon-3.30am) This is the best, and frankly the only, jazz club in South Mumbai. True to its name, there are also live pop, blues and rock performers most nights, but Sunday, Monday and Tuesday are reserved for karaoke.

National Centre for the Performing Arts (NCPA; Map pp78-9; ☎ 66223737; www.ncpamumbai.com; cnr Marine Dr & Sri V Saha Rd, Nariman Point; tickets Rs200-500) Spanning 800 sq metres, this cultural centre is the hub of Mumbai's music, theatre and dance scene. In any given week, it might host Marathi theatre, poetry readings and art exhibitions, Bihari dance troupes, ensembles from Europe or Indian classical music. The Experimental Theatre occasionally has English-language plays. Many performances are free. The box office (☎ 22824567; open 9am to 7pm) is at the end of NCPA Marg.

Prithvi Theatre (Map p94; ☎ 26149546; www.prithvi theatre.org; Juhu Church Rd, Juhu) At Juhu Beach, this is a good place to see both Hindi and English-language theatre. It hosts an excellent annual international theatre festival, too.

The **Nehru Centre** (p88) occasionally stages dance, music and English-language theatre performances.

Sport
CRICKET

To prepare for the Cricket World Cup final in February/March 2011, **Wankhede Stadium** (Mumbai Cricket Association; Map p84; ☎ 22795500; www .mumbaicricket.com; D Rd, Churchgate) is closed until the end of 2010 for a massive renovation. When open, test matches and one-day internationals are played a few times a year in season (October to April). Contact the Cricket Association for ticket information; for a test match you'll probably have to pay for the full five days.

FOOTBALL

The **Cooperage Football Ground** (Map p83; ☎ 22024020; MK Rd, Colaba; tickets Rs20-25) is home to the Mumbai Football Association and hosts national-league and local soccer matches between October and February. Tickets are available at the gate.

SHOPPING

Mumbai is India's great marketplace, with some of the best shopping in the country. Colaba Causeway is lined with hawkers' stalls and shops selling garments, perfumes and knick-knacks. Electronic gear, pirated CDs and DVDs, leather goods and mass-produced gizmos are for sale at stalls on Dr Dadabhai Naoroji Rd between CST and Flora Fountain, and along MG Rd from Flora Fountain to Kala Ghoda.

Antiques & Curios

Small antique and curio shops line Mere-wether Rd behind the Taj Mahal Palace & Tower (Map p83). They aren't cheap, but

THIEVES BAZAAR

Nobody is sure exactly how Mumbai's Chor Bazaar (literally 'thieves market') earned its moniker. One popular explanation has it that Queen Victoria, upon arrival in Mumbai in her steam ship, discovered that her violin/purse/jewellery went missing while being unloaded off the ship. After the city was scoured the missing item was supposedly found hanging in Chor Bazaar's Mutton St, and hence the name.

the quality is a step up from government emporiums.

If you prefer Raj-era bric-a-brac, head to Chor Bazaar (Map pp78-9); the main area of activity is Mutton St, where you'll find a row of shops specialising in antiques (and many ingenious reproductions, so beware) and miscellaneous junk.

Mini Market (Map pp78-9; ☎ 23472427; 33/31 Mutton St; ☷ 11am-8pm Sat-Thu) Sells original vintage Bollywood posters and other movie ephemera as well as odd and interesting trinkets.

Phillips (Map p83; ☎ 22020564; www.phillipsantiques.com; Wodehouse Rd, Colaba; ☷ 10am-7pm Mon-Sat) The 150-year-old Phillips has nizam-era royal silver, wooden ceremonial masks, Victorian glass and various other gorgeous things that you never knew you wanted. It also has high-quality reproductions of old photos, maps and paintings, and a warehouse of big antiques.

Clothes

Bag a bargain backpacking wardrobe at Fashion Street, a strip of stalls lining MG Rd between Cross and Azad maidans (Map p84), or in Bandra's Linking Rd, near Waterford Rd (Map p94); hone your bargaining skills. Kemp's Corner has good shops for designer threads.

Fabindia (Map p84; ☎ 22626539; Jeroo Bldg, 137 MG Rd, Kala Ghoda; ☷ 10am-7.45pm) Founded as a means to get traditional fabric artisans' wares to market, Fabindia has all the vibrant colours of the country in its cotton and silk fashions, materials and homewares, all in a modern-meets-traditional Indian shop. The Santa Cruz outpost (Map p94) is also good.

Khadi & Village Industries Emporium (Khadi Bhavan; Map p84; ☎ 22073280/8; 286 Dr Dadabhai Naoroji Rd, Fort; ☷ 10.30am-6.30pm Mon-Sat) All dusty and old school, Khadi Bhavan is 1940s time-warp with ready-made traditional Indian clothing,

material, shoes and handicrafts that are so old they're new again.

More good shopping:

Anokhi (☷ 10am-7.30pm Mon-Sat) Chowpatty (Map pp78-9; ☎ 23685761; AR Rangnekar Marg, off Hughes Rd) Bandra West (Map p94; ☎ 26408261; Waterfield Rd) Gets the East–West balance just right, with men's and women's clothes and bedding in block-printed silk and cotton.

Biba (Map pp78-9; ☎ 23894184; 1 Hughes Rd, Kemp's Corner; ☷ 10.30am-9pm Mon-Sat) Gorgeous salwar kurtas with just the right amount of bling.

Cotton Cottage (Map p84; ☎ 22674026; Agra Bldg, MG Rd, Kala Ghoda; ☷ 10am-8.30pm) Stock up on simple cotton kurtas and various pants – salwars, churidars, patiala – for the road.

Cottonworld Corp (Map p83; ☎ 22850060; Mandlik Marg; ☷ 10.30am-8pm Mon-Sat, noon-8pm Sun) Small chain selling stylish Indian–Western-hybrid goods. Entrance is behind the State Bank of India.

Courtyard (Map p83; SP Centre, 41/44 Minoo Desai Marg; ☷ 11am-7.30pm) A collection of couture boutiques. Good if you're interested in India's fashion design scene.

Kala Niketan (Map p84; ☎ 22005001; 95 MK Rd; ☷ 10am-8pm Mon-Sat) Sari madness on Queens Rd.

Mélange (Map pp78-9; ☎ 23534492; 33 Altamount Rd, Kemp's Corner; ☷ 10am-7pm Mon-Sat) High-fashion garments from 70 Indian designers in a chic exposed-brick space. Payal Singhal, next door, is also good.

Telon (Map pp78-9; ☎ 23648174; 149 Warden Rd, Kemp's Corner; ☷ 10.30am-8.30pm Mon-Sat) Fine gents tailor. Suits to order start at Rs13,000.

Handicrafts & Gifts

Various state-government emporiums sell handicrafts in the World Trade Centre Arcade (Map pp78-9) near Cuffe Parade.

Bombay Store (Map p84; ☷ 40669999; Western India House, Sir PM Rd, Fort; ☷ 10.30am-7.30pm Mon-Sat, to 6.30pm Sun) A classy selection of rugs, clothing, teas, stationery, aromatherapy and brass sculptures.

Bombay Paperie (Map p84; ☎ 66358171; 59 Bombay Samachar Marg, Fort; ☷ 10.30am-6pm Mon-Sat) Sells handmade, cotton-based paper crafted into charming cards, sculptures and lampshades.

Shrujan Juhu (Map p94; ☎ 26183104; Hatkesh Society, 6th North South Rd, JVPD Scheme; ☷ 9.30am-7pm Mon-Sat) Breach Candy (Map pp78-9; ☎ 23521693; Sagar Villa, Warden Rd, opposite Navroze Apts; ☷ 10am-7.30pm Mon-Sat) Selling the intricate embroidery work of women in 114 villages in Kutch, Gujarat, the nonprofit Shrujan aims to help women earn a livelihood while preserving the spectacular embroidery traditions of the area. The sophisticated clothing, wall hangings and purses make great gifts.

Other stores worth popping into:

Central Cottage Industries Emporium (Map p83; ☎ 22027537; Chhatrapati Shivaji Marg, Colaba; ☺ 10am-7pm) Easy-breezy souvenir shopping.

Chimanlals (Map p84; ☎ 22077717; Dr Dadabhai Naoroji Rd, Fort; ☺ 9.30am-6pm Mon-Sat) Writing materials made from traditional Indian paper. Enter from Wallace St.

Inshaallah Mashaallah (Map p83; ☎ 22049495; Best Marg, Colaba; ☺ 10.30am-8pm) Local oils and perfumes in antediluvian bottles; the rose is popular (Rs250 for 12ml).

Markets

You can buy just about anything in the dense bazaars north of CST (see Map pp78-9). The main areas are Crawford Market (fruit and veg), Mangaldas Market (silk and cloth), Zaveri Bazaar (jewellery), Bhuleshwar Market (fruit and veg) and Chor Bazaar (antiques and furniture), where Dhabu St is lined with fine leather goods and Mutton St specialises in antiques, reproductions and fine junk.

Crawford Market (Mahatma Phule Market) is the last outpost of British Bombay before the tumult of the central bazaars begins. Bas-reliefs by Rudyard Kipling's father, Lockwood Kipling, adorn the Norman Gothic exterior. The meat market is strictly for the brave.

Music

LM Furtado & Co (Map pp78-9; ☎ 22013163; 540-544 Kalbadevi Rd, Kalbadevi; ☺ 10am-8pm Mon-Sat) The best place in Mumbai for musical instruments – sitars, tablas, accordions and local and imported guitars. It also has a branch around the corner on Lokmanya Tilak Rd.

For nonpirated CDs and DVDs, visit **Planet M** (Map p84; ☎ 22071148; Dr Dadabhai Naoroji Rd, Fort; ☺ 10.30am-10.30pm) or, our fave, **Rhythm House** (Map p84; ☎ 22842835; 40 K Dubash Marg, Fort; ☺ 10am-8.30pm Mon-Sat, 11am-8.30pm Sun), which also sells tickets to concerts, plays and festivals.

GETTING THERE & AWAY
Air
AIRPORTS

Mumbai is the main international gateway for travellers to Goa and South India, and has the busiest network of domestic flights. The **Chhatrapati Shivaji International Airport** (☎ domestic 26264000, international 26813000; www.csia.in), about 30km from downtown, comprises two domestic and two international terminals. The domestic side is accessed via Vile Parle and is known locally as Santa Cruz airport, while the international, with its entrance 4km away in

Andheri, goes locally by Sahar. Terminals have ATMs, foreign-exchange counters and tourist-information booths (p80). A free shuttle bus runs between the two every 30 minutes.

INTERNATIONAL AIRLINES

Travel agencies are often better for booking international flights, while airline offices are increasingly directing customers to their call centres.

Air France (off Map pp78-9; ☎ 1800 180033; Sarjan Plaza, 100 Dr Annie Besant Rd, Worli; ☺ 9am-1pm & 1.30-5pm Mon-Fri)

Air India (Map p84; ☎ 26818098, airport 26168000; Air India Bldg, cnr Marine Dr & Madame Cama Rd, Nariman Point; ☺ 9.30am-5.30pm)

American Airlines (off Map pp78-9; ☎ 18002001800; 114 Nirman Kendra, Dr E Moses Rd, Mahalaxmi; ☺ 9am-6pm Mon-Fri, 10am-2pm Sat)

British Airways (Map p94; ☎ 9892577470, 1800 10235922; Notan Plaza, Turner Rd, Bandra West; ☺ 9.30am-1pm Mon, Wed, Fri)

Cathay Pacific (off Map pp78-9; ☎ 66572222, airport 66859002/3; 2 Brady Gladys Plaza, Senapati Bapat Marg, Lower Parel; ☺ 9.30am-6.30pm Mon-Sat)

Delta Airlines (Map pp78-9; ☎ 22839712 5; Interglobe Enterprises Ltd, 12th fl, Bajaj Bhawan, Nariman Point; ☺ 9am-5.30pm Mon-Sat)

El Al Airlines (Map pp78-9; ☎ 22154701, airport 66859425/6; 57 The Arcade, World Trade Centre, Cuffe Parade; ☺ 9.30am-5.30pm Mon-Fri, to 1pm Sat)

Qantas (Map p84; ☎ 22007440; Godrej Bhavan, 2nd fl, Home St, Fort; ☺ 9am-1.15pm & 2.30-5.30pm Mon-Fri)

Thai Airways (Map pp78-9; ☎ 66373737; Mittal Towers A Wing, 2A, Nariman Point; ☺ 9.30am-5pm Mon-Fri, to 4pm Sat)

Virgin Atlantic (Map p84; ☎ 67523701-5; Poddar House, 10 Marine Dr, Churchgate; ☺ 9.15am-5.30pm)

DOMESTIC AIRLINES

Flights to Goa's Dabolim Airport, just outside Vasco da Gama, cost around Rs4100 and take about 45 minutes. There are around 20 flights per day. The following all have ticket counters at the domestic airport; most are open 24 hours.

Go Air (☎ 9223022111)

IndiGo (☎ call centre 18001803838, airport 26156774)

Jet Airways (Map p83; ☎ 39893333, airport 26266575; Amarchand Mansion, Madame Cama Rd; ☺ 9am-7pm Mon-Fri, 9am-5.30pm Sat, 9.30am-1.30pm Sun) Also handles JetLite bookings.

Kingfisher (Map p84; ☎ 40340500, airport 26262605; Nirmal Bldg, Marine Dr, Nariman Point; ☺ 9am-7pm Mon-Sat, 10am-2pm Sun)

SpiceJet (☎ call centre 9871803333, 18001803333)

Bus

Numerous private operators and state governments run long-distance buses to and from Mumbai.

Private buses are usually more comfortable and simpler to book but can cost significantly more than government buses; they depart from Dr Anadrao Nair Rd near Mumbai Central train station (Map pp78-9). Fares to Goa (and other popular destinations) are up to 75% higher during holiday periods. To check on departure times and current prices, try **National Travels** (Map pp78-9; ☎ 23015652; Dr Anadrao Nair Rd; ☉ 7am-10pm).

Most convenient for Goa and southern destinations are the private buses (Map p84) that depart twice a day from in front of Azad Maidan, just south of the Metro cinema. Ticket agents are located near the bus departure point. Bus tickets to Panaji (Panjim) in Goa cost between Rs410 and Rs800. The trip takes around 15 hours.

Long-distance government-run buses depart from **Mumbai Central bus terminal** (Map pp78-9; ☎ 23074272/1524) by Mumbai Central train station.

Train

Three train systems operate running out of Mumbai, but the most important services for travellers to Goa are the *Konkan Kanya Express*, the *Mandovi Express* and the *Jan Shatabdi Express*, which all head to Margao's Madgaon train station. See also p240 for more information

Central Railways (☎ 134), handling services to the east and south, plus a few trains to the north, operates from Chhatrapati Shivaji Terminus (CST). The **reservation centre** (Map p84; ☎ 137; ☉ 8am-8pm Mon-Sat, to 2pm Sun) is around the side of CST where the taxis gather. **Foreign tourist-quota tickets** (Counter 52) can be bought up to 90 days before travel, but must be paid in foreign currency or with rupees backed by an encashment certificate or ATM receipt. You can buy nonquota tickets with a Visa or MasterCard at the much faster credit-card counters (10 and 11) for a Rs30 fee.

GETTING AROUND
To/From the Airports
INTERNATIONAL

The prepaid-taxi booth that is located at the international airport has set fares for every neighbourhood in the city; Colaba, Fort and Marine Dr are Rs325, Bandra and Juhu Rs200. There's a 25% surcharge between midnight and 5am and, at all times, a Rs10 service charge and a charge of Rs10 per bag. The journey to Colaba takes about 45 minutes at night and 1½ to two hours during the day. Tips are not required.

Autorickshaws queue up at a little distance from Arrivals, but don't try to take one to South Mumbai: they can only go as far as Mahim Creek. You can catch an autorickshaw (around Rs30) to Andheri train station, though, and catch a suburban train (Rs9, 45 minutes) to Churchgate or CST. Only attempt this if you arrive during the day outside of rush 'hour' (6am to 11am) and are not weighed down with luggage. At the very least, buy a 1st-class ticket (Rs86).

Minibuses outside Arrivals offer free shuttle services to the domestic airport and Juhu hotels.

A taxi from South Mumbai to the international airport shouldn't cost more than Rs400 with the meter by negotiating a fixed fare beforehand; official baggage charges are Rs10 per bag. Add 25% to the meter charge between midnight and 5am. We love the old-school black-and-yellows, but there's also **Meru** (☎ 44224422; www.merucabs.com), AC, metered call taxis charging Rs15 for the first kilometre and Rs13 each kilometre thereafter (25% more at night). Colaba to the airport will cost around Rs400, and the route is tracked by GPS, so no rip-offs!

DOMESTIC

Taxis and autorickshaws queue up outside both domestic terminals. There are no prepaid counters, but both queues are controlled by the police – make sure your driver uses the meter and conversion card. A taxi to Colaba costs around Rs350.

If you don't have too much luggage, bus 2 (limited) stops on nearby Nehru Rd and passes through Colaba Causeway (Rs18). Coming from the city, it stops on the highway opposite the airport.

A better alternative is to catch an autorickshaw between the airport and Vile Parle train station (Rs15), and a train between Vile Parle and Churchgate (Rs9, 45 minutes). Don't attempt this during rush hour (6am to 11am).

Boat

Both **PNP** (☎ 22885220) and **Maldar Catamarans** (☎ 22829695) run regular ferries to Mandwa

(Rs110 one way), useful for access to Murud-Janjira and other parts of the Konkan Coast, avoiding the long bus trip out of Mumbai. Their ticket offices are at Apollo Bunder (near the Gateway of India; Map p83).

Bus

Mumbai's single- and double-decker buses are good for travelling short distances. Fares around South Mumbai cost Rs3 for a section; pay the conductor once you're aboard. The service is run by **BEST** (Map p83; ☎ 22856262; www .bestundertaking.com), which has a depot in Colaba (the website has a useful search facility for bus routes across the city). Just jumping on a double-decker bus (such as bus 103) is an inexpensive way to see South Mumbai. Day passes are available for Rs15.

In the table below are some useful bus routes; all of these buses depart from the bus stand at the southern end of Colaba Causeway and pass Flora Fountain.

LOCAL BUSES IN MUMBAI (BOMBAY)	
Destination	**Bus No**
Breach Candy	132, 133
Chowpatty	103, 106, 107, 123
Churchgate	70, 106, 123, 132
CST & Crawford Market	1, 3, 21, 103, 124
Haji Ali	83, 124, 132, 133
Hanging Gardens	103, 106
Mani Bhavan	123
Mohammed Ali Rd	1, 3, 21
Mumbai Central train station	124, 125

Car

Cars are generally hired for an eight-hour day and an 80km maximum, with additional charges if you go over. For an AC car, the best going rate is Rs1000.

Agents at the Apollo Bunder ticket booths near the Gateway of India can arrange a non-AC Maruti with driver for a half-day of sightseeing for Rs700 (going as far as Mahalaxmi and Malabar Hill). Regular taxi drivers often accept a similar price.

Motorcycle

Allibhai Premji Tyrewalla (Map pp78-9; ☎ 23099313; www.premjis.com; 205/207 Dr D Bhadkamkar Rd, Opera House; ☻ 10am-7pm Mon-Sat), around for almost 100 years, sells new and used motorcycles with

a guaranteed buy-back option. For two- to three-week 'rental' periods you'll still have to pay the full cost of the bike upfront. The company prefers to deal with longer-term schemes of two months or more, which work out cheaper anyway. A used 350cc or 500cc Enfield costs Rs25,000 to Rs80,000, with a buy-back price of around 60% after three months. A smaller bike (100cc to 180cc) starts at Rs25,000. It can also arrange shipment of bikes overseas (around Rs24,000 to the UK).

Taxi & Autorickshaw

Every second car on Mumbai's streets seems to be a black-and-yellow Premier taxi (India's version of a 1950s Fiat). They're the most convenient way to get around the city, and in South Mumbai drivers almost always use the meter without prompting. Autorickshaws are confined to the suburbs north of Mahim Creek.

Drivers don't always know the names of Mumbai's streets (especially new names) – the best way to find something is by using nearby landmarks. The taxi meters are out of date, so the fare is calculated using a conversion chart, which all drivers must carry. The rate during the day is around 13 times the meter reading, with a minimum fare of Rs13 for the first 1.6km (flag fall) and Rs7 per kilometre after this. Add 30% between midnight and 5am.

If you're north of Mahim Creek and not heading into the city, catch an autorickshaw. They're also metered: the fare is 10 times the meter reading, minus one. Flag fall is Rs9 (the meter will read 1.00). Add 25% between midnight and 5am.

Train

Mumbai has an efficient but overcrowded suburban train network.

There are three main lines, making it easy to navigate. The most useful service operates from Churchgate heading north to stations such as Charni Rd (for Chowpatty), Mumbai Central, Mahalaxmi (for the dhobi ghat; p87), Vile Parle (for the domestic airport), Andheri (for the international airport) and Borivali (for Sanjay Gandhi National Park). Other suburban lines operate from CST to Byculla (for Veermata Jijabai Bhonsle Udyan, formerly Victoria Gardens), Dadar and as far as Neral (for Matheran). Trains run from 4am till 1am. From Churchgate, 2nd-/1st-class fares are Rs6/44 to Mumbai Central, Rs9/78 to Vile Parle or Andheri and Rs11/104 to Borivali.

'Tourist tickets' are available, which permit unlimited travel in 2nd/1st class for one (Rs50/180), three (Rs90/330) or five (Rs105/390) days.

Avoid rush hours when trains are jam-packed, even in 1st class; watch your valuables, and gals, stick to the ladies-only carriages.

GREATER MUMBAI

ELEPHANTA ISLAND

In the middle of Mumbai Harbour, 9km northeast of the Gateway of India, the rock-cut temples on **Elephanta Island** (Map p76; http://asi .nic.in/; Indian/foreigner Rs10/250; ☽ caves 9am-5pm Tue-Sun) are a Unesco World Heritage Site and worth crossing the waters for. Home to a labyrinth of cave-temples carved into the basalt rock of the island, the artwork represents some of the most impressive temple carving in all of India. The main Shiva-dedicated temple is an intriguing latticework of courtyards, halls, pillars and shrines, with the magnum opus a 6m-tall statue of Sadhashiva – depicting a three-faced Shiva as the destroyer, creator and preserver of the universe. The enormous central bust of Shiva, its eyes closed in eternal contemplation, may be the most serene sight you witness in India.

The temples are thought to have been created between AD 450 and 750, when the island was known as Gharapuri (Place of Caves). The Portuguese renamed it Elephanta because of a large stone elephant near the shore, which collapsed in 1814 and was moved by the British to Mumbai's Veermata Jijabai Bhonsle Udyan.

The English-language guide service (free with deluxe boat tickets) is worthwhile; tours depart every hour on the half-hour from the ticket booth. If you explore independently, pick up Pramod Chandra's *A Guide to the Elephanta Caves* from the stalls lining the stairway. There's also a small **museum** on site, which has some informative pictorial panels on the origin of the caves.

Getting There & Away

Launches (economy/deluxe Rs100/130) head to Elephanta Island from the Gateway of India every half-hour from 9am to 3.30pm Tuesday to Sunday. Buy tickets at the booths lining Apollo Bunder. The voyage takes just over an hour.

The ferries dock at the end of a concrete pier, from where you can walk (around three minutes) or take the miniature train (Rs10) to the stairway (Rs5) leading up to the caves. It's lined with handicraft stalls and patrolled by pesky monkeys. Wear good shoes.

SANJAY GANDHI NATIONAL PARK

It's hard to believe that within 90 minutes of the teeming metropolis you can be surrounded by this 104-sq-km **protected tropical forest** (Map p76; ☎ 28866449; adult/child Rs30/15, 2-/4-wheeler vehicle Rs15/50; ☽ 7.30am-6pm). Here, bright flora, birds, butterflies and elusive wild leopards replace pollution and crowds, all surrounded by forested hills on the city's northern edge. Urban development and shantytowns try to muscle in on the edges of this wild region, but its status as a national park has allowed it to stay green and calm.

One of the main attractions is the **lion & tiger safari** (adult/child Rs30/15; ☽ every 20min 9.20am-12.40pm & 2-5.30pm Tue-Sun), departing from the tiger orientation centre (about 1km in from the main entrance). Expect a whirlwind 20-minute jaunt by bus through the two separate areas of the park housing the tigers and lions.

Inside the main northern entrance is an information centre with a small exhibition on the park's wildlife. The best time to see birds is October to April and butterflies August to November.

Another big draw is the 109 **Kanheri Caves** (Indian/foreigner Rs5/100; ☽ 9.30am-5pm Tue-Sun) lining the side of a rocky ravine 5km from the northern park entrance. They were used by Buddhist monks between the 2nd and 9th centuries as *viharas* (monasteries) and *chait-yas* (temples), but don't compare to the caves at Ajanta, Ellora or even Lonavla, all in neighbouring Maharashtra.

Mumbai's main conservation organisation, the Bombay Natural History Society (p88) can provide more information on the park and occasionally offers trips here.

Getting There & Away

Take the train from Churchgate to Borivali (Rs11, one hour). From there take an auto-rickshaw (Rs15) or catch any bus to the park entrance. It's a further 10-minute walk from the entrance to the safari park.

Central Goa

However much you do like to be beside the seaside, the magnificent attractions of central Goa – which come in the manifold eating, drinking, shopping, historic, natural and architectural varieties – are as quintessentially Goan as a dip in the sparkling Arabian Sea. What hedonism is to the north and relaxation is to the south, culture, scenery and vibrancy is to this central portion of the state, eased in between the Mandovi and Zuari Rivers.

Panaji (or Panjim, its former Portuguese name, by which it's still commonly known) is Goa's lazy-paced state capital, perfect for a spell of 'lifestyle' shopping, a stroll in the Portuguese-flavoured Latin Quarter, and a hearty meal topped off with a photogenic sunset cruise or a night out at a floating casino. As Indian towns go, it's an understated gem, well worth an overnight stay away from the beach, or a late night spent in a hole-in-the-wall bar.

But Panaji is only one facet of Central Goa's dazzling charms. Just 9km to the town's east, along one of its most atmospheric riverside byways, sits Old Goa, once known as Ela, the 17th century's 'Rome of the East'. Here, towering churches and cathedrals are all that's left of a once grand and glorious city, home to more people, in its heyday, than London, but with a lingering legacy of disease, disaster and Inquisition.

Top all this off with visits to the temples and spice plantations around Ponda, two of Goa's most beautiful wildlife sanctuaries further out east, time-untouched inland islands, a hidden forest temple and India's second-highest, gushing waterfalls, and it would be possible to spend a fortnight here without even making it to a single beach.

CENTRAL GOA

HIGHLIGHTS

- Dine in old-fashioned Portuguese style in **Panaji** (Panjim; p109), India's most charismatic state capital
- Explore **Divar Island** (p130) on a pootling scooter, a little land that time forgot
- Stroll a fragrant, and organic, **spice farm** (p134) near Ponda, then stock up on magnificent masalas
- Seek out the sole remnant of the once-glorious Kadamba empire at the hidden **Shri Tambdi Surla Mahadeva Temple** (p139)
- Float it out in a dugout canoe, spying fantastic feathered friends at **Dr Salim Ali Bird Sanctuary** (p122)

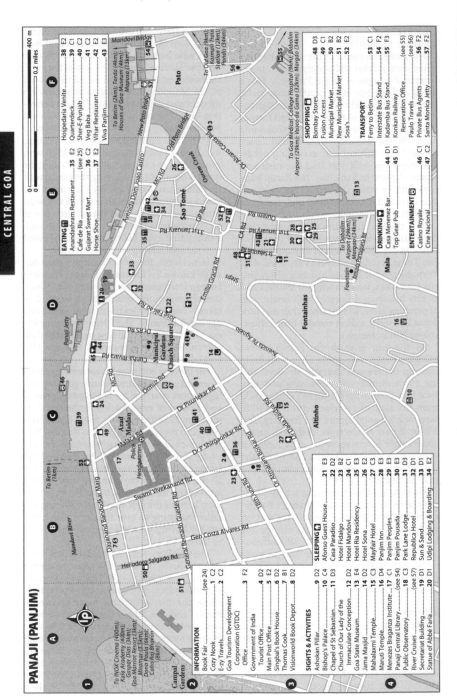

labour, making Panjim a feasible alternative to the capital when finally, 200 years later, Old Goa was abandoned due to the repeated epidemics that ravaged its population. As you drive the beautiful Ribandar Causeway today (now part of the NH4A highway), you can see that the ground remains marshy; the area south of the road is used for saltpans, where sea water floods in and evaporates, leaving yellow-brown deposits of sea salt.

Further limited land reclamation took place in the late 17th century, mostly private projects undertaken by wealthy landowners who reclaimed land to enlarge their own estates. However, as conditions in Old Goa became increasingly desperate (see p123), the land began to support increasing numbers of refugees from the capital.

Finally, in 1759 the viceroy moved to Panjim, where he took the old Idalcaon's Palace as his own residence. Though few traces of Adil Shah's original structure are visible today, the residence, which now serves as Panaji's Secretariat, remains the oldest building in the city. Hot on the heels of the viceroy, those who could afford to escape Old Goa also moved to Panjim, and more land was reclaimed to fit their needs.

By the early 19th century the city was taking shape, courtesy of viceroy Dom Manuel Portugal e Castro, who oversaw the creation of numerous schools, squares and streets. In 1834 Panjim became known as Nova Goa, and in 1843 was finally recognised by the Portuguese government as Goa's state capital. A spate of building took place to make the new capital worthy of its title; among the public buildings erected were the army barracks (now the police headquarters and government offices) and today's public library. In essence though, Goa was fast becoming a forgotten corner of the Portuguese empire, and lack of money and political interest meant that building work was somewhat low key in comparison to the glory days of Old Goa.

Strolling the streets of central Panaji today, you'll find that little has really changed in the ensuing century-and-a-half. Modern building and development, for the most part, remains low level and reasonably well planned, and Panaji's main streets are as wide and leafy as they were under Portuguese dominion. Following the final exit of the Portuguese in 1961, the town's name was officially changed to the Maratha title, Panaji, though today most locals still refer to it as Panjim, as it was christened some 500 years ago on Albuquerque's determined arrival.

Orientation

Panaji is a manageable-sized city, all the more so because only two or three distinct areas have much of interest to visitors. The central, pretty districts of Sao Tomé and Fontainhas are where you'll likely spend most of your time, with 31st January Rd providing the central spine to link them. On this road you'll find plenty of (somewhat grim) budget accommodation, tiny thali joints, hole-in-the-wall bars, internet outlets, a supermarket or two, and several places for making cheap international calls.

The wide riverside road (Dayanand Bandodkar Marg to the west, Avenida Dom Joao Castro to the east) is another good destination for eating and bar-hopping, and to the eastern end, just across the New Pato Bridge, you'll find the Santa Monica Jetty for river cruises, and the local and long-distance bus stands. To the south, incongruously tucked away on the banks of Ourem Creek, is the Goa State Museum.

In the centre of town, clustered around the Municipal Gardens, there are a range of cheap and cheerful food joints for vegetable thalis, fish fry and *fish-curry-rice*, and also the impressive Church of Our Lady of the Immaculate Conception, a number of travel agents, many shopping opportunities, and a crop of ATMs.

Another area where you might like to spend some time is along 18th June Rd, which runs southwest from the bottom corner of the Municipal Gardens. Here you'll find more accommodation options, eating places, ATMs, travel agents and the like, heading off down towards Kala Academy.

Information
BOOKSHOPS
Book Fair (Dayanand Bandodkar Marg; ☿ 9am-9pm) A small, well-stocked bookshop in the Hotel Mandovi lobby, with plenty of well-illustrated books on Goa.

Singbal's Book House (☎ 2425747; Church Sq; ☿ 9.30am-1pm & 3.30-7.30pm Mon-Sat) A good selection of international magazines and newspapers, and lots of books on Goa, are offered at this slightly grumpy establishment.

Visionworld Book Depot (☎ 2182865; Church Sq, ☿ 9.30am-9pm) Offers a good selection of self-help

and spiritual titles, novels and children's books, as well as
selling an assortment of locally made snacks to provide
sustenance for browsing.

INTERNET ACCESS
Internet operations change hands thick and
fast in Panaji, and you won't have any trouble
locating one. Below is one reliable, long-
standing option.
Cozy Nook (☎ 9822001270; 18th June Rd; per hr Rs35)

MEDICAL SERVICES
Goa Medical College Hospital (☎ 2458700; Bambo-
lin) Situated 9km south of Panaji on NH17.

MONEY
As with most places in Goa, you can't walk
far without finding an ATM, with its usually icy air-conditioning and sleepy security
guard. Most take international cards, and
you'll find a particularly bumper crop on the
18th June Rd.
Thomas Cook (☎ 2221312; Dayanand Bandodkar Marg;
🕙 9.30am-6pm Mon-Sat year-round, 10am-5pm Sun
Oct-Mar) Changes travellers cheques commission-free and
gives cash advances on Visa and MasterCard.

POST
Hidden in the lanes around the main post office, there are privately run parcel-wrapping
services that charge reasonable prices for their
artistic services.
Main post office (MG Rd; 🕙 9.30am-5.30pm Mon-Fri,
9am-5pm Sat) Offers swift parcel services and Western
Union money transfers.

TOURIST INFORMATION
Goa Tourism Development Corporation office
(GTDC; ☎ 2424001; www.goa-tourism.com; Dr Alvaro
Costa Rd; 🕙 9.30am-5.45pm Mon-Fri) This GTDC office,
just south of the Old Pato Bridge, is a decent place to pick
up maps of Goa and Panaji, and to book GTDC's host
of tours.
Government of India tourist office (☎ 2223412;
www.incredibleindia.com; Communidade Bldg, Church Sq;
🕙 9.30am-1.30pm & 2.30-6pm Mon-Fri, 10am-1pm Sat)
The staff here is extremely helpful, and can provide a list

of qualified guides for tours and trips in Goa. A half-day
tour (up to four hours) for two people costs around Rs600.

TRAVEL AGENCIES
There are several travel agencies where you
can book and confirm flights; many are along
18th June Rd.
E-zy Travels (☎ 2435300; www.ezytravels.com; Shop
8-9, Durga Chambers, 18th June Rd) A professionally run
travel agent that can book international flights.

Sights
FONTAINHAS & SAO TOMÉ
The oldest, and by far the most atmospheric,
Portuguese-flavoured districts of Panaji are
squeezed between the hillside of Altinho
and the banks of Ourem Creek, and make
for attractive wandering with their narrow
streets, overhanging balconies and quaint air
of Mediterranean yesteryear.

Fontainhas, said to take its name from the
Fountain of Phoenix spring, which stands
near the Maruti Temple, is the larger of the
two districts, comprising pastel-shaded houses
that head up Altinho hill. The land here was
originally reclaimed in the late 18th century
by a returning self-made Goan, known as 'the
Mosmikar', so-called for the riches he had
amassed during a stay in Mozambique.

Aside from its general old-world charms,
Fontainhas is notable for being home to
the pretty **Chapel of St Sebastian** (St Sebastian
Rd; 🕙 Mass 6.45am daily), built in 1818. This
small whitewashed church at the end of a
lovely lane contains one of only a few relics remaining as testament to the Goan
Inquisition, which terrorised the state's
population for more than two centuries. A
striking crucifix, which originally stood in
the Palace of the Inquisition in Old Goa.
Christ's unusual open eyes are said to have
been conceived to strike fear into the hearts
of 'heretical' suspects brought before the
Inquisitors, and awaiting their usually grisly
fate. Following the end of the Inquisition in
Goa in 1814 – due to an Anglo-Portuguese
treaty to that effect – the crucifix was
brought to Panaji's Secretariat, before finally
being moved to the chapel in the early 20th
century, when the viceroy's residence shifted
from the Secretariat to Cabo Raj Bhavan, on
the coast. Nowadays, each mid-November
sees a happy street fair set up outside the
little chapel. to celebrate the Feast of Our
Lady of Livrament.

ABBÉ FARIA

What looks like a scene from a Hammer House of Horror hit is actually a testament in statue form to one of Goa's most famous exports, 18th-century Candolim-born Abbé Faria, displayed in full dramatic throes, 'pouncing', as Graham Greene once noted, 'like a great black eagle on his mesmerised female patient'.

Abbé Faria, born the humble son of a monk and a nun in a Candolim mansion in 1756, is one of history's fabulously enigmatic figures, having hovered handsomely on the sidelines of the greatest events of the 18th century and flirted with its main players (the Portuguese royal family, Robespierre, Marie Antoinette and Napoleon being just some of them), somehow ingratiating himself with every successive regime while remaining an elusive outsider, caught in a world of black magic and esoteric pursuits. He was considered the 'father of modern hypnotism' for his explanations on the power of suggestion – uncharted territory at the time. Next time you see a stage hypnotist parading the tricks of the trade, watch too for the ghost of shape-shifting Custodio Faria, flitting restively in the wings.

Located to the north of Fontainhas, the tiny area around the main post office is known as Sao Tomé. The post office was once the tobacco-trading house for Panaji, and the building to the right of it was the state mint. The square that these buildings face once housed the town pillory, where justice turned into spectacle when executions took place. It was here that several conspirators involved in the Pinto Revolt (p147) were put to death, for plotting to overthrow Portuguese rule in 1787.

SECRETARIAT BUILDING
The oldest colonial building in Goa and, as this book went to press, undergoing extensive and much-needed restoration, is the stolid Secretariat. It stands on the site of the grand summer palace of Goa's 15th-century sultan Yusuf Adil Shah, which was originally fortified and surrounded by a saltwater moat.

After falling to the Portuguese in 1510, the palace was further reinforced and used as a customs post, also serving as temporary accommodation for incoming and outgoing Portuguese viceroys. After the viceroys finally abandoned Old Goa to disease and the elements, the building was adopted as their official residence from 1759 until 1918, when they moved on to the grander coastal buildings at Cabo Raj Bhavan (p120).

From this time onwards the building housed the State Assembly, which now meets in the newer, grander **Assembly Complex**, located on the hill across the river. Today, it's home to dry-as-dust government offices, which make for thoroughly unfascinating exploration.

Standing just beside the Secretariat is a far more interesting curiosity: an unusual **statue** of a man appearing to leer tall over a prone and floundering woman. It's a tribute to hypnotist Abbé Faria, one of Goa's most famous sons; see above.

CHURCH OF OUR LADY OF THE IMMACULATE CONCEPTION
Panaji's spiritual, as well as geographical, centre is its gleamingly picturesque main **church** (🕑 9am-7pm), built in 1619 over an older, smaller 1540 chapel and stacked like a fancy white wedding cake to the southeast of the ragged municipal gardens. When Panaji was little more than a sleepy fishing village, this place was the first port of call for sailors from Lisbon, who would clamber up here to thank their lucky stars for a safe crossing, before continuing to Ela (Old Goa), the state's capital until the 19th century, further east up the river.

By the 1850s the land in front of the church was being reclaimed and the distinctive crisscrossing staircases were added in the late 19th century. Nowadays, entrance to its gloriously technicolour interior – as gold-plated, floral and multicoloured on the inside as it's perfectly white on the outside – is along the left-hand side wall. The itchy-fingered should note the small sign requesting 'please do not ring the bell' beside a tangle of ropes leading up to the enormous shiny church bell in the belfry, saved from the ruins of the Augustinian monastery at Old Goa and installed here in 1871.

If your visit coincides with 8 December, be sure to head here for the **Feast of Our Lady of the Immaculate Conception**, which sees a special

CENTRAL GOA

LUÍS VAZ DE CAMÕES

Luís Vaz de Camões (1524–80), who is regarded as Portugal's greatest poet, was banished to Goa in 1553 at the age of 29, after being accused of fighting with, and wounding, a magistrate in Lisbon. He was obviously no soft touch, for he enlisted in the army and fought with some distinction before attracting further official disapproval for publicly criticising Goa's Portuguese administration.

His reward this time was to be exiled to the Moluccas, and he returned to Goa only in 1562 to write his most famous work, *Os Lusíadas*, an epic poem glorifying the adventures of Vasco da Gama, which, classical in style and imperialist in sentiment, has since become an icon of Portuguese nationalism.

A statue of Camões, erected in 1960, stood at the centre of Old Goa until 1983, when many Goans decided that it was an unacceptable relic of colonialism. An attempt by radicals to blow it up met with failure, but the authorities took the hint and removed the statue. It now stands, along with Afonso de Albuquerque and various other disgraced Portuguese colonials, in the State Archaeological Museum in Old Goa.

---

church service and a lively fair spilling away from the church to mark the date.

MUNICIPAL GARDENS & JAMA MASJID

Panaji's central square is the leafy but unkempt **Municipal Gardens**, also called Church Square (Largo da Igreja). The **Ashokan Pillar** at the gardens' centre was once topped by a bust of Vasco da Gama, the first Portuguese voyager to set foot in Goa in 1498, but he was replaced, upon independence in 1961, by the seal of present-day India: four lions sitting back to back, atop an abacus, and the inscription 'Truth Alone Triumphs'.

Nearby, be on the lookout for the tiny **Jama Masjid** mosque, barely 100m south of the Municipal Gardens, built about two centuries ago. Keep vigilant in your search – it's easy to walk past without even realising it's there. The exterior of the building is plain, its entrance blending in with the small shops on either side, but the interior is extremely ornate in classical white-marble Islamic style.

To the west of the Municipal Gardens, the grassy **Azad Maidan** (Freedom Park) wouldn't, sadly, win any prizes at a flower show. It's centred on a small pavilion (whose Corinthian pillars were reclaimed from the rubble in Old Goa), which houses a modern sculpture dedicated to freedom fighter and 'Father of Goan Nationalism' Dr Tristao de Braganza Cunha (1891–1958). The domed edifice formerly held a statue of Afonso de Albuquerque, 1510 Portuguese conqueror of Goa, now relegated to the State Archaeological Museum in Old Goa.

MENEZES BRAGANZA INSTITUTE & PANAJI CENTRAL LIBRARY

At the northwest corner of the Azad Maidan, the **Menezes Braganza Institute** and the city's **Central Library** (⊗ 9.30am-1.15pm & 2-5.45pm Mon-Fri), the oldest public library in India, occupy part of the old buildings that were once the Portuguese army headquarters.

It's worth poking your head in at the building's west entrance, to examine the grand and dramatic *azulejos* (traditional painted ceramic tiles) adorning the wall, which depict scenes from *Os Lusíadas*, a famously epic and glorious Portuguese poem by Luís Vaz de Camões that tells the tale of Portugal's 15th- and 16th-century voyages of discovery, see above for more on the poet himself.

Much of the upper floor of the building is given over to the Menezes Braganza Institute, which was founded in 1871 as a scientific and literary institution. Originally called the Institute Vasco da Gama, it was renamed in 1963 in honour of the champion of the Goan Independence movement, Luís de Menezes Braganza. The institute has a small **art gallery** that contains some rare prints and paintings.

GOA STATE MUSEUM

An eclectic collection of items awaits visitors to this large, though not bursting-at-the-seams, **museum** (☎ 2438006; www.goamuseum.nic .in; EDC Complex, Pato; admission free; ⊗ 9.30am-5.30pm Mon-Fri), in a strangely uncentral area southwest of the Kadamba bus stand. As well some beautiful Hindu and Jain sculptures and bronzes, there are a few nice examples of Portuguese-era furniture, some ancient coins and quirky antique lottery machines. The gruesome star exhibit for most, however, is the elaborately carved table and high-backed chairs used by the notoriously brutal Portuguese Inquisition in Goa during its reign of terror.

MARUTI TEMPLE

Dedicated to the monkey god Hanuman, this modern temple is resplendently lit at night, and affords pleasant views over the city's Old Quarter from its verandah by day. It forms the epicentre of a roughly 10-day festival celebrated in February, when enormous and colourful statues of Hanuman are placed in the street, and festive street stalls are set up throughout the surrounding Hindu quarter of Mala.

MAHALAXMI TEMPLE

This modern, technicolour temple off Dr Dada Vaidya Rd is not particularly imposing, but is worth a look inside as the first Hindu shrine established in the city during Portuguese rule, and amply demonstrates that among Panaji's ubiquitous whitewashed churches there is a large and thriving Hindu community. The temple was built in 1818 and is devoted to the goddess Mahalaxmi, the Hindu deity of Panaji.

ALTINHO HILL

On the hillside above Panaji is the district known as Altinho. Apart from good views over the city and river, the main attraction here is the **Bishop's Palace**, a huge and imposing building completed in 1893.

The archbishop of Goa came to reside in Panaji early in the 20th century, laying claim to the palatial residence at Cabo Raj Bhavan, on the promontory that looks out over the confluence of the Mandovi and Zuari Rivers. This, however, was not to be: when the Portuguese governor-general realised that it was the best property in Goa, the archbishop was forced to change his plans and settle instead for the palace here in Panaji.

Today, the crumbling mansions of Altinho constitute the most prestigious place to live in Panaji; the pope stayed here at the Bishop's Palace during his visit to Goa in 1999.

CAMPAL GARDENS

The road to Miramar from Panaji runs through the Campal district. Just before you reach the Kala Academy, on the seaward side of the road are the strollable **Campal Gardens**, also known as the Children's Park. The gardens offer a nice view over to Reis Magos Fort (p145) and the boats that cruise along the Mandovi River each evening.

PUBLIC OBSERVATORY

For anyone interested in checking out the incredibly clear night skies over Goa, the local branch of the Association of Friends of Astronomy has a **public observatory** (7th fl, Junta House, Swami Vivekanand Rd; ☽ 7-9pm 14 Nov-31 May). The local enthusiasts are only too happy to welcome visitors and explain what you're looking at. The view of Panaji by night is lovely, especially around dusk.

Courses

London-based **Holiday on the Menu** (www.holiday onthemenu.com; Ⓥ) offers a range of Goan cooking holidays, ranging from a Saturday 'Curry Morning' to a whole-week program including trips out to a spice plantation and a local market, based in the picturesque village of Betim, just across the river from Panaji. Prices start at £59 per person for the Curry Morning. All courses are suitable for vegetarians.

Tours & Cruises

GTDC (see p235) operates a range of really quite entertaining daily hour-long **cruises** (Rs150; ☽ dusk cruise 6pm & 6.30pm, sundown cruise 7.15pm & 7.45pm) along the Mandovi River aboard the *Santa Monica* and *Shantadurga*. All include a live band – sometimes lively, sometimes lacklustre – performing Goan folk songs and dances. There are also twice-weekly, two-hour **dinner cruises** (incl snacks & buffet dinner Rs400; ☽ 8.30pm) and regular two-hour **dolphin-watching trips** (incl refreshments Rs250; ☽ 8.30am Wed, Sat & Sun). All cruises depart from the Santa Monica Jetty next to the huge Mandovi Bridge. Tickets can be purchased here.

Various other companies offer virtually identical cruises also from Santa Monica Jetty. Head down to the jetty to see what's on offer; in general, though, the GTDC cruises are a little more staid, while others – perhaps because of the promise of 'free beer' – can get a bit rowdier with groups of local male tourists.

GTDC also runs a two-hour **Goa by Night bus tour** (Rs200; ☽ 6.30pm), which leaves each evening from the same jetty spot and includes a river cruise. As ever, its breakneck speed allows it to pack in as many sights as possible; in this case, in just two hours you'll experience a river cruise, a long string of churches, a palace, a temple and a panoramic view.

Other GTDC trips – of which there are many – depart daily from outside the thoroughly unremarkable GTDC Hotel Panaji Residency.

Sleeping

BUDGET

Panaji's not a city brimming with good budget accommodation, and most of what you'll find at the lower end of the accommodation spectrum is fairly poor quality, or, at best, entirely forgettable. If you're looking for rock-bottom budget, the best options run the length of the 31st January Rd. Don't expect atmospheric old Portuguese haunts: most consist of nothing much but a cell-like room, no view and a 9am or earlier checkout, with doubles going for around Rs500. Wander up and down and check out a few before you decide; there's little to choose between them, though some may let you barter down the price.

Udipi Lodging & Boarding (☎ 228047; Sao Tomé; d Rs200) For a really basic stay, without quite so much of a disturbing prison-like feel as some of the budget options along the 31st January Rd, check into one of the eight rooms at the Udipi, just around the corner from the main post office. Don't expect any home comforts, but it's a decent enough place to lay down your backpack for a night or two.

Republica Hotel (☎ 2224630; Jose Falcao Rd; d Rs600) You may not receive a warm welcome or a well-decorated room at the dilapidated Republica; indeed, the service is charismatically gloomy and the decor decidedly grim, but that's all part of the charm of this elderly, ramshackle wooden building. If you're not craving comforts, check in for a basic, but atmospheric, stay you're unlikely to forget.

Park Lane Lodge (☎ 2227154; St Sebastian Rd; d Rs755-1025; 🔀) Set in an old and rambling bungalow near the Chapel of St Sebastian, the Park Lane has been popular with travellers for years, despite its seemingly ever-extending list of rules. Current formidable warnings include 'No Laundry', 'No Internet', 'Gates Closed 10pm' and '8am Checkout'. If you can work with all this, it makes a characterful – if crumbling – place to stay.

Mayfair Hotel (☎ 2223317; Dr Dada Vaidya Rd; s/d/tr from Rs780/980/1300; 🔀) With its bright, cheerful balconies, beautiful ground floor oyster-shell

windows and general, slightly musty air of yesteryear, the Mayfair is an atmospheric central option. Note the 'hot water timings' chart at reception, and be sure to arrange your showers accordingly.

MIDRANGE

Hotel Ria Residency (☎ 2220002; www.riaresidency .co.nr; Ourem Rd, Fontainhas; d from Rs945; 🔀) In no way spectacular, this place just off the end of 31st January Rd is perfectly acceptable for a comfortable and air-conditioned, if fairly uncharismatic, stay. Don't, however, believe the computer-generated image of the place on the website: the real thing is decidedly less neat and angular.

Hotel Sona (☎ 2222226; www.hotelsonagoa.com; Ourem Rd; d with/without AC Rs1200/990; 🔀) With a nice location near the river in a calm and central part of town, not all of the 30 clinical-but-clean rooms of this four-storey building face the river, so make sure you check out a few first.

Afonso Guest House (☎ 2222359; St Sebastian Rd; d Rs1200) Run by a friendly elderly gentleman, this lovely place set in a pretty old Portuguese town house offers plain but comfortable rooms, and a little rooftop terrace for sunny breakfasting (dishes Rs15 to Rs25). It's a simple, serene stay in the heart of the most atmospheric part of town.

ourpick Casa Paradiso (☎ 2420297; www.casa paradisogoa.com; Jose Falcao Rd; d Rs1350-1800; 🔀) A new and terrific stay in the heart of the city, just steps away from Panaji's Church of Our Lady of the Immaculate Conception, with friendly staff and modern, well-decorated rooms; the hotel itself makes for a highly comfortable, cosy stay, but it's the central location that really can't be beat.

Panjim Inn (☎ 2226523, 2435628, 2228136; www .panjiminn.com; 31st January Rd, Fontainhas; s/d from Rs1710/ 1980; 🔀) A long-standing Panaji favourite for its character and charm, this beautiful mansion from the 19th century has spacious, charismatic rooms, some with four-poster beds and all sporting colonial furniture and individual character. The Panjim Inn people also run Panjim Pousada and Panjim Peoples. Though all three could benefit from a basic spruce-up – especially considering the tariffs – they remain atmospheric choices for a stay in the city.

Panjim Pousada (☎ 2226523, 2435628, 2228136; www.panjiminn.com; 31st January Rd, Fontainhas; s/d from

Rs1710/1980; 🔀) Down the road from the Panjim Inn, the nine divine, colonial fantasy rooms at Panjim Pousada are set off a stunning central courtyard. Various doorways and spiral staircases lead to the rooms; those on the upper level are by far the best.

TOP END
Hotel Mandovi (☎ 2426270; Dayanand Bandodkar Marg; standard s/d Rs2500, executive s/d Rs3000, ste Rs7500; 🔀) A Panaji institution (these days with just a touch of the institutional) for more than 50 years, the Mandovi offers comfortable, though dated rooms, many looking out onto the wide Mandovi River. If the urge for sweet things strikes, you'll find A Pastelaria, an old-fashioned cake shop; there's also a little – but well-stocked bookshop, with plenty of titles on Goa and three restaurants, including the pleasant Quarterdeck just across the road. Check-out, unusually for Panaji, is at noon. Courtesy airport drop-off coach available at scheduled times: ask for the latest departure times.

Hotel Fidalgo (☎ 2226291-99; www.hotelfidalgo -goa.com; 18th June Rd; s/d/ste Rs3400/4200/12,000; 🔀 🖵 🖭) The city's smartest (and rather business-traveller-styled) choice is the Fidalgo, thoroughly modern, with snappy service and a good range of cuisines courtesy of its 'food enclave'. It's not at all atmospheric, but will guarantee you a very restful, efficient stay.

Sun & Sand (☎ 240000; www.sunnsandhotel.com; Bairo Alto Dos Pilotos, Jose Falcao Rd; d with/without river view Rs5500/6500, ste Rs12,000; 🔀 🖵 🖭) Perched high above Panaji, with lovely views from its terrace and small pool, this is a great option for a little bit of luxury in the midst of the city. The price includes breakfast and pick-up/drop-off at the airport or railway station, for stays of more than two nights.

Panjim Peoples (☎ 2226523, 2435628; www.panji minn.com; 31st January Rd; d Rs7200; 🔀) Undeniably atmospheric, if rather pricey for the standard of facilities on offer, this lovely option sports atmospheric rooms with mosaic-covered bathrooms, deep bath tubs, and lots of quaint antiques, arranged around a serene indoor inner courtyard.

Eating
You'll never go hungry in Panaji, where food is enjoyed fully and frequently. A stroll down 18th June or 31st January Rd will turn up a number of great, cheap can-teen-style options, as will a quick circuit of the Municipal Gardens.

Gujarat Sweet Mart (Gujarat Lodge; 18 June Rd; drinks Rs10-30; 🟉) If you're possessed with a sweet tooth, here's the place to indulge it, with a panoply of Indian confectioneries of the sweet, sweeter and sweetest varieties. Wash all that decadence down with a thick milkshake or lassi, which also come in an array of heavenly, sugary flavours.

Vihar Restaurant (MG Rd; veg thalis Rs30-60; 🟉) A vast menu of 'pure veg' food, great big thalis and a plethora of fresh juices make this clean, simple canteen a popular place for locals and visitors alike. Sip a hot chai, invent your own juice combination, and dig into an ice cream for afters.

Anandashram Restaurant (thalis from Rs40; 🕑 noon-3.15pm & 7.30-10.30pm) Just opposite the Hospedaria Venite, this little places dishes up simple, mighty tasty fish curries and veg and nonveg thalis for lunch and dinner.

Cafe de Ria (Ourem Rd; mains from Rs40; 🟉) Just beneath the Hotel Ria Residency sits the unassuming Cafe de Ria, another 'pure veg' place that dishes up delicious, diverse south Indian dishes.

Veg Baba (Vagle Vision Bldg; off 18th June Rd; mains from Rs40; 🟉)This spanking new place down a side street off 18th June Rd dishes up delicious Indian vegetarian delights of all descriptions, and is friendly, cheerful and efficient. A self-declared 'meat-free zone', it's clean, cool and blessed with a good line in proverbs: 'An elephant is 50 times stronger,' it reminds us sagely, 'It is vegetarian.'

Viva Panjim (31st January Rd; mains Rs50-160; 🕑 11.30am-3pm & 7-11pm Mon-Sat, 7-11pm Sun) Though it might be more than a touch touristy these days, this little side-street eatery, with a couple of tables out on the street itself, nevertheless still delivers tasty Goan staples, as well as the standard range of Indian fare. Keep an eye out in the dim interior for Mrs Linda de Souza, restaurant founder and doughty matriarch.

our pick **Sher-E-Punjab** (18th June Rd; mains Rs60-150) A cut above the usual lunch joint, Sher-E-Punjab caters to well-dressed locals with its generous, carefully spiced Indian dishes. There's a pleasant garden terrace out the back, and an icy AC room if you're feeling sticky. Try the delicious *paneer tikka* (Rs90) but note, if you're hungering for snacks, that the fish fingers and chicken fingers are 'seasonal only'.

CARNIVAL CRAZINESS

Panaji's annual carnival has been hitting the city centre for three chaotic days, sometime in late February or early March, since the 18th century, when it was introduced by the Catholic Portuguese as one last opportunity for excess before the strictures of Lent.

However, the origins of Carnival are far older, dating back as far as the Bacchanalias of ancient Rome, and later enlivened by African slaves in the Portuguese colonies. Once introduced into Goa, of course, an entirely local twist was added to the fun-filled goings on, with the inclusion of *tiatrs*, the satirical folk plays which are still performed throughout Carnival today.

Today, Carnival begins – as it has done for centuries – with the arrival in Panaji of a character called King Momo on Fat Saturday (*Sabato Gordo*), and his instruction to the people of the city to, in essence, 'don't worry, be happy'. Dancing, drinking, processions of floats through the streets, cross-dressing, and amiable battles (*assaltos*) – with sticky mixtures of flour, coloured tikka powder and water – ensue.

Though various criticisms of Carnival have emerged over the years – ranging from its post-Independence shunning due to its 'colonialism', to its recent commercialisation and excuse for the overconsumption of alcohol – Panaji's three days of mayhem are still celebrated by many thousands each year, seeing hotels booked solid, streets filled with revellers, and bars doing a brisk trade. Don't come dressed in your best, and prepare to be soaked to the skin.

Hospedaria Venite (31st January Rd; mains Rs65-110) Along with Viva Panjim, this is without doubt the lunch address to which most tourists head, and, though the food isn't exactly excellent, the atmosphere warrants the visit. Its tiny, rickety balcony tables, which look out onto pastel-washed 31st January Rd, make the perfect lunchtime spot, and the Goan *chouriços* (spiced sausages; Rs145) and vegetable vindaloo (Rs95) are really pretty tasty. Order a cold beer or two, munch on a slightly '70s-style salad (think cold boiled vegetables in vinaigrette) and watch lazy Panaji slip by.

Quarterdeck (Dayanand Bandodkar Marg; mains from Rs80) Watch crammed passenger ferries and hulking casino boats chug by from a waterside table at this open-air 'multicuisine' restaurant perched on the Mandovi banks. There's a small playground for children and the multicuisine is tasty enough, though the location is without doubt the restaurant's biggest drawcard.

Horse Shoe (☎ 2431788; Ourem Rd; mains Rs150-350) A well-respected, sweet little Goan-Portuguese place, this is a simple but romantic choice for some traditional dishes and a nice bottle of Portuguese wine. At the time of research Horse Shoe was open for dinner only (7pm to 10.30pm; bookings advised) but this might change, so call ahead to be sure.

Drinking

Panaji's drinking scene is centred in the town's tiny, tucked-away bars, mostly equipped with rudimentary plastic tables, a fridge and a rarely turned-off TV. They're great places to mingle with the locals, and generally open up towards lunchtime, closing for a siesta mid-afternoon, and cranking up again come sundown. Though the local clientele is mainly male, women heading out for a drink won't experience any problems, except for perhaps a curious look or two. The river road and the area around the Municipal Gardens are the best places to instigate a bar crawl.

Casa Menenez Bar (Dayanand Bandodkar Marg; ⊗ 11am-3pm & 7-10.30pm) One of dozens of down-to-earth drinking holes scattered along the river road and around the Municipal Gardens, this friendly place, opening out onto the street and with just a scattering of plastic tables, is great for grabbing a cool Kingfisher.

Top Gear Pub (Dayanand Bandodkar Marg; ⊗ 11am-3pm & 6.30pm-midnight) A few doors down from Casa Menenez, there's a tiny, cool, retro bar hidden behind Top Gear's unassuming doors. Food isn't served here, so don't come hungry, but it's a great place to wet your whistle or whet your appetite.

Entertainment

Panaji doesn't go wild for nightlife, apart from the casino boats that ply the waters of the Mandovi and the quiet imbibing of strong drinks in neighbourhood bars.

Casino Royale (☎ 6659400; www.casinoroyalegoa .com; admission Rs1500 Mon-Thu, Rs1800 Fri-Sun; ⊗ 6pm-8am) The newest and largest of Goa's floating casinos, this upscale floating shrine to all things speculative will have you losing your money all night long. Various age and dress restrictions apply; call to book your slot at the slots.

Cine Nacional (Ormuz Rd; tickets Rs50) If you're feeling up for a bit of grim local grime, you've found the place at the Nacional. It's dismal, dark and dank, but with unique appeal if you're looking for an unforgettable dose of Bollywood. Just make sure you don't have too much soft drink, as the only filmic quality the toilets possess is their likeness to a certain scene in *Trainspotting*. Films are shown about four times daily; check at the box office for current screenings.

INOX Cinema (☎ 2420999; www.inoxmovies.com; Old GMC Heritage Precinct; tickets Rs50-200) This comfortable, plush multiplex cinema shows Hollywood and Bollywood blockbusters alike. If you've internet access, you can even try your hand at online booking and choose your seats in advance.

Kala Academy (☎ 2420451; www.kalaacademy.org; Dayanand Bandodkar Marg) On the west side of the city at Campal is Goa's premier cultural centre, which features a program of dance, theatre, music and art exhibitions throughout the year. Many shows are in Konkani, but there are occasional English-language productions; call to find out what's on when you're in town.

Shopping

Panaji's the place for a quick shopping stop, with international brand-name stores such as Lee Cooper and Wrangler dotting the MG Rd (at around a third of European prices) and a slew of 'lifestyle stores' selling high-end faux antiques, well-made textiles and richly illustrated coffee-table tomes. And just in case you're in need of a new laptop, there's even these days a cool Apple i-Store in town. For a touch more grit and grime head instead to the municipal markets.

Bombay Stores (☎ 2230333; Rua de Natal) Selling high-quality gifts, crafts, textiles, beauty products, tea and jewellery, Bombay Stores makes for good gift shopping, with the slightly befuddling slogan 'Treasures to Gift, Gifts to Treasure'.

Fusion Access (☎ 6650342; www.fusionaccess.com; 13/32 Ormuz Rd) A cool 1st-floor treasure trove, filled with beautiful reproduction antiques – from beds to bedside lamps – textiles, richly

illustrated books on Goa, and lots of other exciting goodies.

Municipal Market (☼ from 7.30am) This atmospheric place, where narrow streets have been converted into covered markets, makes for a nice wander, offering fresh produce, clothing stalls and some tiny, enticing eateries. The fish market is a particularly interesting strip of activity.

New Municipal Market (☼ from 7.30am) Near the Muncipal Market, you'll find everything from fruit and vegetables to tailors, but with a touch less atmosphere than the Municipal Market.

Sosa's (☎ 2228063; E245 Ourem Rd) A chic boutique carrying local labels such as Horn Ok Please, Hidden Harmony and Free Falling, Sosa's is the best place in Panaji to source upscale Indian fashion.

Getting There & Away

AIR

Goa's only airport, Dabolim Airport (see p238), is around 30km from Panaji. See Getting Around (p120) for details on how to get to and from the airport.

BOAT

The rusty, chugging passenger/vehicle ferry across the Mandovi River to the fishing village of Betim makes a fun shortcut en route to the northern beaches. It departs the jetty on Dayanand Bandodkar Marg roughly every 15 minutes between 6am and 10pm (passenger/motorcycle free/Rs4). From Betim there are regular buses onwards to Calangute and Candolim via Reis Magos.

BUS

All local buses depart from Panaji's **Kadamba bus stand**, with frequent local services (running to no apparent timetable) heading out all over the state every few minutes. Fares to almost any Goan destination will rarely cost more than Rs20, and usually in the region of Rs7. Most bus services start at around 6am, running several times an hour until around 10pm. Ask at the bus stand to be directed to the right bus for you, or check the signs on the bus windscreens. To get to the beaches in South Goa, take a bus to Margao (Rs15, 45 minutes) and change; to get to beaches north of Baga, it's best to head to Mapusa and change there (Rs12, 50 minutes).

State-run long distance services also depart from the Kadamba bus stand, but since the prices offered by private operators are about the same, and levels of comfort are far greater on private lines, it makes sense to go private instead. Many private operators have booths outside the entrance to the Kadamba bus stand (head there to compare prices and times), but most private interstate services actually depart from the **interstate bus stand** next to the Mandovi Bridge.

One reliable private operator is **Paulo Travels** (☎ 2438531; www.paulotravels.com; G1, Kardozo Bldg) with offices just north of the Kadamba bus stand. It operates a number of services with varying levels of comfort to Mumbai (Rs350 to Rs700; 11 to 15 hours), Pune (Rs450 to Rs600, 10 to 12 hours), Hampi (Rs450 to Rs650, 10 hours), Bengaluru (Rs450 to Rs750, 14 to 15 hours) and various other long-distance destinations.

TRAIN

The closest train station to Panaji is Karmali (Old Goa), 12km to the east. A number of long-distance services stop here, including services to and from Mumbai (see above). Note that Panaji's **Konkan Railway reservation office** (⏰ 8am-8pm Mon-Sat) is on the 1st floor of the Kadamba bus stand – not at the train station. You can also check times, prices and routes online at www.konkanrailway.com.

Getting Around

It's easy enough to get around Panaji itself on foot, and it's unlikely you'll need even as much as an autorickshaw. A taxi to Old Goa costs around Rs300, and an autorickshaw should agree to take you there for Rs150 to Rs200. Lots of taxis hang around at the Municipal Gardens, making it a good place to haggle for the best price.

TO/FROM THE AIRPORT

There are no direct bus services between Dabolim Airport and Panaji, though some higher-end hotels offer a minibus service, often included in the room tariff. Prepaid taxis from the airport cost Rs480 and take around an hour. Alternatively, when you step out of the airport building, turn left and walk to the main road, where you can catch a bus to Vasco da Gama (Rs4, every 15 minutes or so). From the bus stand at Vasco you can take a bus direct to Panaji (Rs17, 45 minutes) or Margao (Rs15, 45 minutes). Buses leave between about 7am and 7pm, every 10 to 15 minutes.

WEST OF PANAJI
Miramar
☎ 0832

Miramar, 3km southwest of the city (follow Dayanand Bandodkar Marg west along the Mandovi waterfront), is Panaji's nearest beach. The couple of kilometres of exposed sand facing Aguada Bay are hardly inspiring compared to other Goan beaches, but are a popular local place to watch the sun sink into the Arabian Sea.

While there's reasonable swimming to be had at **Miramar Beach**, be warned that the experience might not be an altogether relaxing one. Not many foreigners venture down here, so you'll be something of an attraction – and, in a less-than-modest bathing suit, the most exciting thing that's happened for months.

Along the seafront road, at the start of Miramar Beach, is **Gaspar Dias**. Originally a fort stood here, designed for defence, directly opposite the fort at Reis Magos on the other side of the Mandovi. There's no fort now, but the most prominent position on the beachfront is taken up by a **statue** representing Hindu and Christian unity.

Miramar's plush **Goa Marriot Resort** (☎ 2463333; Miramar Beach; d/ste Rs10,500/23,000; ✖ 🖳 🖭) provides probably the best reason to make the journey here. Luxe and lavish, the Marriot is expertly choreographed, with the five-star treatment beginning in the lobby and extending right up to the rooms-with-a-view. The Waterfront Bar is a great place for a sundowner – whether or not you're staying at the hotel itself – while its Simply Fish restaurant (dinner; bookings advised) is a favourite with well-heeled Panjimites, offering up such exotic fishy delights as lobster cappuccino and mud crab *xacuti* (a spicy dish made with coconut milk).

There are frequent buses to Miramar from Panaji's Kadamba bus stand, and from various points along the Panaji riverfront (Rs4, 20 minutes), setting you down near Miramar's main roundabout. Buses then continue on southwards to Dona Paula.

Dona Paula
☎ 0832

Situated on the headland that divides the Zuari and Mandovi Rivers, 9km southwest of Panaji, Dona Paula allegedly takes its name from Dona Paula de Menenez, a Portuguese viceroy's daughter who threw herself to Davy

Jones' locker from the cliff top after being prevented from marrying a local fisherman. Her tombstone, attesting to her grisly fate, still stands in the chapel at nearby Cabo Raj Bhavan. Though the views out over Miramar Beach and Mormugao Bay are nice enough, the drab village and persistent hawkers could, given enough time, inspire you to consider a fate similar to that of dear Dona.

For the last 40 years, Baroness Yrsa von Leistner's (1917–2008) whitewashed *Images of India* statue has graced a mock acropolis on an outcrop of rock at the end of the Dona Paula road. It portrays a couple looking off in different directions, the man towards the past and the woman towards India's future. Ain't it always the way.

Meanwhile, on the westernmost point of the peninsula stands an old fortress, **Cabo Raj Bhavan** (Cabo Raj Niwas; www.rajbhavangoa.org; chapel Sun Mass 9.30-10.30am, Christmas, Easter & feast days), nowadays the official residence of the Governor of Goa. Plans to build a fortress here, to guard the entrance to the Mandovi and Zuari Rivers, were first proposed in 1540 and, although the 16th century had become the 17th before work on the fortress began, a chapel was raised on the spot almost immediately. The fortress was subsequently completed and the chapel extended to include a Franciscan friary. The fort itself, though equipped with several cannons, was never used in defence of Goa, and from the 1650s was instead requisitioned as a grand and temporary residence for Goa's lucky Archbishop.

From 1799 to 1813 the site (along with Fort Aguada and Reis Magos Fort, to the north) was occupied by the British who, during the Napoleonic Wars, deemed it necessary in order to deter the French from invading Goa. Now all that remains of the British presence is a forlorn little **British cemetery**, with gravestones spanning just over a century. It's tucked away behind the Institute of Oceanography – look for the hand-painted sign to the cemetery and the clam-shaped Oceanography Institute roof. It's off the main roundabout, heading from Dona Paula to Miramar. Cabo Raj Bhavan's 500-year-old chapel also draws thousands of locals to its **Feast of the Chapel** for prayers and festivities each 15 August.

After the departure of the British, the buildings were once again inhabited by the Archbishop of Goa, but didn't remain long in his possession: in 1866 the Portuguese viceroy took a shine to the buildings, and had them refurbished and converted into the governor's palace, packing the poor old Archbishop back to the hilltop Bishop's Palace in Panaji.

SLEEPING & EATING
Though there's no particular need or reason to do so, the Dona Paula vicinity offers several options for higher-end sleeping, popular with wealthy domestic tourists and package-holidayers but not especially enticing, unless you've the need to stick close to Panaji. All three have decent restaurants, in case you're craving lunch; for something rather cheaper, there's a cluster of quite standard cafes all along the seafront.

O Pescador (2453863; www.opescador.com; d with/without AC Rs3000/2500;) Also known as the Dona Paula Beach Resort, O Pescador's site has been well used to create well-decorated mock-Portuguese villas with a nice view of the 'private' (though no beach in Goa is legally private) beach. It's a firm favourite among the UK package-holiday crowd.

Prainha (2453881-3; www.prainha.com; d/ste Rs3000/6500;) Lovely beachside cottages and pleasant rooms in peaceful gardens, all with good views of a little sandy beach.

Cidade de Goa (2454545; www.cidadedegoa.com; d from Rs8000;) Indulgence is the order of the day at this swanky village-style place, designed by renowned local architect Charles Correa, located 1km down the coast from Dona Paula at Vanguinim Beach. All the usual opulence is on offer, including pool, spa and casino, with eight restaurants to satisfy your culinary requirements. Chow down at Portuguese-themed Alfama, complete with wandering minstrels to serenade you as you dine, or drop in for a cool sundowner at the Bar Latino.

GETTING THERE & AWAY
Frequent buses to Dona Paula depart the Kadamba bus stand in Panaji (Rs5, 20 minutes), running along riverfront Dayanand Bandodkar Marg, and passing through Miramar along the way.

You can also make the fun journey across Mormugao Bay, from Dona Paula to Mormugao – just north of Vasco da Gama – by rusty old **ferry** (pedestrians/motorbikes/cars free/Rs10/20), which departs several times daily.

PANAJI TO OLD GOA

Ribandar

The old riverside road joining Panaji to Old Goa, via the quaint village of Ribandar, seems to have changed little since it was first built, on land reclaimed from marshes, some 400 years ago. Driving this route towards Old Goa gives you – despite the modern touches – the distinct impression that time here has stood still. Ribandar makes a nice place to pause, and provides one of several access points, by **ferry** (pedestrians/motorbikes/cars free/Rs4/12; 🕑 every 30min from 8.30am to 8pm), to Chorao (below) and Divar (p130) Islands, beautiful islands supporting old-fashioned communities and a glorious bird sanctuary.

Chorao Island

Lazy Chorao Island, accessible by ferry from Ribandar or Divar Island, is only known for its beautiful bird sanctuary. But if you arrive here under your own steam, to while away the hours spotting chirping, cheeping things, it's worthwhile also taking a detour into little Chorao village itself, with its handful of whitewashed village churches and picturesque Portuguese homes.

DR SALIM ALI BIRD SANCTUARY

Named after the late Dr Salim Moizzudin Abdul Ali, India's best-known ornithologist, this serene **sanctuary** on Chorao Island was created by Goa's Forestry Department in 1988 to protect the birdlife that thrives here and the mangroves that have grown up in and around the reclaimed marshland. Apart from the ubiquitous white egrets and purple herons, you can expect to see colourful kingfishers, eagles, cormorants, kites, woodpeckers, sandpipers, curlews, drongos and mynahs, to name just a few. Marsh crocodiles, foxes, jackals and otters have also been spotted by some visitors, along with the bulbous-headed mudskipper fish that skim across the water's surface at low tide. There's a birdwatching tower in the sanctuary that can be reached by boat when the river level, dependent on the tide, is not too low.

Even for those not especially interested in the birds themselves, a leisurely drift in dugout canoe through the sanctuary's mangrove swamps offers a fascinating insight into life on this fragile terrain, while a peek at the farming and fishing activities of the island is a fascinating contrast to the pace of modern life in nearby Panaji.

The best time to visit is either in the early morning (around 8am) or in the evening (a couple of hours before sunset), but since the Mandovi is a tidal river, boat trips depend somewhat on tide times. You'll find boatmen, in possession of dugout canoes to take you paddling about the sanctuary, waiting around at the ferry landing on Chorao Island; the going rate is anywhere between Rs350 and Rs700 for a 90-minute trip, while entry to the sanctuary – payable to the forest officer – costs another Rs50. Don't forget to bring binoculars and a field guide to all things feathered if you're a keen birdwatcher.

To get to Chorao Island by bus, board a bus from Panaji bound for Old Goa and ask to be let off at the Ribandar ferry crossing (Rs4, 15 minutes).

OLD GOA

☎ 0832

Picture the scene. It's 1760, and you're lucky enough (and pious enough, given the dark penchants of the Inquisition) to be living in the most glorious city in all of Asia – the Rome of the East – filled with ornate cathedrals soaring into the sky at heights unimaginable to most people on the entire subcontinent. Then, suddenly, disaster strikes. All around, people fall ill, eyes bleeding, mouths foaming. Your neighbours die in their dozens, and then your parents, your cousins, your friends. You rush to the cathedral to beg God for help, but the deaths continue. The smell of decay hangs heavy in the hot, breathless air, and it's an all too familiar scene. Ten years ago it happened before, and 15 years before that.

But this time, you decide it's worse; this time, you've your young children to think of. Scrabbling together what you can carry of your belongings, you scoop up your children, praying it's not already too late, and flee the glorious city of dreaming spires. You cast a final glance back as the towers and turrets recede into the distance, and put your mind to the future, and onwards to Panaji.

Life in Old Goa, the capital of the new Portuguese colony and the principal city of the Portuguese eastern empire from 1510 until its abandonment in 1835, was anything but dull. Its rise was meteoric. Over the course of the century following the arrival of the Portuguese in Goa, the city became famous throughout the world. One Dutch visitor compared it with Amsterdam for the volume of its trade and wealth. However, its fall was just as swift, and eventually, plagued by epidemic after deadly epidemic – cholera, malaria and typhoid among them – the city was completely abandoned.

These days in Old Goa, 9km east of Panaji on the course of the broad Mandovi River, only a handful of imposing churches and convents remain in a city that was once so grand and so powerful it was said to rival Lisbon in magnificence. Although some of the churches, the cathedral and a convent or two are still in use, many of the other historical buildings have become museums maintained by the Archaeological Survey of India.

As Goa's top historical attraction and a focal point for pilgrims and domestic bus tours, Old Goa can get very crowded on weekends and feast days. The best time to visit is on a weekday morning, when you can take in Mass at Sé Cathedral or the Basilica of Bom Jesus and explore the rest of the site before the afternoon heat sets in. Remember to cover your shoul-

ders and legs when entering the churches and cathedral, and as you wander the great open spaces between Old Goa's remaining edifices try to conjure up a sense of how everyday life here, grand yet precarious, must have been in its now long-vanished streets.

History

The first records of a settlement on the site of Old Goa date back to the 12th century and a Brahmin colony, known as Ela, established here by the Hindu king. Though continuously occupied, it wasn't until the 15th century that Ela rose to prominence, with the Muslim Bahmani rulers choosing it as the site for a new Goan capital, in place of the ransacked and silted-up port capital of Govepuri (today Goa Velha).

Within a short time the new capital was a thriving city. When the Bahmani sultanate disintegrated and it came into the hands of the Muslim Bijapur sultanate, the capital (still known to some as Ela, but also referred to by a new name: Gove) was so favoured by sultan Yusuf Adil Shah that it became his

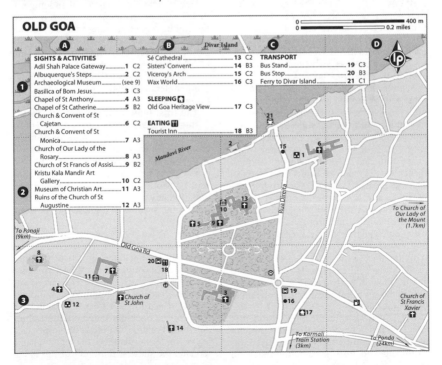

second capital. Contemporary accounts tell of the magnificence of the city and of the grandeur of its royal palace, the city enlarged and strengthened with ramparts and a moat. It became a major trading centre and departure point for pilgrims to Mecca, and also gained prominence for its shipbuilding .

In 1510, with the arrival of the Portuguese, Gove (which, in turn, simply became known to the Portuguese as Goa) was captured, and soon became the region's major colonial base, with waves of immigrants flooding in from Portugal and shipments of spices sailing regularly out. It's estimated that, by mid-century, 2500 new immigrants arrived in Old Goa each year, helping to maintain a population that was already falling prey to the regular epidemics that would eventually be the capital's downfall. With the immigrants came the missionaries (including the young Francis Xavier; see p36), intent on converting the natives, and in 1560 the Inquisition (see p34 and p47), to put paid to the legendary licentious behaviour of both locals and colonials. Though their methods were gruesome, the behaviour they were targeting was widespread: despite the proliferation of churches and cathedrals, Old Goa was a city of drunkenness and adultery, even the clerics themselves sometimes keeping harems of slave girls, and death from syphilis was rife.

Syphilis, however, wasn't to be Old Goa's most widespread disease. The city had been built on swamps, a breeding ground for mosquitos and malaria, while water sources tainted with sewage caused cholera to sweep its streets. In 1543 a cholera epidemic wiped out an estimated 200,000 inhabitants, and further epidemics followed. Undeterred, the missionaries pressed on, building grand churches, hospitals and seminaries, vying with each other to produce the most splendid buildings. All were modelled on European counterparts, with domes, pilasters, barrel arches and flying buttresses by the dozen.

By the late 16th century the city had expanded hugely; the city walls were removed and the moat filled in to allow for the spread. Goa, at this time, had an estimated population of around 250,000.

But it was also during this period that Goa's fortunes began to turn. By the end of the 16th century the Mandovi River was silting up and Portuguese supremacy on

the seas had been usurped by the British, Dutch and French. The city's decline was accelerated by another devastating cholera epidemic, which struck in 1635. Bouts of disease recurred in the following years and eventually led to plans to abandon the city. In 1684, against considerable opposition, the Viceroy Conde do Alvor ordered work to begin on a new capital in Mormugao (north of present-day Vasco da Gama). His successor abandoned the project, only restarting work when ordered to do so by Lisbon, but the plan never really got off the ground.

In 1695 the viceroy himself had had quite enough, and decided to move to Panelim, a village outside Old Goa. Although Old Goa remained the capital, everybody who could afford to do so followed his example to escape the appalling health problems, which had already led to a depleted population of just 20,000 – less than 10% of its inhabitant numbers just a century before. By 1759 Panelim had been struck by the same problems and the successive viceroy again moved residence, this time to Panjim.

Despite Old Goa's virtual abandonment, in 1777 the government in Lisbon ordered the city be rebuilt, arguing that if the water supply and drainage could be thoroughly cleaned and reconstructed the city would be healthy. Work was abandoned five years later when the death toll among the workers from cholera and malaria became too high to continue.

The final blow came in 1835 when the Portuguese government ordered the repression of religious societies, and most of the missionaries were shipped back home. In 1843 Panjim was officially declared the new capital, and by 1846 only Old Goa's convent of Santa Monica was in regular use, though that was also eventually abandoned, leaving the shadow of a grand and desolate city behind.

From the late 19th century until the mid-20th century, Old Goa remained a city of ghosts, empty but for one or two buildings used as military barracks. When archaeological interest started to increase, work was done to clear the area, and some buildings were returned to their former uses. But for many of the once-glorious buildings, plundered for building materials or simply falling victim to the elements, the reprieve came too late; the starkest reminder of this is the skeletal tower of the Church of St Augustine, which can be seen from miles around.

Information

Old Goa possesses no tourist office, but willing tour guides linger outside the main churches. You can also enquire at the Archaeological Museum, which stocks books on Old Goa, including S Rajagopalan's excellent booklet *Old Goa*, published by the Archaeological Survey of India. One of the most comprehensive is *Old Goa: the Complete Guide* by Oscar de Noronha (2004).

Sights

SÉ CATHEDRAL

At over 76m long and 55m wide, this is the largest church in Asia. Building work commenced in 1562, on the orders of King Dom Sebastiao of Portugal, to replace the older church of St Catherine, which had until then served as Old Goa's far less grandiose cathedral. Progress was slow, and beset with financial difficulties; work on the building wasn't completed until 1619 and the altars weren't finished until 1652, some 90 years after their construction had first been ordered.

The exterior of the cathedral is notable for its plain style, after the Tuscan tradition. Also of note is its rather lopsided look resulting from the loss of one of its bell towers, which collapsed in 1776 after being struck by lightning. The remaining tower houses the famous *Sino de Ouro*, **Golden Bell**, the largest in Asia and renowned for its rich tone, which once tolled to accompany the Inquisition's notoriously cruel autos-da-fé (trials of faith), held out the front of the cathedral on what was then the market square.

The huge interior of the cathedral is also surprisingly plain. To the right as you enter is a small, locked area that contains a font made in 1532, said to have been used by St Francis Xavier. Two small statuettes, inset into the main pillars, depict St Francis Xavier and St Ignatius Loyola. There are four chapels on either side of the nave, two of which have screens across the entrance. Of these, the **Chapel of the Blessed Sacrament** is outstanding, with every inch of wall and ceiling gorgeously gilded and decorated – a complete contrast to the austerity of the cathedral interior.

Opposite, to the right of the nave, is the other screened chapel, the **Chapel of the Cross of Miracles**. The story goes that in 1619 a sim-

ple cross (known as the *Cruz dos Milagres*) made by local shepherds was erected on a hillside near Old Goa. The cross grew bigger and several witnesses saw an apparition of Christ hanging on it. A church was planned on the spot where the vision had appeared and while this was being built the cross was stored nearby. When it came time to move the cross into the new church it was found that it had grown again and that the doors of the church had to be widened to accommodate it. The cross was moved to the cathedral in 1845, where it soon became, and remains, a popular place of petition for the sick.

Towering above the main altar is the huge gilded reredos (ornamental screen), its six main panels carved with scenes from the life of St Catherine, to whom the cathedral is dedicated. She was beheaded in Alexandria, and among the images here are those showing her awaiting execution and being carried to Mt Sinai by angels.

Mass takes place from Monday to Saturday at 7am and 6pm; on Sunday it's at 7.15am, 10am (High Mass) and 4pm.

WAX WORLD

If you're a fan of kooky representations of obscure historical figures, look no further than this **waxworks** (☎ 9970 126202; admission Rs30; ☽ 9.30am-7pm), which boasts of a host of 'Life-Size Look-Alike Wax Statues' including a full, waxen version of Michelangelo's *Last Supper*.

CHURCH OF ST FRANCIS OF ASSISI

West of the Sé Cathedral, the Church of St Francis of Assisi is no longer in use for worship, and consequently exudes a more mournful air than its neighbours.

The church started life as a small chapel, built on this site by eight Franciscan friars on their arrival in 1517. In 1521 it was replaced by a church consecrated to the Holy Ghost, which was then subsequently rebuilt in 1661, with only the doorway of the old building incorporated into the new structure. This original doorway, in ornate Manueline style, contrasts strongly with the rest of the facade, the plainness of which had become the fashion by the 17th century. Maritime themes – unsurprising given Old Goa's important port status – can be seen here and there, including navigators' globes and coats of arms, which once adorned ships' sails.

The interior of the church, though now rather ragged and faded, is nevertheless beautiful, in a particularly 'folk art' type style. The walls and ceiling are heavily gilded and decorated with carved wood panels, with large paintings depicting the works of St Francis adorning the walls of the chancel. Look out for the huge arch that supports the choir, painted vividly with floral designs, and the intricately carved pulpit. The reredos dominates the gilded show, although this one is different from others in Old Goa, with a deep recess for the tabernacle. The four statues in its lower portion represent apostles, and above the reredos hangs Christ on the cross. The symbolism of this scene is unmistakable: Jesus has his right arm free to embrace St Francis, who is standing atop the three vows of the Franciscan order – Poverty, Humility and Obedience.

Like many other Old Goa churches, tombstones of long-gone Portuguese gentry are laid into the floor, while the more unusual font, situated just beside the door, is made partly from a fragment of an old pillar from a Hindu temple.

Note, too, the sign inside that reads 'No Photography of Persons'. Presumably, they've no problem with you clicking pictures of any heavenly hosts that decide to put in an appearance.

ARCHAEOLOGICAL MUSEUM
Part of the Franciscan monastery at the back of the Church of St Francis of Assisi is now an **Archaeological Museum** (☺ 9am-6.30pm Sat-Thu), housing some lovely fragments of sculpture from Hindu temple sites in Goa, and some Sati stones, which once marked the spot where a Hindu widow committed suicide by flinging herself onto her husband's funeral pyre. Also here you'll find two large bronze statues: one of the Portuguese poet Luís Vaz de Camões (p114), which once stood more prominently in the central grassy area of Old Goa, and one of Afonso de Albuquerque, the Portuguese conqueror and first governor of Goa, which stood in the Azad Maidan in Panaji, before being moved here after Independence.

Upstairs, a gallery contains portraits of some 60 of Goa's Portuguese viceroys, spanning more than 400 years of Portuguese rule. Not particularly exciting in terms of portraiture, they're an interesting insight into Portugal's changing fashions, each as unsuitable for the tropical heat as the last.

KRISTU KALA MANDIR ART GALLERY
This **gallery** (☺ 9.30am-5.30pm Tue-Sun) sandwiched between the Church of St Francis of Assisi and Sé Cathedral is located in what used to be the archbishop's house, and contains an only mildly diverting collection of modern Christian art.

CHAPEL OF ST CATHERINE
About 100m to the west of the Church of St Francis of Assisi stands the small Chapel of St Catherine. An earlier chapel was erected on

---

OLD GOA'S ARCHITECTURE

In order to make the most of what you encounter in Old Goa, it's worth brushing up quickly on its architectural heritage.

Most churches are made of laterite, a local red and highly porous stone, which was traditionally coated in white lime wash, mixed in with crushed clam shells, in an effort to prevent erosion. Some were embellished with harder-wearing basalt, much of it quarried from Bassein, near Mumbai, though some is thought to have been brought as ballast by ships from Portugal.

Built in an era of glorious colonialism, much of what's on display today is staunchly European, inspired by the building fashions of late-Renaissance Rome. The pinnacle of building here (in the early 17th century) collided with the rise, in Europe, of the baroque movement, characterised by its love of dripping gilt, scrollwork and ornamentation. This pomp and splendour served an important purpose for its priests and missionaries, as it kept the locals awed into submission, feeling dwarfed and vulnerable when confronted with an immense gold altarpiece.

The second style evident at Old Goa is more wholly Portuguese, known as Manueline, after its main patron King Manuel I. This vernacular approach saw the embellishment of buildings with symbols reflecting Portuguese might; anchors, ropes and other maritime motifs represent Portugal's ascendency on the high seas. Though not too much Manueline architecture has survived the test of time, the Church of Our Lady of the Rosary remains a well-preserved example.

this site by Portuguese conqueror Afonso de Albuquerque in 1510 to commemorate his triumphant entry into the city on St Catherine's Day. In 1534 the chapel was granted cathedral status by Pope Paul III and was subsequently rebuilt; the inscribed stone added during rebuilding states that Afonso de Albuquerque actually entered the city at this spot, and thus it's believed that the chapel stands on what used to be the main gate of the Muslim city, then known as Ela. The chapel is currently empty and unused, and thus rarely open to visitors. Check the doors to see if you're in luck.

BASILICA OF BOM JESUS

Famous throughout the Roman Catholic world, the imposing Basilica of Bom Jesus contains the tomb and mortal remains of St Francis Xavier, the so-called Apostle of the Indies (p36), a former pupil of St Ignatius Loyola, founder of the Society of Jesus (the Jesuits). St Francis Xavier's missionary voyages throughout the East became legendary – and, considering the perilous state of transport at the time, were nothing short of miraculous.

Construction on the basilica began in 1594 and was completed in 1605, to create an elaborate late-Renaissance structure, fronted by a facade combining elements of Doric, Ionic and Corinthian design, with pillars carved from basalt brought from Bassein, some 300km away. Prominent in the design of the facade is the intricately carved central rectangular pediment, embellished with the Jesuit emblem 'IHS', an abbreviation of the Latin 'Iesus Hominum Salvator' (Jesus, Saviour of Men).

This is the only church in Old Goa not plastered on the outside, the lime plaster having been stripped off by a zealous Portuguese conservationist in 1950. Apparently his notion was that exposed to the elements, the laterite stone of which the basilica is built would become more durable and thus the building would be strengthened. Despite proof to the contrary, no one has got around to putting the plaster back yet; hence, some of the intricate carving is eroding with the dousing of each successive monsoon.

Inside, the basilica's layout is simple but grand, contained beneath a simple wooden ceiling. The huge and ornate gilded reredos, stretching from floor to ceiling behind the altar, takes pride of place, its baroque ornament contrasting strongly with the classical, plain layout of the cathedral itself. It shows (a rather portly) St Ignatius Loyola, protecting a tiny figure of the infant Jesus. His eyes are raised to a huge gilded sun above his head, on which 'IHS' is again emblazoned, above which is a representation of the Trinity.

To the right of the altar is the slightly grisly highlight for the vast majority of visitors: the body of St Francis Xavier himself. The body was moved into the church in 1622, and installed in its current mausoleum in 1698 courtesy of the last of the Medicis, Cosimo III, Grand Duke of Tuscany, in exchange for the pillow on which St Francis' head had been resting. Cosimo engaged the Florentine sculptor Giovanni Batista Foggini to work on the three-tiered structure, constructed of jasper and marble, flanked with stars, and adorned with bronze plaques that depict scenes from the saint's life. Topping it all off, and holding the shrivelled saint himself, is the casket, designed by Italian Jesuit Marcelo Mastrili and constructed by local silversmiths in 1659, whose sides were originally encrusted with precious stones which, over the centuries, have been picked off.

Crowds are heaviest at the basilica during the **Feast of St Francis Xavier**, held annually on 3 December and preceded by a nine-day devotional novena, with lots of light-hearted festivity alongside the more solemn open-air Masses. Once every 10 years, the saint is given an exposition, and his body hauled around Old Goa before scores of pilgrims; the next is scheduled for 2014.

Passing from the chapel towards the sacristy there are a couple of items relating to St Francis' remains and, slightly further on, the stairs to a **gallery** of highly dubious and infinitely missable modern art.

Next to the basilica is the **Professed House of the Jesuits**, a two-storey laterite building covered with lime plaster. It actually pre-dates the basilica, having been completed in 1585. It was from here that Jesuit missions to the east were organised. Part of the building burned down in 1633 and was partially rebuilt in 1783.

Mass is held in the basilica in Konkani at 7am, 8am and 6pm Monday to Saturday, at 8am and 9.15am on Sunday, and at 10.15am in English on Sunday. Confession is held daily in the sacristy from 5pm to 6pm.

CENTRAL GOA

CHURCH & CONVENT OF ST CAJETAN

Modelled on the original design of St Peter's in Rome, this church was built by Italian friars of the Order of Theatines, sent here by Pope Urban VIII to preach Christianity in the kingdom of Golconda (near Hyderabad). The friars, however, were refused entry to Golconda, so settled instead at Old Goa in 1640. The construction of the church began in 1655, and although it's perhaps less interesting than the other churches, it's still a beautiful building and the only domed church remaining in Goa.

Though the altar is dedicated to Our Lady of Divine Providence, the church is named after the founder of the Theatine order, St Cajetan (1480–1547), a contemporary of St Francis Xavier. Born in Vicenza, St Cajetan spent his life whole in Italy, establishing the Order of Theatines in Rome in 1524. He was known for his work in hospitals and with 'incurables', and for his high moral stance in an increasingly corrupt Roman Catholic church. He was canonised in 1671.

The facade of the church is classical in design and the four niches on the front contain statues of apostles. Inside, clever use of internal buttresses and four huge pillars have given the interior a cruciform construction, above the centre of which is the towering dome. The inscription around the inside of the base of the dome is a verse from the Gospel of St Matthew. The largest of the altars on the right-hand side of the church is dedicated to St Cajetan himself. On the left side are paintings illustrating episodes in the life of St Cajetan; in one it appears, quite peculiarly, that he is being breastfed at some distance by an angel whose aim is remarkably accurate. Traditionally, the last mortal remains of deceased Portuguese governors were kept in the church's crypt, beneath the reredos, in lead coffins until their shipment home to their final resting place. The last few, forgotten for more than three decades, were finally sent back to Lisbon in 1992.

Adjoining the church, the Convent of St Cajetan is nowadays a college for recently ordained priests; next door, immediately to the west, you'll see a freestanding basalt doorway, atop five steps, which forms the only remains of Goa's 16th-century Muslim ruler Adil Shah's grand palace. This was later converted into the notorious Palace of the Inquisition, in whose dungeons countless

'heretics' languished, awaiting their dreadful fate. The palace was torn down in the 18th century and its materials repurposed for building in Panaji.

RUINS OF THE CHURCH OF ST AUGUSTINE

Standing on Holy Hill (Monte Santo) is perhaps the most mournful memorial to Old Goa's fallen might. All that's left today of the Church of St Augustine is the 46m-high tower, which served as a belfry and formed part of the church's facade. The few other remnants are choked with creepers and weeds, making picking your way among them rather difficult.

The church was constructed in 1602 by Augustinian friars who had arrived in Old Goa in 1587. It was abandoned in 1835, mostly due to the repressive policies of the Portuguese government that resulted in the eviction of many religious orders from Goa. As Old Goa emptied due to a continual series of deadly epidemics, the church fell into neglect and the vault collapsed in 1842. In 1931 the facade and half the tower fell down, followed by more sections in 1938. The tower's huge bell was moved in 1871 to the Church of Our Lady of the Immaculate Conception in Panaji, where it can be seen (and heard) today.

CHURCH & CONVENT OF ST MONICA

Work on this three-storey laterite church and convent, also standing on the hill, commenced in 1606 and was completed in 1627, only to burn down nine years later. Reconstruction began the following year and it's from this time that the current buildings date. Once known as the 'Royal Monastery' because of the royal patronage that it enjoyed, the building comprised the first nunnery in the East but, like the other religious institutions, it was crippled by the banning of the religious orders and, though it didn't immediately close, it was finally abandoned when the last sister died in 1885. During the 1950s and '60s the buildings housed first Portuguese and then Indian troops, before being returned to the church in 1968.

The building is now used by nuns of the Mater Dei Institute, and visitors are welcomed if they're suitably dressed. The high point of a visit is a peek at the 'miraculous' cross behind the high altar, said to have opened its eyes in 1636, when blood began to drip from its crown of thorns.

MUSEUM OF CHRISTIAN ART

Adjacent to the Convent of St Monica, this **museum** (adult/child Rs15/free; ☉ 9.30am-5pm) contains a collection of statues, paintings and sculptures, most of it transferred here from the Rachol Seminary (p185). Interestingly, many of the works of Goan Christian art made during the Portuguese era, including some of those on display here, were produced by local Hindu artists; this might explain a tiger-skin-wrapped John the Baptist, fitted out in the style of Hindu god Shiva. Among the other items on show are richly embroidered priest vestments, a number of devotional paintings and carvings, a portable Mass kit for travelling priests, and a fair amount of silverware, including crucifixes, salvers and crowns.

CHURCH OF OUR LADY OF THE ROSARY

Passing beneath the buttresses of the Convent of St Monica, about 250m further along the road is the Church of Our Lady of the Rosary, which stands on the top of a high bluff. It's one of the earliest churches in Goa; legend has it that Albuquerque surveyed the action during his troops' attack on the Muslim city from this bluff and vowed to build a church there in thanks for his victory. It's also thought to be here that St Francis Xavier gave his first sermon upon his arrival in Old Goa.

The church, which has been beautifully restored, is Manueline in style and refreshingly simple in design. There are excellent views of the Mandovi River and Divar Island from the church's dramatic position, but unfortunately the building is frequently locked.

The only ornaments on the outside of the church are simple rope-twist devices, which bear testimony to Portugal's reliance on the sea. Inside the same is true; the reredos is wonderfully plain after all the gold decorating those in the churches down in the centre of Old Goa, and the roof consists simply of a layer of tiles. Set into the floor in front of the altar is the tombstone of one of Goa's early governors, Garcia de Sá, and set into the northern wall of the chancel is that of his wife, Caterina a Piró.

CHAPEL OF ST ANTHONY

Opposite the ruins of the Church of St Augustine is the Chapel of St Anthony, which is now partly in use as a convent. The chapel, dedicated to the saint of the Portuguese army and navy, was one of the earliest to be built in Goa, again on the directions of Afonso de Albuquerque in order to celebrate the assault on the city. Like the other institutions around it, St Anthony's was abandoned in 1835 but was brought back into use at the end of the 19th century. St Anthony's statue inside the church was afforded the honorary rank of army captain and, for many years before the church's abandonment, was paraded out each year to collect its military wages.

VICEROY'S ARCH

Perhaps the best way to arrive in Old Goa is the same way that visitors did in the city's heyday. Approaching along the wide Mandovi River (and probably giving thanks for having made it at all), new arrivals would have first glimpsed the city's busy wharf just in front of the symbolic arched entrance to the city.

This archway, known as the Viceroy's Arch, was erected by Vasco da Gama's grandson, Francisco da Gama, who became viceroy in 1597. On the side facing the river the arch (which was restored in 1954 following a collapse) is ornamented with the deer emblem

CENTRAL GOA

WHEN A MAN LOVES A WOMAN

Sex and scandal aren't solely a modern fascination – Old Goa, in particular, at one time was full of it – and the graves of Garcia de Sá and Caterina a Piró, in Old Goa's demure Church of Our Lady of the Rosary, have their own lascivious tale to tell.

Caterina a Piró, a 'commoner' by birth, was the first Portuguese woman to arrive in the new colony of Old Goa, apparently departing Portugal in an attempt to flee the scandal surrounding her affair with a Portuguese nobleman named Garcia de Sá, The star-crossed pair, however, were destined to meet again, when de Sá was made one of Goa's earliest governors.

Under pressure from the newly arrived St Francis Xavier, de Sá was finally persuaded to do the honourable deed and marry Caterina, who, unfortunately, was already on her deathbed at the time. Her finely carved tomb, at a 'respectful' distance from Garcia's, might suggest to some that the relationship was never *exactly* true love.

on Vasco da Gama's coat of arms. Above it in the centre of the archway is a statue of da Gama himself. On the side facing the city is a sculpture of a European woman wielding a sword over an Indian, who is lying under her feet. No prizes for guessing the message here, as the Inquisition made its way liberally across the city. The arch originally had a third storey with a statue of St Catherine.

The road running from the dock through the Viceroy's Arch and into the city was known as the Rua Direita (so-named for being the only straight, 'direct' street in the city), and was lined, in its prime, with shops, a bazaar, a customs house, foundry and other businesses. The waterfront was fully built-upon, with the whitewashed, red-roofed homes of wealthy merchants thronging its shores, all now figments of a long-vanished past.

CHURCH OF OUR LADY OF THE MOUNT

There is one other church in Old Goa, often overlooked due to its location on a wooded hilltop, some 2km east of the central area. Approached by a long and overgrown flight of steps, the hill on which the church stands commands an excellent view of the whole of Old Goa down below. This is reputedly where Yusuf Adil Shah placed his artillery during the assault to recapture his city in May 1510, and again when he was defending the city (to no avail) in November. The church was built shortly afterwards by Afonso de Albuquerque, completed in 1519, and has been rebuilt twice since; it now makes the perfect, suitably sorrowful place to watch the sunset over the ruins of once-mighty Old Goa.

Sleeping & Eating

There's no particular reason to stay overnight in Old Goa when Panaji is so close by, and the city can be easily accessed as a day trip from elsewhere in the state.

Old Goa Heritage View (Old Goa Residency; ☎ 2285327, 2285013; d with/without AC Rs975/775; 🕸) If you find you need, for any reason, to spend the night in Old Goa, the GTDC's offering may not be exciting, but it's reasonably good value and is a comfortable distance from everything you're here to see in Old Goa.

Tourist Inn (Old Goa Rd; mains from Rs80) One in a string of little tourist restaurants, all dispensing decent, basic food at surprisingly reasonable prices, Tourist Inn has the edge on the others, allowing you to enjoy a cold beer while contemplating the view over St Francis of Assisi.

Getting There & Away

There are frequent buses to Old Goa (Rs5, 25 minutes) from the Kadamba bus stand at Panaji; buses from Panaji to Ponda also pass through Old Goa. Buses to Panaji or Ponda leave when full (around every 10 minutes) from either the main roundabout or the 'Bus Stop-cum-ATM' just beside the Tourist Inn restaurant. Alternatively, Old Goa has plenty of free parking if you're coming under your own steam.

DIVAR ISLAND

Stepping off the ferry from Old Goa onto beautiful little riverine Divar Island, you have the distinct feeling of entering the land that time forgot. Its marshy waters, crisscrossed with sleepy single-lane roads, make for lovely, languid exploration, and though there's not much particularly to see, it's a wonderful, and seldom-visited place to drink in the atmosphere of old-time Goa.

The largest settlement on the island, **Piedade**, is sleepy but picturesque; filled with lazy old Portuguese palaces, and ladies gos-

---

BUT WHERE ARE THE MEN?

Most of the inhabitants of Divar Island, whom you'll see out and about on its sleepy streets, are women, since a large number of Divar's male population have left their home turf to seek their fortunes on the construction sites of the Middle East and elsewhere in Asia. Each year, in January, they return home to celebrate the Festa das Bandeiras (Flag Festival), during which they parade around Piedade, waving flags from their adoptive homes. The tradition is thought to stem from an ancient pagan Harvest Festival, during which the villagers marked the boundaries of their land by marching about it, wielding weapons. Today the most dangerous part of the proceedings is the brandishing of pea-shooters, an only mildly hazardous part of the gleeful event.

siping at the roadside. But Divar, whose name stems from the Konkani *dev* and *vaddi* (translated as 'place of the Gods'), has an important Hindu history that belies its modern day tranquillity.

Before the coming of the Portuguese, Divar was the site of two particularly important temples – the Saptakoteshwara Temple (moved across the river to Bicholim when the Portuguese began to persecute the Hindus), as well as a Ganesh temple that stood on the solitary hill in Piedade. The former contained a powerful Shivalingam (phallic symbol representing the god Shiva) which was smuggled during the Inquisition to Naroa on the opposite side of the river, just before more than 1500 Divar residents were forcibly converted to Christianity. It's likely that the Ganesh temple, meanwhile, was destroyed by Muslim troops near the end of the 15th century, since the first church on this site was built in around 1515.

The church that occupies the hill today, the **Church of Our Lady of Compassion**, is in fine condition. It combines an impressive facade with an engagingly simple interior. The ceiling is picked out in plain white stucco designs, and the windows are set well back into the walls, allowing only a dim light to penetrate into the church; the views alone, however, make Piedade and its church worth the trip.

Just behind the church, a little **cemetery** offers one of only a few fragments of the once grand Kadamba dynasty (see p30). The small chapel in its grounds was converted from an older Hindu shrine, and the carving, painted plaster ceiling and faint stone tracery at the window all date from before the death of the Kadamba dynasty in 1352. Look around for the priest, who'll unlock the chapel for you to take a look.

Divar Island can only be reached by one of three ferry services. A boat from Old Goa (near the Viceroy's Arch) runs to the south side of the island, while the east end of the island is connected by ferry to Naroa (p143) in Bicholim taluka (district). Another ferry operates to Ribandar from the southwest of the island. All ferries run every 30 minutes, from around 7am to 8pm, and are free for pedestrians, Rs5 for motorbikes and scooters, and Rs12 for cars.

GOA VELHA
☎ 0832

Though it's hard to believe it today, the small and sleepy village of Goa Velha – nowadays just a blur of roadside buildings on a trip south towards Margao along the national highway NH17 – was once home to Govepuri, a grand international port and capital city, attracting Arab traders who settled the surrounding area, rich from the spoils of the spice trade.

Before the establishment of Old Goa (then known as Ela) as Goa's Muslim capital around 1472, Govepuri, clinging to the banks of the Zuari River, flourished under the Hindu Kadamba dynasty. It was only centuries later, long after grand Govepuri had fallen, that the place was renamed Goa Velha by the Portuguese, to distinguish it from their new capital, Old Goa, known to them simply as Goa.

The city, which, in its heyday, was southwest India's wealthiest, was established by the Kadambas around 1054, but in 1312 was almost totally destroyed by Muslim invaders from the north, and over the following years was repeatedly plagued by Muslim invasions. It wasn't until Goa came under the control of the Hampi-based Vijayanagar Empire in 1378 that trade revived, but by this time the fortunes of the old capital had declined beyond repair, due to both its crushing destruction and the gradual silting-up of its once lucrative port. In 1472 the Muslim Bahmani sultanate took Goa, destroyed what

---

DETOUR: TRACES OF THE KADAMBAS

Little remains today of Govepuri, its exact site lying 3km north of the small village of Agassaim, on the northern side of the bridge over the Zuari River. But if you're determined to seek out its traces, look for signs of the original harbour walls, which can sometimes be spotted amid the mud of the estuary at low tide. Also ask around in Goa Velha for directions to the *fatrar*, a carved Kadamba millstone used for the extraction of coconut oil, one of the Kadambas' major exports. It's not much, but it's almost the only proof, along with Tambdi Surla (p139) and some traces on Divar Island (opposite) of this once grand and powerful local dynasty.

WORTH A DETOUR: CHURCH OF ST LAWRENCE

About 3km south of Goa Velha, at the south end of the small village of Agassaim, is the **Church of St Lawrence**, a plain and battered-looking building that houses one of the most flamboyantly decorated reredos (ornamental screen) in Goa. The heavily gilded construction behind the altar is unique not only for its wealth of detail but also for its peculiar design, which has multitudes of candlesticks projecting from the reredos itself. The panelled blue-and-white ceiling of the chancel sets the scene. Also interesting are the Jesuit IHS motifs set into the tiled walls, representing, as at Old Goa's Basilica of Bom Jesus, 'Iesus Hominum Salvator' (Jesus, Saviour of Men).

---

remained of Govepuri, and moved the capital to Old Goa.

Just off the main road at the northern extent of Goa Velha is the **Church of St Andrew**, which hosts an annual festival. On the Monday a fortnight before Easter, 30 statues of saints are taken from their storage place in Old Goa and paraded around the roads of the village. The festivities include a small fair, and the crowds that attend this festival are so vast that police have to restrict movement on the NH17 highway that runs through the village.

The procession has its origins in the 17th century when, at the prompting of the Franciscans, a number of lavishly decked-out life-sized statues were paraded through the area as a reminder to locals of the lives of the saints and as an attempt to curb the licentiousness of the day. Originally the processions started and ended at Pilar, but in 1834 the religious orders were forced to leave Goa and the statues were transferred to the Church of St Andrew. Processions lapsed and many of the original sculptures were lost or broken, but in 1895 subscriptions were raised to obtain a new set, which is still used today, and the procession was reinstated with gusto.

Buses running between Panaji and Margao pass through Goa Velha and Agassaim. They leave from the Kadamba bus stand in Panaji (Rs5, 20 minutes).

TALAULIM

About 5km north of Goa Velha, in the small village of Talaulim, the massive **Church of St Anne** (known to the local people simply as Santana) is an imposing 17th-century structure which, though spectacular, has suffered gravely from years of rain and neglect. A handpainted sign by the side door still boasts the claim made by some observers that this is one of the greatest churches of its type (baroque, with Indian influences). However, it's hard to feel anything other than sorry for the appalling state it's in now. Even so, mildewed and languishing as it is, the place is still undeniably impressive. Its massive five-storey facade is covered in intricate carving, and if you peek through the doors you can see that the interior – largely dating from the 18th and 19th centuries – is still intact, though with more than a touch of the ghostly about it. If you find the chapel locked, tug on the church bell to summon the key-holder.

It's easiest to get here under your own transport, or to ask around at the Kadamba bus stand for a bus from Panaji.

PILAR

A few kilometres north of Goa Velha, and 12km southeast of Panaji, set on a hill high above the surrounding countryside, is **Pilar Seminary**, one of four theological colleges built by the Portuguese. Only two of these seminaries still survive, the other being Rachol Seminary (p185) near Margao. The hill upon which the seminary stands was once the site of a large and ancient Hindu temple, dedicated to Shiva; it's thought that this was the Goveshwar Mandir, from whose name Goa is thought to have derived. The college was established here in 1613 by Capuchin monks, naming it Our Lady of Pilar, after the statue they brought with them from Spain.

Abandoned in 1835 when the Portuguese expelled the religious orders, the seminary was rescued by the Carmelites in 1858 and became the headquarters of the Missionary Society of St Francis Xavier in 1890. The movement gradually petered out and in 1936 the buildings were handed over to the Xaverian League. Today the seminary is still in use, these days as a training centre for missionaries, and is also the site of local pilgrimages by those who come to give thanks for the life of Father Agnelo de Souza, a director of the seminary in the early 20th century who was beatified after his death.

Aside from the beautiful views afforded from its roof terrace, the seminary is home to a small **museum** (admission free; ☉ 8am-1pm & 3-6pm Mon-Sat), which holds some of the Hindu relics discovered on-site, as well as some lovely religious paintings, carvings and artefacts. The first floor of the building houses a small, but brilliantly lit, chapel.

At the bottom of the hill is the old **Church of Our Lady of Pilar**, which still contains that original statue brought from Spain, along with lots of tombstones of Portuguese nobility, the grave of the locally famed Father Agnelo, and some attractive paintings in an alcove at the rear of the chapel.

Getting to Pilar is easiest with your own transport; alternatively, take a bus to Goa Velha and bargain hard for a taxi or autorickshaw to take you the couple of kilometres up to Pilar Seminary.

PONDA
☎ 0832

Scruffy, workaday Ponda is the urban gateway to Goa's interesting Hindu temple heartland, as well as to the fragrant spice plantations that pepper the countryside all around. As such, the pleasant but unremarkable town makes a useful stopping-off point for a quick lunch, an ATM cash stop or a hot shot of chai on the way out to view temples and vanilla groves.

The only real reason to linger in Ponda is to take a look at the **Safa Shahouri Masjid** (also known as the Safa Masjid), Goa's oldest remaining mosque, 2km from the town centre, on Ponda's northern outskirts. Built by Bijapuri ruler Ali Adil Shah in 1560 (and conveniently close to today's NH4A highway for a quick visit) it was originally surrounded by gardens, fountains and a palace, and is said to have matched the mosques at Bijapur in size and quality. The buildings were damaged and then left to decay when the Portuguese moved into the area – though they remained the only Muslim structures to escape the Inquisition's destructive influence. Today little remains of the mosque's former grandeur, despite attempts at restoration by the Archaeological Survey of India.

The mosque itself, a tiny white building with graceful Islamic arches, set on a stone platform well back from the road, is usually kept locked except when prayers are under way. In front of it is a water tank, constructed of laterite and thought to date from the same time as the mosque. Apart from these two elements, only a few broken pillars and random blocks of stone mark the extent of the original site. But what the mosque lacks in sights, it makes up for in legend: it's said that it's connected, by way of an underground passage, to a ruined hilltop fort, some 2km away. It hasn't been discovered yet, though this shouldn't discourage those with a flashlight and a penchant for adventure.

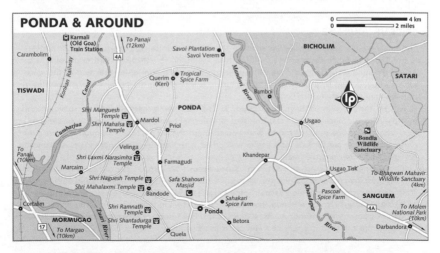

PONDA & AROUND

CENTRAL GOA

Sleeping & Eating

Given that Ponda is just 30km from Panaji, there's little reason to stay overnight. In case you do decide you want to, a scattering of unremarkable hotels are ranged along the main road, with budget rooms priced from Rs200 to Rs300; wander along and take your pick of a fairly dingy crop.

Hotel Sungrace (☎ 2311238, 2311239; s/d/ste with AC Rs600/700/1500, s/d without AC Rs500/600; ❄) At the heart of town, the Sungrace advertises itself as 'the Elegant Hotel in Ponda' and, in contrast with the rest of Ponda's offerings, it's not far wrong. Clean, efficient and bright modern rooms are stacked atop a busy restaurant, serving up the usual range of Indian and Chinese dishes. It's wise to book ahead during festival and holiday periods, as its 28 rooms are frequently filled with Indian tourists. The Sungrace is located one road to the left of the main road if you're coming into Ponda from the south.

Cafe Bhonsle (☎ 2318725; thalis from Rs33; ❂ 7am-10pm Mon-Sat, 7am-3pm Sun) This all-vegetarian restaurant, on the right-hand side of the main road when entering town from the south, makes a great all-day stop in the midst of Ponda, whipping out high-speed thalis to a hungry lunchtime crowd, with an extensive menu of Indian and Chinese food – and a mean *bhaji-pau* (fluffily white bread roll with a small chickpea-based curry for dipping). Clean, quick and efficient, it's sure to satisfy.

Sumudra Pub & Family Restaurant (❂ 11am-3pm & 7-11pm) Near the popular Bhonsle, this is another good option for a cheap and tasty lunch, with the added advantage of a 1st-floor open-air eating area offering a pleasant bird's-eye view of Ponda's busy main road.

Getting There & Away

There are regular buses, via Old Goa, between Panaji and Ponda (Rs18, 1½ hours), and to and from Margao (Rs15, one hour). To explore the region's surrounding temples and spice farms, you'll need your own transport, or to take one of the GTDC's lightning day trips (see p235).

AROUND PONDA

For nearly 250 years after the arrival of the Portuguese in 1510, Ponda taluka remained under the control of Muslim or Hindu rulers, and many of its temples in the hinterland came into existence when Hindus were forced to escape Portuguese persecution by fleeing across its district border, bringing their sacred temple deities with them as centuries-old edifices were destroyed by the new colonial regime.

Here the temples remained, safe from the destruction that occurred in the Velhas Conquistas (Old Conquests), and by the time that Ponda itself came under Portuguese control, increased religious tolerance meant that no threat was posed to the temples.

But despite the temples' intrepid history, true temple junkies may be disappointed with the area's architectural collection. Most were built during the 17th and 18th centuries, mak-

---

SPICE UP YOUR LIFE

Though there are several spice plantations in the general Ponda area, one of the most popular is the **Tropical Spice Farm** (☎ 0832-340329; admission Rs300; ❂ 9am-5pm), 5km north of Ponda. An entertaining (especially so if Martin happens to be your guide) 45-minute tour of the spice plantation, followed by a banana-leaf buffet lunch, is included in the price, and elephant rides/ bathings are available for Rs500/600 extra.

Nearby, the 200-year-old **Savoi Plantation** (☎ 2340272; www.savoiplantations.com; ❂ daily), whose motto is 'Organic Since Origin', is less touristed and elephant-free, but you'll find a warm welcome from knowledgeable guides keen to walk you through the 40-hectare plantation at your own pace. Local crafts are for sale, and you're welcomed with fresh pomegranate juice, cardamom bananas and other organic treats.

Two further options are the **Sahakari Spice Farm** (☎ 0832-2312394; www.sahakarifarms.com; ❂ daily), just 2km from Ponda near the village of Curti, equipped with elephants and enthusiastic staff, and the restful, organic **Pascoal Spice Farm** (☎ 9422055455, 9422643449; www.pascoalspice village.com; ❂ daily) 7km from Ponda, in a secluded area of Khandepar. There is also some accommodation (rooms with/without AC Rs1400/700) on this 23-hectare property; the rooms are not too fancy, but the farm is a very peaceful place to while away a day or two.

ing them modern compared to those elsewhere in India. Nevertheless, what they lack in ancient architecture they make up for with their highly holy ancient deities, salvaged on devout Hindus' flights from probable death at the hands of the Inquisition.

The temples are clustered in two main areas: the first in the countryside 5km west of town, and the second north along the route of the NH4A highway. If you're not a true temple-traipser, the two with most appeal are the Shri Mahalsa and Shri Manguesh temples, both near the villages of Priol and Mardol. Close to the busy highway, they are easy to reach by bus; take any bus between Panaji and Margao that runs via Ponda and ask your driver to drop you off near the temples. To get to others of the region's temples, it may be easiest to visit with your own car or motorbike, or negotiate a day rate with a taxi from Panaji, Ponda or Margao.

The other reason to visit Ponda taluka is to visit one of the aromatic spice plantations that await in the heart of the countryside, welcoming you with lavish lunches, elephants and informative tours (see opposite).

SHRI MANGUESH TEMPLE

Around 9km north of Ponda, this temple is one of the most visited of Goa's Hindu temples, admirably combining two key features of Goan Hinduism: first, it's dedicated to a solely Goan deity (in this case the local god Manguesh), and second, it exhibits the mixture of architectural styles that typifies the region's temples.

The temple's original location was on the south side of the Zuari River, near the present-day village of Cortalim. When the Portuguese took control its ancient Shivalingam stone was brought to Priol and installed in a new temple, enlarged later in the mid-18th century, an effort that saw Hindus from Portuguese-held districts risking death, arriving in the dead of night, to worship here. Today the temple has grown to encompass a substantial complex that includes accommodation for pilgrims and administrative offices.

Architecturally, Shri Manguesh shows the influences of both Christian and Muslim styles. There's evidence of Christian influence in the octagonal tower above the sanctum, the pillared facade of the impressive seven-storey *deepastambha* (lamp tower), the largest in Goa, and the balustrade design around the roof, while the domed roofs indicate a Muslim influence. The tank (reservoir) in front of the temple is the oldest part of the complex, while if you walk down to the right-hand side of the temple you can also see the giant chariots (raths) that are used to parade the deities during the temple's festival, which takes place in the last week of January or the first week of February.

Manguesh, the temple's god, is said in Goan Hindu mythology to be an incarnation of Shiva. The story goes that Shiva, having lost everything to his wife Parvati in a game of dice, came to Goa in a self-imposed exile. When Parvati eventually came looking for him, he decided to frighten her and disguised himself as a tiger. In horror, Parvati cried out *'trahi mam girisha!'* (Oh lord of mountains, save me!), whereupon Shiva resumed his normal form. The words *mam girisha* became associated with the tale and Shiva's tiger incarnation, with time, became known as Manguesh. The Shivalingam left to mark the spot where all this happened was eventually discovered by a shepherd, and a temple was built to house it at the temple's original location near Cortalim.

SHRI MAHALSA TEMPLE

The Mahalsa Temple, 1km down the road from the Shri Manguesh Temple, is in the tiny village of Mardol. This temple's deity originally resided in an ancient shrine in the village of Verna in Salcete taluka in the south. The buildings were reputedly so beautiful that even the Portuguese priest whose job it was to oversee their destruction requested that they should be preserved and converted into a church. Permission was refused, but before the work began in 1543 the deity was smuggled away to safety.

Again, Mahalsa is a uniquely Goan deity, this time an incarnation of Vishnu in female form. Various legends suggest how Mahalsa came into being. In one, Vishnu, who was in a particularly tight corner during a struggle with the forces of evil, disguised himself as Mohini, the most beautiful woman ever seen, in order to distract his enemies. The trick worked and Mohini, with her name corrupted to Mahalsa, was born. To complicate matters, Mahalsa also fits into the pantheon as an incarnation of Shiva, the destroyer. In general, however, she is regarded by her devotees as a representative of peace; for this, and for her multifaceted identity, she has many devotees.

CENTRAL GOA

GOA'S TEMPLE ARCHITECTURE

Though Goa's temples often exhibit a strange and colourful blend of traditional Hindu, Christian and Muslim architectural elements, several of their key components remain constant.

On entering a temple, you'll first reach the courtyard (prakara), which surrounds the whole complex, often encompassing a water tank (tirtha), in which worshippers bathe before continuing into the temple. Next you'll pass one or two pillared assembly halls (mandapas), used for music, dancing and congregational prayer.

Through these, you'll arrive at the main shrine (antaralya), surrounded by a passage (pradak-shena) for circumambulation, and flanked by two shrines of the temple's lesser deities. Within the main shrine is the shrine room (garbhagriha), which houses the devta (sacred deity) – in elaborate statue or simple stone form – and forms the most sacred part of the temple. Only high-caste Brahmin priests are admitted to the Shrine Room, where they perform regular ritual purifications. Topping off the shrine room is the sanctuary tower (shikhara), which symbolises the Divine Mountain, the source of the sacred River Ganges.

Just as Goan food is a heady mix of influences, so too is its architectural fusion, and Goa's temples also sport some features specific to the sunny state. Sanctuary towers tend to have been influenced by Portuguese church trends (despite the fact that those same conquerors were responsible for the destruction of many of the originals), often resulting in octagonal towers topped by a copper dome. Mandapa roofs are often terracotta-tiled, decorated with oriental images imported from Macau, another Portuguese colony, and embellished with Muslim motifs. The most unique of all, however, are the Maratha-conceived light towers, deepastambhas or deepmals, multistoreyed pagodas usually standing beside the temple's main entrance, whose multiple cubby holes hold dozens of oil lamps stunningly illuminated on special occasions and during the weekly ceremonial airing of the devta.

Once you pass through the entrance gate, off the busy side street, the temple is pleasantly peaceful. The inner area is impressive, with huge wooden pillars and slatted windows and, like most of the other temples in this area, an ornamented silver frame surrounds the doorway to the sanctum. Walk around to the back of the main building and peer through the archway to the water tank; the combination of the ancient stonework, palm trees and paddy fields beyond is quite a sight.

In front of the temple stands a large *deepastambha* (lamptower) and a 12.5m-high brass oil lamp that is lit during festivals; it's thought to be the largest such lamp in the world.

In addition to the annual chariot procession held in February for the **Zatra festival**, the temple is also famous for two other festivals. Jasmine flowers are offered in tribute to the god Mahalsa during the **Zaiyanchi Puja festival**, which falls in August or September. The full-moon festival of **Kojagiri Purnima** is also celebrated here; on this particular night (usually in September) the goddess Lakshmi (Laxmi) descends to earth to bestow wealth and prosperity on those who stayed awake to observe the night-time vigil.

SHRI LAXMI NARASIMHA TEMPLE

Almost immediately after leaving the village of Mardol on the main road, a side road to the right takes you up a hill towards the little village of Velinga and the Laxmi Narasimha Temple, one of the most attractive and secluded temples around Ponda. It's dedicated to Narasimha or Narayan, a half-lion half-human incarnation of Vishnu, which he created to defeat a formidable adversary. The deity was moved here from the district of Salcete in 1567, and the most picturesque part of the temple is the old water tank, to the left of the compound as you enter, spring-fed and entered via a ceremonial gateway. Although the temple has a sign by the door announcing that entry is for the 'devoted and believers only', respectful nonbelievers will probably be allowed to have a look. If ushered out, however, you'll get the best overall view of the place from the gateway to the tank, looking through the *mandapa* (pillared assembly hall) to the inner area and the sanctum beyond.

SHRI NAGUESH TEMPLE

A short distance further south, in the village of Bandode, is the small and peaceful Naguesh Temple. The most striking part of the temple is the ancient water tank, with its overhanging palms, fishy depths and weathered stones together making an attractive scene. Also of note are colourful images in relief around the base of the *deepastambha*, and the frieze of Ramayana scenes running inside along the tops of the pillars. Unlike its neighbours, this temple was in existence well before Albuquerque ever set foot in Goa, but the buildings you see today are newish and rather uninteresting. The temple is dedicated to Shiva, known in this incarnation as Naguesh, and is particularly rich in animal representation: note Shiva's Nandi bull lying at the entrance porch, the subsidiary shrine to elephant god Ganesh, and the peacocks and elephant heads adorning the corners of the *shikhara* (sanctuary tower) roofs.

SHRI MAHALAXMI TEMPLE
Only 4km outside Ponda, and a stone's throw from the Naguesh Temple, is the relatively uninspiring Mahalaxmi Temple. The goddess Mahalaxmi, looked upon as the mother of the world, was particularly worshipped by the Shilahara rulers and by the Kadambas, and thus has featured prominently in the Hindu pantheon in southern India. Here she wears a lingam (phallic symbol of Shiva) on her head, symbolising her connection with Shiva.

SHRI RAMNATH TEMPLE
Though undoubtedly one of Ponda's all-round uglier temples, Shri Ramnath is notable for the impressive and extravagant silver screen on the door to the sanctum. Although other temples have similar finery, the work here is exceptional, in particular the two unusual scenes depicted at the top of the lintel. The lower of the two depicts kneeling figures worshipping a lingam, while the upper one shows Vishnu lying with Lakshmi, his consort, on a couch made up of the coils of a snake. The lingam installed in the sanctum was brought from Loutolim in Salcete taluka in the 16th century.

SHRI SHANTADURGA TEMPLE
Surrounded by forest and paddy fields, the Shri Shantadurga Temple is one of the most famous shrines in Goa and is consequently packed with those who come to worship, as well as day trippers brought in by the bus load. Hustle past the rows of roadside hawkers to get a look at this heavily European-inspired creation, built in 1738, 200 years after its deity had been smuggled in from Quelossim, not far from present-day southern Colva.

The goddess Shantadurga is another form taken by Parvati, Shiva's consort. As the most powerful of the goddesses, Parvati could either adopt a violent form, Durga, or she could help to bring peace, as Shanta. The legend goes that during a particularly savage quarrel between Shiva and Vishnu she appeared in her Durga form and helped to make peace between the two gods – thus embodying the contradiction that the name Shantadurga implies. In Goa she has come to be worshipped as the goddess of peace and has traditionally had a large following.

Features to look out for here are the lavishly decorated interior, complete with marble, chandeliers and an intricately worked silver screen, while outside you'll find massive raths (chariots) used in the annual Yatra festival held here each February, and a beautiful, six-storey *deepastambha*.

BONDLA WILDLIFE SANCTUARY
Small and hard-to-get to **Bondla Wildlife Sanctuary** (entry Rs5, motorcycle/car Rs50/100, camera/video camera Rs25/100; ✆ 9am-5.30pm Fri-Wed) is undeniably beautiful, but its out-of-the-way location makes it only an option for those with their own transport or those committed public-transport–travelling naturalists with plenty of time on their hands. Its location remains even more hidden due to a dearth of signposts as to its whereabouts, off the main, truck-blown NH4A road from Ponda to Molem.

You're unlikely to see animals just by wandering around the sanctuary, though the park's jungly reaches are home to wild boar, gaurs (Indian bison), monkeys, jackals and deer, but it's a butterfly-spotter and birdwatcher's paradise, and a great place to peaceably stake out both if you're staying at nearby Backwoods Camp (p140). Entry to the park's forlorn little zoo, nature interpretation centre and botanical gardens (none of which are worth the trip out here in themselves, unless you've a penchant for caged animals and ornamental lawns) are all included in your sanctuary entrance fee.

If you're opting to reach the park by public transport, there are buses from Ponda to Usgao village (Rs5), from which you'll need to take a taxi (Rs200) the remaining 10km.

MOLEM & AROUND
☎ 0832

If you're keen to visit Goa's largest protected wildlife area, the state's oldest temple, or the second-largest waterfalls in the whole of India, chances are you'll end up in Molem, a dusty, truck-blown village on the main road east into Karnataka state. Despite the tourist magnets at its dishevelled doorstep, Molem does little in the way of cashing in on its advantages.

Accessible by bus from Ponda and by private car or motorbike along the NH4A, the drive out here is made quite unpleasant by the constant stream of wagons emerging from iron ore mines in the area, and shuddering, like Dark Crystal beasts of burden, along heavily pot-holed roads. This can make the journey excruciatingly slow, and the eventual arrival in Molem even more anticlimactic.

Bhagwan Mahavir Wildlife Sanctuary (admission Rs5, motorcycle/car Rs10/30, camera/video camera Rs30/130; ⊙ 8.30am-5.30pm) lies a stone's throw from Molem and, with an area of 240 sq km, this is the largest of Goa's four protected wildlife areas; it also encompasses the 107-sq-km Molem National Park. Unless you're on a guided tour, however, you might also have problems actually gaining access to the park's quiet, shady, unmarked trails. In theory, tickets are available at the Forest Interpretation Centre, 2km before the park entrance, close to Molem town. In practice,

though, there are usually only a couple of bewildered-looking men sitting about, who will have enough trouble interpreting your request to purchase a ticket, let alone finding the keys to the park gates. Beware, too, that aside from the top-end Azuska Retreat (see opposite), Molem is unequipped with anywhere to stay.

But, along with dogged persistence, there are three distinct ways to gain access to the sanctuary. The first, organise a tour through a travel agent, hotel or tour guide, and head out here on a day trip, most of which confine themselves to Dudhsagar Falls and the Devil's Canyon. The second, hop aboard the GTDC's lightning tour of the region (see p235), which again only involves a trip to the falls. And the third, spend a plush night or two at Azuska Retreat, where staff can arrange trips into the park's seldom-trodden jungly interior.

If you do make it into the thick of the park, you'll be rewarded with lush and deserted tracts of forest populated by jungle cats, Malayan giant squirrels, gaurs, sambars, leopards, chitals (spotted deer), slender loris, Malayan pythons and cobras. Though the wildlife is confoundedly shy and hard to spot, with wildlife numbers still recovering from devastation during Goa's colonial rule, there's an observation platform a few kilometres into the park. The best time to see wildlife is in the early morning or late evening.

DETOUR: INDIAN(A) JONES AND THE CAVES OF KHANDEPAR

For archaeological enthusiasts and spelunkers, a trip out to the small village of Khandepar will prove rewarding.

Khandepar is 5km northeast of Ponda on the NH4A national highway. Set back in the dense forest behind the Mandovi River you will find (with some persistent asking around) four small rock-cut caves believed to have been carved into the laterite stone around the 12th century, though some archaeologists date their origin back as early as the 9th century. Thought to have been used by a community of Buddhist monks, each of the four caves consists of two simple cells, with tiered roofs added in the 10th or 11th centuries by the Kadamba dynasty who, it's thought, appropriated the caves and turned them into Hindu temples. The fourth cave confirms the Buddhist theory, containing a pedestal used for prayer and meditation. There are also niches in the walls for oil lamps, and pegs carved for hanging clothes. The first cave, meanwhile, has a lotus medallion carved into its ceiling, typical of the later Kadambas.

These are among Goa's oldest remaining historical treasures, and yet (herein lies the excitement) they were only rediscovered in 1970.

Don't be surprised if no one knows what you're talking about when you get to the Khandepar junction (preferably with your own transport). Be persistent and ask around until you find someone knowledgeable enough to take you to the site; it's worth the effort to get here before it becomes a prime tourist attraction. Bring a torch. And perhaps a whip.

THE DHANGARS

Goa's green eastern reaches are home to the Dhangars, one of the state's nomadic tribes who have lived, for centuries, on buffalo-herding. Their lifestyle, like that of many other nomadic tribes, is today threatened, in their case by deforestation and high levels of alcoholism, and many have been forced to move to cities in search of work, or attempt settled forms of agriculture. You might, however, still see them in far-flung stretches of the park, tending their lowing, leathery livestock as they have for centuries.

Molem's sole and upscale accommodation option, **Azuska Retreat** (☎ 2612319; www.azuska retreat.com; d/tent incl breakfast Rs3750/7500; ✖ ⬜ ⬜) is a newly renovated and luxurious series of bungalows and huge luxury tents, set up around a lovely, if slightly municipal-feeling, garden. The tents at Azuska (which means 'clean and green' in Sanskrit) are a delight, with huge beds, sleek modern furnishings and gorgeous deep baths, set on the quiet side of the site amid tall trees brimming with monkeys. It's situated near the Molem forest checkpoint. The highly obliging folks here can organise all sorts of excursions into the park, including elephant rides, night-time forest forays, along with trips out to Dudhsagar Falls. There are also a spa with steam baths and sauna, three restaurants and a nice garden pool.

Molem and the gateway to the sanctuary lie 55km east of Panaji (54km from Margao), with its main entrance on NH4A. To reach here by public transport, take any bus to Ponda, then change to a bus to Belgaum or Londa (both in neighbouring Karnataka state), getting off at Molem (Rs10, two hours).

Dudhsagar Falls

Situated in the far southeastern corner of the Bhagwan Mahavir Wildlife Sanctuary, Goa's most impressive waterfalls splash down just west of the border with Karnataka state, and at 603m are the second highest in India after Jog Falls (see p216). They're best visited as soon after monsoon as possible (October is perfect), when the water levels are highest and the cascades earn their misty nomenclature, Dudhsagar meaning, in Konkani, 'Sea of Milk'.

Aside from taking a day trip, it's not all that difficult to reach the falls. First, you need to get to the village of Colem, around 7km south of Molem, either by car or by train from Margao (p181). It's best to check return train times at the Margao railway station in advance, since they vary seasonally. From Colem, pick up a shared jeep (Rs4000 per jeep, divided by up to six people) for the highly scenic, highly bumpy, approximately 45-minute journey. After this, it's a quick clamber up over the rocks to reach the falls themselves.

The jeep takes you into the sanctuary, through a number of extremely scenic jungle and forest areas (there are three streams to be forded, which would make this trip tricky – though not impossible – by Enfield or other motorbike). En route, you might be driven past **Devil's Canyon**, a beautiful gorge with a river running between the steep-sided rocks. Though some intrepid souls do don their costumes and take a dip, locals say it's named through being a dangerous spot to swim, with strong underwater currents and the odd 'mugger' crocodile.

At the falls themselves swimming is quite possible and very refreshing, but don't picture yourself taking a romantic swim on your own – there'll be plenty of other bathers joining in. You can also walk the distance to the head of the falls (though it's unwise without a local to guide you), a real uphill slog, but affording beautiful views, and really earning you the pleasure of the swim at the end of it.

If all this seems like too much hard work, the GTDC (p235) runs one of its trademark whirlwind tours, the 'Dudhsagar Special' (with/without AC Rs800/700) to the waterfall, throwing in, for good measure, Old Goa, Ponda and lunch at Molem (not included in the cost), with a visit, too, to the Shri Tambdi Surla Mahadeva Temple on the return leg. Tours depart Calangute, Mapusa, Panaji or Miramar on Wednesdays and Sundays, departing 9am and returning 6pm.

TAMBDI SURLA

If you're a history or temple buff, don't miss the atmospheric remains of the unusual little Hindu **Shri Mahadeva Temple** at Tambdi Surla, 12km north of the truck-stop town of Molem. Built around the 12th century by the Kadamba dynasty, who ruled Goa for around seven centuries, it's the only temple of dozens of its type to have survived both the years and the various conquerings and demolishings by Muslim and Portuguese forces, and probably only made it thus far due to its remote jungle setting, only accessible, until recently, after trekking through dense jungle.

No one quite knows why this spot was chosen, since historically there was no trade route passing here and no evidence of there having been any major settlement nearby. Furthermore, the high-quality, weather-resistant black basalt of which the temple is constructed must have been brought a considerable distance – probably all the way across the Western Ghats themselves – since rock of this sort isn't generally found in Goa. Consequently the origins of the temple are something of a mystery, and although it hasn't survived completely unscathed (the headless Nandi bull in the *mandapa* is evidence of some desecration), it remains a beautiful insight into a long lost world.

The temple itself is very small, facing eastward so that the rays of dawn light up its deity. At the eastern end, the open-sided *mandapa* is reached through doorways on three sides. The entrance to the east faces a set of steps down to the river, where ritual cleansing was carried out before worship. Inside the *mandapa* the plain slab ceiling is supported by four huge **carved pillars**. The clarity of the designs on the stone is testimony not only to the skill of the artisans, but also to the quality of the rock that was imported for the construction; look out for the image on one of the bases of an elephant crushing a horse, thought to symbolise Kadambas' own military power at the time of the temple's inauguration.

The best examples of the carvers' skills, however, are the superb lotus-flower **relief panel** set in the centre of the ceiling, and the finely carved pierced-stone **screen** that separates the outer hall from the *antaralya* (main shrine), flanked by an image of Ganesh and

several other deities. Finally, beyond the inner hall is the *garbhagriha* (shrine room), where the lingam resides.

The exterior of the temple is plain, with a squat appearance caused by the partial collapse of its *shikhara* tower. On the remains of the tower are three relief carvings depicting the three most important deities in the Hindu pantheon: on the north side (facing towards the access road) is Vishnu, to the west is Shiva and on the south is Brahma. On the level above are three further carvings, depicting each of the deities' consorts.

Given its somewhat out-of-the-way location, Tambdi Surla makes the easiest day trip with your own wheels (though GTDC tours also stop here). It's a scenic drive, and quite well signposted, from Molem. Otherwise, take a bus to Molem from Ponda, and negotiate a taxi fare from there. If you roll up on a weekday, when it's not inundated with quick-stopping, fast-snapping day trippers, this remote place remains a solitary and stirring memorial to a once grand and glorious era.

Sleeping

Backwoods Camp (☎ 9822139859; www.backwoods goa.com) For birdwatching enthusiasts, this quiet, rustic camp in the village of Matkan near Tamdi Surla offers one of Goa's richest sources of feathered friends, with everything from Ceylon frogmouths and Asian fairy bluebirds, to puff-throated babblers and Indian pittas putting in a regular appearance. Accommodation comes in the form of tents on raised forest platforms, bungalows, and farmhouse rooms, and the camp makes a valiant attempt to protect this fragile bit of the Goan ecosystem, through measures including waste recycling, replanting indigenous tree species, and employing local villagers. Three-day birdwatching excursions, including guide, transport, accommodation at the camp and all meals, cost from Rs5500 per person.

North Goa

Packaged neatly between the Terekhol and Mandovi Rivers, North Goa encompasses most of what many folks come to Goa seeking: the relentless action of Calangute and Baga, the kooky hippie vibe of Arambol and Anjuna, the remnants of the trance-party scene at Vagator, the thick *charas* (cannabis or hashish) smoke at Chapora, the laid-back beach paradises of Aswem and Mandrem, the five-star havens at Candolim and Sinquerim, and the hideaway luxury boltholes interspersed neatly throughout, many in gorgeously atmospheric heritage homes.

It was not, however, always this way. Until the 1960s Calangute, nowadays Goa's most raucous package resort, was the watering hole of the Portuguese elite, who arrived in May for their annual *mudança* (movement), to 'take the air' along the sedate seaside promenade. Aside from Calangute, the northern coastal strip remained a simple string of fishing villages, bounded to the south by the Portuguese Fort Aguada, and to the north by Terekhol Fort. Towards the end of the '60s came the heady hippie days of naked revellers, drugs and 'flower power'; next came the all-night trance parties of the '80s and '90s, and, simultaneously, the package-holiday hordes.

Today, the key to enjoying North Goa lies in knowing exactly what you're after. If you're here for spiritually slanted tranquillity, don't go to Baga on a Friday night, more Ibiza than Inner Peace. Similarly, if you're here to live it up a little, don't roll up at Mandrem, where the liveliest thing you'll find is a high-energy ashtanga yoga session. Meanwhile, head inland and you'll find enchanting, undiscovered villages, churches and temples alongside all the morphing and mayhem of the coast. Choose carefully, then, and North Goa still has plenty of delights in store, whatever your holiday inclination.

HIGHLIGHTS

- Barter for a bargain at **Anjuna flea market** (p168), a fun day out despite the tourist trappings

- Explore emotive forts, churches and villages along the seldom-explored northern banks of the **Mandovi River** (p143)

- Salute to the sun at mellow **Mandrem** (p174), a cool, calm yoga-infused gem of the northern coast

- Dine in candlelit opulence at one of Calangute or Baga's top-notch **international eateries** (p158)

- Spend a night in a history-heavy heritage hotel in pretty **Siolim** (p173)

★ Mandrem
★ Siolim
★ Anjuna
★ Baga
★ Calangute

Mandovi River

NORTH GOA

NORTH GOA

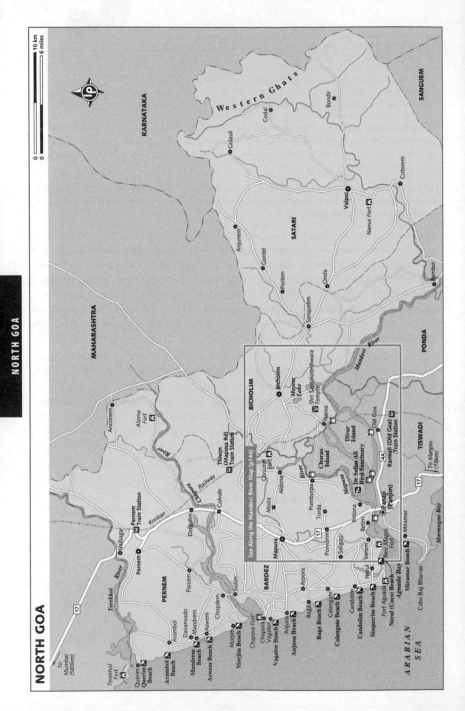

ALONG THE MANDOVI RIVER

The northern banks of the broad Mandovi River, just across the slow-moving waters from state capital Panaji (Panjim), hold a host of unexplored delights, running from the riverside village of Naroa in Bicholim taluka (district) in the east, to Fort Aguada, in Bardez taluka in the west, where the Mandovi finally meets the sea. Exploring under your own steam, by motorbike, car or scooter, allows you the freedom to meander like the tributaries of the river itself, stopping off here and there to seek out the plentiful, seldom-visited hidden treasures that this sleepy stretch has to offer. The listings below follow an east-to-west route, in the order you'd visit them on the 'Grand Day Out' day trip below, from Naroa in the east all the way west along to Fort Aguada.

Naroa & Shri Saptakoteshwara Temple

The little village of Naroa, clinging to the banks of the Mandovi, makes a good entry point for exploring the region; for the most scenic entry, venture here by **ferry** (pedestrians/motorbikes/cars free/Rs5/12; ☼ every 20-30 min) from picturesque Divar Island (p130).

Just 2km from the ferry point, the Shri Saptakoteshwara Temple is tiny and beautifully complemented by its natural surroundings, tucked away in a narrow emerald-green valley and undisturbed by anything apart from a few mopeds and the occasional tour bus.

The deity worshipped here is a lingam (phallic symbol of Shiva, the destroyer). According to Hindu legend, it was cast from seven different metals by the Saptarishis (Seven Great Sages), who performed penance for 70 million years, a feat that pleased Shiva so much that he came to earth personally to bless them. The incarnation in which he appeared at the time was Saptakoteshwara, which was to become a favourite deity of the great – but doomed – Kadamba dynasty (p30).

The lingam underwent considerable adventures before arriving here. Having been buried to avoid early Muslim raids, it was recovered and placed in a great Kadamba temple on Divar Island, but when the Portuguese desecrated the spot in 1560 it was smuggled away and subsequently lost. Miraculously discovered again in the 17th century by Hindus who found it being used as part of a well shaft, it was smuggled across the Mandovi River to safety in Bicholim, and placed in the simple new Shri Saptakoteshwara Temple. It's said that the great Maratha rebel leader Shivaji used to come here to worship, and personally saw to it that the temple was reconstructed in 1668, creating the small, solid structure that stands here today.

To find the temple, follow the road from the ferry point at Naroa (from Divar Island) for approximately 2km, before forking right down a small tarmac lane. You'll find the temple about 1.5km along, to your left; follow the red and green archaeology arrows until you arrive. You'll know it from its shallow, Mughal-style dome, tall lamp tower, and vaulted arches. Look out for the equestrian mural of Shivaji, above the entrance.

If you don't have your own transport, it's easiest to reach the temple on the GTDC's daily North Goa bus tour (see p235), which departs Panaji at 9.30am and calls first at the temple, then at Mayem Lake before continuing on a whistlestop tour of North Goa.

A GRAND DAY OUT

For a long, full day's exploration of the Mandovi River and inland Bicholim district, fill up first on breakfast at **Panaji** (p117), then head east along the Ribandar Causeway (now the NH4A) to **Old Goa** (p122). From here, take a ferry to **Divar Island** (p130) and a ferry off the island at the other end, to **Naroa**. From here, visit the **Shri Saptakoteshwara temple** and **Mayem Lake**, then head west across bridge-bound **Corjuem Island** to **Aldona**, and south, via **Pomburpa**, to **Britona**. Just after Britona, detour north up to the **Houses of Goa Museum** at Torda, stopping off for lunch at Porvorim's once-infamous **O'Coqueiro**. Backtrack south, to continue along the coast road, via **Betim**, **Reis Magos** and **Nerul**, and finish the busy day off with a spectacular sunset from the clifftop remains of **Fort Aguada** (p148). After all this, stay on for dinner and a cool Kingfisher or two at nearby **Candolim** (p147).

To give yourself more time, and make a lazy two-day jaunt of it, consider stopping off for the night at Britona village's swish **Casa Britona** (p145) along the way.

Mayem Lake

East of Naroa and about 35km from Panaji, glistening Mayem Lake is a pleasant sort of place that's popular among local picnickers, while the GTDC's North Goa bus tour also sets down daily for lunch here. Despite the occasional midday rush, the lake's a quiet spot, offering a lovely bit of R&R, and makes a great place to munch your own packed lunch.

If you're keen to stay for longer than lunchtime, the GTDC's **Mayem Lake View** (☎ 0832-2362144; www.goa-tourism.com; d with/without AC Rs975/775, ste Rs1620; 🕱) is almost certainly the nicest of all the GTDC's hotels. Its rooms are cheerful, clean and good value, particularly those perched at the lake's edge.

Corjuem Island

From Naroa or Mayem Lake, head northeast to Corjuem, an inland island now accessible by modern road bridges. Here you'll find the only still-intact inland fort, the abandoned and atmospheric **Corjuem Fort**. Around 1705 Corjuem came to mark the easternmost boundary of Portugal's colonial conquest, and the small fort on Corjuem Island was quickly built to protect the territory from raids by the Rajputs and Marathas.

Squat and thick walled, standing alone on a small hillock, the fort has a lonely element of *beau geste* about it, and although there's not a whole lot to see here, it's easy to imagine this place as a solitary outpost in the jungle nearly three centuries ago, filled with homesick Portuguese soldiers just waiting to be overrun by bloodthirsty attackers.

Aldona
☎ 0832

The large and picturesque village of Aldona is home to the **Church of St Thomas** on the banks of the Mapusa River, which makes a grand sight, particularly when viewed from the village's now-defunct ferry crossing. The church, built in 1596, is attached to a strange, saintly legend: the story goes that one day, as a group of thieves crossed the river to Aldona to strip the church of its riches, they were met by a young boy who warned them to reconsider carrying out their crime. While they were nonetheless attempting to remove valuables, the church bells began to peal; fleeing in a panic, some

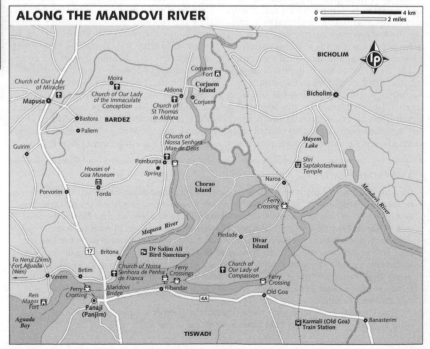

ALONG THE MANDOVI RIVER

DEFENDER OF HEARTH AND HOME

Corjuem Fort's most famous Portuguese defender was Ursula e Lancastre, a Portuguese noblewoman who travelled the world disguised as a man, eventually finding herself stationed here as a soldier. It was not until she was suspected and stripped that her secret was discovered. However, this did not put an end to her military career. She promptly went on to marry the captain of the guard, following what was, in retrospect, probably one of the most interesting strip searches in the history of warfare.

---

of the thieves drowned, while the others were captured. As the leader was led sorrowfully away, he recognised the church's statue of St Thomas as the boy who had cautioned him against his misdeeds.

Pomburpa & Britona
☎ 0832

Passing through the village of Pomburpa, about 5km north of Britona, peek in at its beautiful **Church of Nossa Senhora Mae de Deus** (Our Lady Mother of God), noteworthy for its stunning interior and elaborate gold-leaf reredos (ornamental screen).

Further on, the parish church at the pretty riverside village of Britona, **Nossa Senhora de Penha de Franca** (Our Lady of the Rock of France), is an equally grand old dame, occupying a fine location at the confluence of the Mandovi and Mapusa Rivers, looking across to Chorao Island on one side and to the Ribandar Causeway on the other.

Nossa Senhora de Penha de Franca was a Spanish saint who, after one hair-raising voyage in which the sailors saved themselves from certain death by appealing to Nossa Senhora, became associated with seafarers, and thus was favoured by many of those who had survived the voyage to India.

The interior of the church is beautifully decorated, with a high vaulted ceiling and a simple reredos embellished with painted scenes. The church is best visited in the morning and holds one service (in Konkani) on most days.

Britona itself, meanwhile, has plenty of old-fashioned village character, despite its proximity to the state capital Panaji, and makes a nice place to stay for the night. **Casa**

Britona (☎ 2416737, 2410962; www.casaboutiquehotels .com; deluxe/luxury d Rs5000/7000; 🖾 🖵 ⍲) is a 300-year-old converted customs warehouse, with luxurious antique-filled rooms, fine outdoor dining beneath the stars and a lovely riverside swimming pool.

Torda
☎ 0832

Turning right to take the main highway north just after Britona, it's worth a quick detour away from the Mandovi riverbanks to reach the little village of Torda, where you'll find the interesting **Houses of Goa Museum** (☎ 2410711; 🕙 10.30am-7.30pm Mon-Sat), created by well-known local architect Gerard de Cunha to illuminate the history of Goan homes, apparent statewide in various states of picturesque decrepitude. Marooned shiplike in the middle of a traffic island, the museum is hard to miss; to find it, turn right at the O'Coqueiro junction and then left at the fork, and you'll find it just there. If you don't have your own transport, a taxi here from Panaji (p109) should cost around Rs200.

Betim

As you return from Torda to the course of the Mandovi River, the busy village of Betim hugs tight to its banks, looking out to Panaji on the other side. Here, you can take a cooking course courtesy of **Holiday on the Menu** (see p115) and fill up on petrol or snacks for your onward travels.

The village can also be reached by passenger **ferry** from Panaji; see p120 for details.

Reis Magos
☎ 0832

A couple of kilometres west from Betim, the riverside road reaches a crossroads at the small village of **Verem**, unmistakable because of its colourful Hindu banyan-tree shrine on the left-hand side of the road. Take a left here, and the road will lead you up to tiny Reis Magos (meaning Three Wise Men) village, with its classic Portuguese **fort** and 16th-century **Reis Magos Church** (🕙 9am-noon & 4-5.30pm Mon-Sat, for services Sun), dedicated to St Jerome.

It's easy to appreciate the strategic importance of the site that this fort occupies, since it overlooks – and once afforded protection to – the narrowest point of the Mandovi River estuary. Built in 1551, after the north bank of the river came under Portuguese control,

CRIME PAYS AT O'COQUEIRO

On your right-hand side on the main road north from Panaji you'll reach **O'Coqueiro** (☎ 2417806), a well-known Goan restaurant in Alto Porvorim (Upper Porvorim), which boasts more than just a decent pomfret *recheiado* (fish stuffed with red masala filling). It was once the scene of one of India's most famous captures (or at least recaptures), and nowadays boasts a life-sized statute of Charles Sobhraj, the elusive captive, to commemorate the event.

Sobhraj (also known as 'the Serpent') was a notorious con man, thief, murderer and suspected serial killer. In the mid-1970s this Vietnamese-Indian-French man was Asia's most wanted criminal, facing arrest for murdering travellers in Thailand, Nepal, Afghanistan and India. Sobhraj would charm foreign tourists with his charismatic personality, but one by one they would disappear, and their bodies would be found drugged and disfigured.

After being jailed briefly in Bombay in 1973 over a bungled jewellery theft, Sobhraj flitted around Asia pulling off various scams, establishing a cultlike family of followers and travelling under enough disguises and stolen passports to elude police and the International Criminal Police Organization (Interpol) for years. He finally came unstuck after attempting to drug a group of French tourists in Delhi in 1977. Amazingly, he was charged just with that offence and one count of manslaughter, and was jailed for only 12 years.

With a 20-year warrant for his arrest outstanding in Thailand (and a certain death penalty), he bided his time in Delhi's gruelling Tihar Prison, where he lead a relatively comfortable life by befriending and manipulating prison guards and fellow prisoners. In 1986 he threw a party, drugged the prison guards and walked out.

Not long after, Sobhraj was spotted by a policeman in Goa, where authorities swooped on him in O'Coqueiro and sent him back to Tihar Prison for another 10 years. Sobhraj later claimed he had allowed himself to be caught to escape extradition to Thailand, where he would have faced a possible death penalty.

In 1997 he was freed from prison and fled to France, a free man at the age of 52. But in August 2004, Sobhraj was rearrested, this time in a Nepalese casino, for the 1975 murder of an American tourist, and remains in prison in Nepal today. During his time in France, Sobhraj made a fortune living off his notoriety; he was reportedly paid US$15 million for a book and movie deal. Nowadays, the proprietors of O'Coqueiro are also cashing in, by association, on his crimes.

If you're keen to learn more about the undeniably charismatic criminal, pick up Australian writer Richard Neville's *The Life and Crimes of Charles Sobhraj*, which makes for some tasty lunchtime reading.

it was rebuilt in 1703, in time to assist the desperate Portuguese defence against the Hindu Marathas (1737–39), during which the whole of Bardez taluka, with the exception of the fort itself, and Fort Aguada further west, was taken.

Though Reis Magos had survived Maratha attack, it was occupied by a foreign army in 1799 when the British requisitioned Reis Magos, Cabo Raj Bhavan and Fort Aguada in anticipation of a possible attack by the French.

After the British withdrawal in 1813 the Reis Magos fort gradually lost importance, and was eventually abandoned by the military. Like Fort Aguada further up the coast, modern Goans have paid homage to Portugal's penchant for fort-building in their own special way: by locking up present-day prison-

ers within the structure originally designed to keep the naughty folk out. Though it's out of bounds to law-abiding citizens, it makes an imposing sight – from a safe distance – and is worth the trip up here for the excellent views.

The little church standing below the fortress walls is made all the more attractive by the imposing black fort bastions that loom above it. The first church was built in 1555, shortly after the fort itself. A Franciscan seminary was later added, and over the years became a significant seat of learning.

Nowadays the seminary is gone but the church is worth a look, with its steep steps up from the road and fine views of the Mandovi River from the main doors. Outside the church, the lions portrayed in relief at the foot of the steps show signs of Hindu influence (these might, in fact, be evidence of an early Hindu temple on the same spot), and a crown tops off the facade. The colourful interior of the church contains the tombs of three viceroys, including Dom Luis de Ataíde, famous for holding 100,000 Muslim attackers – along with their 2000 elephants – at bay for 10 months in 1570, with his own force of just 7000 men.

Reis Magos nowadays is the scene of a colourful **Reis Magos festival** on 6 January, when the story of the three kings is recreated with young local boys acting the parts of the Magi, complete with gifts for the infant Jesus.

If you're coming here by public transport, buses run regularly between Betim and Candolim or Calangute; coming from either direction, ask to be let off at the Reis Magos junction and then walk the short distance to the church and fort.

Nerul (Coco) Beach

Nerul Beach, known to tourists as Coco Beach, with its rather murky tidal waters, affords a great view across the water to Miramar and Panaji, and makes a nice spot for a quick paddle. Though a few beach operations set up camp here seasonally, there's no particular reason to stay here, especially with the beaches of the north beckoning.

CANDOLIM, SINQUERIM & FORT AGUADA

☎ 0832 / pop 8600

Candolim's long, narrow, busy beach, which curves round to join smaller Sinquerim Beach to the south, is largely the preserve of slow-

basting package tourists from the UK, Russia and Scandinavia, and is fringed with an unabating line of beach shacks, all offering sun beds and shade in exchange for your custom. There are some great independent budget hotels, which make for a terrific stay in the area if you've got your own transport.

Though Candolim, for a beach resort, has its fair share of non-sand-based attractions, by far the most bewildering sight here is the hulking wreck of the *River Princess* tanker, which ran aground in the late 1990s. Nothing can quite prepare you for the surreal sight of this massive industrial creature, marooned just a few dozen metres offshore, with tourists sunbathing in her sullen shadow.

Back from the beach, bustling Fort Aguada Rd is the best place to head for shops and services, and is home to dozens of restaurants that awaken each evening to provide cocktails, dinners of different culinary persuasions and the odd spot of live music. The beach, meanwhile, is Candolim's other option for nightlife, where the shacks host happy hours and jam sessions well beyond sunset.

Orientation & Information

The post office, supermarkets, travel agents, pharmacies and plenty of banks with ATMs are all located on the main road, known as Fort Aguada Rd, which runs parallel to the beach. Internet outfits change seasonally; ask around for the year's latest. **Davidair** (☎ 2489303/4; www.com2goa.com) is a reputable travel agency specialising in flights out of Goa and organised tours throughout India; it pride itself on its service to foreign

---

THE PINTO REVOLT

In 1787 Candolim was the scene of the first serious local attempt to overthrow the Portuguese. The founders of the conspiracy were mostly churchmen, angry at the ingrained racial discrimination that meant they were not allowed to occupy the highest clerical positions. Two of them, Father Caetano Francisco Couto and Jose Antonio Gonsalves, travelled to Portugal to plead their case in the court at Lisbon. Unsuccessful in their attempts to remove the injustice, they returned to Goa and began plotting at the home of the Pinto family in Candolim. Gradually the number of conspirators grew, as army officers and others disaffected with their Portuguese overlords joined the cause.

The plans were near enough to completion for a date to have been fixed for the proposed coup, when the plot was discovered by the Portuguese authorities. A total of 47 conspirators, including 17 priests and seven army officers, were arrested. The lucky ones were sentenced to the galleys or deported to Portugal for a 20-year-or-so prison stint, while 15 of the lowlier and less fortunate were hanged, drawn and quartered in Panaji and their heads mounted on stakes as a deterrent to other would-be revolutionaries.

tourists, pointing out sagely on the organisation's website: 'It's a long way to Goa from Cheltenham, Galliwasted, Ashby-de-la-Zouch or wherever.'

Sights & Activities
FORT AGUADA

Standing on the headland overlooking the mouth of the Mandovi River, Fort Aguada occupies a magnificent and successful position, confirmed by the fact that it was never taken by force. A highly popular spot to watch the sunset, with uninterrupted views both north and south, the fort was built in 1612, following the increasing threat to Goa's Portuguese overlords of attacks by the Dutch, among others.

The fort covers the entire headland, and the Mandovi River below was once connected with the coast at Sinquerim to form a moat, entirely cutting off the headland. One of the great advantages of the site was the abundance of water from natural springs on the hillside, making the fort an important first watering point for ships freshly arrived from Portugal; the spring also gave the fort its name, *agua* being Portuguese for 'water'. Like Reis Magos and Cabo Raj Bhavan, the British occupied the fort in 1799 to protect Goa from possible French invasion.

Today visitors flock to the **bastion** that stands on the hilltop, although, when compared with the overall area surrounded by defences, this is only a fraction of the original

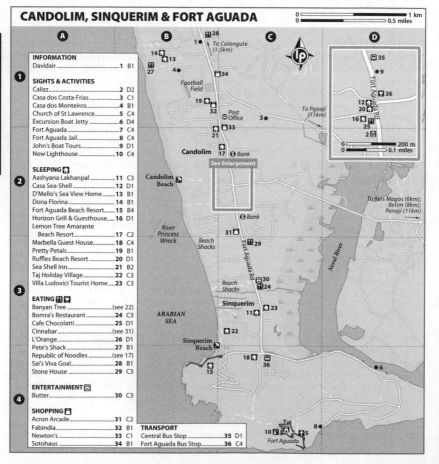

CANDOLIM, SINQUERIM & FORT AGUADA

0 ————— 1 km
0 ————— 0.5 miles

INFORMATION
Davidair.................................1 B1

SIGHTS & ACTIVITIES
Calizz.....................................2 D2
Casa dos Costa-Frias................3 C1
Casa dos Monteiros.................4 B1
Church of St Lawrence............5 C4
Excursion Boat Jetty...............6 D4
Fort Aguada...........................7 C4
Fort Aguada Jail.....................8 C4
John's Boat Tours....................9 D1
New Lighthouse.....................10 C4

SLEEPING
Aashyana Lakhanpal...............11 C3
Casa Sea-Shell.......................12 D1
D'Mello's Sea View Home.......13 B1
Dona Florina..........................14 B1
Fort Aguada Beach Resort......15 B4
Horizon Grill & Guesthouse....16 D1
Lemon Tree Amarante
    Beach Resort.....................17 C2
Marbella Guest House.............18 C4
Pretty Petals..........................19 B1
Ruffles Beach Resort..............20 D1
Sea Shell Inn.........................21 B2
Taj Holiday Village.................22 C3
Villa Ludovici Tourist Home....23 C3

EATING
Banyan Tree......................(see 22)
Bomra's Restaurant................24 C3
Cafe Chocolatti......................25 D1
Cinnabar...........................(see 31)
L'Orange...............................26 D1
Pete's Shack..........................27 B1
Republic of Noodles...........(see 17)
Sai's Viva Goa!......................28 B1
Stone House..........................29 C3

ENTERTAINMENT
Butter....................................30 C3

SHOPPING
Acron Arcade.........................31 C2
Fabindia................................32 B1
Newton's................................33 C1
Sotohaus...............................34 B1

TRANSPORT
Central Bus Stop....................35 D1
Fort Aguada Bus Stop.............36 C4

To Calangute
(1.5km)

Football
Field

Post
Office

To Panaji
(11km)

Candolim

See Enlargement

Candolim
Beach

Candolim
Beach

Bank

To Reis Magos (6km);
Betim (8km);
Panaji (11km)

River
Princess
Wreck

Beach
Shacks

Bank

ARABIAN
SEA

Sinquerim

Sinquerim
Beach

Beach
Shacks

Nerul River

Fort Aguada Rd

Fort Aguada Rd

Fort Aguada

0 ————— 200 m
0 ————— 0.1 miles

NORTH GOA (side tab)

fort. Once protected by a battery of 200 cannons, steps in the main courtyard lead down to vast underground water tanks, able to hold 10 million litres of drinking water. These huge echoing chambers indicate just how seriously the architects of the fort took the threat of a prolonged period of siege.

The **old Portuguese lighthouse**, which stands in the middle of the fort, was built in 1864 and once housed the great bell from the Church of St Augustine in Old Goa before it was moved to the Church of Our Lady of the Immaculate Conception in Panaji. It's the oldest of its sort in Asia, and it is occasionally open to the public, allowing you to climb the spiral steps and enjoy the view from the top. Nearby, the **new lighthouse** (adult/child Rs5/3; ☪ 4-5.30pm), built in 1976, can also usually be visited; cameras are not allowed inside.

A short way to the east of the bastion is the pretty **Church of St Lawrence**, which also occupies a magnificent viewpoint. The church was built in 1643 to honour St Lawrence, the patron saint of sailors, whose image stands on the gilded reredos, holding a model ship.

Down below the fort, gazing out melancholically to the broad Mandovi River is **Fort Aguada jail**, Goa's largest prison, whose cells stand on the site that once formed the square-shaped citadel of the hilltop Fort Aguada. Today the prison houses inmates mostly serving sentences for drug possession or smuggling, including a dozen or so long-staying foreigners. The road down to the jail's entrance – which is as far, thankfully, as most people ever get – passes a weird and wonderful compound known as Jimmy's Palace, home to reclusive tycoon Jimmy Gazdar. Designed by Goan architect Gerard de Cunha, it's a closely guarded froth of fountains, foliage and follies, of which you'll catch glimpses as you whiz past.

To get to the hilltop fort, take the 4km winding road that heads east from Sinquerim Beach and loops up around the headland. Otherwise there's a steep 2km walking trail to the fort that starts just past Marbella Guest House (see p152).

CALIZZ

Those with a thirst for Goan history and architecture shouldn't miss a visit to Candolim's **Calizz** (☎ 325000; www.calizz.com; admission Rs300; ☪ 10am-7pm). An illuminating insight into Goan heritage, its roomy compound is filled with traditional, transplanted Goan houses, complete with authentic interiors. Tours last for 45 minutes and are conducted by historians who bring the state's cultural history to life in a National Tourism Award–winning project.

RIVER PRINCESS

Back at the beach, and an eyesore or an engaging oddity depending on your point of view,

---

CANDOLIM'S MANSIONS

You'd be forgiven for thinking that architecture starts and ends with hotels and beach shacks in Candolim, but despite the wholesale development of this once-sleepy seaside village, some intriguing architectural remnants of a rather different past remain hidden in its quiet back lanes.

In the 17th and 18th centuries, Candolim saw the arrival of a number of wealthy Goan families, fleeing from the capital at Old Goa due to the ravages of typhoid, cholera and malaria epidemics. The homes they built were lavish and ornate, filled with oyster-shell windows, fine materials from Macau and China, and scrolling carved stonework.

Though it's not open to the public, seek out the beautiful **Casa dos Costa-Frias**, down a side road just opposite Candolim's football field, which belonged to relatives of the influential Pinto family (see the boxed text, p147). It was built in the early 18th century, and stands behind a white, cross-topped gateway, with a family chapel tucked behind it. The recently renovated facade's architectural ornament gives a good indication of what Candolim's grand *palácios* (palaces) must have looked like in their heyday.

Nearer the beach, the **Casa dos Monteiros** is another tucked-away example of the peak of Candolim's architectural splendour, built by Goa's most powerful family, the Monteiros, with the pretty 1780 Nossa Senhora dos Remedios (Our Lady of Miracles) chapel standing opposite the entrance to the house. Still occupied by descendants of the Monteiros, the house is sadly not open to visitors, but is worth a look from the outside in any case.

the rusty run-aground **River Princess** tanker has been blighting (or gracing) Candolim's beachfront for years, and though plans often surface to haul her off, they never quite seem to come to fruition. If you're an adventurous sort, there's little to stop you swimming or wading out to the ship and climbing the ropey rope ladder; landlubbers might prefer to admire her from rather more of a distance.

BOAT TRIPS

If you're looking to haggle for an on-the-spot dolphin-spotting trip, head up to the **Excursion boat jetty** on the banks of the Nerul River, where lots of independent local boatmen operate, selling their services to a domestic holidaying crowd. Prices vary, so bargain hard.

Meanwhile, **John's Boat Tours** (☎ 5620190, 9822182814; Fort Aguada Rd) offers one of the most organised of Candolim's day-tripping options. John's has been offering a variety of boat and jeep excursions for years, as well as arranging fabulous river-based houseboat

cruises (Rs4300 per person per day including full board). A dolphin-watching trip costs Rs795; a return boat trip to the Wednesday Anjuna market is Rs500, and a 'Crocodile Dundee' river trip, to catch a glimpse of the Mandovi's crocodile 'muggers', costs Rs1000 per person.

WATER SPORTS

The southern stretch of Candolim Beach, and Sinquerim Beach beyond it, are home to plenty of independent water-sports operators, who offer jet skis, parasailing, waterskiing and the usual host of watery activities. Operations change seasonally; compare several to plump for the best rate.

Sleeping

Though Candolim is largely frequented by package tourists bussed straight in from Dabolim Airport, there's a great range of accommodation for the independent traveller, with the added bonus that many midrange

---

BEACH FINDER: THE NORTH

Goa's northern beaches vary dramatically in character within short distances, and whether you're looking for backpacker-filled beach huts, silent sands or plenty of party people, you'll likely find what you're looking for. Here's a quick rundown to help you.

Candolim & Sinquerim

Busy Candolim is a favourite with British package tourists, who set up camp for their fortnightly dose of sun 'n' sand at one of its dozens of beach shacks. Away from the beach, you'll find some surprisingly good budget accommodation options, making Candolim a good base for exploring the coast if you've your own set of wheels. Sinquerim, at its north end, is dominated by the Taj Group hotel's two resorts, and is a little less buzzing, but a popular location for arranging water sports through ever-changing independent operators.

Calangute & Baga

If you're in Goa for the action, or are in the mood for a good dose of 'oh, I do like to be beside the seaside', Calangute and Baga are without doubt the places for you. Here you'll find bars open – unusually, these days, for Goa – until 4am, unbroken lines of beach shacks, international brand shops, scores of tourist-orientated restaurants, and some pretty classy dining and accommodation options tucked in between. The beaches are busy (think sunlounger central), but the bustle appeals to many who've been returning year after year for decades.

Anjuna

Famed for its weekly Wednesday flea market, slightly scruffy Anjuna remains a firm backpacker favourite week-round, with its nice rocky beaches, great eating options, and general sense of chilledness. It might not be as hip or hippie as in years past, but it still makes a terrific place to hang out, eat, and drink into the wee hours with travellers and long-stayers from across the globe.

places include nice little swimming pools. Most of the best value budget choices are situated either in the northern part of Candolim or in the Sinquerim area further south; the little road up to Marbella Guest House (see p152) has lots of private houses offering double rooms for around Rs500 per night.

BUDGET

Villa Ludovici Tourist Home (☎ 2479684; Fort Aguada Rd; d incl breakfast Rs650) For 30 years Ludovici's has been welcoming travellers into its well-worn, creaky rooms in a grand old Portuguese villa. This is the place for a four-poster bed on a budget; rooms are vast, if definitely faded, and the hosts (and ghosts) are kind and amiable.

D'Mello's Sea View Home (☎ 2489650; dmellos_sea view_home@hotmail.com; d small/large Rs700/1200) Lovely breezy rooms are the principal attraction at D'Mello's, which has the advantage of being just a stone's throw from the beach. A great choice for a simple, serene stay, especially when nearby Dona Florina is fully booked.

our pick Dona Florina (☎ 2489051; www.donaflorina .com; Monteiro's Rd; s/d/seaview d Rs750/950/1500) It's hard to get better value in Candolim than friendly Dona Florina, just a quick walk from the sea and situated in the quiet northern part of the village. Front-facing rooms have spectacular sea views, there's daily yoga on the roof terrace, and the lack of vehicle access ensures a quiet night's repose.

Sea Shell Inn (☎ 2489131; seashellgoa@hotmail .com; Fort Aguada Rd; d Rs850) You won't miss this beautiful white-painted Portuguese mansion, just opposite the massive Newton's supermarket. Its eight plain rooms might come as a bit of a disappointment, however, after visiting the reception; they're in a '70s-style annexe around the back. Still, they're clean, fan-cooled and reasonable value. Rates include breakfast.

MIDRANGE

Pretty Petals (☎ 2489184; www.prettypetalsgoa .com; d with/without AC Rs1200/900; ❷) Despite the

---

Vagator & Chapora

Once the centre of Goa's trance-party scene, things are quieter these days on Vagator's three small covelike beaches, ranged around a rocky headland, though remnants of the state's fabled parties do still occur over Christmas and New Year. Small Chapora, just north of Vagator and dominated by the hilltop remains of a Portuguese fort, has more puff than a magic dragon, and the scent of *charas* (cannabis or hashish) hangs thick in the air at the centre of the village.

Morjim & Aswem

Stretching down to the Chapora River, the sandy beaches of Morjim and Aswem might be beautiful, but the village resorts behind them are decidedly lacklustre. Morjim, particularly popular with young Russians, has a somewhat desolate aura, though it's a scenic place for a walk along the mouth of the Chapora River and is a breeding site for endangered olive ridley sea turtles. Aswem's beach is wide and lovely, but the strip of development behind it is distinctly lacking atmosphere, and some of its sandy stretches are getting pretty grubby these days. Nevertheless, Aswem, like Arambol, is very popular with long-stayers.

Mandrem

South from Arambol, Mandrem is a long and palm-edged ribbon of clean, uncluttered sand, and although it's certainly been discovered it still makes a great choice for getting away from it all. The best digs here are in the midrange budget, many offering yoga courses, ayurvedic massage and other ways to help you relax, release and rejuvenate.

Arambol (Harmal) & Querim

Little Arambol is backpacker central, with its simple huts scattered across a rocky headland. It is the most northerly of Goa's developed beaches, and a popular choice for long-stay hippies and travellers, as well as for those looking for somewhere cheap and chilled to rest up for a while. A little further north, quiet Querim is still just a fishing village with a scattering of beach shacks, and makes a nice change of pace if you're looking to bask in peace.

cutesy name, it's not at all twee here. Instead, bright, simply furnished rooms, some with separate kitchenette and dining room, are ranged around a lovely grassy garden, which is just perfect for days when the beach seems too much bother.

Ruffles Beach Resort (☎ 6641039; www.rufflesgoa .com; d/tr Rs1500/1800; ✹ ♨) 'Welcome to your abode in Paradise', declares Ruffles' website; that might be a slight overstatement, but this decent place does have a pleasant courtyard pool and well-equipped rooms that are good value.

Horizon Grill & Guesthouse (☎ 2479727; www.horizon view.co.in; d with/without AC Rs1800/1200; ✹ ♨) One of the few midrange places in town catering solely to independent tourists, this small hotel is a new good-value option run by British expats, with simple rooms set around a small swimming pool. Don't expect luxury, but for the price it can't be beaten.

Casa Sea-Shell (☎ 2479879; seashellgoa@hotmail.com; Fort Aguada Rd; d with/without AC Rs1850/1150; ✹ ♨) This modern, rather characterless choice, run by the same people as the Sea Shell Inn, represents good value with its efficient service, nice little pool and comfortable rooms.

TOP END

Marbella Guest House (☎ 2479551; www.marbellagoa .com; d from Rs2700; presidential ste Rs4700; ✹) You might be put off by the name – particularly if you've already noticed the similarities on the sands – but this place hasn't the slightest touch of the Costa del Sol about it. A stunning Portuguese villa filled with antiques and backed by a peaceful courtyard garden, this is a romantic, redolent old-world remnant. Its kitchen serves breakfast, lunch and dinner daily, with some imaginative touches, and its penthouse suite is a dream of polished tiles and four-posters. Sadly for kids with a keen sense of style, guests under 12 aren't permitted.

Fort Aguada Beach Resort (☎ toll-free 1800111825; www.tajhotels.com; d from Rs9000; ✹ ♨ ♨) Dominating the headland above Sinquerim Beach, the Taj Group's sprawling beach resort isn't the best the Taj name has to offer, but its service is still top-notch even where its rooms are showing signs of wear and tear. Its Jiva Spa offers a host of soothing balms and palms, and the resort has a gym and pool, and offers adventure sports.

Taj Holiday Village (☎ toll-free 1800111825; www .tajhotels.com; cottages from Rs10,000; ✹ ♨ ♨) Next

door to the Fort Aguada Beach Resort, this newly renovated set of cottages – also owned by the Taj Group – is a smart variation on a five-star theme, possessing all the luxuries you'd expect from this top-end chain, though lacking some of the individual character.

Lemon Tree Amarante Beach Resort (☎ 3988188; www.lemontreehotels.com; r Rs10,500-21,000; ✹ ♨ ♨) Squeezed in on the main strip, this boutiquey, luxey place conjures up a strange mixture of Thai-spa style and medieval motifs, intended to echo, apparently, 'the history and romance of 15th-century Portugal'. Whatever the mix, it works, with swish rooms equipped with wi-fi and DVD players, a luxurious spa and a roomy courtyard pool with swim-up bar.

Aashyana Lakhanpal (☎ 2489225; villa/casinha per week Rs199,500/84,000; ✹ ♨ ♨) An art-filled five-bedroom villa and three smaller two-bedroom 'casinhas', set amid 1.6 hectares of lush, landscaped grounds spilling down to the beach, Aashyana makes the perfect retreat (especially grand for a family or large group of friends) from the brashness and bustle of Candolim. Featured in *Vanity Fair*, this is high-society luxe at its best, with a perfect pool, organic herbs and vegetables direct from the kitchen garden, and a staff keen to cater to your every desire.

Eating

There's a delicious variety of dishes on offer in Candolim, including high-level international cuisine as well as the obligatory all-encompassing beach-shack menus down on the sands. Much of the best on offer is ranged along Fort Aguada Rd, though if you take to the side streets to the east you'll also come across local joints for a cheap and tasty breakfast *bhaji-pau* (bread roll with a small curry for dipping) or lunchtime thali.

Pete's Shack (dishes from Rs60) Amid an ocean of beach shacks (with shacks dedicated to Peter Stringfellow, Jim Morrison and Bob Marley vying for business alongside Pete's), Pete's stands out at the northern end of the strip as one of the sleekest, coolest beachfront operations. Good tunes, tasty salads, and scrumptious desserts keep the holidaying crowds coming back for more.

Sai's Viva Goa! (Fort Aguada Rd; mains from Rs60; ☺ 11am-midnight) This cheap, locals-oriented little place serves flipping-fresh fish and Goan seafood specialities such as a spicy mussel fry.

our pick **Cafe Chocolatti** (Fort Aguada Rd; cakes from Rs80; 9am-7pm) When you're tired of thalis or simply seeking sanctuary, there's nowhere better in Candolim to treat yourself than this lovely tea room, set in a green garden seemingly light years from the bustle of the beach. Though the cafe serves sandwiches and salads, the clue to its speciality is in the name. Order a ginger fizz (Rs60) and a slice of double chocolate cake (Rs80) and sink back into cocoa heaven.

Cinnabar (Fort Aguada Rd; dishes from Rs80) This corner joint set in the Acron Arcade shopping centre makes for a calm pit stop on the shady terrace. Choose snacks from an uncomplicated bistro menu of pastas, soups and salads, then top it off with a black forest ice cream and a frothy coffee.

L'Orange (Fort Aguada Rd; mains from Rs90; noon-midnight) A cute, and largely orange, bar, restaurant and art gallery next to John's Boat Tours. Check it out on Tuesday and Thursday nights when there's 'live music by Elvis', who's apparently alive and well and living in Candolim.

Stone House (Fort Aguada Rd; mains Rs90-240; 6pm-midnight) Surf 'n' turf's the thing at this venerable old Candolim venue, inhabiting a stone house and its leafy front courtyard, and the improbable sounding 'Swedish Lobster' tops the list. There's live music most nights of the week, amid the twinkle of fairy lights.

Republic of Noodles (Fort Aguada Rd; appetisers Rs200, mains from Rs425; 11.30am-3pm & 7-11pm) For a sophisticated dining experience, the RoN delivers with its dark bamboo interior, Buddha heads and floating candles. Delicious, huge noodle plates are the order of the day, and if you're feeling flush there's an exquisite brunch on Sunday mornings: Rs1200 buys you an extensive southeast Asian buffet, along with unlimited mimosas and Bloody Marys.

Bomra's Restaurant (Fort Aguada Rd; mains from Rs250) Fabulously unusual cuisine is on offer at this sleek little place, tucked into a courtyard next door to Candolim's Butter nightclub (look for the huge golden saxophone), and serving interesting Burmese cuisine with a fusion twist. Try the curries, and a killer cocktail, and you'll undoubtedly be back for more.

Banyan Tree (6645858; Taj Holiday Village; 7.30-10.30pm; mains from Rs500) Refined Thai food is the trademark of the Taj's romantic Banyan Tree, its swish courtyard set, unsurprisingly, beneath the branches of a vast old banyan tree. If you're a fan of green curry, don't miss the succulent, signature version on offer here; it's a good idea to book during high season, as it's very popular.

Drinking & Entertainment
Candolim's drinking scene is largely hotel-based, but its plentiful beach shacks are a popular place for a relaxed lunchtime beer or a happy-hour sunset cocktail or two. For something a little livelier, a golden saxophone marks the entrance to the huge **Butter** (7pm-late) lounge-bar complex, which gears up each night during high season, sometimes hosting international guest DJs.

For the last couple of years, Butter has also been one of the venues for the stellar **Sunburn Festival** (www.sunburn-festival.com), billing itself as 'Asia's biggest music festival', which has set up camp in Candolim over Christmas and New Year. Check the website for details, and if it continues to run to form, don't miss it for a four-day dance-music extravaganza filled with international DJs and all-day partying.

Shopping
Acron Arcade (Fort Aguada Rd) A swish shopping arcade with a bookshop, clothing, jewellery,

NORTH GOA

art and textiles. This is also a good place to pick up international designer brands at half (or less) the price you'll pay in many other countries.

Fabindia (Seashell Arcade, Fort Aguada Rd; ☯ 10.30am-9pm) Part of a nationwide chain selling tempting fair-trade bed and table linens, home furnishings, clothes, jewellery and toiletries. Fabindia makes for a great, colourful browse, and is perfect for picking up high-end gifts or treating yourself to a traditional kurta or *salwar kameez* outfit.

Newton's (Fort Aguada Rd; ☯ 9.30am-midnight) If you're desperately missing Edam cheese or Pot Noodles, don't delay in dashing to Newton's, to stock up on homely goods of all descriptions. This vast supermarket also has a good line of toiletries, wines and children's toys, and expat folks travel miles just to peruse its goodies-lined shelves.

Sotohaus (☎ 2489983; www.sotodecor.com; Fort Aguada Rd) Offering cool, functional items dreamed up by a Swiss expat team, this is the place to invest in a natural-form-inspired lamp, mirror or dining table, to add a twist of streamlined India to your pad back home.

Getting There & Around

Buses run about every 10 minutes to and from Panaji (Rs7, 45 minutes), and stop at the central bus stop near John's Boat Tours. Some continue south to the Fort Aguada bus stop at the bottom of Fort Aguada Rd, then head back to Panaji along the Mandovi River road, via the villages of Verem and Betim.

Frequent buses also run from Candolim to Calangute (Rs3, 15 minutes) and can be flagged down on Fort Aguada Rd.

CALANGUTE & BAGA
☎ 0832 / pop 15,800

Depending on your definition of 'fun in the sun', the twin resorts of Calangute and Baga – once the habitat of naked, revelling hippies and nowadays package-holiday central – can prove holiday heaven or the Bosch-like depths of Hell.

Calangute was, long ago, the place to which well-heeled Goan townsfolk would retreat to escape the oppressive heat of the pre-monsoon hinterlands, and later became Goa's first heady '60s hippie-hangout hot spot. Meanwhile Baga, to the north, remained a sleepy fishing village until well into the 1980s, until it was seized upon by package-holiday

developers. These days, though, Calangute and Baga's wide, continuous strip of sand sees relentless action, crowded with beach shacks, bars, water-sports operators, hawkers, sunbathers, and revellers of both the domestic and foreign varieties.

While Calangute's northern beach area is very much bucket-and-spade territory, its southern beach is more relaxed, refined and upscale. To the north, Baga has a younger beach-shack crowd and is the place for drinking and dancing with clubs open until 4am – very unusual these days in Goa. To escape the Baga beat, head north across the Baga river to some budget accommodation bargains clinging to the coast.

If you're coming to Goa seeking spiritual solitude and swathes of quiet tropical sand, you'll find quite the reverse here, with Calangute's main beach drag being India's modern 'Kiss Me Quick' capital, closer to Blackpool than Blissed-Out. But if you're looking for Ibiza-style action, dance-around-your-handbag clubbing, exquisite cuisine and nonstop shops (with the occasional holy cow or temple elephant thrown in to remind you where you really are) you simply couldn't hope for better.

Orientation & Information

Calangute is divided into two basic areas, with very different characters. Its main beach, along with the road leading to it, is a kitsch delight of tacky souvenirs, cheap eats, dingy local bars, soft-serve ice creams, and milling, bewildered coach-tour visitors. Here you'll find touts vying for water-sports custom, buckets and spades being wielded with enthusiasm, and plenty of domestic-tourist-orientated seaside fun. Don't expect any kind of R&R but it's undeniably atmospheric, if only for a pint-sized dose.

Far more sophisticated than its main beach counterpart, Calangute's south beach is the preserve of classier joints. Its sands are quieter (though by no means deserted), its restaurants are more upscale, and its pace altogether more relaxed. The south's the place for sundowners, shopping and sumptuous dining, away from the tourist tat a tad further north.

Baga is also not the ideal place to come for tropical tranquillity. Though wide and roomy, Baga's beach consists of jostling shacks, peppered with water-sports and boat-trip touts, and row upon row of sun-beds. The crowd here is young and excitable, the music loud, and the atmosphere runs from cheerful to chaotic.

CALANGUTE & BAGA

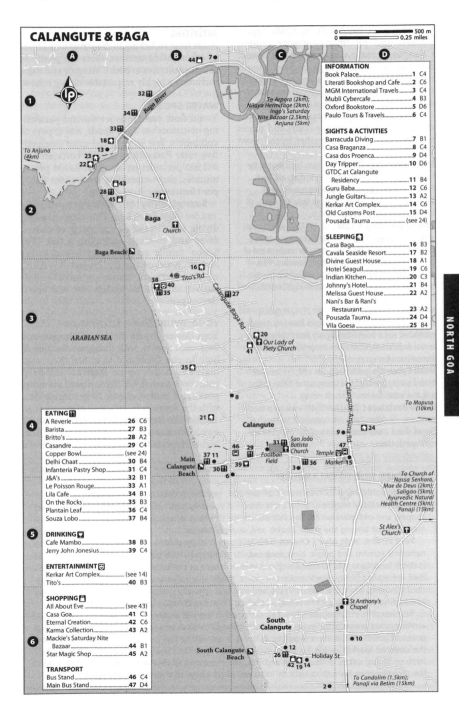

0 ————— 500 m
0 ————— 0.25 miles

INFORMATION
Book Palace.................................**1** C4
Literati Bookshop and Cafe.........**2** C6
MGM International Travels.............**3** C4
Mubli Cybercafe..........................**4** B3
Oxford Bookstore.........................**5** D6
Paulo Tours & Travels...................**6** C4

SIGHTS & ACTIVITIES
Barracuda Diving..........................**7** B1
Casa Braganza.............................**8** C4
Casa dos Proenca.........................**9** D4
Day Tripper................................**10** D6
GTDC at Calangute
    Residency...............................**11** B4
Guru Baba.................................**12** C6
Jungle Guitars............................**13** A2
Kerkar Art Complex....................**14** C6
Old Customs Post.......................**15** D4
Pousada Tauma....................(see **24**)

SLEEPING
Casa Baga...................................**16** B3
Cavala Seaside Resort.................**17** B2
Divine Guest House......................**18** A1
Hotel Seagull..............................**19** C6
Indian Kitchen............................**20** C3
Johnny's Hotel...........................**21** B4
Melissa Guest House...................**22** A2
Nani's Bar & Rani's
    Restaurant.............................**23** A2
Pousada Tauma..........................**24** D4
Vila Goesa................................**25** B4

EATING
A Reverie...................................**26** C6
Barista.......................................**27** B3
Britto's......................................**28** A2
Casandre....................................**29** C4
Copper Bowl.......................(see **24**)
Delhi Chaat...............................**30** B4
Infanteria Pastry Shop................**31** C4
J&A's...**32** B1
Le Poisson Rouge........................**33** A1
Lila Cafe....................................**34** B1
On the Rocks.............................**35** B3
Plantain Leaf.............................**36** C4
Souza Lobo...............................**37** B4

DRINKING
Cafe Mambo..............................**38** B3
Jerry John Jonesius....................**39** C4

ENTERTAINMENT
Kerkar Art Complex.............(see **14**)
Tito's...**40** B3

SHOPPING
All About Eve......................(see **43**)
Casa Goa...................................**41** C3
Eternal Creation........................**42** C6
Karma Collection........................**43** A2
Mackie's Saturday Nite
    Bazaar..................................**44** B1
Star Magic Shop.........................**45** A2

TRANSPORT
Bus Stand..................................**46** C4
Main Bus Stand..........................**47** D4

To Arpora (2km);
Nilaya Hermitage (2km);
Ingo's Saturday
Nite Bazaar (2.5km);
Anjuna (5km)

To Anjuna
(4km)

Baga River

Baga

Church

Baga Beach

ARABIAN SEA

Tito's Rd

Calangute-Baga Rd

Our Lady of
Piety Church

To Mapusa
(10km)

Calangute

Calangute-Anjuna Rd

Main
Calangute
Beach

São João
Batista
Church

Football
Field

Temple

Market

To Church of
Nossa Senhora,
Mae de Deus (2km);
Saligao (5km);
Ayurvedic Natural
Health Centre (5km);
Panaji (15km)

St Alex's
Church

St Anthony's
Chapel

South
Calangute

South Calangute
Beach

Holiday St

To Candolim (1.5km);
Panaji via Betim (15km)

NORTH GOA

our pick **Indian Kitchen** (☎ 2277555; ikitchen2602@ yahoo.co.in; d Rs880; 🖳 🖳) If a colourful stay is what you're after, look no further than this family-run guest house, which offers basic, rather ramshackle rooms with much attempt at individual charm, set around a sparkly, spangly central courtyard. Each room has its own terrace or sit-out, but what really tips the budget scales in its favour is the small, sparklingly clean swimming pool out the back and the free wi-fi. Roomy air-conditioned apartments are also available for long-stayers, for Rs15,000 to Rs18,000 per month.

Baga

Melissa Guest House (☎ 2279583; d Rs500) Neat little rooms, all with attached bathroom and hot-water showers, comprise this quiet, good-value little place, pleasantly situated just past Nani's & Rani's.

Divine Guest House (☎ 2279546; www.indivinehome .com; d from Rs800; 🖳 🖳) You'll get the general optimistic air of this place as soon as you see the 'Praise the Lord' gatepost, and the happiness continues indoors with quietly cheerful rooms embellished with the odd individual touch amid a quiet riverside location.

Nani's Bar & Rani's Restaurant (☎ 2276313; www .naniranigoa.com; r Rs1000; 🖳) Situated on the tranquil north side of the Baga River, just a short hop from the Baga beach action, Nani's is as charming as it is well situated, with simply furnished rooms set around a garden and a gorgeous colonial bungalow.

MIDRANGE & TOP END
Calangute

Hotel Seagull (☎ 2179969; www.villatheresagoa.com; Holiday St, Calangute; with/without AC Rs2500/2300; 🖳 🖳) Bright, friendly and welcoming, the Seagull's rooms, set in a cheerful orange-painted house in quieter South Calangute, are light and airy, with antique bits and pieces of furniture to give them much character. Downstairs there's a popular bar-restaurant with meals served all day.

Vila Goesa (2277535; www.vilagoesa.com; d with/without AC Rs3250/2750; 🖳 🖳) Nicely situated between south Baga and north Calangute and hidden in the palm thickets 200m back from the beach, this is a great place for lingering with a good book by the pool. Rooms are simple but pleasantly furnished; the higher the tariff, the closer you get to the beach.

Pousada Tauma (☎ 2279061; www.pousada-tauma .com; d from €225; 🖳 🖳 🖳) If you're looking for luxury with your ayurvedic regime, check right into this gorgeous little boutique hotel in Calangute. Costs for treatments range from €45 for a 1½ hour treatment, up to €495 for a 14-day 'Pizhichil' course to treat complaints such as arthritis and sciatica.

Nilaya Hermitage (☎ 2276793; www.nilaya.com; Arpora; d incl breakfast & dinner €320; 🖳 🖳 🖳) Ultimate Goan luxury, set 3km inland from the beach at Arpora, a stay here will see you signing the guestbook with the likes of Giorgio Armani, Sean Connery and Kate Moss. Eleven beautiful red-stone rooms undulate around a swimming pool, alongside four stunning tents. The food is as dreamy as the surroundings, and the spa will see you spoiled rotten.

Baga

Cavala Seaside Resort (☎ 2276090; www.cavala.com; s/d without AC from Rs 850/1100, d with AC from Rs2200; 🖳 🖳) Idiosyncratic, ivy-clad Cavala has been charming Baga-bound travellers for over 25 years, and continues to deliver clean, simple, nicely furnished rooms, ranged about a large complex with two central swimming pools. Rates include a hearty breakfast. The bar-restaurant also cooks up a storm most evenings.

Casa Baga (☎ 2253205; www.casaboutiquehotels.com; d Rs6000-7000; 🖳 🖳 🖳) Twenty Balinese-style rooms, some with huge four-poster beds, make for a classy and tranquil stay, with all the little stylish touches the Casa boutique team is so adept at providing.

Eating

Calangute and Baga boast probably the greatest concentration of dining options of anywhere in Goa, with everything on offer from the simplest kerbside *bhelpuri* (a Mumbai snack food, made with fried noodles, lime juice, onions and spices) to the finest Scottish smoked salmon.

For the best of the area's street food, try the main Calangute beach strip, which is thick with vendors grilling sweet corn, serving up *bhaji-pau,* and spinning luminescent fairy floss. Dining gets more sophisticated further towards both the north and south, with a number of Mediterranean stunners, while all along the beach you'll find the usual gamut of beach-shack cuisine. The market area, meanwhile, is filled with little local chai-and-thali joints, where an all-veg lunch costs a mere Rs30 or so.

CALANGUTE

Delhi Chaat (snacks from Rs20) In the thick of the seaside action, this highly popular takeaway joint dispenses all manner of spicy, savoury snacks to the milling masses, as well as delicious hot, sweet chai (Rs10). A *bhaji-pau* comes in at Rs40; an *aloo fry masala chaat* (spicy fried potato) at Rs20.

Barista (coffee Rs45-79; ⏲ 10am-4am) For a cup of Joe and a piece of cake around the clock, rest weary feet on the pleasant terrace of this countrywide coffee chain, and kick back with a cappuccino.

Infanteria Pastry Shop (cake Rs50-100; ⏲ 7.30am-midnight) Next to the Sao João Batista church is this scrummy bakery, loaded with homemade cakes, croissants and little flaky pastries. The noticeboard here is a hotbed for all things current and countercurrent.

Plantain Leaf (thali Rs55) In the heart of the market area, this clean, popular *udupi* (vegetarian restaurant serving South Indian dishes) dishes up South Indian breakfast classics – don't miss the *masala dosas* – and abundant thalis to a constant stream of hungry locals.

Souza Lobo (dishes from Rs90) OK, so the food and service might not be the most tip-top in town, but Souza Lobo wins hands-down for longevity. Serving up seafood to Calangute's seaside parade since 1932, it's still a hit for its location facing the sea and its decent dinners.

Casandre (mains from Rs100; ⏲ 9am-midnight) Housed in an old Portuguese bungalow, this dim and tranquil retreat seems mightily out of place amid the tourist tat of Calangute's main beach drag. With a long and old-fashioned menu encompassing everything from 'sizzlers' to Goan specialities, and a cocktail list featuring the good old gimlet, this is a loveable time-warp, with a pool table to boot.

Copper Bowl (Pousada Tauma; mains from Rs250; ⏲ lunch & dinner) Cute boutique hotel Pousada Tauma is the venue for this intimate little open-air restaurant, which serves up delicious coconut and spice-infused Goan cuisine in the copper bowls after which it's named. Try the spicy *balchão* (seafood in spicy tomato sauce) or coconutty *xacuti*,

and revel in the romance of the candle- and fairy-lit location.

our pick **A Reverie** (mains from Rs320; ⏲ 7pm-late) A gorgeous lounge bar, all armchairs, cool jazz and sparkling crystals, this is the place to spoil yourself, with the likes of Serrano ham, grilled asparagus, French wines and Italian cheeses. Try the delectable forest mushroom soup with truffle oil (Rs255) or go for a bowl of wasabi-flavoured guacamole (Rs215).

BAGA

Lila Cafe (mains from Rs70; ⏲ 8.30am-6pm Wed-Mon) This airy, white and enticing place located along the river is run by German long-term expats and serves up great home-baked breads and perfect frothy cappuccinos. The restful river view is somewhat obscured by the cafe's own guest parking places, but it still makes for a soothing place for a quiet cuppa.

Britto's (mains Rs70-250; ⏲ 8am-late) Long-running, usually packed to the gills, and sometimes open as late as 3am, this Baga institution tumbles out onto the beach, serving up a healthy mixture of Goan and Continental cuisines, satisfying cakes and desserts, and live music several nights a week.

J&A's (mains from Rs250) A pretty cafe set around a gorgeous little Portuguese villa, this little slice of Italy is a treat even before the sumptuous, if rather pricey, food arrives. Owned by a wonderful couple originally from Mumbai, the jazz-infused garden and twinkling evening lights makes for a place as drenched in romance as a tiramisu is in rum. Add to this triple-filtered water, the owners' electric car and composted leftovers, and you've got an experience almost as good for the world as it is for your tastebuds.

Le Poisson Rouge (mains from Rs250; ⏲ 7pm-late) Baga manages to do fine dining with aplomb, and this French-slanted experience is one of the picks of the place. Simple local ingredients are combined into winning dishes such as beetroot carpaccio and red snapper masala, and served up beneath the stars.

Drinking & Entertainment

Boisterous, brash and booming, Baga's club scene somehow manages to bubble on long after the trance parties of further north have been locked down for good by late-night noise regulations. Just how this little strip of night-owls' nirvana has managed to escape the lockdown is anybody's guess, but escape it has, and if you're up for a night of decadent drinking or dancing on the tables, don your glad rags and hit the hot spots with the best of them.

If you're seeking something lower-key, go for the main Calangute beach access road, where simple bars are populated with a captivating mix of frazzled foreigners, heavy-drinking locals and tipsy out-of-towners.

Cafe Mambo (☎ 9822765002; www.titos.in; Tito's Rd, Baga; cover charge before/after 10pm free/Rs200; ☽ 8pm-late) Owned and managed by Tito's, this is a – very slightly – more sophisticated version of the same thing, with nightly DJs pumping out house, hip-hop and Latino tunes.

Indian music and dance recitals (Kerkar Art Complex; per person Rs300; ☽ 6.45-8pm Tue) Held in the outdoor courtyard of the Kerkar Art Complex, these soothing recitals seem a world away from the brasher, bolder side of Calangute, and offer a little glimpse into local traditional music and dance forms.

Jerry John Jonesius (JJJ; Calangute; ☽ 7am-10.30pm) Largely the preserve of locals, JJJ is a suitably dingy and atmospheric bar to down a few beers. Snacks and basic Indian meals (from Rs50) are also available, if you need to line your stomach with something more substantial than *feni* (palm liquor).

On the Rocks (☎ 2277879; Baga; ☽ 8pm-late) Further down toward Baga Beach from Tito's, On the Rocks offers a slicker, more stylish alternative to the mayhem found at the marauding mammoth up the road.

Tito's (☎ 9822765002; www.titos.in; Tito's Rd, Baga; cover charge men/women from Rs300/free; ☽ 8pm-3am) Tito's, the titan on Goa's clubbing scene, is trying its hardest to escape the locals-leering-at-Western-women image of yesteryear, though it's still hardly the place for a hassle-free girls' night out. Thursday's Bollywood Night and Friday's Hip Hop are the pick of the bunch, for the closest thing to Ibiza this side of Star TV.

Shopping

In line with its status as the tourist capital of Goa, Calangute has likewise grown to become the shopping capital. Flashy brand shops familiar to numerous international travellers have sprouted up along the main road to Candolim, just south of Calangute's market. Also here are upmarket gold and jewellery shops, bou-

---

> ### THE FUTURE OF
> ### GOA'S NIGHT MARKETS
>
> Until recently, the highlight of any Calangute or Baga Saturday night came in the form of a trip to one of two lively local night markets: **Mackie's Saturday Nite Bazaar** and **Ingo's Saturday Nite Bazaar**, held each Saturday from 6pm to midnight and filled with vendors, street food, live music and garlands of fairy lights. During the 2008 to 2009 season, however, both were cancelled, though their grounds remained vacant, and opinion was divided on whether they might be reinstated. Ask around to find out, since they're well worth a shopping spree if they're up and running once more.

---

tique fashion stores and dozen upon dozen of arts-and-craft emporia.

However, it's probably the small-time stalls that will catch the eye of most foreign visitors. Calangute and Baga have been swamped by Kashmiri traders eager to cash in on the tourist boom. There is a fantastic range of things to buy – Kashmiri carpets, embroideries and papier-mâché boxes, as well as genuine and reproduction Tibetan and Rajasthani crafts, bronzes, carvings and miniature paintings. This is all the same sort of stuff, however, that you'll see in abundance at Anjuna flea market (p168), so it might be worth comparing prices.

CALANGUTE

Casa Goa (☎ 2281048; ☽ 10am-8pm) A treasure trove of furniture, jewellery, textiles and home accessories housed in an old Portuguese mansion. Browse Casa Goa for a pair of vintage-style candlesticks, a cute picture frame, or clothes by renowned Goan designer Wendell Rodricks.

Eternal Creation (www.eternalcreation.com; Holiday St; ☽ 9am-7pm) Stop in at Eternal Creation to pick up beautiful Australian-designed fair-trade clothes, jewellery and children's wear, ethically produced in the northern Indian mountains by a multifaith workforce and sold here at this cheerful, colourful little store.

BAGA

All About Eve (☎ 2275687; ☽ 10am-8pm) Just next door to Karma Collection, and owned and operated by the same proprietors, All About

Eve stocks unusual clothes, bags and accessories, unlike any of the usual array you'll find on a beach road stall.

Star Magic Shop (☺ daily till late) While strolling Calangute, Baga and Anjuna market, you're sure to spot Star's shop or one of its stalls, promising to teach you magic tricks in a startlingly brief two minutes. Stop off to purchase tricks and illusions to thrill your great aunties and uncles next Christmas, or simply to satisfy that inner thirst to be Thurston.

Karma Collection (☎ 2275687; ☺ 10am-8pm) Beautiful home furnishings, textiles, ornaments, bags and other enticing stuff – some of it antique – has been sourced from across India, Pakistan and Afghanistan and gathered at Karma Collection, which makes for a mouth-watering browse. Fixed prices mean there's no need to bargain, a welcome relief after a stint amid the hard-haggling stalls.

Getting There & Away

There are frequent buses to Panaji (Rs7, 45 minutes) and Mapusa (Rs6, 30 minutes) from the bus stand near Calangute's main beach entrance, and some services to Panaji also stop at the bus stop near the temple, close to the covered market on the Calangute-Anjuna Rd. A taxi from Calangute or Baga to Panaji costs around Rs350 and takes about 45 minutes. A prepaid taxi from Dabolim Airport to Calangute costs Rs645. **Paulo Tours & Travels** (☎ 2281274) has a small office near the beach. It's the main operator for private buses to Hampi, Mumbai and Bengaluru; pick-up is available in Calangute.

Getting Around

Motorcycle and moped hire is easy to arrange in Calangute, and if you're here outside the peak season, you should be able to bargain a reasonable price. Try to pay around Rs100 a day for a Honda Kinetic if you hire it for a week or more, though you're doing well if you manage to get one for Rs150. Expect to pay Rs250 a day around Christmas. Ask around near the steps to the beach in central Calangute, near the roundabout or at the market area where taxis hang out. Up in Baga, taxis congregate towards the end of the road near Britto's.

Take particular care riding on the Calangute–Baga road and near the market area, which gets congested with buses and taxis. Bicycles can also be hired (around Rs40 per day) in the market area – there are no shops as such, just ask around and look for signs.

MAPUSA

☎ 0832 / pop 40,100

The market town of Mapusa (pronounced 'Mapsa') is the largest town in northern Goa, and is most often visited for its busy Friday market, which attracts scores of buyers and sellers from neighbouring towns and villages, and a healthy intake of tourists from the northern beaches. It's a good place to pick up the usual slew of embroidered bed sheets and the like, at prices far lower than in the beach resorts.

There's not a lot else to see here, though it's a pleasant, bustling and typically Indian town to wander for a while, and if you're interested in learning more about the admirable work of International Animal Rescue (see p73) or the Goa Foundation (see p68), both of which have their headquarters close by.

Information

There are plenty of ATMs scattered about town, and you won't have any trouble locating

---

THE MAGIC TOUCH: SHAMIM KHAN

How long have you been practising magic? For 20 years, or maybe more – since I was a small child back in Delhi.

And 20 years on, how many tricks do you know? I'd say 1000, perhaps more.

What's your favourite? A snooker ball, which becomes five balls, then three, then four, then appears from my mouth, then my ear, then vanishes. But then, of course, there's the Magic Key, and the Indian Rope Trick…it's hard to choose just one.

What's the best thing about being a professional magician? My hobby is also my job – not many people can say that. And magic makes people happy: I love making people happy. I've got my shops, as well as this stall every Wednesday at Anjuna Market, and everyone always leaves smiling. What better job can you get?

Shamim Khan is a professional magician and proprietor of Star Magic Shop, Baga.

one. There's a bumper crop around the Municipal Gardens and the market area.

Mapusa Clinic (☎ 2263343; ☯ consultations 10am-noon & 4-6pm) A well-run medical clinic, and the place to go in an emergency.

Other India Bookstore (☎ 2263306; www.otherindia bookstore.com; Mapusa Clinic Rd; ☯ 9am-5pm Mon-Fri, to 1pm Sat) A little hard to find: go up the steps on the right as you walk down Mapusa Clinic Rd, and follow signs. This friendly and rewarding little bookshop is at the end of a dingy corridor.

Pink Panther Travel Agency (☎ 2250352, 2263180; panther_goa@sancharnet.in) A very helpful agency, selling bus, train and air tickets (both international and domestic) as well as performing currency exchange and property consultancy services.

Softwy (☎ 2262075; per hr Rs20; Chandranath Apts, opp Police Station) In a small shopping complex to the left just after the post office, this place has fast internet connections, and sells ice creams to keep you cool while surfing.

Sights & Activities

Founded in 1594 and rebuilt several times since, the **Church of Our Lady of Miracles** (also known as St Jerome's) is famous more for its annual festival than for its architecture. It was built by the Portuguese on the site of an old Hindu temple, and thus the Hindu community still holds the site as sacred. On the 16th day after Easter, the church's annual feast day is celebrated here by both Hindus and Christians – one of the best examples of the way in which Hinduism and Christianity often coexist merrily in Goa.

In the centre of town, the small, pastel-coloured **Maruti temple** was built in the 1840s at a site where the monkey god Hanuman was covertly worshipped during more oppressive periods of Portuguese rule. After temples had been destroyed by the Portuguese, devotees placed a picture of Hanuman at the fireworks shop that stood here, and arrived cloaked in secrecy to perform their *pujas* (prayers). In April 1843 the picture was replaced by a silver idol and an increasing number of worshippers began to gather here. Eventually the business community of Mapusa gathered enough funds to acquire the shop, and the temple was built in its place. The intricate carvings at the doorway of the temple are the work of local artisans.

The **Mapusa market** (☯ 8am-6.30pm Mon-Sat) goes about its business daily, except Sundays, but really gets going on Friday mornings. It's a raucous affair that attracts vendors and shoppers from all over Goa (and interstate) with an entirely different vibe to the Anjuna market. Here you'll find locals haggling for clothing and produce, and you can also find antiques, souvenirs and textiles. So significant is the market locally that the town's name is derived from the Konkani words *map* meaning 'measure' and *sa* meaning 'fill up', in reference to the trade in spices, vegetables and fruit that's plied here daily.

If you're still not shopped-out after a visit to the market, browse the handful of antique and junk shops that dot the Municipality Rd, to the north of the Municipal Gardens, or the couple of chappal (old-fashioned Indian leather san-

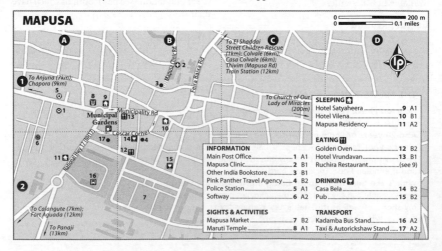

MAPUSA

0 ——— 200 m
0 ——— 0.1 miles

To El Shaddai Street Children Rescue (1km); Colvale (6km); Casa Colvale (6km); Thivim (Mapusa Rd) Train Station (12km)

To Anjuna (7km); Chapora (9km)

Municipal Gardens

Municipality Rd

Coscar Corner

To Church of Our Lady of Miracles (200m)

To Calangute (7km); Fort Aguada (12km)

To Panaji (13km)

INFORMATION	
Main Post Office	1 A1
Mapusa Clinic	2 B1
Other India Bookstore	3 B1
Pink Panther Travel Agency	4 B2
Police Station	5 A1
Softwy	6 A2

SIGHTS & ACTIVITIES	
Mapusa Market	7 B2
Maruti Temple	8 A1

SLEEPING ⬛	
Hotel Satyaheera	9 A1
Hotel Vilena	10 B1
Mapusa Residency	11 A2

EATING ⬛	
Golden Oven	12 B2
Hotel Vrundavan	13 B1
Ruchira Restaurant	(see 9)

DRINKING ⬛	
Casa Bela	14 B2
Pub	15 B2

TRANSPORT	
Kadamba Bus Stand	16 A2
Taxi & Autorickshaw Stand	17 A2

dals) shops, which have been dispensing their utilitarian wares for generations.

Sleeping

There's no particular or pressing reason to stay overnight in Mapusa, since the northern beaches are all so easily accessible from here. In case you have the need or inclination, Mapusa offers a couple of passable choices.

Hotel Vilena (☎ 2263115; Feira Baixa Rd; d with/without bathroom Rs450/300) Friendly owners run Mapusa's best budget choice, though best not bring a cat since there won't be room to swing it in any of the 14 plain double rooms. The hotel's quaint Obsession Pub is open for bar-propping each evening.

Hotel Satyaheera (☎ 2262849; hotelsatyaheera@hotmail.com; d with/without AC from Rs1000/700; ⚋) Just next to the little Maruti temple, this is widely considered Mapusa's best hotel – and don't they know it. Disinterested staff dole out comfy, yet dated, rooms, and the most thrilling thing about the entire experience is the forest-scene wallpaper in the elevator. Note the 9am checkout time and the stipulation that children up to age 12 will be charged Rs50 per day to share a room with their parents, though 'no extra linen will be provided'.

Mapusa Residency (☎ 2262794, 2262694; d with/without AC Rs1155/870, ste Rs1550; ⚋) Service is indifferent and rooms are in the bland-but-functional mould you'd expect from GTDC accommodation, but if all else fails it's a clean place to spend the night, conveniently placed beside the bus stand for an easy getaway the next morning.

Eating & Drinking

There are plenty of nice, old-fashioned cafes within the market area, serving simple Indian snacks, dishes and cold drinks to a local clientele. Thalis come in at the Rs40 mark, and chai at Rs5.

Golden Oven (pastries from Rs6; ☯ 9am-6.30pm) For some clean and shiny comfort, duck into this bakery, which is a civilised respite from the chaos of the market.

Hotel Vrundavan (dishes Rs8-50; ☯ 7am-late; Ⓥ) An all-veg place bordering the Municipal Gardens, this is a great place for a hot chai and a quick breakfast. Dip your *pau* (fluffy white bread roll) or *puri* (deep-fried, puffed-up bread) into a cashew nut *bhaji* (small curry) for just Rs10, or try the tomato version for a more modest Rs9.

DETOUR: A LITTLE LIGHT LUXURY

If the thought of a night in one of Mapusa's hotels is just too much to bear, detour a measly 7km north up the NH17, to reach the small inland village of **Colvale**. Pretty and peaceful, it's the location of boutique hotel **Casa Colvale** (☎ 2299021, 2299028; www.casaboutiquehotels.com; d from Rs7000; ⚋ ▢ ⚌). With a stunning infinity pool, yoga and massage options, and just 12 river-view rooms, it's got all the luxe that Mapusa's accommodation options are lacking. If you really want to arrive in style, however, arrange to be picked up instead from Siolim (p173) by the hotel's speedboat and whisked off down the river to where tranquillity awaits.

Casa Bela (☯ 9.30am-3pm & 6-10.30pm) A windowless remnant of more mahogany-clad era, the dingy Casa Bela is a good place to escape the Mapusa blather and sip silently on a cold Kingfisher (Rs25). The service is surly, but this only enhances the slightly bizarre charm of this little scrap of days gone by. There's a simple menu to help wash down the drinks.

Ruchira Restaurant (mains Rs30-100; ☯ 11am-11pm) On the top floor of Hotel Satyaheera, this place is very popular with tourists and is widely deemed one of Mapusa's best restaurants, serving Indian and Continental dishes. Though the views alone make a visit worthwhile, beware the occasional slightly bewildered, lacklustre service.

Pub (mains from Rs70; ☯ 9am-10.30pm) Don't be put off by the dingy entrance or stairwell; this place is great for watching the milling market crowds over a cold beer or long glass of *feni*. Eclectic daily specials (Rs108) include roast beef and goulash with noodles.

Getting There & Away

If you're coming to Goa by bus from Mumbai, Mapusa's Kadamba bus stand is the jumping-off point for the northern beaches. Private operators sell tickets to Mumbai (with/without AC Rs700/500, 14 hours) and Bengaluru (with/without AC Rs700/500, 12 hours) from next to the bus stand. There's generally little difference in prices, comfort or duration between services, but shop around for the best fare.

Frequent local services – express and regular – also arrive and depart from the

---

A HELPING HAND: ANITA EDGAR

How did your charity begin? I came here in 1996 to recharge my batteries after driving aid trucks for 15 years. Three days into my holiday, I saw some homeless children, fending for themselves, near my hotel. That day, God gave me a vision to open homes to help these children.

What's the most rewarding thing about your work? To rescue a child from a tragic situation, and when they come to you with their exam results or admission to university, to know that without our help, they would be dead.

And the hardest? Endless bureaucracy, and the fact that most holidaymakers just aren't aware of the terrible lives these children lead.

How can foreigners best help? Adopt a child, or get in touch to find out more. It costs us £25 per month to give them everything, and offer a desperate child the chance of life.

Anita Edgar is the co-founder/director of El Shaddai Street Children Rescue (see p73).

Kadamba bus stand; just look for the correct destination on the sign in the bus windscreen. Express services to Panaji (Rs9, 25 minutes), Calangute (Rs8, 20 minutes) and Anjuna (Rs8, 20 minutes) all depart every 30 minutes or so. For buses to the southern beaches, take a bus to Margao (Rs10, 1½ hours) and change there.

An autorickshaw to Anjuna or Calangute should cost Rs150; a taxi'll be at least Rs250.

Thivim, about 12km northeast of town, is the nearest train station on the Konkan Railway. Local buses to Mapusa meet trains (Rs10); an autorickshaw into town from Thivim costs around Rs120.

ANJUNA
☎ 0832

Dear old Anjuna, that stalwart on India's hippie scene, still drags out the sarongs and sandalwood each Wednesday for its famous – and once infamous – flea market. Though it continues to pull in droves of backpackers, midrange tourists are increasingly making their way here for a dose of hippie-chic without the beach-hut rusticity of Arambol further up the coast.

Meanwhile Anjuna remains filled with a weird and wonderful – if these days somewhat diminished – collection of defiant ex-hippies, overlanders, monks, gentle lunatics, artists, artisans, seers, searchers and itinerant expatriates who have wandered far from the organic confines of health-food emporia in San Francisco and London.

The village itself might be a bit ragged around the edges these days, but that's all part of its charm, and Anjuna remains a favourite of long-stayers and first-timers alike.

Orientation & Information

Anjuna is spread out over a wide area, its most northerly point being the main Starco crossroads – where most buses stop and around which many eating options are dotted – and the southernmost point being the flea market site, about 2km to the south. Most accommodation and other useful services are sprinkled along the beach, or down shady inland lanes, in between.

Internet access in Anjuna – away from the midrange hotels – is perilously slow and unreliable and internet joints thus open and close down regularly. Ask around for the best new option on the scene, or head to the German Bakery which offers wireless access (for a cost) for those with their own laptops.

Something important to consider – especially on market day – is that there are no ATMs in Anjuna; the closest are in Mapusa or Calangute. The **Bank of Baroda** (☼ 9.30am-2.30pm Mon-Sat) gives cash advances on Visa and MasterCard, but won't exchange currency. For this, try one of the travel agents below.

There are plenty of reliable travel agents in town. Try **Speedy Travels** (2273266) near the post office, or the excellent **MGM Travels** (☎ 2274317; www.mgmtravels.com; Anjuna-Mapusa Rd; ☼ 9.30am-6pm Mon-Sat).

Dangers & Annoyances

Anjuna is a well known place for procuring drugs and illicit substances, though they're not quite so freely available as in Goa's trance-party days gone by. Participate at your peril – the police Anti-Narcotics Cell has been known to carry out checks on foreigners.

Take great care of your wallet, camera and the like on market day, when pickpocketing can be a problem.

Activities

If you're in the mood for a dip, Anjuna's charismatic, rocky beach runs for almost 2km from the northern village area to the flea market. The northern end shrinks to almost nothing when the tide washes in, when it's fun to watch local tourist ladies hopping perilously from rock to rock in strappy sandals and saris, in search of a scenic photo opportunity. When the tide goes out, it becomes a lovely – and surprisingly quiet – stretch of sand, with lots of room to escape the presence of other sunbathers. Stay away from the southern end of the beach, near the market site, which is sadly blighted with rubbish and engine oil.

Anjuna's activities are many and varied. For an adrenalin rush, **paragliding** usually takes place off the headland at the southern end of the beach on market days; tandem rides cost Rs1500.

If you're looking to embellish yourself while in town, try **Andy's Tattoo Studio** (www.andys -tattoo-studio-goa.com; 11am-7pm), attached to San Francisco Restaurant, where the Anjuna cliffside slides down to meet the beach. Drop in to make an appointment and receive a price quote for your permanent souvenir.

YOGA & AYURVEDA

There's lots of yoga, ayurveda and other alternative therapies and regimes on offer, seasonally, in town; look out for notices posted at Cafe Diogo, Cafe Orange Boom and the German Bakery.

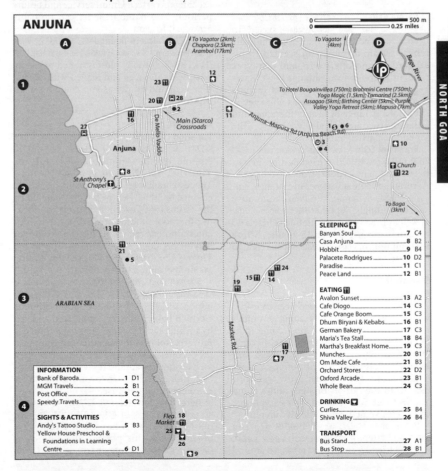

ANJUNA

0 — 500 m
0 — 0.25 miles

To Vagator (2km);
Chapora (2.5km);
Arambol (17km)

To Vagator
(4km)

To Hotel Bougainvillea (750m); Brahmini Centre (750m);
Yoga Magic (1.5km); Tamarind (2.5km);
Assagao (5km); Birthing Center (5km); Purple
Valley Yoga Retreat (5km); Mapusa (7km)

Anjuna–Mapusa Rd (Anjuna Beach Rd)

De Mello Vaddo

Main (Starco)
Crossroads

Anjuna

St Anthony's
Chapel

Church

To Baga
(3km)

ARABIAN SEA

Market Rd

Flea
Market

NORTH GOA

INFORMATION
Bank of Baroda.............................1 D1
MGM Travels.................................2 B1
Post Office....................................3 C2
Speedy Travels.............................4 C2

SIGHTS & ACTIVITIES
Andy's Tattoo Studio....................5 B3
Yellow House Preschool &
  Foundations in Learning
  Centre..6 D1

SLEEPING
Banyan Soul..................................7 C4
Casa Anjuna..................................8 B2
Hobbit...9 B4
Palacete Rodrigues.....................10 D2
Paradise.......................................11 C1
Peace Land...................................12 B1

EATING
Avalon Sunset..............................13 A2
Cafe Diogo...................................14 C3
Cafe Orange Boom.......................15 C3
Dhum Biryani & Kebabs..............16 B1
German Bakery.............................17 C3
Maria's Tea Stall..........................18 B4
Martha's Breakfast Home.............19 C3
Munches.......................................20 B1
Om Made Cafe.............................21 B3
Orchard Stores.............................22 D2
Oxford Arcade..............................23 B1
Whole Bean..................................24 C3

DRINKING
Curlies...25 B4
Shiva Valley.................................26 B4

TRANSPORT
Bus Stand....................................27 A1
Bus Stop......................................28 B1

LITTLE LEARNERS IN ANJUNA

Parents intending on arriving in Goa for the season might be keen to learn of the existence of the **Yellow House Pre-school & Foundations in Learning Centre** (☎ 09326127423; near the Bank of Baroda, Anjuna; www.theyellowhouseschool.com), a small kindergarten and preschool that runs each season, in Anjuna, from October through to April. Created by a British parent, the school offers fun, stimulating learning for kids from two to eight years old, with morning classes running from 9am to 1pm. Check the school's website to find out more about what's on offer at the Yellow House this season.

Purple Valley Yoga Retreat (☎ 2268364; www .yogagoa.com; 142 Bairo Alto, Assagao), based in nearby Assagao village, is a popular upscale retreat set amid frangipani-scented tropical gardens and offers one- and two-week residential courses in ashtanga yoga. Rates begin at £390 for one week, and include accommodation and delicious all-vegetarian meals. A range of beauty therapies and ayurvedic treatments is also available on-site for course participants.

Brahmani Centre (www.brahmaniyoga.com; classes Rs500, 10-class pass Rs3500) is a friendly drop-in centre, which opens its doors from November to April, and offers daily classes in ashtanga, vinyasa, hatha, dynamic, kundalini, restorative and, intriguingly 'superhero acro-flow' yoga, as well as pranayama meditation. There's no need to book: just turn up 15 minutes before the beginning of class, to secure space enough to spread your yoga mat.

Sleeping
BUDGET

Dozens of rooms of the largely concrete-cell variety string themselves along Anjuna's northern clifftop stretch; most come in at Rs250 to Rs500 per night. There are also plenty of small, family-run guest houses tucked back from the main beach strip, offering nicer double rooms for a similar price; take your pick from the dozens of signs announcing 'rooms to let'. We've listed these three exceptional choices for something a little bit different.

Peace Land (☎ 2273700; s/d Rs300/500; 🖳) You can't get better on a budget than Peace Land, run by a friendly couple and arranged around

a tranquil courtyard garden. Rooms are small but spotlessly clean and comfortable, and their little restaurant cooks up some great Indian food. There's internet access for Rs30 per hour, and a small shop selling basic provisions.

Paradise (9922541714; janet_965@hotmail.com; d without AC Rs400–800, d with AC Rs1500) This place is a paradise for animal-lovers, since proprietor Janet is a keen collector of all things canine, feline and avian. This friendly place is fronted by an old Portuguese home and offers good, clean rooms with well-decorated options in the newer annexe. And Janet doesn't stop at accommodation: her enterprising family can service your every need, with their pharmacy, general store, restaurant, internet access (Rs40 per hour), Connexions travel agency, money exchange, Western Union service and beauty parlour. You name it, Janet can probably arrange it for you.

ourpick Palacete Rodrigues (☎ 273358; www .palacetegoa.com; s/d without AC Rs850/950, d with AC Rs1050; 🕮) This beautifully old-fashioned mansion, filled with antiques and loaded with charm, is as cool and quirky as you could hope for in Anjuna.

MIDRANGE

Tamarind (☎ 2274319; www.thetamarind.com; r from Rs1200; 🖳) A couple of kilometres out of Anjuna on the Anjuna–Mapusa Rd, the Tamarind has 22 rooms in a lovely setting. The restaurant is set on the verandah of an old colonial building, but the building containing the rooms is of Tuscan-style stone overlooking the pool. Rooms are TV-free, but your entertainment can come, instead, from four playful pet dogs: Basil, Parsley, Ginger and Thyme. Children under 12 (even dog-lovers) are not permitted to stay here.

Banyan Soul (☎ 9820707283; sumityardi@theban yansoul.com; d Rs1500; 🕮) A slinky new 12-room option, tucked just behind Anjuna's scrummy German bakery, lovingly conceived and run by a young escapee of the Mumbai technology rat race. Rooms are chic and well equipped, the decor is flawless, and there are plans afoot for a rooftop restaurant. It's without doubt the best midrange choice in town, and the staff is extremely keen to please.

Hotel Bougainvillea (☎ 2273270; www.granpas inn.com; d incl breakfast Rs1950-3250; 🕮 🖳) An old-fashioned hotel housed in a centuries-old mansion, this place – also known as Granpa's Inn – offers charm with a touch of luxury with a lovely pool and well-decorated rooms.

TOP END

Yoga Magic (☎ 6523796; www.yogamagic.net; tent/villa per person twin share Rs2750/3500) Solar lighting and compost toilets are just some of the worthy initiatives practised in this ultraluxury bamboo hut-and-villa village, where hand-printed textiles, locally made ironwork furniture and organic gourmet vegetarian food are the order of the day. Prices include breakfast and afternoon tea; daily yoga classes cost an extra Rs300 per session.

Casa Anjuna (☎ 2274123-5; www.casaboutiquehotels .com; d from Rs5000; ▓ 🖳 🖳) Yet another of the chain's decent top-end boutique hotels, this branch offers all the comfort you'd expect from a Casa, with a lovely pool and light, airy rooms.

Hobbit (☎ 9820055053; www.thehobbitgoa; house per night Rs14,400; ▓ 🖳) Bilbo himself would be proud of a hobbit hole like this, nestled away in the very southern part of Anjuna, known as St Michael's Waddo, with terrific views out to sea. This hidden gem of a three-bedroom house, with its own meditation room and cool, curvaceous spaces, is perfect for a big family or for a group of friends seeking respite from the Goan hustle.

Eating & Drinking

Anjuna has a whole host of great eating options, with jostling cliffside cafes sporting the standard traveller-orientated menus, happy hours and stunning coastal views. The area around the Starco crossroads is also thick with dining options, as is Anjuna–Mapusa Rd (Anjuna Beach Rd).

Though Anjuna is no longer party central, and drinking is largely confined to hotel and clifftop bars, inside the flea market on market days you'll also find a number of boozy

bars, one with a stage manned by cover-version-singing foreigners. For a quick market shopping stop, look out for teensy **Maria's Tea Stall** (Flea Market; snacks from Rs10; ☾ market day), selling tasty chai and snacks made by colourful elderly local Maria.

Self-caterers will likely be excited to note that Anjuna is home to two great expat-slanted stores. The smaller **Orchard Stores** is a small, jam-packed (in both senses of the phrase) village shop that dispenses familiar grocerial all-and-sundry to those in need of Heinz baked beans, Marmite or proper pesto, washed down with a nice glass of Ribena. Meanwhile, the massive **Oxford Arcade** (☎ 2273436), just next to the Starco crossroads, is a fully fledged supermarket, complete with shopping trolleys, ice-cold air-conditioning and checkout scanners. Hallowed ground for foreigners who pay dearly for little luxuries, it also sports a bakery, toiletries department, pet food, wine department and children's toys. Come Christmas, this is the place to buy your tinsel and baubles, fake tree and kids' gifts to stack beneath it.

Dhum Biryani & Kebabs (Biryani Palace, Anjuna-Mapusa Rd; mains Rs50-150) Next door to the cheekily titled Come Look My Shop, this place is loved by visitors and locals alike, for its consistently good and fantastically tasty kebabs.

German Bakery (dishes from Rs60; 🖳) Leafy and filled with prayer flags and jolly lights, this is a perfect place for a huge lunch chosen from an equally huge menu. Tofu balls in mustard sauce with parsley potatoes and salad is a piled-high winner at Rs150. Wi-fi is available for a fairly steep Rs100 per hour.

Avalon Sunset (dishes from Rs60; 🖳) Good food, a pool table, a chill-out area, free wi-fi and rooms for rent (Rs400 and up) make this a great representative of Anjuna's clifftop restaurant parade. There's daily yoga on the roof, too; call in for class times.

THE ALBUQUERQUE CURSE

Though two-and-more-storey buildings are slowly beginning to creep their way into Anjuna's periphery, every self-respecting Anjuna villager is aware of a local curse, which prophesies doom and gloom on anyone who dares build an upper level atop their ground-floor dwelling. Though no one knows quite where the curse originated, many locals tell the tale of Dr Manuel Albuquerque, physician to the Sultan of Zanzibar, who in 1920 built a two-storey replica of the Sultan's palace to serve as his retirement home. Soon beset with misfortunes, Albuquerque failed to produce an heir and fell into dire financial straits; his mansion – though still standing – remains a warning to Anjunans to keep their feet firmly on the ground.

GOA'S FLEA MARKET EXPERIENCE: GOAN, GOAN, GONE?

Wednesday's weekly **flea market** at Anjuna is as much part of the Goan experience as a day on a deserted beach. More than two decades ago, it was still the sole preserve of hippies smoking jumbo joints and convening to compare experiences on the heady Indian circuit.

Nowadays things are far more staid and mainstream, and package tourists seem to beat out independent travellers both in numbers and purchasing power. The market sprawls on hawking stuff that is much of a muchness: a couple of hours here and you'll never want to see a mirrored bedspread, peacock-feather fan, or floaty Indian-cotton dress again in your life. That said, though, it's still a great place for a spot of people-watching, and you can find some interesting one-off souvenirs and pieces of clothing in among the tourist tat. Remember to bargain hard and take along equal quantities of patience and stamina, applicable to dealing with local and expat vendors alike.

Until recently, great evening-time alternatives to the Anjuna experience were Mackie's and Ingo's Saturday 'Nite Bazaars', both set up in the region of Calangute and Baga. At the time of research, however, both had been cancelled. Reasons for the cancellations remained unclear – reports range from licences being revoked to the ongoing threat of terrorism – but ask around to double-check, since in seasons past they made for a pleasant evening mix of live music, food and shopping.

Cafe Diogo (dishes from Rs70; ☾ 9am-4pm) Probably the best fruit salads in the world are sliced and diced at Cafe Diogo, a small locally run cafe on the way down to the market. Also worth a try are the generous toasted avocado, cheese and mushroom sandwiches, the jumbo fry-ups, and the unusual gooseberry lassi.

Cafe Orange Boom (dishes from Rs70; ☾ breakfast & lunch) Just past Cafe Diogo, on the opposite side of the road, this nice little place has the same good food and friendly service at equivalent prices, with a useful noticeboard for catching up on Anjunan goings-on.

Martha's Breakfast Home (breakfasts from Rs70) As the name suggests, Martha's speciality are her all-day breakfasts, served up in a quiet garden on the way down to the flea-market site. The porridge and juice may be mighty tasty, but the star of the breakfast parade is undoubtedly the piping-hot plates of waffles, just crying out to be smothered in real maple syrup.

Munches (dishes from Rs70; ☾ 24hr) Near the Starco crossroads, this ever-popular place, serving up the full list of travellers' favourites, is a good choice for whenever any attack of the munchies demands you munch. Next door, Eatopia offers much the same sort of thing, with the added benefit of a nightly movie screening.

Whole Bean (dishes Rs70-130; Ⓥ) This simple, tasty, tofu-filled health-food cafe – which proudly announces itself as 'Anjuna's premier soy destination' – focuses on all things created from that most versatile of beans.

our pick **Om Made Cafe** (dishes Rs90-190; ☾ 8.30am-sunset) A highlight on Anjuna's clifftop strip, this cheery little place offers striped deck-chairs from which to enjoy the views and the simple, sophisticated breakfasts, sandwiches and salads. Go for a raw papaya salad with ginger and lemongrass (Rs170), accompanied by a chickoo (small, sweet fruit of the sapodilla tree) and coconut smoothie or a glass of 'perfumed water' (Rs20).

Down on the beach, past the flea-market site, **Curlies** (mains from Rs50; ☾ till late) and nearby **Shiva Valley** (☾ till late) are two very popular places for an evening drink, an alternative crowd and the odd impromptu party. Head down to either to find out what's on.

Getting There & Away

There are buses every 30 minutes or so from Mapusa to Anjuna (Rs6), stopping at the end of the road to the beach and continuing on to Vagator and Chapora, while some continue to Arambol. Plenty of motorcycle taxis gather at the main crossroads and you can also easily hire scooters and motorcycles here. A prepaid taxi from Dabolim Airport to Anjuna costs Rs860.

VAGATOR & CHAPORA
☎ 0832

Dramatic red stone cliffs, dense green jungle and a crumbling 17th-century Portuguese fort provide Vagator and its diminutive village neighbour Chapora with one of the prettiest settings on the North Goan coast. Once known for their wild trance parties and heady, hippie lifestyles, things have slowed down considerably these days, but Chapora – still reminiscent of *Star Wars'* Mos Eisley Cantina – remains a fave for hanger-on hippies and long-staying smokers, with the smell of *charas* clinging heavy to the light sea breeze.

Chapora is a working fishing harbour nestled at the mouth of the Chapora River, and hence is basically beachless, whereas Vagator has three small, charismatic coves to choose from. The most northerly and largest is Vagator Beach, a beautiful stretch of sand, which only fills up for a few hours each afternoon when domestic coach tours unload their swift-clicking tourist hordes making the most of its good swimming. Avoid this time of day and you'll have plenty of room for lounging on its pretty, boulder-studded sands.

South from here, Vagator's two southerly coves are known as Little Vagator Beach and Ozran Beach; both are accessible by steep footpaths running down from near the Nine Bar. Both make upbeat, and sometimes cramped, places for a beach-shack lunch, a snooze on a sun lounge or a dip in the sea. With shacks dominating the sands, Goa Trance heavy on the sound systems, and cows thronging among the people, there's a distinctly laid-back backpacker vibe, overseen at Ozran by the huge, happy carved Shiva face that gazes out serenely from the rocks.

Information

Neither Vagator nor Chapora is outfitted with an ATM, though you'll find that a number of shops and travel agencies offer foreign exchange. The nearest ATM facilities are in Mapusa.

In Vagator you'll find the lovely little **Rainbow Bookshop** (☎ 2273613; ⏲ 9.30am-10pm), which is run by a charming elderly gentleman and stocks a good range of secondhand and new books, including this very guide.

Plenty of internet places are scattered along the road to Little Vagator Beach; **Tanu Communications** (per hr Rs50; ⏲ 9am-late), just before the Alcove Resort at Little Vagator, is one reliable option.

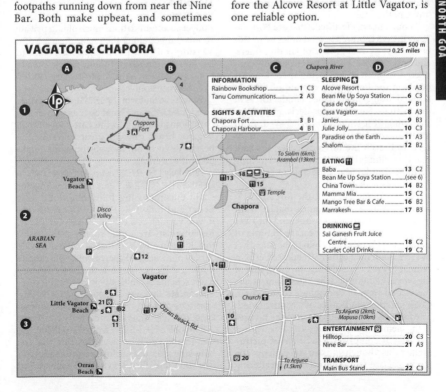

VAGATOR & CHAPORA

INFORMATION	
Rainbow Bookshop	1 C3
Tanu Communications	2 A3

SIGHTS & ACTIVITIES	
Chapora Fort	3 B1
Chapora Harbour	4 B1

SLEEPING	
Alcove Resort	5 A3
Bean Me Up Soya Station	6 C3
Casa de Olga	7 B1
Casa Vagator	8 A3
Janies	9 B3
Julie Jolly	10 C3
Paradise on the Earth	11 A3
Shalom	12 B2

EATING	
Baba	13 C2
Bean Me Up Soya Station	(see 6)
China Town	14 B2
Mamma Mia	15 C2
Mango Tree Bar & Cafe	16 B2
Marrakesh	17 B3

DRINKING	
Sai Ganesh Fruit Juice Centre	18 C2
Scarlet Cold Drinks	19 C2

ENTERTAINMENT	
Hilltop	20 C3
Nine Bar	21 A3

TRANSPORT	
Main Bus Stand	22 C3

NORTH GOA

PREGNANT IN GOA

If you're planning on visiting Goa while pregnant, you might find yourself tempted to do a birth-related course at the **Birthing Center** (☎ 2268144; www.birthing-center.com) in the village of Assagao, just 5km or so away from Anjuna. Run by German midwife Corinna Stahlhofen, this tranquil place offers pre- and post-natal courses, along with holistic birthing and water births, and has welcomed dozens of happy, healthy babies into the world.

Sights & Activities

CHAPORA FORT

Chapora's windswept old laterite fort, standing guard over the mouth of the Chapora River, was built by the Portuguese in 1617, to protect Bardez taluka, in Portuguese hands from 1543 onwards, from the threat of invaders. It was built over the remnants of an older Muslim structure, hence the name of the village itself, from 'Shahpura', meaning 'town of the Shah'.

Though heavily fortified, Chapora Fort was nevertheless captured several times by invaders: first by several groups of Hindu raiders, and next, in 1684, when it was reportedly conquered without a shot being fired. On this occasion the Portuguese captain of the fort decided to surrender to the Maratha forces of the chieftain Sambhaji, his decision perhaps stemming, if legend is to be believed, from the manner in which Sambhaji's forces managed to breach the fort's defences: it's said that they clung tight to tenacious 1.5m-long monitor lizards, who were able to scale the rocky walls with ease.

The Portuguese rebuilt the fort in 1717, adding features such as tunnels that led from the bastion down to the seashore and the river bank to enable resupply or escape in times of trouble, but Chapora fell again to the Marathas in 1739. Soon the northerly taluka of Pernem came into Portuguese hands, forming part of the Novas Conquistas (the 'New Conquests', the second wave of Portuguese conquests in Goa), and the significance of Chapora faded. The fort was finally abandoned to the ravages of the elements in 1892.

Today it comprises a crumble of picturesque ruins, though you can still pick out the mouths of two escape tunnels and a scattering

of pre-Portuguese Muslim tombstones. The main reason, though, to make the climb up the hill is for the stunning views out along the coast, especially enticing at sunset.

CHAPORA HARBOUR

The narrow road northwest of the village leads you past lots of village homes with rooms for rent, up to a small harbour where the day's catch is hauled in from colourful, bobbing fishing boats. Self-caterers with the desire for fresh fish can haggle for their supper direct with fishermen, while for most others, it makes for a scenic photo opportunity and provides an interesting window into traditional village life.

YOGA & AYURVEDA

There's plenty of yoga and ayurveda on offer seasonally in both Vagator and Chapora; check the noticeboards at Bean Me Up Soya Station or Scarlet Cold Drinks for up-to-date details.

Sleeping

VAGATOR

Budget accommodation, much of it in private rooms, ranges along the Ozran Beach Rd in Vagator; you'll see lots of signs for 'rooms to let' on the side roads, too, in simple private homes and guest houses. Most charge Rs300 to Rs500 per double.

Paradise on the Earth (☎ 2273591; www.moondance .co.nr; huts Rs300) Simple bamboo huts with shared bathrooms clinging to the cliff above Small Vagator beach offering great value for the beachside location, though the name might be a little overkill.

Julie Jolly (☎ 2273357; www.hoteljollygoa.com; r & apt Rs528-3360; 🔀 🖳 🖳) Part of a local Vagator chain encompassing Julie Jolly, Jolly Jolly Lester and Jolly Jolly Roma (try saying that if you've just come back from Chapora). Receptionists are a little snooty at this comfortable place with a small pool and a wide variety of rooms and apartments. Still, despite a bit of a bleak location, the barber's-shop paint scheme is faultlessly jolly.

Bean Me Up Soya Station (☎ 2273479; www .myspace.com/beanmeupindia; d with private/shared bathroom Rs550/350) The rooms around a leafy courtyard might look a bit cell-like from the outside, but step in and you'll be pleased to find that the billowing silks and mellow, earthy shades follow you there. Bicycles (Rs1000 deposit, and

Rs100 per day) and motorbikes (Rs250 per day) are both available for hire, and there's a nice vegetarian restaurant.

Janies (☎ 2273635; janiesricardo@hotmail.com; d Rs800, 1-/2-bed bungalow Rs1000/1200) A great choice for long-stayers, run by a very friendly lady and with a simple but homely vibe. The three double rooms each have a small kitchen, bathroom and TV. There are also two large bungalows, the first with one double bedroom and the second with two.

our pick Shalom (☎ 2273166; d with/without TV & fridge Rs1500/800, 2-bed apt per month Rs25,000) Arranged around a placid garden not far from the path down to Little Vagator beach, this place run by a friendly family (who lives on-site) offers a variety of well-kept rooms, and a two-bedroom apartment for long-stayers.

Alcove Resort (☎ 2274491; www.alcovegoa.com; d with/without AC Rs2200/1800, cottages with/without AC Rs2500/2000, ste with/without AC Rs3500/3000; ✖ ☒) With attractively furnished rooms, slightly larger cottages and four suites within striking distance of Little Vagator beach, this place is for those who want a touch of luxury at surprisingly reasonable prices. When you tire of the sands there's a cool central pool.

Casa Vagator (☎ 2416738; www.casaboutiquehotels .com; d Rs7000-13,000; ✖ ☒ ☒) A successfully rendered outfit in the deluxe Casa boutique mould, this is Vagator's most stylish accommodation option, with gorgeous rooms offering equally gorgeous views out to the wide blue horizon. The only downside is its proximity to techno-heavy Nine Bar, which pumps out Goa Trance every night until the 10pm shutdown; great, if you like that sort of thing, gruesome if you don't.

CHAPORA

Head down the road to the harbour and you'll find lots of rooms – and whole homes – for

---

TRANCE PARTIES

Goa has a far longer and more vibrant history of hosting parties than most people realise. As far back as the 16th century, the Portuguese colony was notorious as an immoral outpost where drinking, debauching and dancing lasted till dawn, and, despite a more strait-laced interlude at the hands of the notorious Goan Inquisition, the tradition was finally resurrected full-force when the 'Goa Freaks' arrived on the state's northern beaches in the 1960s.

But the beach parties and full-moon raves of the 1970s and '80s came to seem like innocent affairs compared with the trance parties that replaced them in the '90s. At the peak of Goa's trance period, each high season saw thousands of revellers choosing synthetic substances such as ecstasy over marijuana and dancing to techno beats in Day-glo stupors, sometimes for days at a time.

In 2000 the country decided it was time to crack down, instigating a central government 'noise pollution' ban on loud music in open spaces between 10pm and 6am. This, combined with increasing crackdowns on drug possession, effectively put an end to the trance-party scene, with police teams swooping in to close down parties before they even began. This has largely been greeted with relief from locals, who were becoming increasingly worried at the peak of the trance-party phenomenon about the effects of drug dealing, alcohol and attendant promiscuity on Goa's own youth population.

With a tourist industry to nurture, the police still tend to turn a blind eye to a handful of parties during the peak Christmas–New Year period, their opinion swayed by a hefty hand-outs of baksheesh. Some monster mainstream clubs of Baga (p159) have managed to circumvent the ban, and pump on each weekend till 4am or later. Meanwhile in Vagator the once legendary Nine Bar (p172) still limps along, but nowadays turning off the techno at 10pm sharp. Down south in Palolem, however, several people have found an ingenious way around the loud music restrictions: see the boxed text, p209 for more on Palolem's 'silent parties'.

If, though, you're determined to experience the remnants of Goa's true trance scene, hang around long enough in Vagator and you'll likely be handed a flyer for a party (many with international DJs), which can range from divine to dire. You may also catch wind of something going down in a hidden location – if you're lucky, it won't have been closed down by police by the time you manage to get there. In other words, keep your ear close to the ground, your fingers crossed and pray for a trance-music miracle.

rent, far nicer than setting yourself up in the congested village centre; be sure to thoroughly trawl what's on offer before you land your catch.

Casa de Olga (☎ 2274355, 9822157145; d from Rs250) This welcoming choice ranged around a nice garden offers clean rooms of a variety of sizes and states of equipped-ness. You'll pay more for the best of them, which come with hot showers, kitchenette and balcony.

Baba (☎ 2273213; d with/without bathroom Rs300/150) The gaggle of men owning this place, with simple but serviceable rooms, seem a little like rulers of their own small empire. Nevertheless, they're a one-stop destination for most material needs, with their restaurant (serving the usual menu hodgepodge of Indian, Italian and just about everything else), internet cafe (Rs40 per hour) and money-exchange service.

Eating & Drinking
VAGATOR
There are a few eating options clustered around the entrance to Little Vagator beach, along with the usual slew of much-of-a-muchness beach shacks down on the sands themselves.

China Town (mains from Rs70) Brightly painted and dispensing traveller favourites from its long menu, this simple place offers good chow mein and sweet-and-sour, as well as some decent seafood.

Mango Tree Bar & Cafe (mains Rs100-120) An ever-popular place for its big breakfasts and far-ranging menu, with films screened here most evenings around 7.30pm.

Marrakesh (mains Rs120-160; ☉ 11am-11pm) Billing itself as the 'Heart of Moroccan cuisine', this is the place to pick up a tasty tagine or a delectable veg couscous (Rs150) in what seems to be Goa's only Moroccan restaurant.

Bean Me Up Soya Station (mains from Rs150; Ⓥ) A delicious, all-vegetarian restaurant at this popular place to stay, with lots of carefully washed salads and a wealth of tasty tofu and tempeh treats.

CHAPORA
Scarlet Cold Drinks (drinks & desserts Rs5-50) Vending juice, lassis and snacks to munchies-driven travellers, a rickety table at Scarlet offers a perfect vantage point from which to observe Chapora's comings and goings; there's also an extremely useful noticeboard, pinned to

bursting with news of the latest local yoga classes, reiki courses and the like.

Sai Ganesh Fruit Juice Centre (juices Rs15-30) Offering similar stuff to Scarlet, in equally close proximity to the thickest gusts of *charas* smoke, this diminutive juice centre is a great place for a vitamin fix and a fascinating spot of people-watching.

our pick Mamma Mia (☉ 8am-9pm Tue-Sat; panini & pizza Rs100) The best of the Chapora bunch is Mamma Mia, run by Marco who makes his own focaccia fresh every night ready for the next day. The cappuccinos are perfect, the pizza is simple and filling, and the smoke puffed out by customers is, well, heady.

Entertainment
Aside from secretive parties, there's not too much going on in Vagator and Chapora these days, though you might have more luck tracking down an event or two over the busy Christmas and New Year period. Beach shacks and the small local bars lining Chapora's main street make good choices for a cool evening Kingfisher.

Hilltop (☎ 2273025, 2273665; ☉ sunset-late) Deserted by day, this place comes alive after nightfall, its edge-of-town location allows it on occasion (and for now, at least) to gleefully flout 10pm noise regulations to host concerts, parties and the occasional international DJ. Venture up to the site by day, and wander about until you find someone who'll tell you what's on and when.

Nine Bar (Sunset Point, Little Vagator Beach; ☉ till 10pm) Once the epicentre of Goa's trance scene, custom has cooled at the open-air Nine Bar, though the trance still thumps away each evening until it's turned off promptly at 10pm. On a good night, a trace of parties past can still be found; on bad, its atmosphere is akin to a wedding reception, long after the bride and groom have gone home.

Getting There & Away
Fairly frequent buses run to both Chapora and Vagator from Mapusa (Rs12) throughout the day, many via Anjuna. The bus stand is near the road junction in Chapora village. Many people hire a motorcycle to buzz back and forth; enquire wherever you see a man with a scooter. Prices tend to be around Rs150/200 per day for a scooter/motorbike.

SIOLIM

☎ 0832 / pop 12,000

The large village of Siolim, lying on the road north between the traveller epicentres of Anjuna and Arambol, is often overlooked by travellers, due to its riverside location some way from the nearest beach. If you're looking for a change from sea and sand, it makes a pleasant place to stay, with lots of budget and midrange-priced houses for rent (just wander about a bit, and look out for handwritten signs) and a growing range of top-end heritage home hotels.

Siolim is home to an atmospheric **daily market** near the ferry landing stage on the banks of the Chapora River, where you can watch women open the shells of mussels at a speed that will impress. On Wednesday mornings another small **market** (◷ 7.30-10am), full of homegrown produce, sets up near central **St Anthony Church**, which dates back to the 16th century.

Sleeping

Solar Monte Verde (☎ 2182305; www.solarmonte verdegoa.com; d from Rs2000; ☒) Located on the right-hand side of the road into Siolim from Chapora, you'll find yet another of Siolim's beautifully restored heritage houses. Here, you've a choice of five simple rooms, each with canopied wooden beds and antique touches, and a broad garden containing a cool little pool.

Hilario Heritage Inn (☎ 2540508; www.hilarioinn goa.com; d from Rs4500; ☒ ☒) You won't miss Hilario's bright blue-painted mansion, built a century ago by local landlord Hilario Fernandes and now lovingly administered by his great-great-grandson. Seven rooms, with cool-tiled floors and four-poster beds, and a decent-sized swimming pool, make this another nice heritage choice, though not quite as luxurious as the Raj Angan and Siolim House.

Siolim House (☎ 2272138; www.siolimhouse.com; d from Rs6600; ☒) Comprising the seven-room Siolim House hotel and the smaller, three-bedroom Siolim Villa, Siolim House is without doubt one of North Goa's boutique treats. Situated in an old *palácio* once home to the Governor of Macau, the hotel is elegant and carefully restored, and, though it has a pool, is devoid of many 'luxury' trappings; there's no AC or vast plasma TV to be found in its antiquey rooms, and the dining, while delicious, is decidedly local.

Raj Angan (☎ 2272547; www.rajangan.com; ☒ ☒) An air of exclusivity pervades Raj Angan (Sanskrit for 'Royal Courtyard'), a historic, 150-year-old four-bedroom villa rescued from decay by its current German owners. Go for the Rani room with its circular bathtub, or

---

SIOLIM ZAGOR FESTIVAL

Held annually on the first Sunday after Christmas, Siolim's **Zagor Festival** offers a happy glimpse into the peaceful coexistence that manages to exist within Goa's diverse religious communities.

Taking place on the Christian feast day of Nossa Senhora de Guia, the night-time festival blends both Hindu and Christian traditions, centring on a small Hindu shrine near the ferry dock, which is believed to house Zagoryo, the village deity. The guardian of the village *bunds* (the dams that keep the river from the rice fields), Zagoryo is offered thanks during the festival by every Siolim family. Hindu families offer the deity oil; Christians bring candles, and everyone also offers up *pohe* (small cakes of pressed rice).

Beginning with a candlelit procession, villagers file through the streets of Siolim bearing an effigy of Zagoryo, stopping at both roadside Hindu and Christian shrines for blessings along the way. Next comes a traditional dance drama, during which legends are re-enacted by members of two important Siolim families – the Catholic D'Souzas and Hindu Shirodkars – who've inherited the roles from their forebears.

At first light the next morning, Hindu and Christian blessings are chanted by village priests, and the deity is carried back to his shrine, amid a shower of further offerings. Once complete, the festivities are topped off with a Konkani *tiatr* (play) or two, a party and usually a performance by Siolim born-and-bred celebrity, Remo Fernandes (see p48). If you're in the area at the right time of year, don't miss a visit to the Zagor along with what is, at present, only a thin trickle of foreign tourists.

the Clara room for its wide, white open space, or simply rent the whole thing with a group of friends and kick back in the lovely pool all by yourselves. Call ahead for prices.

MORJIM
☎ 0832

Greetings from Morjim, where the Arabian Sea meets the Baltic: for reasons perhaps known best to itself, the tiny village has become the destination of choice for young, long-staying Russians and receives only a trickle of visitors from other beaches. Situated at the mouth of the Chapora River, the south end of Morjim beach (also known locally as Temb) has lovely views down the headland to Chapora Fort, and makes for a pretty stroll down the estuary. This area is also where ever-decreasing numbers of olive ridley marine turtles come to lay their annual clutches of eggs. Drop into the Goa Forestry Department's hut, set up to protect the eggs, to learn more. See also p65.

Though it's a reasonably nice place to spend an afternoon on the sands, and is certainly quite laid-back, the whole place gives off a distinct whiff of desolation (not helped by some decidedly lacklustre 'resorts'), and there's very little bucolic charm in evidence. The beach, in parts, is no longer pristine, and Cyrillic language skills will go a long way to help you decipher some menu boards.

Nevertheless, it could be a good place to look if you're seeking a full-season house rental; look for 'house to rent' signs around the village. The other good reason to come here is if you're in need of a serious spiritual fine-tuning: Morjim's **Yoga Village** (☎ 2244546; www.yogavillage.org; two-week retreat €800) offers popular two-week retreats. Price includes ayurvedic meals, cottage accommodation, yoga and daily metaphysical discussion.

ASWEM
☎ 0832

A wide stretch of quiet beach backed by a rather scruffy village strip, the quiet Aswem sands are popular with long-staying foreigners and play host to an annually changing parade of beach-hut accommodation and beach-shack restaurants. Though some stretches of the beach are becoming distressingly grubby, development here is generally low-key, swimming is usually safe, the sands are quiet and the vibe very, very mellow.

Aside from a good and growing range of beach huts (operations change annually, but a basic hut should cost between Rs300 and Rs500 and up, depending on the view, facilities and proximity to the beach), you'll find one top-notch sleeping option at **Yab Yum** (☎ 6510392; www.yabyumresorts.com; domes from £60), whose unusual, stylish, dome-shaped huts are made of a combination of all-natural local materials, including mud, stone and mango wood. There are also cottages on offer, and a stellar 'double suite pod' with two bedrooms and an amazing view out to sea. A whole host of yoga and massage options are also available, and parents will appreciate the kids' tepee, full of children's toys.

Though you'll find no end of beach shacks offering the usual traveller-orientated menus, one place stands out above the rest. **La Plage** (mains from Rs100; ☾ lunch & dinner) is renowned by those in the know, and has been dishing up sumptuous gourmet Mediterranean food in simple surroundings since 2003, concocted by a genuine French chef.

MANDREM

Mellow Mandrem has in recent years become an in-the-know bolt-hole for those seeking respite from the relentless traveller scene of Arambol and Anjuna. The beach is wide and beautiful, and there's little to do but laze on it, and here's hoping that it stays that way. So far, Mandrem has resisted expansion, remaining small and perfectly formed, with rare olive ridley marine turtles still turning up annually to lay their eggs in its soft sands.

Information

Facilities remain basic at beachside Mandrem, and most people head up to Arambol – or to little Madlamaz-Mandrem village at the top of the hill, set inland from the beach – for all their basic supplies and services. But down on the single, accommodation-lined lane to the beach, **SS Travels** (☎ 2242712), near the Shri Gopal Supreme Pure Juice Centre & Cafe, offers bus tickets, internet at Rs40 per hour and Western Union money transfer.

Getting to Mandrem and getting around by public transport isn't all that easy. Your very best bet is to hire a scooter at Arambol.

Activities

Mandrem has become Spiritual Central in the last few years, and there's more yoga here than you could shake an iyengar block at. Many classes and courses change with the season, but there are a few spiritually slanted places that reappear year after year. ayurvedic massage, too, is widely available throughout the fledgling resort: ask around for recommendations.

Amalia Camp (www.neeru.org) Its slogan – 'Meeting Yourself' – might give you a clue as to what's going on at Amalia Camp, where local guru Neeru hosts *satsangs*, (devotional speech and chanting sessions) to help ease you towards ever-elusive enlightenment. Her own personal three-point plan invites you to join her in 'Step One: Realization of Truth; Step Two: Liberation of the Mind; Step Three: Integration Into Life'. Check her website for upcoming opportunities to do so.

Ashiyana Retreat Centre (☎ 9850401714; www.ashiyana-yoga-goa.com) This 'tropical retreat centre' situated right on Mandrem Beach has a long list of classes and courses available from November to April, from retreats and yoga holidays to daily drop-in workshops, meditation and yoga sessions, along with a spa, massage and 'massage camp' for those wanting to learn the tricks of the tickly trade. Its largely organic, vegetarian restaurant dishes up tasty buffet brunches and dinners daily to guests and drop-in casuals alike.

Fabulous Body Care (☎ 9420896843; behind Oasis Restaurant; massage from Rs800; ⏲ 9am-8pm) Ayurvedic massage is to be had here from the delightful Shanti, whose clients have included Dawn French. Try the rejuvenating 75-minute massage and facial package, or go for an unusual 'Poulti' massage, using a poulticelike cloth bundle containing 12 herbal powders, which is dipped in warm oil and comes especially recommended for treating back pain.

Sleeping & Eating

There are lots of coco-huts for Rs400 or thereabouts down on the beach; as with most destinations in Goa, the huts change appearance, owner and prices seasonally, so it's best to do a bit of trawling for the best before you take your pick. Dining options are largely of the standard beach-shack variety, with most places dishing up a decent range of Indian and international cuisine.

Shree Gopal Supreme Pure Juice Centre & Cafe (juices Rs30-35; ⏲ 7am-10pm) On the road down to the beach, thirst-quenching juicy combi-

nations are squeezed and served up in a cute little chill-out area. Lots of notices are posted in the vicinity, with info on the latest yoga class locations.

Dunes Holiday Village (☎ 2247219; www.dunes goa.com; huts/family r from Rs630/1500) An established place with 20 huts of various shapes and sizes, the accommodation here, while unspectacular, is comfortable and well equipped, making it a good fall-back in busy high season. Staff here can also arrange day trips by boat to Anjuna's Wednesday flea market, and dolphin-watching expeditions.

Cuba Retreat (☎ 2645775; www.cubagoa.com; d with/without AC Rs1500/1050; ⚡ 🖳) Those enterprising folks from Cuba seem to get everywhere, including to this spick and span set of suites just a few moments walk from the beach. Though it didn't seem too pricey to us, Cuba's website claims it serves up 'exorbitant seafood delicacies' in its great courtyard bar-restaurant.

Villa River Cat (☎ 2247928; www.villarivercat.com; d Rs1700-3600; ⚡ 🖳) This fabulously unusual circular guest house, filled with art, light and antiques, makes for a wonderful and extremely popular – stay. Hence, the management advises to book an astonishing eight months ahead for a stay during high season.

Elsewhere (www.aseaescape.com; tents/houses per week from US$759/1308; 🖳) Though the exact location of this heavenly set of historic beachfront houses, and Otter Creek Tents (its canvas alter ego), is a quite closely guarded secret, it's safe to say that somewhere around Mandrem, on a secluded spit of land, lies Elsewhere. Choose from four beautiful beachfront houses, enticingly entitled the Piggery, Bakery, Priest's House and Captain's House, or from three luxury tents, each sleeping two (both houses and tents are only available for weeklong stays) and revel in the delightful solitude that comes with a hefty price tag and a 60m walk across a bamboo bridge.

ARAMBOL (HARMAL)

☎ 0832

Arambol (also known as Harmal) first emerged in the 1960s as a mellow paradise for long-haired long-stayers. Today, things are still decidedly cheap and cheerful, with much of the village's mostly budget accommodation ranged in simple little huts along the cliff sides, but it's a bit more mainstream festival in style than in days gone by, and you have a feeling that many of today's 'hippies' shave off their fortnight's beards and take off their tie-dye once they're back to the nine-to-five.

The village's main covelike beach is gently curved and safe for swimming, perhaps the reason why, in recent years, Arambol has become popular among families with young children, who hang out happily with the uniformly dreadlocked, tattooed and creatively pierced individualists. Some people love Arambol for all this; others turn up their pierced noses and move along, leaving today's long-stayers to enjoy the pretty beach and extensive 'alternative' shopping opportunities provided by nonstop stalls all the way down the beach road and along round the cliff. If you're looking for a committed traveller vibe, this is the place to come; if you're seeking laid-back languidness, you might be better heading on down the coast to Mandrem.

Orientation & Information

If you're arriving in Arambol with your own transport from further south, the road from the NH17 highway takes you through the pleasant, parochial town of Pernem. Take a right here when you arrive at the large temple complex, unmistakeable for its large elephant sculptures, and wind your way along a scenic high road beside the lazy, island-studded Terekhol River where fishermen in dugouts ply the waters. This trip alone almost makes a visit to Arambol worthwhile.

Buses from Mapusa stop on the main road at the 'backside' (as locals are fond of saying) of Arambol village, where there's a church, a school and a few local shops. From here, a side road leads 1.5km down to the rest of the village, and the beach is about another 500m further on.

Everything you'll need in the way of services – dozens of internet outfits, travel agents, moneychangers and the like – you'll find in abundance on Glastonbury St, the road leading down to Arambol's beach. Internet access here generally costs Rs30 to Rs40 per hour, and money-changing commission rates are all comparable. There are also several agencies towards the top of the road offering parcel services with Federal Express and DHL deliveries, and by air and sea mail.

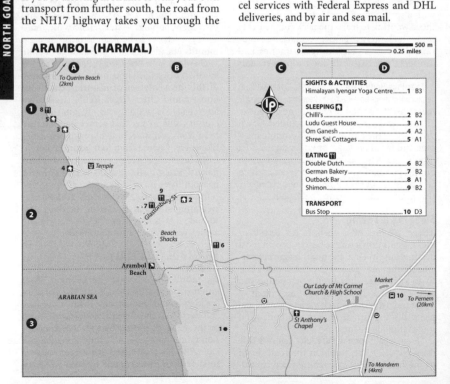

ARAMBOL (HARMAL)

| SIGHTS & ACTIVITIES | |
| Himalayan Iyengar Yoga Centre | 1 B3 |

SLEEPING	
Chilli's	2 B2
Ludu Guest House	3 A1
Om Ganesh	4 A2
Shree Sai Cottages	5 A1

EATING	
Double Dutch	6 B2
German Bakery	7 B2
Outback Bar	8 A1
Shimon	9 B2

| TRANSPORT | |
| Bus Stop | 10 D3 |

To Querim Beach (2km)

Temple

Glastonbury St

Beach Shacks

Arambol Beach

ARABIAN SEA

Our Lady of Mt Carmel Church & High School

Market

To Pernem (20km)

St Anthony's Chapel

To Mandrem (4km)

Activities

On the sand dunes of Arambol Beach is **Himalayan Iyengar Yoga Centre** (www.hiyogacentre .com; Arambol Beach), which runs five-day courses in hatha yoga from mid-November to mid-March. This is the winter centre of the iyengar yoga school in Dharamsala, and is run by the same teacher, Sharat Arora. Five-day courses for new and more-experienced students cost Rs1800, with additional days of instruction available at a reduced rate. Booking and registration must be done in person at the centre on Tuesday at 2pm. Courses start on Friday. There are also intensive two- to three-week courses for more experienced hatha yoga devotees and special short courses combining yoga with ayurvedic treatment.

Aside from yoga and beach lounging, the most popular pursuits in Arambol these days are **paragliding** and **kite surfing**. Several operators give lessons and rent equipment on the very south of Arambol beach; walk down there, or check out some noticeboards, to find out who's renting what this season.

Sleeping

Accommodation in Arambol is plentiful, almost all of the budget variety, and it pays to trawl the cliffside to the north of Arambol's main beach stretch for the best of numerous hut options. Here you can expect simple accommodation, mostly without private bathroom but with the benefit of incredible sea views (along with attendant breezes). Most cost around Rs350 to Rs500 in high season, and it's almost impossible to book in advance – simply turn up early in the day to check out who's checking out of your dream hut.

Chilli's (☎ 9921882424; Glastonbury St; d Rs300) This clean and simple place, owned by friendly and helpful Derek Fernandez, is one of Arambol's best nonbeachside bargains. Chilli's offers 10 nice, no-frills rooms on the road down to the beach, all with attached bathroom, fan and a hot water shower. There's an honour system for buying self-service bottled water from the fridge on the landing.

Om Ganesh (☎ 2297675; r Rs350-400) Popular huts, especially those on the sea-side of the coastal path, as well as a great place for lunch or dinner, with almost everything you can think of on the menu (if you can manage to decode entries such as 'gokomadi' in the Mexican section).

Shree Sai Cottages (☎ 2262823; shreesai_cottages @yahoo.com; huts Rs400) A good example of what's

VIPASSANA – THE ART OF SILENCE

Chances are that during your Goan sojourn you'll see Vipassana courses on offer, and wonder what exactly they involve. Vipassana, roughly meaning 'to see things for what they really are', is a meditation technique most often taught in Goa as a 10-day residential retreat, concentrating on 'self-transformation through self-observation'. In practice, this translates as 10 days of meditation, clear thought and near silence, abstaining from killing, stealing, lying, sexual activity and intoxicants, and concentrating at length on one's own breathing. Sounds like your cup of decaffeinated tea? Consult www.dhamma .org for more detailed information.

on offer, Shree Sai has simple sea-facing huts a short walk north from the main Arambol Beach, with lovely views out over the water, and a calm, easygoing vibe.

Ludu Guest House (☎ 2242734; r Rs700-1000) A cut above many other Arambol options, Ludu offers simply decorated, clean and bright cliffside rooms with attached cold-water showers. Hot water can be ordered by the bucketful.

Eating & Drinking

Plenty of cute, sparkly little places are dotted along the top part of the road curving down towards the beach. Many change annually; stroll along and see what organic, glitter-ball and parachute-silk destination takes your fancy. For simpler fare, head up to the village, where chai shops and small local joints will whip you up a chai for Rs4 and a thali for Rs40.

Meanwhile, all along the beach you'll find the usual assortment of traveller-friendly menus, attempting (with wildly varying levels of success) everything from thick Tibetan *thukpa* (noodle soup) to crunchy Korean *kimchi* (pickled vegetable dish). Most drinking is undertaken in beach shacks, which often serve happy-hour cocktails alongside a dose of live music or a DVD film screening or two.

German Bakery (cake from Rs40; ☺ 7am-late) This rather dim and dingy corner cafe is exceptionally popular, with great cakes including lemon cheese pie (Rs50) and a scrummy chocolate biscuit cake (Rs40). Big breakfasts come in at around the Rs90 mark.

Outback Bar (mains from Rs50) Seafood is a speciality at this nice place tucked away from the Arambol action; it also makes a fantastic spot for a sundown cocktail or two.

Blue Sea Horse (mains from Rs70) Situated just where beach meets street, Blue Sea Horse serves a solid all-day menu with extensive seafood options when the catch comes in, but its popularity soars come sunset, with mean cocktails and a nightly movie (usually screened around 7pm) on offer.

Double Dutch (mains from Rs70) An ever-popular option for its steaks, salads and famous apple pies, this is a great place to peruse the noticeboard for current Arambolic affairs, while munching on a plateful of cookies or a huge, tasty sandwich.

Fellini (pizza from Rs90) A long-standing Italian joint, perfect for when you're craving a carbonara or calzone, Fellini delivers all your wood-fired pizza and fresh pasta requirements in the thick of the Arambol action.

Shimon (8am-midnight) If you can navigate the sometimes surly service, Israeli-owned Shimon's is a good place to fill up on a tasty felafel (Rs70) before hitting the beach. For something more unusual, go for *sabich* (Rs70), crisp slices of eggplant stuffed into pitta bread along with boiled egg, boiled potato, salad and spicy relish.

Getting There & Away

Buses from Mapusa stop on the main road at Arambol (Rs12). From here, follow the road about 1.5km through the village to get to the main road down to the beach, or hop into a rickshaw for Rs20. Places in the village advertise scooters and motorbikes for hire, for Rs150 and Rs200, respectively, per day. A prepaid taxi to Arambol from Dabolim Airport costs Rs975.

NORTH OF ARAMBOL
Querim

Quiet Querim's beach is the place to come to while away the hours in peace, with only the occasional beach shack for company. Backed by a shady cover of fir and casuarina trees – though sadly this hinterland is becoming a little litter-blown – there's not much to do here but have a leisurely swim, settle back with a book, and revel in the tranquillity that descends so close, yet so far, from the Arambol action.

If you're keen to stay here, wander around the village set back from the beach, where you'll find a scattering of 'rooms for rent' signs, and some entire village houses up for grabs.

To get to Terekhol (the most northerly point in Goa) and its fort, it's fun to hop on board Querim's **ferry** (pedestrians/motorbikes/cars free/Rs4/Rs10; 7am-10pm, every 30 min) that chugs passengers and vehicles across the Terekhol River from the ferry landing at the very end of the village. If you find yourself stranded at low tide on the opposite side – when services are suspended for several hours – head downstream several kilometres to a second ferry point, winding your way through a surreal amber landscape of iron-ore mines.

Terekhol Fort

At the northernmost point of Goa is Terekhol (Tiracol) Fort, perched high above the banks of the river of the same name.

Originally built by the Marathas in the early 17th century, the fort was captured by viceroy Dom Pedro de Almeida in 1746. The fort was rebuilt and the glum little Chapel of St Anthony, which takes up almost all of the available space within it, was added.

The fact that the fort falls on the 'wrong' side of Goa's natural northern border, the Terekhol River, led it to be involved in considerable controversy. In the late 18th century the British demanded that it be handed over to the Empire, and in 1825, when the first Goan-born governor, Dr Bernardo Peres da Silva, was ousted, his supporters took over the fort. His own forces mutinied at the last moment, and met their deaths at the hands of the Portuguese. Finally, in 1954 Goa's entire northern border came to be at the centre of anti-Portuguese demonstrations. Several pro-India supporters hoisted an Indian flag over the fort's ramparts, and two were killed as a result; a plaque here still attests to this today.

Today the fort is far more peaceable and better known as the **Fort Tiracol Heritage Hotel** (2276793; www.nilaya.com/tiracol.htm), run by the same folks who run the exclusive Nilaya Hermitage (p158). The hotel is a hit with travellers for its romantically decked-out rooms, impeccable service and stunning views out over Querim, the Terekhol River and the Arabian Sea. With only seven rooms, each one named after a day of the week, this is your chance to really get the feel for life in one of Portugal's maritime bastions, and perhaps live out all those Rapunzel fantasies. Call or email for prices.

South Goa

South Goa, bounded to the north by the wide Zuari River and to the south by the neighbouring state of Karnataka, could well be seen as the quieter, shyer sister of her older, party-friendly North Goa sibling. Though the resorts have made it here too – Colva and Cavelossim being the two biggest – the pace never reaches the frenetic levels of Calangute or Candolim further north, and the resorts still peter out quickly into palm groves and paddy fields.

At the region's northern end stands shabby, workaday Vasco da Gama, its biggest city and major port. Further south you'll find Margao, the region's other main urban conurbation and administrative and transport hub. What Margao lacks in sights, it makes up for in its easygoing atmosphere, with all the bustle, but none of the hassle, of a true Indian town.

Taking to the coast, the northern half of the region, from the Zuari River down to the Sal River, is the most developed. The coast is punctuated with top-end five-star resorts, which, for all their sins, have managed to keep the beautiful shoreline free from midrange concrete-block development. Looming large on the traveller radar are uncharming Colva – a favourite among domestic tourists – and only slightly more appealing Cavelossim – a big winner with package-holiday Brits.

Below the Sal River, things slow down considerably, and Palolem, though well and truly 'discovered', remains an alluring and appealing backpacker favourite. Along this stretch you'll still be able to find the beach solitude you're seeking, and villages little changed by the impact of tourism. Inland you'll find some fabulous historic sights, plenty of bucolic bliss and Goa's most easily accessible wildlife reserve, making the south a redolent, rewarding and re-energising place to base yourself.

SOUTH GOA

HIGHLIGHTS

- Laze the weeks, or months, away on still lovely, still laid-back **Palolem Beach** (p204)
- Head out into the hinterland to seek out the little-visited **Usgalimal rock carvings** (p189)
- Explore a colonial *palácio* (palace) relic or two in the village of **Chandor** (p187)
- Spend the afternoon with four-legged friends, playing with the puppies at **GAWT dogs' home** (p199) in Curchorem
- Seek out your own stretch of empty sands on the coastline somewhere between **Mobor** (p201) and **Varca** (p198).

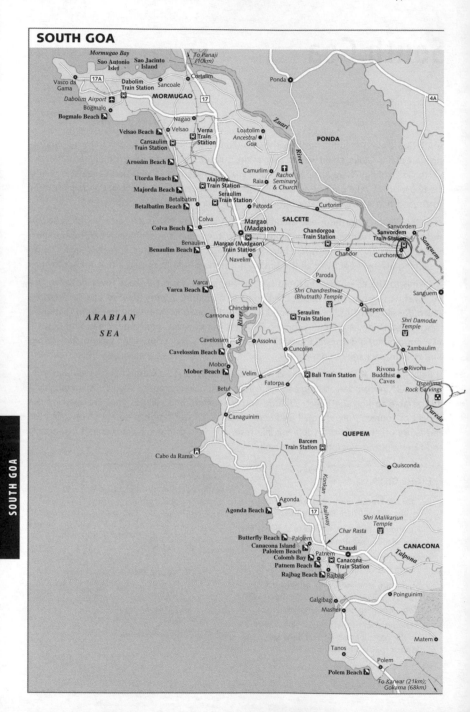

SOUTH GOA

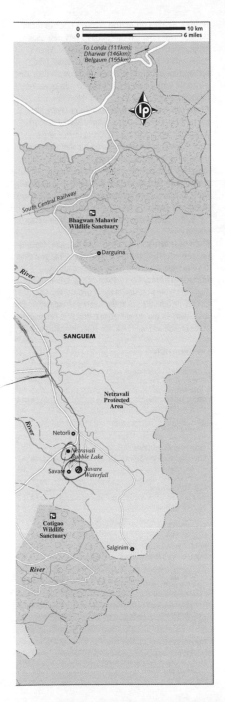

MARGAO

☎ 0832 / pop 94,400

The capital of Salcete province, Margao (also known as Madgaon) is, along with coastal Vasco da Gama, the main population centre of South Goa and is a happy, bustling market town of a manageable size for getting things done. If you're basing yourself in Goa's south, it's a useful place for shopping, organising bus and train tickets, checking emails or simply enjoying the busy energy of big-city India in manageable small-town form.

Though the modern town favours commerce over culture, this wasn't always the case. Before the Portuguese conquests of the 16th century onward, Margao was a centre for both pilgrimage and learning, with dozens of Hindu temples and a library of thousand upon thousand of volumes. However, all traces were destroyed by the Portuguese, as Margao became absorbed into their 17th-century Novas Conquistas (New Conquests).

Today, it nevertheless makes for a nice wander, while its small Shiva temple, just south of the covered market, still attracts Hindus each evening, to light candles and incense, and leave offerings of garlanded marigolds and coconuts to the ever-popular god. If you happen to be in town towards Christmas, Margao's Christians also hold a large fair to celebrate the Feast of Our Lady of the Immaculate Conception around 8 December.

Orientation

Margao's town centre, ranging around the Municipal Gardens, is quite small and compact, with its shops, restaurants, ATMs and covered market all within easy reach. To the north of town, the old Portuguese-flavoured Largo de Igreja district, with its Church of the Holy Spirit, is worth a stroll; about 1km north beyond it is the main (Kadamba) bus station.

About 1.5km southeast of the Municipal Gardens is Margao's train station (also known as Madgaon train station), a main stop on the north-to-south Konkan Railway (see p240), which has replaced the now-defunct Old Margao train station, just to the east of the flyover on the south end of town.

Information

There are plenty of banks offering currency exchange and 24-hour ATMs ranged around the Municipal Gardens, and on the western extension of Luis Miranda Rd. GTDC trips

SOUTH GOA

(see p235) can be booked at the front desk of the Margao Residency hotel, also on Luis Miranda Rd.

Cyberlink (Caro Centre, Abade Faria Rd; per 20 min Rs8, per hr Rs20; ☉ 8.30am-7pm Mon-Sat) Reasonably swift internet access on the central square. Be sure to heed the notice that requests you to 'Register yourself before sitting on the PC'. Fax and international call services are also available.

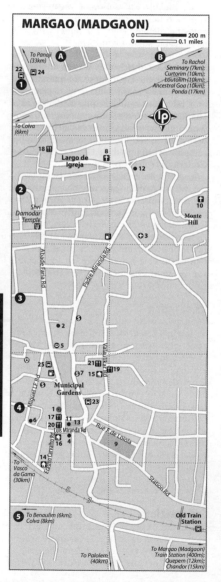

MARGAO (MADGAON)

Golden Heart Emporium (☎ 2734250; Confidant House, Abade Faria Rd) One of Goa's very best bookshops, crammed with fiction, nonfiction, children's books, and illustrated volumes on the state's food, architecture and history. It's situated down a little lane off Abade Faria Rd, on the right-hand side as you're heading north.

Grace Cyber Cafe (1st fl, Reliance Trade Centre, Valaulikar Rd; per hr Rs20; ☉ 9.30am-7.30pm Mon-Sat) A spanking new place in the centre of town, Grace has reliable, fast connections and a number of other services including CD writing and DVD direct from USB.

Hospital (Hospicio; ☎ 2705664; Padre Miranda Rd) Has a casualty department and a well-stocked 24-hour pharmacy. It's about 500m northeast of the Municipal Gardens.

Maharaja Travels (☎ 2732744; Luis Miranda Rd; ☉ 9am-1pm & 3-6pm Mon-Sat) Great for long-distance bus tickets.

Main post office (☉ 9am-1.30pm & 2-4pm Mon-Sat) On the north side of the municipal gardens. The post office can also arrange Western Union money transfers.

Municipal library (☉ 9.15am-1pm & 2.45-6.30pm Mon-Fri) On the west side of the Secretariat Building, you'll find respite from the sun at the library's newspaper reading room, wherein you're required to collect your newspaper at the counter and then sit in the seat designated only for

INFORMATION
Cyberlink	**1**	A4
Golden Heart Emporium	**2**	A3
Grace Cyber Cafe	(see 15)	
Hospital	**3**	B2
Maharaja Travels	**4**	A4
Main Post Office	**5**	A3
Paramount Travels	**6**	A4
Thomas Cook	**7**	A4

SIGHTS & ACTIVITIES
Church of the Holy Spirit	**8**	A2
MC New Market	**9**	B4
Mount Church	**10**	B2
Municipal Library	**11**	A4
Sat Burnzam Ghor	**12**	B2
Secretariat Building	**13**	A4

SLEEPING
Hotel La Flor	**14**	A5
Hotel Tanish	**15**	A4
Margao Residency	**16**	A4

EATING
Casa Penguim de Gelados	**17**	A4
Casa Vaz Tea Shop	**18**	A2
Gaylin	**19**	A4
Longhuino's	**20**	A4
Tato	**21**	A4

TRANSPORT
Bus Stand	**22**	A1
Buses to Palolem, Colva, Benaulim & Betul	**23**	A4
Kadamba Bus Stand	**24**	A1
Old Bus Stand	**25**	A4

readers of that particular paper; you'll be pleased to know it's a 'No Spitting and No Smoking Zone'.

Paramount Travels (☎ 2731150; paramount5@yahoo .com; Shop 5, Commerce House, Luis Miranda Rd; ⏱ 9am-1.30pm & 3-6pm Mon-Sat) A few doors down from Longhuino's, this well-established and reliable agency handles international and domestic flight tickets.

Thomas Cook (☎ 2714768) A reliable place to change money, on the eastern side of the Municipal Gardens.

Sights

CHURCH OF THE HOLY SPIRIT

Margao's main church also comprises probably its most interesting attraction, first built in 1565, on the site of an important Hindu temple. Before demolition started on the temple, local Hindus managed to rescue the statue of the god Damodara, to whom the building was dedicated. It was secretly moved to a new site in the village of Zambaulim, around 30km southeast, where there is still a large temple today.

However, the new church didn't last long and was burned to the ground by Muslim raiders the same year it was built. It was soon replaced and a seminary was established, but both were subsequently destroyed, again by Muslim forces, after which the seminary was moved to Rachol, to the northeast.

The present church, built in 1675, has lasted rather longer. It remains in use as a parish church and is finely decorated inside. The impressive reredos (ornamental screen) is dedicated to the Virgin Mary, rising from ground level to the high ceiling, made more distinguished by the gilded and carved archway that stands in front of it. The church doors are usually unlocked throughout the day, and access is via the side entrance on the northern side. Outside, in the centre of a dusty square nowadays most often used for volleyball games, stands a 17th-century cross, atop a pedestal carved with images depicting the story of Easter.

LARGO DE IGREJA

Largo de Igreja, the area around the Church of the Holy Spirit, features a number of traditional old Portuguese mansions, in various states of decay or repair. The most famous is the grand, 1790 **Sat Burnzam Ghor** (Seven Gabled House). Originally, as its name suggests, there were seven of the distinctive high-peaked gables, of which only three remain, though it remains an impressive edifice.

Built by Sebastiao da Silva, private secretary to the viceroy, it sports an especially beautiful private chapel, dedicated to St Anna, and noteworthy for being the first private chapel in which a Goan family was permitted to privately perform Mass. Its upstairs salons are filled with a stunning assortment of porcelain, chandeliers, marble and damask. Though it's not open daily to the public, your best bet to arrange a visit is to contact the GTDC (p235) about a tour.

MONTE HILL

Located about 500m southeast of Sat Burnzam Ghor and a fair climb up Monte Hill, Margao's only hill, **Mount Church** is a simple whitewashed building, faced by a similarly diminutive piazza cross. A detour up here is worth it for the view: from the shade of a grove of palm trees in front of the church, it's possible to see straight across the coastal plain to the beaches of Colva and Benaulim.

MC NEW MARKET

Margao's crowded, covered canopy of colourful stalls (perfect for self-caterers) is a fun place to wander around, sniffing spices, sampling soaps and browsing the household merchandise.

Sleeping

Margao doesn't have the range of accommodation that you'd expect in a town of this size, and with the beaches of the south beckoning, there's no pressing reason to stay here. Most of the budget options in town are really of the rock-bottom variety: a few are strung between the Municipal Gardens and an area near the old train station, in case you're feeling hardy enough to inspect a few. Otherwise, the three choices listed present solid value for a night's sojourn.

Margao Residency (☎ 2715528; Luis Miranda Rd; s/d Rs425/500, d with AC Rs650; ⚡) The omnipresent GTDC's outfit in town, this is another reasonable midrange choice, with clean, fairly comfy rooms and a great central location just opposite Longhuino's. Other GTDC hotels and its vast range of tours can be booked at reception.

Hotel La Flor (☎ 2731402; laflorgoa@gmail.com; Erasmo Carvalho Rd; s/d from Rs550/650, with AC Rs690/800; ⚡) Tucked away in a quiet corner of town, despite its proximity to the railway line, the slowly ageing La Flor has certainly seen better days, but its light, clean rooms (the AC options with ominous-looking AC boxes) still offer a relaxing stay in the big city. All rooms come with a TV and many with AC. There's also a little leafy garden out the front for an afternoon Kingfisher.

Hotel Tanish (☎ 2735656; Reliance Trade Centre, Valaulikar Rd; s/d without AC Rs900/1500, s/d/ste with AC Rs1300/1900/2500) Without doubt the best place to stay in town, this top-floor hotel offers great views of the surrounding countryside, with stylish, well-equipped rooms. Suites come with a bathtub, a big TV and a view all the way to Colva.

Eating

Casa Vaz Tea Shop (Abade Faria Rd; dishes from Rs8; ☺ breakfast & lunch) Run by a lovely local, this teensy tea joint on the edge of the Largo de Igreja district serves up the best caramelised-oniony *bhaji-pau* (bread roll with a small curry for dipping) in South Goa for an equally teensy Rs12.

Casa Penguim de Gelados (opposite Municipal Gardens; veg thali Rs30; ☺ 8.30am-8pm Mon-Sat) Tea and ice creams are really the thing here, but this clean, fan-cooled place also does a decent vegetarian thali and an array of dosas and *idlis*.

Gaylin (Valaulikar Rd; mains from Rs40; ☺ noon-3pm & 6.30-11pm) Hidden behind opaque glass doors decorated with dragon motifs, you'll find generous, garlicky renditions of Chinese favourites dispense by friendly Darjeeling-derived owners, with recipes suitably spiced up to cater to resilient Indian palates.

Tato (Apna Bazaar Complex, off Valaulikar Rd; thalis from Rs40; ☺ Mon-Sat; Ⓥ) Down a small street east of the Municipal Gardens is this excellent, and highly fragrant, vegetarian restaurant popular with lunching locals. If you're indecisive, order a thali (traditional South Indian all-you-can-eat meal), though the *paneer chilli* (spicy Indian cheese) is the manager's personal favourite. It costs slightly more to eat upstairs in the icy AC, but the fan-cooled ground floor is perfectly fine too.

Longuinho's (☎ 2739908; Luis Miranda Rd; mains Rs40-90) Every day since 1950, quaint old Longhuino's has been serving up tasty Indian and Chinese dishes, popular with locals and tourists alike. To thoroughly hark back to the '50s, order the tongue roast for Rs80 (and that doesn't mean a very spicy masala) and follow it up with a rum ball (Rs15).

Getting There & Around

BUS

Local buses arrive and depart from the Kadamba bus stand 2km north of the Municipal Gardens. Many services also stop at the old bus stand in the town centre. Buses to Palolem, Colva, Benaulim and Betul stop at the Kadamba bus stand and at the bus stop on the east side of the Municipal Gardens. Services run to no particular timetable, but are cheap and frequent.

Though there are daily public buses to Mumbai (Rs700, 16 hours) and Bengaluru (Rs400, 14 hours), a better bet is to take a long-distance private bus, which are more comfortable, quicker and cost about the same. You'll find booking offices all over town; Maharaja Travels is one helpful choice.

Private buses to Mumbai (AC/non-AC Rs750/650, 12 hours), Bengaluru (AC/non-AC Rs700/350, 12 hours), Pune (AC/non-AC Rs750/650, 11 hours) and Hampi (sleeper/luxury Rs750/650, eight hours) all leave from the bus stand opposite the Kadamba bus station.

TAXI

Taxis are plentiful around the Municipal Gardens and Kadamba bus stand, and are a quick and comfortable way to reach any of Goa's beaches, including Palolem (Rs650), Calangute (Rs1000), Anjuna (Rs1000) and Arambol (Rs1700). Be sure to wear your best bargaining cap for negotiating your fare.

TRAIN

Margao's well-organised train station (also known as Madgaon train station), about 1.5km south of town, serves both the Konkan Railway and local South Central Railways routes. Its **reservation hall** (☺ 8am-2pm & 2.15-8pm Mon-Sat, 8am-2pm Sun) is on the 2nd floor of the main building. See p240 for details of Konkan Railway services.

A taxi or autorickshaw from the town centre to the station should cost Rs50.

AROUND MARGAO

As tempting as it is to head directly west to the beach from Margao, the area to the east and northeast of town is a rich patchwork of rice paddy fields, lush countryside, somnolent rural villages, superb colonial houses, and a smattering of historical and religious sites. With a day to spare and a hired motorcycle, car or taxi, you can cover most of the sights of interest, and still get back to the beach in time for your happy-hour cocktail.

Rachol Seminary & Church

Built in 1580 atop an old Muslim fort, the Rachol Seminary and Church stands near the village of Raia, 7km from Margao. Although it's not officially open to visitors, you'll likely be able to find a trainee priest to show you around its beautiful church and cloistered theological college.

Built by the Jesuits, the seminary soon became a noted centre of learning, graced with one of India's first printing presses. Among the seminary's most famous members were Father Thomas Stevens, who by 1616 had busily translated the Bible into Konkani and Marathi, to help with the conversion of the locals, and Father Ribeiro, who produced the first Portuguese-Konkani dictionary in 1626.

Work on the church, dedicated to Jesuit founder St Ignatius Loyola, began in 1576, four years before the founding of the seminary, and it has been maintained in excellent condition. Its splendid gilded reredos fills the wall above the altar, featuring an image of St Constantine, the first Roman emperor to convert to Christianity; fragments of St Constantine's bones are on display near the main doorway. One of the side altars also displays the original Menino Jesus (see p196), which was first installed in the Colva church, before being taken up to Rachol amid much controversy and general hoo-hah.

Not much evidence remains of the old Muslim fort, though the archway spanning the road up to the seminary is one remnant, as is the still discernible old moat at the bottom of the hill. Bits of Hindu sculpture also grace the hallways of the theological college, as does an ancient water tank beneath its central courtyard.

Loutolim
☎ 0832

Architectural relics of Goa's grand Portuguese heritage can be seen around the unhurried village of Loutolim, some 10km northeast of Margao. The village hosts a number of

---

TAKE THE LOW ROAD

Take your moped, your Enfield Bullet, your Ford Ambassador taxi or your little hired Hyundai and hit the open road – avoiding cows, pedestrians, careening trucks, chickens, dogs and the assorted other obstacles that make Goan roads something of a thrilling ride. Take your time, take a hot chai here and there, and savour the stunning scenery – and a local lunch at your own, newly discovered roadside cafe – on one of the state's most gorgeous southern stretches of pot-hole-plentiful tarmac.

- **Cavelossim to Agonda** Hop aboard the rusty rub-a-dub ferry at Cavelossim (p199), and meander the coastal road – with stunning views down to the sea – stopping off at windswept Cabo da Rama fort (p202), all the way down to sleepy, seaside Agonda (p202).

- **Cotigao Wildlife Sanctuary** (p210) Though its roads are bumpier than most, a trip out along the lanes of this sanctuary, towards the Western Ghats, takes you through tiny villages, tracts of forest and farmland, and miles of untouched countryside, complete with haystacks and oxen pulling the plough.

- **Quepem to Usgalimal** Delve deep into the Goan hinterland with a drive out from busy little Quepem's Portuguese palace (p188) to Usgalimal's ancient rock carvings (p189), hidden away along the course of a lazy stream.

- **Colva to Velsao** Head north from busy beachfront Colva (p194), up the scenic coast road past dozen upon dozen of crumbling Portuguese palaces. Stop off here and there to discover deserted stretches of beach, and climb up to Velsao's Our Lady of Remedios chapel (p192) for the view back down.

- **Vasco da Gama to the NH17** Hug tight to the southern bank of the Zuari River, heading east from Vasco da Gama (p189) to take an interesting drive past shipbuilders, rusting trawler hulks and a couple of tiny riverine islands.

- **Heading east to Netravali** Embrace the spirit of adventure, with a jaunt down south off the NH17 highway to the 'bubble lake' and a hidden waterfall at Netravali (p210). You'll likely get lost several times along the way, but getting there, through thick forest, is more than half the fun.

impressive Portuguese mansions but just one, **Casa Araujo Alvares** (admission Rs125; ☺ 10am-6pm), which was built in 1757, is officially open to the public. It may not be as brimming with atmosphere as some of the other examples you'll find scattered across the state, but it's still well worth looking in on. Though Loutolim's other mansion masterpieces – Miranda House, Roque Caetan House and Salvador Costs House among them – aren't officially open to the public, you never know – linger longingly long enough outside the great wrought gates, and you might just be invited inside. Start out up at the central village square, with its scruffy, brooding whitewashed church, and wander from there.

If you're keen for high kitsch, be sure to drop in at **Ancestral Goa** (☎ 2777034; admission Rs20, camera Rs10; ☺ 9am-6.30pm), which encompasses a host of attractions including – but not limited to – 'Big Foot', a wishing rock, Mini Goa (as if the full-sized version weren't mini enough), and the 'longest laterite sculpture' in India.

Big Foot aside, the best reason to visit Loutolim is to bask in slow, sleepy Goan village life and gaze at the privately owned jewels of mansions scattered along the foliage-thick lanes. Without your own wheels, Loutolim is best accessed by taxi from Margao; a one-way fare should be about Rs120.

SLEEPING

our pick **Casa Susegad** (☎ 2106341; www.casasusegad goa.com; s/d from Rs3685/5170; ☒ ☒) With just four lovely, antique-filled rooms, this place makes a wonderful place to wind down, with an organic vegetable garden supplying delicious dinners; parakeets, monkeys, cats and dogs inhabiting the extensive gardens and a swimming pool glittering on the terrace.

Garça Branca (White Heron; ☎ 2777064; www.garca branca.com; d with/without AC US$70/60; ☒ ☒) This friendly option offers comfortable B&B accommodation in a nicely renovated ancestral home, still operated by descendants of its original owner.

BEACH FINDER: THE SOUTH

South Goa conceals (and reveals) the state's best beaches, perfect for picnicking, paddling, and peace and quiet. Here's a brief rundown of the south's main destinations, to help you decide where you're headed.

Bogmalo

What was once a small but perfectly formed bay roared to life (quite literally) with the arrival nearby of Dabolim Airport and its attendant hordes of weekenders, not to mention a rather ugly five-star hotel dipping its toes in the shallows. Nevertheless, if you've a night to kill before an early flight it makes an acceptable stop, and is best known for its respected diving operation, which offers a long list of dives, tours and certification courses.

Arossim & Velsao

Quiet, cool and happily undeveloped, both Velsao and Arossim are perfect for a picturesque paddle with just seabirds and the occasional shack for company. The only blight on the horizon is the scowling, spluttering petrochemical plant to the north, something only *The Simpsons'* Mr Montgomery Burns himself could have conceived.

Utorda, Majorda & Betalbatim

Clean and quiet stretches of sand, offering lots of space to frolic away from the sun-lounging crowds, characterise these three villages heading down south towards Colva. Perfect for exploring by scooter, they're dotted with beach shacks and backed by slowly crumbling Portuguese mansions. If you're keen to explore on four legs, rather than two wheels, seek out Frank, Goa's only horse-riding operator, based in Majorda (see p193).

Colva & Benaulim

Not the loveliest, nor the liveliest, of Goa's bigger resorts, Colva is a hit with domestic tourists, though its busy beach and raggle-taggle beach road are distinctly lacking in charm. Benaulim

Chandor

About 15km east of Margao, on the border between Salcete and Quepem talukas (districts), stands the small village of Chandor, a higgledy-piggledy collection of once-grand Portuguese mansions, ranged along a dusty main road, which now sees more long-distance trucks than grand, embroidered palanquins. It's a photographer's dream, with its paint-peeling gables – many topped with typically Portuguese carved wooden roosters – dripping ivy and the looming white Nossa Senhora de Belem church.

A kilometre east past the church, and open to the public, is the **Fernandes House** (☎ 2784245; ◷ 10am-5pm Mon-Sat), whose original building dates back more than 500 years, while the Portuguese section was tacked on by the Fernandes family in 1821. The secret basement hideaway, full of gun holes and with an escape tunnel to the river, was used by the family to flee attackers. A minimum Rs100-per-visitor donation is expected.

Despite modern appearances, Chandor was once far more than a picturesque, but decrepit, countryside village. Between the late 6th and mid-11th centuries it was better known as Chandrapur, the most spectacular city on the Konkan coast. This was the grand seat of the ill-fated Kadamba dynasty (see p30) until 1054 when the rulers moved to a new, broad-harboured site at Govepuri, at modern-day Goa Velha. When Govepuri was levelled by the Muslims in 1312, the Kadambas briefly moved their seat of power back to Chandrapur, though it was not long before Chandrapur itself was sacked in 1327, and then its glory days were finally, definitively, over.

Few signs remain of once-glorious Chandrapur, though the village has an archaeological site, where the foundations of an 11th-century Hindu temple and a headless stone Nandi bull (the vehicle of Shiva) still mark the spot.

The best way to reach Chandor is with your own transport, or by taxi from Margao

---

next door is quieter, though a little wind-blown and desolate, and offers better options for the budget and midrange traveller. The sands aren't exceptional, but both make decent bases for exploring this stretch of southern coast.

Varca, Cavelossim & Mobor

A string of luxury resorts, running south from Varca to the river mouth at Mobor, lead onto relatively empty, undeveloped beaches, with lots of room to stretch out unhassled by crowds. Cavelossim, while not a pretty development, sports a good range of eating and drinking options for night-time satiation.

Palolem

Palolem's golden crescent of sand remains one of Goa's gems, despite the hut-to-hut development along its entire length. The seas are shallow and swimmable, the days are long and languid, and there's little to do except indulge in a slow pace and perhaps a spot of beach volleyball, if you're feeling energetic.

Agonda, Colomb & Patnem

Patnem, a short distance south, is a quieter (if less picturesque) alternative to Palolem, with a wide sandy beach and good surf on windy days. South of here, small Rajbag Beach is dominated by the presence of the Intercontinental hotel, but makes a nice jaunt across the rocky headland. Colomb, meanwhile, a tiny bay between Patnem and Palolem, makes for relaxed beach-hut repose, though it's too rocky to be good for swimming. Agonda to the north is gorgeous, expansive, idyllically undeveloped and shuts up shop well before 10pm.

Polem

Tucked away at the southern end of the state, this empty little bay of golden sand, though notorious as a smugglers' den, makes for a nice day trip, by bus or scooter, from Palolem.

CHANDOR'S COLONIAL JEKYLL & HYDE

Braganza House, built in the 17th century and stretching along one whole side of Chandor's village square, is possibly the best – and worst – example of what Goa's scores of once grand and glorious mansions have today become. Granted the land by the King of Portugal, the house was divided from the outset into the east and west wings, to house two sides of the same big family.

The **West Wing** (☎ 2784201; 🕙 10am-5pm) belongs to one set of the family's descendants, the Menezes-Braganças, and is filled with gorgeous chandeliers, Italian marble floors and antique treasures from Macau, Portugal, China and Europe. The elderly, rather frail, Mrs Aida Menezes-Bragança nowadays lives here alone, but will show you around with the help of her formidable assistant. Between them, they struggle valiantly with the upkeep of a beautiful but needy house, whose grand history oozes from every inch of wall, floor and furniture.

Next door at the **East Wing** (☎ 2784227; 🕙 10am-5pm), prepare for a shock. Owned by the Pereira-Braganza family, descendants of the other half of the family, it's as shabby and decaying as the other is still grand. Paint peels from windows; ceilings sag; antiques are mixed in willy-nilly with a jumble of cheap knick-knacks and seaside souvenirs. The only high point here is the small family chapel, which contains a carefully hidden fingernail of St Francis Xavier (see p127), and even this – the chapel, not the fingernail – is beginning to show signs of neglect. You're unlikely to see a more stark architectural contrast at such close quarters for quite a while. It's a moving, if somewhat melancholy, experience.

Both homes are open daily, and there's almost always someone around to let you in. Though there are no official entry fees, the owners rely on contributions for the hefty costs of maintenance: Rs100 per visitor per house is reasonable, though anything extra would, of course, be welcome.

(Rs200, round trip). On 6 January, Chandor hosts the colourful **Feast of the Three Kings**, during which local boys re-enact the arrival of the three kings from the Christmas story.

Curtorim

About 5km north of Chandor is the small village of Curtorim, another of Goa's many peaceful pastoral places. If you're passing through, stop to have a look at the **Church of St Alex**, a large whitewashed affair with a rusty tin-roofed porch and a lovely, lavish interior, which looks out serenely onto a vast lily-studded lake. It's one of Goa's oldest churches and makes a grand spot to break a countryside journey.

Quepem

About 8km southeast of Chandor, in the busy small town of Quepem, stands the **Palácio do Deão** (☎ 2664029/9823175639; www.palaciododeao.com; admission free, but donation appreciated; 🕙 10am-6pm Sun-Thu, Fri by appointment). This recently renovated 18th-century palace, just opposite the Holy Cross Church, was once the home of the town's founder himself, and sits on the banks of the small Kushavati River, a tributary of the Pareda River. Plans are afoot to create a cultural centre here, but for now the house

and its beautiful, serene gardens make a great place for a stop-off between Chandor and the Usgalimal rock carvings further south. Call ahead to book a tour or arrange a delicious Portuguese-inspired lunch or afternoon tea on its lovely terrace.

Shri Damodar Temple

Approximately 12km southeast of Chandor and 22km from Margao, on the border of Quepem and Sanguem talukas, is the small village of **Zambaulim**, home to the Shri Damodar Temple.

Though the temple itself is uncompromisingly modern, the deity in its sanctum is anything but, having been rescued in 1565 from the main temple in Margao, which was destroyed by the Portuguese to make way for their Church of the Holy Spirit.

The ablutions area, built 200m back from the main buildings on the banks of the Kushavati River, is an ancient Hindu site, and its water – if you're feeling simultaneously brave and under the weather – is said to have medicinal properties.

Rivona Buddhist Caves

Continuing south from Zambaulim for about 3km, the road passes through **Rivona**, which consists of little more than a few houses spread out along the roadside. As the road leaves the village, curling first to the left and then right, there is a small sign on the left, pointing to Shri Santhsa Gokarn. A short way up the dirt track, which comes to an end at a tiny temple, the **Rivona caves** (also called Pandava caves) are on the left. Look out for strips of red cloth, hung auspiciously from an old tamarind tree nearby. The main caves entrance is just beside an ablutions tank and small well.

It's thought that the caves were occupied by Buddhist monks, who settled here some time in the 6th or 7th century AD. There's little to see, but the tiny compartments are an interesting reminder that religions other than Hinduism, Islam and Christianity also made it to Goa. There's a small staircase cut through the rock between the upper and lower levels of the caves. If you plan to have a poke about inside, you'll need a torch and be mindful to keep a very sharp eye out for snakes – the caves are teeming with these modern-day tenants.

Usgalimal Rock Carvings

One of Goa's least visited but most fascinating sights is tucked far into the depths of the countryside at Usgalimal, seeing only a teeny trickle of adventurous visitors and, so far, no busloads of tour groups whatsoever.

Make the effort to head out here and you'll be rewarded not only with some beautiful countryside driving, but also with a series of prehistoric **petroglyphs** (rock art), carved into the laterite stone ground on the banks of the Kushavati River, and depicting various scenes including bulls, deer and antelope, a dancing woman, a peacock and 'triskelions' – a series of concentric circles thought by some archaeologists to have been a primitive means of measuring time.

These underfoot carvings are thought to be the work of one of Goa's earliest tribes, the Kush, and were only discovered by archaeologists in 1993, after being alerted to their existence by locals. The images are thought to have been created some 20,000 to 30,000 years ago, making them an important, if entirely unexploited, prehistoric site. In order for you to make out the carvings better, you'll likely have a helping hand from a local, who sits patiently at the site waiting to drizzle water from a plastic bottle into the grooves; he appreciates a tip for his efforts.

To get here, continue past Rivona for about 6km and keep an eye out for the circular green-and-red Archaeological Survey of India signs. An unsealed road off to the right of the main road leads 1.5km down to the river bank and carvings, passing a large abandoned ore pit to the left, its flood waters deep and luminescent.

Shri Chandreshwar (Bhutnath) Temple

Approximately 14km southeast of Margao near the village of Paroda, a number of hills rise out of the plain, the highest of which is Chandranath Hill (350m). At the top, in a small clearing stands the Shri Chandreshwar (Bhutnath) Temple, a small but attractive 17th-century building in a lovely solitary setting.

Although the present buildings date from the 17th century, legend has it that there has been a temple here for almost 2500 years, since the moment a meteor hit the spot. The site is dedicated to Chandreshwar, an incarnation of Shiva who is worshipped here as 'Lord of the Moon'. Consequently it's laid out so that the light of the full moon shines into the sanctum and illuminates the deity, glittering gold. At the rear of the shrine, two accessory stone deities keep Chandreshwar company: Parvati, Shiva's consort, to the west, and Ganesh, his son, to the east. It's said that when the moonlight falls on it, the shrine's lingam (phallic symbol of Shiva) oozes water.

Leaving through the side entrance there is another small shrine standing separately that is dedicated to the god Bhutnath, who is worshipped in the form of a simple stone pinnacle that sticks out of the ground.

To get here, you'll need your own transport, since buses don't service this road. Head to Paroda, and ask there for the turn-off that takes you up the narrow, winding hillside road. There's a small parking area near the top, from which the approach to the temple is via a steep flight of steps.

VASCO DA GAMA
☎ 0832 / pop 150,000
Industrial Vasco da Gama is a busy port town, and was once a major transport hub for travellers, until its train station was eclipsed by Margao's, further south. Situated at the base of the isthmus leading to Mormugao Harbour, Vasco sports an oil refinery and Goa's biggest red-light district at Baina, where there's also a small (dirty) beach and a steady influx of

sailors and truck drivers. The city also has a reputation for being the crime centre of Goa, largely because of its outlying shanty towns, inhabited by migrant workers looking for employment in its port, iron-ore and barge-building industries. All that said, it's not a truly unpleasant place, and the city centre, though unkempt, is perfectly fine. But, with no sights of interest, it's just that there's no reason, as a visitor to Goa, to bother to come here at all.

Orientation & Information

Vasco da Gama's city centre is arranged along three parallel roads, bordered to the south by the railway line and to the north by Mormugao Bay. All the services you need – including ATMs, pharmacies and plenty of cheap *udupi* (South Indian vegetarian) restaurants – should you find yourself here and in need, are arranged along the most southerly road, Swatantra Path. Next, to the north you'll find Pe José Vaz Rd, and further again, FL Gomes Rd, off which, to the north again, is the fruit and vegetable market and a minibus stand. About 200m south of the minibus stand you'll find Vasco da Gama train station on Swatantra Path; from here the main bus stand is 400m east.

Sleeping & Eating

Vasco Residency (☎ 2513119; Swatantra Path; s/d Rs870/1155; ⌘) Secure, central and bland as they come, the GTDC's Vasco offering is serviceable if, for some reason, you find yourself stuck in Vasco. British visitors might feel at home with a trip to its Little Chef bar and restaurant.

Hotel La Paz Gardens (☎ 2512121; www.hotel lapazgardens.com; Swatantra Path; s/d standard Rs1400/1800, premium Rs1900/2400, deluxe ste Rs4000/4500; ⌘) This is the top place in town; a comfortable but unexceptional business hotel comprising 72 rooms with AC and satellite TV. Other facilities include a gym, sauna and three restaurants, including the locally popular Chinese restaurant, Sweet-n-Sour.

Getting There & Away

Express minibuses run nonstop from the minibus stand off FL Gomes Rd to Margao (Rs15, 45 minutes) and Panaji (Rs17, 45 minutes). There are also regular buses from here to the airport (Rs5) and Bogmalo (Rs6). Long-distance state buses don't depart from here,

but private buses to Mumbai (Rs300) and Bengaluru (Rs500) depart daily from outside the train station, where you'll find booking agents' offices. At the eastern end of Swatantra Path is a second bus stand, from which you can flag down eastbound buses.

A taxi from the airport costs around Rs100 and an autorickshaw Rs50.

AROUND VASCO DA GAMA
Sao Antonio Islet

If you've the taste for truly local flavour on a Sunday afternoon, venture about 6km east from Vasco da Gama, on the riverside road that takes you to the NH17 highway, where you'll find the tiny Sao Antonio islet in the middle of the Zuari estuary, joined by a thin isthmus to the main land. Here, at low tide, hundreds of locals converge to pick clams, wading waist-deep into the muddy tidal waters, accompanied by copious quantities of *feni* (palm liquor) and general merry-making.

Sao Jacinto

Another 1km along from Sao Antonio, you'll reach Sao Jacinto, a second little river island connected to the mainland by a causeway where you'll find an old lighthouse and two small whitewashed chapels. It's home to a small village of mostly fishermen and toddy (palm beer) tappers, and makes a pleasant place to pause for a few minutes, to have a quick look around.

Sancoale

A mournful monument to Portugal's past glories is on display at Sancoale, another 1km past Sao Jacinto, where you'll find all that's left of **Nossa Senhora de Saude** (Our Lady of Health), a once-impressive 1566 church, built to commemorate the spot where the first Jesuits touched down in Goa in 1560. A fire ravaged the church in 1834, and all that's left now is a highly decorative part of the facade, worth stopping off to see by following the Archaeological Survey of India sign that leads the way off the main road.

BOGMALO TO BETALBATIM

The northern section of South Goa's coastline extends from Bogmalo, just a few kilometres south of Dabolim Airport, down to Mobor, perched on the headland above the mouth of the Sal River. The main village-based resorts here are Colva and Benaulim, both rather lacklustre compared to the smaller villages dotting the coastal road, but nevertheless equipped with decent facilities and a good range of restaurants. Colva, in particular, tends to attract a domestic holidaying crowd, while Benaulim is a lower-budget, marginally more atmospheric choice. Meanwhile, Cavelossim, further south, is a firm favourite on package-holiday itineraries, with a scruffy village, quietly buzzing nightlife and a long, uninterrupted beach.

To experience the beauty of this area, head to the deserted stretches of beach between the local villages and sprawling five-star resorts between Velsao and Betalbatim, where you'll find little other than seabirds floating on the thermals and scuttling sand crabs to keep you company.

Bogmalo
☎ 0832

So close and yet so far, Bogmalo is a world away from the hubbub of Dabolim Airport and its polluted surroundings, though in fact it's just a 4km, 20-minute taxi ride. The roar of the surf is joined by the roar of arriving and departing planes, both from the civilian airport and from its military neighbour. Its beach is a small, pretty bay, tragically marred by the '70s-style Bogmalo Beach Resort, which somehow evaded the restriction requiring all hotels to be built at least 500m from the high-tide line.

It makes a decent stop if you've got an hour or two to kill before a flight, or if you're keen to experience Goa's underwater scene, courtesy of its highly respected diving outlet. Otherwise it's not especially appealing, cramped with ragtag stalls, beach cafes and spluttering busloads of excitable domestic day-trippers.

SIGHTS & ACTIVITIES

Though there's not an extensive range on offer, there are usually a couple of jet skis available for hire on the beach, along with a windsurfer or two. Ask around, or wander along the beach to find a vendor and negotiate a price.

Full Moon Cruises (☎ 9764625198, 9764762988; Full Moon Cafe; boat trip per couple Rs3500). Despite the name, these boat trips aren't held at full moon, and nor are they really cruises. They're daily boat trips, tailored to their customers' requirements, usually involving a spot of dolphin-watching, a bit of fishing and a visit to Bat

Island (the name giving you a clue to its sole inhabitants), which floats, lush and calm, just off the Bogmalo coast. Trips usually last from 9am to 12pm, but affable organisers Rahul and Umesh will throw in more time for free if you'd like to stay out longer. Contact them at the Full Moon Cafe at the southern end of Bogmalo Bay.

Goa Diving (☎ 2555117, 2538204, 9822100380; www .goadiving.com) is an internationally respected outfit (with the distinction of having been the first dive school in the whole of India), with a range of dives to suit novices and would-be Jacques Cousteaux alike. Its booth is at the southern entrance to the beach, diagonally opposite the Full Moon Cafe. It offers lots of courses; some off local Grande Island, where you can explore the remains of the British-built SS *Mary*, and others at Pigeon Island, 85km to the south. Local dives start at Rs1700 for a one-tank dive; four dives plus transfers and one night's accommodation near Pigeon Island comes to Rs14,000. An introductory pool lesson plus four guided dives is Rs14,000 (or Rs16,000 for more advanced divers) and an open-water course costs Rs18,000.

If you've exhausted your options or your patience for hawkers down on Bogmalo Beach, the **Naval Aviation Museum** (☎ 5995525; adult/child Rs20/5, camera/video Rs10/25; ☺ 10am-5pm Tue-Sat) at the naval base on the road above the beach makes an interesting diversion. Full of men idling about, especially around its Cockpit Cafe, the museum offers a neat and interesting presentation of India's naval history, and its connection to machines of the air. Make sure to turn left into the museum gates, rather than heading on straight ahead, where you'll likely encounter a goose-stepping naval officer complete with snow-white socks pulled up to his knees, intent on making sure you don't get much further.

SLEEPING & EATING

If you've got a particularly early flight from nearby Dabolim Airport, you might consider spending a night at Bogmalo. Otherwise, there's no pressing reason to check in here. For lunch, three beach shacks – each offering a standard Indian menu and decent seafood – stand in a row: take your pick from the Full Moon Cafe, Stiff Waves and Dom's Cuisine.

Sarita's Guest House (☎ 2538965; saritasguest house@rediffmail.com; d Rs900) Sarita's has clean but unremarkable rooms, with a common balcony offering an unimpeded view of the beach.

Joets Guest House (☎ 2538036, 2538090; joets@san charnet.in; d Rs3950, extra adult/child Rs850/650) Down on the beachfront, this clean and simple guest house, run by the same operators as Coconut Creek, offers simpler rooms, but has nice views out over the bay. Rates also include airport transfers, that same American breakfast, and free use of the swimming pool and fitness room at Coconut Creek.

Coconut Creek (☎ 2538090, 2358100; coconut creek@dataone.in; cottages with/without AC Rs6000/5250; ❌ 🖳 🐟) Stylish cottages set up largely for package tourists are set up around a pool in a coconut grove, for a laid-back, but rather overpriced, stay. Rates include transfer to/from Dabolim Airport and a hearty 'American breakfast'.

GETTING THERE & AWAY

An irregular bus service runs between Bogmalo and Vasco da Gama (Rs6, 25 minutes). Buses depart from the car park in front of the entrance to the Bogmalo Beach Resort. Taxis and autorickshaws wait around in the same area; a taxi to the airport should cost a very steep Rs200 and an autorickshaw will be an equally pricey Rs100.

Velsao
☎ 0832

South from Bogmalo, Velsao marks the northerly starting point of South Goa's beautiful beaches. Despite the gloomy presence of the vast and looming Zuari Agro chemical plant to the north, Velsao's beach makes a quiet place to get away from it all, in the company of just a lifeguard, a scattering of tourists and a flock or two of milling seabirds.

The beach road travels through thick coconut groves past dozens of old bungalows, while the coastal road around this stretch makes for a delicious countryside drive, fringed with lily-pad-studded lakes and paddy fields and coconut groves stretching gently down to the sea.

If you're travelling the coast under your own steam, it's the view, rather than the plain little chapel itself, that should entice you to take the steep road east off the coastal road up to **Our Lady of Remedios** at the

top of the hill. On clear days, you'll have a gorgeous, camera-clicking view south along the calm, quiet sands – studiously ignoring the uglier northerly and easterly views up towards the monstrous fertiliser factory and surrounding industrial sprawl.

Arossim
☎ 0832

Quiet and clean Arossim, like Velsao to its north, is a good place to settle into solitude with a good book. Here, the simple **Starfish Beach Shack** (mains from Rs90) is the only place for a drink or lunch, with its sun beds and beach umbrellas occupying a very quiet patch. To get to the beach, follow signs for the Heritage Village Club hotel, then hop across the sandbags, over a rather desultory creek.

On Arossim Beach's approach road you'll also find the **Treasure** (☎ 2754228; thetreasure @rediffmail.com; Arossim Beach Rd, near Heritage Village Club). If you're a fan of the gorgeous Goan vintage furniture you'll see gracing many of the state's old homes and higher-end hotels, pick up your own pieces here from a selection that ranges from dripping chandeliers to carved four-poster beds. Don't miss the small shrinelike chapel on this converted mansion's staircase, a feature that graces the very best of Goa's colonial homes.

The top sleeping option in Arossim is the 18-hectare **Park Hyatt Resort & Spa** (☎ 2721234; www .goa.park.hyatt.com; d from Rs7500; ❌ 🖳 🐟) Rooms here are lavish and large, and the resort has plenty of features that would entice even the most adventurous to stay put. Its Sereno Spa, voted 'World's Number One Spa' by *Condé Nast Traveller* magazine readers in 2006 and spread over a series of stunning outdoor pavilions, offers a magical *Abhyanga* – 'four-hands' massage – performed simultaneously by two therapists. Gorgeous upmarket Goan cuisine is dished up at fantastic **Casa Sarita** (mains from Rs400; ☽ dinner), offering the piquant flavours of Goa in all their glory. Make for the *vindalho* or the Kingfish curry. You won't be disappointed.

Utorda
☎ 0832

A clean, if slightly characterless, stretch of beach, approached on sandbag stepping-stones and rickety bridges over a series of fairly stagnant pools, Utorda makes for a pleasant afternoon on its sands, taking your pick from a ragtag bunch of beach shacks, many of whose sun beds you can use. Though the pretty coast is offset by the hulking Zuari Agro chemical plant further north, it's still popular with holidaymakers from the surrounding swish resorts, and the beach has the added bonus of an on-duty lifeguard.

Daily **fishing and dolphin-watching trips** are in no short supply in Utorda. Take your pick from the seasonal offerings sold in and around the beach shacks that line the main stretch of sands.

SLEEPING & EATING

Zeebop by the Sea (dishes from Rs60; ☺ 10.30am-11.30pm) Renowned for its excellent seafood – or 'underwater treasures', as the restaurant itself describes its cuisine – simple Zeebop, just back from Utorda's main beach and opposite Kenilworth, is a firm favourite with locals in the know. Closed Good Friday.

Dom Pedro's House (☎ 713251; r with/without AC Rs600/500; ✵) A down-to-earth option, unusual on this strip of coast, on the left- hand side at the entrance to the beach road. It's a simple six-room affair run by a local family; note that it closes down annually between June and September.

Kenilworth (www.kenilworthhotels.com; d from US$120) Utorda's ritziest resort is a pleasant upmarket affair backing directly onto the beach with all the standard five-star bells and whistles. Its Mallika restaurant, open from 7pm till 11pm, offers 'Northern frontier' fine dining, with succulent kebabs, thick fluffy tandoori-oven breads, and other Punjabi- and Kashmiri-inspired delights.

Majorda
☎ 0832
Approached through pleasant, leafy Majorda village, Majorda Beach is a smarter, more-organised option than neighbouring Utorda. Here, the stagnant streams and puddles that blight the division between road and beach have been arranged to form a moat, which flows round into a pleasant stream, forded by small, bamboo bridges. The beach itself has about half-a-dozen Russian-oriented beach shacks, all serving up the standard beach fare with menu boards chalked up in Cyrillic. To get here, take the left-hand curve of the beach approach; the right-hand curve takes you down to the highly swish Majorda Beach Resort.

ACTIVITIES
Horse riding (☎ 9822586502; 20-min beach ride Rs200) Keen equestrians shouldn't pass up the chance for a sunset or sunrise ride along Goa's sands, and Majorda is currently the only place in the state to do it. Bookings with Frank, the proprietor, are essential, for rides ranging from beginner to advanced. The horses are tethered outside Greenland Bar & Restaurant (see below).

Treat Yourself Health Centre (☎ 9850183319; ☺ 6am-9pm) This spick and span little place in the heart of Majorda village offers a well-equipped gym, swimming pool and ayurvedic massage centre, run by a British expat. Rates for the gym and pool start at Rs100 per day, while massages begin at Rs700 for an hour-long session. Take a left-hand turn off the beach approach road.

SLEEPING
Rainbow's End (☎ 9822586596; r from Rs800) A great-value place for those looking to stay for a while, these simple self-contained units, situated in a characterful building amid a lovely garden, are on the left-hand side as you turn down towards the beach road.

our pick **Vivenda Dos Palhaços** (☎ 9881720221; www.vivendagoa.com; d from Rs4750; ▢ ✿) No beach bar or five-star facilities here, but this upmarket boutique hotel, run by a British brother-and-sister team whose family brews the superstrength Indian truck driver favourite Hayward's 5000 beer, is a gem of the south Goan coast. Rooms inhabit an old Portuguese mansion and older Hindu house, with sparkling courtyard pool and resident basset hound. There's also a top-end tent and self-contained cottage on offer.

Majorda Beach Resort (☎ 2754871; www.majorda beachresort.com; s/d from Rs7200/7700; ✵ ▢ ✿) Though rooms at this five-star could definitely do with a thorough overhaul, the Majorda Beach Resort gets consistently good feedback from domestic tourists, and while some aren't impressed with the high tariffs, almost everyone agrees that it's (almost) worth it for the beach stretching out at the end of the garden.

EATING & DRINKING
Greenland Bar & Restaurant (mains from Rs70; ☺ 10am-10pm) On Majorda's southern 'Cabana Beach', across a little bamboo bridge, you'll find cute Greenland, run by a lovely British couple from Kent. The Goan chef cooks up a range of local specialities including *xacutis* and *vindalhos*,

along with yummy banana fritters. It must be said, though, the couple are probably proudest of their spotlessly clean toilet. You'll find Frank's steeds (see p193) resting up just outside the restaurant.

Raj's Pentagon Restaurant & Garden Pub (mains from Rs90; ☺ till midnight) Opposite the Majorda Beach Resort on the right-hand side as you head to the beach, there's decent garden dining at this large, friendly place, worth stopping in at for a filling lunch or evening drink. Live music hits the stage here every night; on Thursday, it's acoustic tunes courtesy of the Friendly Brothers.

Betalbatim
☎ 0832

Though the beaches along this entire strip – from Mobor in the south right up to Velsao further north – are actually just different patches of one long and continuous stretch of sand, each place manages to retain its own very distinct and individual character. Betalbatim, just to the north of Colva, is a good example of what a difference a few hundred metres can make, as calm, quiet and pastoral as Colva is touristed and dust-blown. And even Betalbatim itself consists of several different smaller strips of beach – try **Sunset Beach**, or **Lovers' Beach**, which is suitably lovely: the only lovers to be seen when we visited were a pair of wheeling seagulls, along with the odd solitary dog and a lone lovelorn sea eagle. To get to Lovers' Beach, follow signs from the main road, passing a less lovely rash of time-shares on the way.

As well as Sunset and Lovers', there are a couple of other entrance points onto Betalbatim beach from the village, all more or less guaranteeing peace and quiet.

A local legend and also popular with Indian tourists, **Martin's Corner** (www.martins cornergoa.com; mains from Rs60; ☺ 11am-3pm & 6.30-11pm), near Sunset Beach, is a great place to try out Goan cuisine, in a relaxed and quite upmarket setting. The *xacutis* and *vindalhos* here are superb, and there are plenty of tasty vegetarian options on offer. There's live music most nights from 8pm. Plump for, or avoid, Wednesday, depending on your relationship with karaoke.

COLVA
☎ 0832 / pop 10,200

If it's a beach paradise you're after, you'll likely be disappointed with what's waiting to greet you in Colva. A large concrete roundabout marks the end of the beach road and the entrance to the beach, filled with day-trippers and listless hawkers. The main beach drag is lined with dreary stalls and shabby cafes; sure, it's got all the material needs you're seeking, but as far as atmosphere goes it's sorely lacking.

Perhaps the biggest reason to stay at Colva (or Benaulim, a touch south) is its central location if you're keen to explore this part of the coast (which stretches north as far as Velsao and south as far as the mouth of the Sal River at Mobor), which in many parts is empty and gorgeous. The inland road that runs this length is perfect for gentle scootering, with lots of picturesque Portuguese mansions and whitewashed churches along the way.

Information

Colva has plenty of banks and ATM machines strung along Colva Beach Rd, and a post office on the lane that runs past the eastern end of the church.

Hello Mae Communication (Colva Beach Rd; 15 min Rs10, per hr Rs30; ☺ 8am-10pm) Internet access, money exchange, and weekly Wednesday trips to Anjuna market for Rs150 per person. Keep in mind the stern warning: 'No Surfing of Porn Websites.'

Sights & Activities

Colva's beach entrance throngs with young men keen to sell you **parasailing** (per ride Rs500), **jet-skiing** (15 min Rs700) and **dolphin-watching trips** (per person around Rs250). There's little to choose between operators, which gives you significant leeway in terms of haggling for the best deal.

One place to stop off is at the **Goa Animal Welfare Trust (GAWT) Shop** (www.gawt.org; ☺ 10am-12.30pm & 5-7pm Mon-Sat) in Colva where you can borrow books from its lending library, or peruse the new and secondhand goods on offer. There's also a newly opened **GAWT Information Centre & Office** (☺ 9.30am-1pm & 3-5pm Mon-Sat), also in Colva, located below the Infant Jesus Church Hall, where you can find out more about the work of this wonderful organisation.

Sleeping

It's hard to recommend many budget or midrange options in Colva, since the majority are either horribly overpriced or, more simply, horrible. Indeed, since there's nothing midrange up-to-scratch enough to include, unless you're lying low in one of the town's groovier top end choices you're far better off heading down to Benaulim or pushing on further south.

BUDGET

Casa Mesquita (r Rs300) With just three rooms that go beyond simple and no telephone for bookings, this atmospheric old mansion on the main coast road is certainly the place to go if you thrive on the atmosphere that Colva lacks. Goodness knows when the rooms were last cleaned; nevertheless, the elderly owners are friendly, the paint's suitably peeling and the ghosts of better days linger lovingly in the shadows.

Sam's Cottages (☎ 2788753; r Rs350) Up where the countryside begins you'll find Sam's, painted a cheerful bright orange and with decent, clean rooms. If your name also happens to be Sam, prepare yourself for a particularly ebullient welcome.

La Ben (☎ 2788040; www.laben.net; r with/without AC Rs965/575; ❄) Neat, clean and not entirely devoid of atmosphere, this place is particularly known for its rooftop restaurant, though its rooms represent reasonable value.

TOP END

Beleza (☎ 2781300; www.belezagoa.com; d from Rs5000; ❄ ▢ ▨) Right out at the north end of Colva is self-contained Beleza, a smart new 30-room resort with well-equipped rooms in spacious

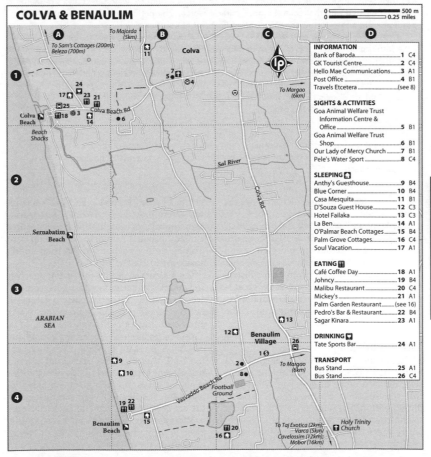

COLVA & BENAULIM

0 — 500 m
0 — 0.25 miles

INFORMATION
Bank of Baroda...............................**1** C4
GK Tourist Centre...........................**2** C4
Hello Mae Communications......**3** A1
Post Office..**4** B1
Travels Etcetera ....(see 8)

SIGHTS & ACTIVITIES
Goa Animal Welfare Trust
  Information Centre &
  Office...**5** B1
Goa Animal Welfare Trust
  Shop..**6** B1
Our Lady of Mercy Church **7** B1
Pele's Water Sport **8** C4

SLEEPING
Anthy's Guesthouse......................**9** B4
Blue Corner **10** B4
Casa Mesquita...............................**11** B1
D'Souza Guest House...................**12** C3
Hotel Failaka.................................**13** C3
La Ben **14** A1
O'Palmar Beach Cottages..........**15** B4
Palm Grove Cottages..................**16** C4
Soul Vacation **17** A1

EATING
Café Coffee Day............................**18** A1
Johncy...**19** B4
Malibu Restaurant **20** C4
Mickey's..**21** A1
Palm Garden Restaurant .....(see 16)
Pedro's Bar & Restaurant...........**22** B4
Sagar Kinara..................................**23** A1

DRINKING
Tate Sports Bar.............................**24** A1

TRANSPORT
Bus Stand.......................................**25** A1
Bus Stand.......................................**26** C4

To Majorda (5km)

To Sam's Cottages (200m); Beleza (700m)

Colva

To Margao (6km)

Colva Beach Rd

Colva Beach

Beach Shacks

Sal River

Colva Rd

Sernabatim Beach

ARABIAN SEA

Benaulim Village

To Margao (6km)

Vasvaddo Beach Rd

Football Ground

Benaulim Beach

Holy Trinity Church

To Taj Exotica (2km); Varca (5km); Cavelossim (12km); Mobor (16km)

SOUTH GOA

COLVA'S MENINO JESUS

If the only miracle you've experienced in Colva is finding a nice budget bed, the village's 18th-century **Our Lady of Mercy Church** has been host to several miracles of its own, of the rather more celestial kind.

Inside, closely guarded under lock and key, lives a little statue known as the 'Menino' (Baby) Jesus, which is said to miraculously heal the sick. Legend has it that the statue was discovered by a Jesuit priest named Father Bento Ferreira in the mid-17th century, after he was shipwrecked somewhere off the coast of Mozambique. The plucky missionary swam to shore, to see vultures circling a rocky spot. On closer inspection, he discovered the statue, apparently washed ashore after having been tossed overboard as worthless by Muslim pirates.

When he was posted to Colva in 1648, Father Ferreira took the Menino Jesus along with him, and had it installed on the high altar, where it promptly began to heal the sick and soon acquired some serious local celebrity. It wasn't long before it was worshipped with its own special **Fama de Menino Jesus festival**, which still occurs each year on the second Monday in October.

However, all was not smooth sailing for the Menino. When the Portuguese suppressed many religious orders in 1836, the Jesuits were forced to flee Colva, and took the Menino with them to their seminary in Rachol (see p185), where both they – and it – were safe. Colva's residents weren't pleased with the removal of their miracle-worker, and petitioned the head of the Jesuits in Rome, then the viceroy, then the king of Portugal himself for its return.

Finally they got the answer they hoped for, orders for the statue to go back to Colva. However, the Jesuits didn't quite seem to get around to returning it, and finally the Colvan villagers clubbed together and had their own replica made, furnished with a diamond ring that had fallen off the finger of the original Menino during the move to Rachol. Meanwhile, in Rachol, the first statue slowly appeared to lose its healing powers, while the newcomer healed away merrily, prompting the delighted villagers to claim it had been the ring, and not the statue, that was the source of its miraculous powers all the while.

These days, the distinctly unmiraculous Menino is still kept at Rachol Seminary, while its more successful successor only sees the light of day during the annual Fama festival. Then, the little image is removed from deep within the church's vaults, paraded about town, dipped in the river, and installed in the church's high altar for pilgrims to pray to, hoping for their own personal miracle.

---

villas, complete with huge flat-screen TVs, heavenly pillows and chilly AC.

Soul Vacation (☎ 2788144, 2788147; www.soul vacation.in; d from Rs5500; ✖ 🖳 🖳) Thirty restful white rooms arranged around nice gardens and a great pool are the trademarks of sleek Soul Vacation, set 400m back from Colva Beach. Equipped with all mod cons, it's a great – if slightly pretentious – place to unwind without ever even having to venture out of the resort itself.

Eating & Drinking

There are plenty of wooden beach shacks lining the Colvan sands, offering the extensive standard range of fare, and you'll spot this season's best by the crowds already dining within. For simpler eating, head up to the roundabout just before the church, where tourist joints are replaced by simple chai shops and thali places, and there are plenty of fruit, vegetable and fish stalls for self-caterers. At night, *bhelpuri* (crisp fried thin rounds of dough with lentils, puffed rice and onions) vendors set up camp here, dishing up big portions of the fried noodle snack for just a few rupees.

Sagar Kinara (mains Rs30-100; Ⓥ) A pure-veg restaurant with tastes to please even committed carnivores, this great place is clean, efficient and offers cheap and delicious North and South Indian cuisine all day long.

Café Coffee Day (cakes & coffees from Rs40; ☯ 8am-midnight) A pleasant enough place to escape the heat, this wannabe sleek joint offers a half-decent cappuccino (Rs44) along with a range of cakes, including the suitably '70s black forest gateau (Rs44), reminiscent of the era when Colva was still cool.

Mickey's (mains from Rs60) An ever-popular place to drink the afternoon away or munch lunch from the extensive Indian/Continental/

Chinese menu, Mickey's is usually busy and the food dispensed is fresh and filling.

Tate Sports Bar (mains from Rs100; ☺ 8am-midnight) Hearty English breakfasts, draught Kingfisher on tap and football on TV inhabit a comfier, more cosmopolitan drinking option than Colva is used to.

Getting There & Away
Buses run from Colva to Margao roughly every 15 minutes (Rs12, 20 minutes) from 7.30am to about 7pm, departing from the parking area at the end of the beach road.

BENAULIM
☎ 0832
A long stretch of largely empty sand, peppered with a few hawkers and stray dogs, laid-back, windswept Benaulim has the distinct feeling of an off-season Welsh seaside resort, were global warming ever to get that far. That said, it's a reasonable-enough place to relax on the sands, with a lifeguard present and plenty of sunbed-equipped beach shacks lining the stretch to the north of the main beach entrance. It might not be tropical bliss, but it's definitely decent.

Benaulim also has a special place in Goan tradition: legend has it that it was here that the god Parasurama's arrow landed when he fired it into the sea to create Goa. Modern-day archers, however, might choose a prettier spot.

Orientation & Information
Though Benaulim as a whole is sprinkled over a large area, most accommodation, eating options, grocery shops and pharmacies are concentrated along the Vasvaddo Beach Rd along the stretch around the crossroads and football ground. There are a couple of reliable travel agents in Benaulim that can arrange air, bus and train tickets, and will also change money.

Bank of Baroda (Vasvaddo Beach Rd) Just east from the junction of the Colva Rd, the ATM here professes to be 24-hour, but on our visit, at least, was closed. Since this is the only machine in town, it might be wise to stock up on cash at Cavelossim, Margao or Colva, just in case.
GK Tourist Centre (☎ 2770476, 2771221, 2770471; gktouristcentre@hotmail.com; Vasvaddo Beach Rd)
Travels Etcetera (New Horizons; ☎ 2770635, 2771218; newhorizonsgoa@sancharnet.in; Vasvaddo Beach Rd)

Activities
Water sports in Benaulim are not as prevalent as they are at more-crowded Colva, though some operators hang around the beach shacks. One of the most prolific is **Pele's Water Sport** (☎ 9822080045, 9822686011); jet skis cost Rs500 per 10 minutes, parasailing costs Rs500 per ride, and dolphin trips are Rs250 per person.

Sleeping
BUDGET
Lots of budget rooms for rent throng the main road towards the beach, and the lanes around it: walk around, shop around and bargain if you're even slightly outside high season (Christmas and New Year). Prices have slowly crept up, but there are still lots of family-run places with just a handful – or less – of rooms with bargain-basement prices.

Blue Corner (☎ 9850455770; www.blue-cnr-goa.com; huts from Rs600) One of only a handful of truly beachside places on this entire strip of coast, Blue Corner offers simple beach huts. Its restaurant gains stellar reviews from guests.

O'Palmar Beach Cottages (☎ 2770631; opalmar@ sancharnet.in; r Rs600; 🖳) Set amid a huge, dusty lot, the holiday-camp-style rooms, with odd, dark little sitting rooms, have the benefit of being close to the beach and possessing very friendly management. Internet access is available for Rs50 per hour.

our pick **D'Souza Guest House** (☎ 2770583; d Rs700) As you may guess from the name, this traditional blue-painted house is run by a local Goan family and comes with bundles of homely atmosphere, a lovely garden and just three spacious, clean rooms – making it best to book ahead.

Hotel Failaka (☎ 2771270; hotelfailaka@gmail.com; r Rs800) A fair walk from the beach, but good value if you have wheels. Don't be put off by the rather gloomy lobby: upstairs, the rooms at red-and-white painted Failaka are bright and sunny, and well equipped with hot water, TV and balconies.

MIDRANGE & TOP END
Anthy's Guesthouse (☎ 2771680; anthysguesthouse@ rediffmail.com; r Rs1300-1800) One of just a handful of places lining Benaulim's beach itself, Anthy's is a firm favourite with travellers for its warm service (manager Prabot is extremely friendly and helpful), its good restaurant, and its well-kept chalet-style rooms, which stretch back from the beach surrounded by a pretty

garden. Ayurvedic massage is available here for Rs500 per, um, squeeze.

Palm Grove Cottages (☎ 2770059; www.palmgrove goa.com; d with/without AC from Rs1575/1460; 🕸) Old-fashioned, secluded charm is on offer amid the dense foliage at Palm Grove Cottages, hidden among a thicket of trees on a road winding slowly south out of Benaulim. Guest rooms are atmospheric, and the ever-popular Palm Garden Restaurant graces the garden.

Taj Exotica (☎ 2771234; www.tajhotels.com; d from US$300; 🕸 🖳 🖭) If your budget runs to it, don't hesitate: here's one of Goa's plushest resorts, set in 23 hectares of tropical gardens 2km south of Benaulim, and just aching to pander to your every whim. It's probably best to just relinquish the struggle and let it.

Eating

Johncy (mains Rs60-120) Like Pedro's beside it, Johncy dispenses standard beach-shack fa-vourites from its location just back from the sand. Staff are obliging and food, if not exciting, is fresh and filling.

Pedro's Bar & Restaurant (mains Rs60-120) Set amid a large, shady garden on the beachfront and popular with local and international travellers alike, Pedro's offers standard Indian, Chinese and Italian dishes, as well as a good line in Goan choices and some super 'sizzlers'.

Palm Garden Restaurant (mains Rs60-140; ☺ lunch & dinner) A spotlessly clean and some-times pleasantly sociable restaurant set in a gazebo-shaped building in the gardens of Palm Grove Cottages.

Malibu Restaurant (mains Rs90-150) This place offers one of Benaulim's more sophisticated dining experiences in its secluded garden set-ting just a short walk back from the beach. It does great renditions of Italian favourites and has live jazz and blues on Tuesday evenings.

Getting There & Around

Buses from Margao to Benaulim are frequent (Rs8, 15 minutes); some continue on south to Varca and Cavelossim. Buses stop at the crossroads quite a distance from the main action (such as it is) and beach; it's best to hail a rickshaw (Rs20) for the five-minute ride to the sea.

VARCA, CAVELOSSIM & MOBOR

☎ 0832

Heading south from Benaulim, you'll travel a road lined with beautiful Portuguese rel-ics, paddy fields, whitewashed churches and farmland, encountering first the town of Varca – a sleepy village outside which sev-eral five-star resorts have sprung up. Next up is Cavelossim, an ever-increasing (but still quite pleasant and friendly) strip of stalls, malls, and midrange to top-end hotels running parallel to the beautiful white-sand beach. Finally, where the Sal River meets the ocean, you'll find little Mobor, dominated by the presence of the Leela, one of Goa's costliest hotels, and the peninsula tipped by a tiny fishing settlement of poor migrant fishermen from Orissa state.

These three destinations back a 10km stretch of beautiful, pristine beach, where it's little effort to find a comfy sun lounge or a deserted patch of virgin sands, de-pending on your preference. Luckily, the presence of these luxury residences (and the high precedent set for the price of sea-facing real estate here) seems to have saved this swathe of sands from tacky, midrange development. Even if you're not staying at one of the swanky addresses along it, with your own transport you've got plenty of opportunity to enjoy the sands (which belong to everyone, despite what some hotels might assert). Moreover, many re-sorts employ their own staff to keep the beachfront litter-free.

Locals report that some hotels have a nasty habit of assuring their comfortably cocooned guests that there's nothing to see and nowhere to go in the vicinity and that, if you do venture out far from its pearly gates, you'll likely be mugged – or worse. But wan-der the beaches or back lanes a little, and you'll likely come across a great places for a *bhaji-pau* breakfast (Rs6), a perfect spot for a cold beer or a friendly fisherman willing to take you out on his sunset adventures.

There are regular buses that serve the main coastal road, from Margao, via Colva or Benaulim, all the way down to Mobor. They run daily between around 8am and 10pm, every few minutes, and can be flagged down along the road. The furthest stop south drops you outside the grounds of the Leela, from which it's an easy walk to the beach or the Blue Whale, for a bite to eat.

Varca

A seemingly endless palm-backed strip of sand punctuated, here and there, by the

IT'S A DOG'S LIFE

The small town of **Curchorem**, situated inland in Goa about 6km past Chandor, is as sleepy and unremarkable as they get – except in one way. Here, housed in the old police station on the right-hand side of the main road, is the main dogs' home of the **Goa Animal Welfare Trust** (GAWT; ☎ 2653677; www.gawt.org) where southern Goa's sick and stray animals find rare solace.

It's almost impossible that you'll complete a visit to Goa without seeing an adorable stray puppy, or its older, desperately thin relative, and GAWT (along with International Animal Rescue in the north; see p72) tries its best to help them out, providing veterinary help for sick animals, shelter for puppies and kittens, sterilisation programs for street dogs and low-cost veterinary care (including anti-rabies injections) for Goan pets. It also deals with animal cruelty cases, and runs school 'pet awareness' programs.

The shelter is open daily from 9am to 5pm and volunteers are welcome, even just for a few hours on a single visit, to walk or play with the dogs. No donation is too small, and even your old newspapers – all those copies of the *Times of India* and the *Herald* you've bought from beach vendors – will be gratefully received for lining kennel floors, as will old sheets, towels and anything else you might not be taking home.

Saleable goods and old books will find a home at the **GAWT Information Centre & Charity Shop** (see p194) in Colva.

If you fall madly in love with that doe-eyed street dog that adopts you during your stay, it is possible – though lengthy and expensive – to take him or her with you back home. You'd need to satisfy quarantine requirements, which vary from country to country, but there are plenty of ways to do it if you're determined. The Trust can probably provide you with advice, and phone numbers of people who undertake animal transportation regularly. If all that seems too difficult, you can also adopt (and name) one of the shelter's long-term residents for about £50 per year.

'I just hope that this will continue,' says Charmian Byrne, GAWT's founder and driving force. 'We can't do this without tourists; it's the tourists that keep us going.' GAWT's happy to take long-term volunteers (though it can't provide housing or meals); there's also the chance for a male veterinary volunteer to work alongside its own current vet. It's a great idea for the recently veterinarily qualified, wanting to rack up some pro-bono experience – and extremely good karma to boot.

grounds of a luxury resort or a whitewashed Christian shrine, Varca is quiet, calm and almost entirely hawker-free, making it easy to find a quiet spot all to yourself. Outside the resorts, one good access point is the portion known as **Zalor Beach**. Follow signposts from Varca village, near the church. When you arrive a final sign declares: 'You are being watched. No Spitting or Abusing Children.'

SLEEPING

Dona Sa Maria Holiday Home (☎ 2745290; www.dona samaria.com; d Rs1000; 🄲 🖵 🖭) Further south from Varca, you'll pass the pretty village of Tamborim, comprising a stretch of beautifully rundown old Portuguese-style homes. Here you'll find this pleasant midrange hotel with a small pool, bar and restaurant. The family that runs it is very friendly, and the rooms are all well decked out with very nice balconies. It's a good place if you're seeking peace, and is located just a quick walk across from a quiet patch of Varca's long beach.

Ramada Caravela (☎ 2745200; www.caravela beachresort.com; d from Rs12,000; 🄲 🖵 🖭) This standard, opulent five-star, with its enormous lobby, manicured gardens stretching to the beach, pool, spa, tennis courts and golf course, is exactly what you'd expect from a resort of its kind: good, but not exactly atmospheric. Add to that plentiful restaurants and a casino ship that heads off nightly to ply the Mandovi River and you'll definitely have an all-round entertaining stay.

Cavelossim

Cavelossim village, a straggling strip of jewellery and souvenir shops, with a strange proliferation of dentists, is a place of large, down-at-heel hotels and time-share complexes strung along the main road. It's here that pinkish browsers shop for sandals and sarongs, and the two-week brigade settle in to their plain back-from-the-beach abodes. For all that, though, the beach remains long, wide and beautiful, dotted with water-sports

---

GOA'S FERRIES

One of the joys of day-tripping in Goa is a quick ride on one of the state's slowly shrinking selection of passenger ferries, which, until the recent addition of road bridges to span Goa's wide and wonderful rivers, formed a crucial means of transport for locals.

Though slowly disappearing altogether, and often in rather bad, rusty, fume-ridden condition, they're still a great way to see Goa's waterways without the need to sign up for an organised boat trip, and make a fab, thrifty way of getting about. Most ferries run every half an hour or so from around 7am to 8pm, some stopping between 1pm and 2pm for lunch. Pedestrians travel free; motorbikes and scooters cost Rs4; and cars are Rs10 to Rs12. Hop aboard, and experience life on the water the truly local way.

- Querim to Terekhol Fort (p178)
- Old Goa to Divar Island (p130)
- Cavelossim to Assolna (p199)
- Panaji to Betim (p109)

- Dona Paula to Mormugao Bay (p120)
- Divar Island to Naroa (p143)
- Ribandar to Chorao Island (p122)

---

vendors and beach shacks, and makes a nice place for a paddle.

Look out, on the road south, for the Old Anchor Hotel, allegedly the first ever resort in South Goa (a questionable accolade in itself). This place is worth a glance solely for its extreme Las Vegas–outskirts style kitsch value, shaped, as it is, to resemble a huge boat. Ahoy there, me hearties.

ACTIVITIES

Betty's Place Boat Trips (☎ 2871456, 2871038; ☺ restaurant 7-11pm) A restaurant by night, Betty's offers a wide range of boat cruises by day, including a full day combined dolphin-watching and birdwatching trip (Rs750 including lunch and drinks), fishing trips, sunset boat rides, and a two-hour birdwatching trip on the River Sal (Rs250; departs daily at 4pm). It can also arrange multiday scuba excursions to Pigeon Island, in the neighbouring state of Karnataka (Rs12,000 to Rs22,000 all-inclusive). Drop in or call in advance to book your boat trip. Meanwhile, the restaurant is known for its seafood and tandoori dishes (tiger prawns are Rs500); its hosts karaoke on Thursday and live music on Tuesday and Sunday.

For a slightly less sophisticated watery experience, hop on the 10-minute **ferry** (pedestrians/motorbikes/cars free/Rs4/7; ☺ 8am-8.30pm, every 30 min) across the Sal River to Assolna. To reach it, turn east at the ferry timetable sign, near Cavelossim's whitewashed church, then continue on for 2km to the river. Outside operational hours, you can charter the ferry to reach the opposite shore for a princely Rs50.

SLEEPING

Cavelossim is squarely aimed at package tourists, and most midrange places have little interest in renting rooms separately to individual travellers. Unless you're really keen to stay here, consider instead basing yourself either to the north or further south.

Sao Domingo's Holiday Home (☎ 2871461; www .saodomingosgoa.com; d with/without AC Rs2000/1600, ste Rs2500; ☒) Down a laneway opposite Goan Village, this tidy hotel is in a pleasant area of coconut palms just a few minutes' walk from the River Sal. Rooms have balconies and hot water, and some have AC. If it's full, there are a further eight rooms on offer, with similar prices and facilities, at its neighbouring complex, Luciana.

Casa de Cris (☎ 2685909; www.casadecris.com; d from Rs2200; ☒ ☐) A smart new option, this place, near Sao Domingo's, has crisply painted, well-maintained rooms, with nice homely touches. A great choice for a relaxed, comfortable stay.

Holiday Inn Resort (☎ 2871303; www.holidayinngoa .com; d from Rs10,200; ☒ ☐ ☒) On the road south towards Mobor, you'll reach the Holiday Inn, yet another sleek place on this coastal strip, with great service, a large pool and plenty of Thai and ayurvedic spa treatments on offer.

EATING

There are plenty of decent beach shacks strung along the beach, including the popular Mike's Beach Oasis Shack, owned by the village-based Mike's Place. All serve up the usual mix of seafood, traveller favourites and Indian dishes.

Papa Joe's (mains from Rs70; ☺ daily) 'Nothing fancy, just friendly', say the Papa Joe folks who serve great, spicy Goan cuisine in an open-air restaurant at Orlim, situated just north of Cavelossim on the right-hand side of the coastal road. Even the seafood seems happy to be there: their lively specialities include 'laughing squid' and 'jumping prawns'. And if their publicity blurb is to be believed, they've been chefs to the stars: 'Lovely Music Best Food,' allegedly said 'David Beckam [sic] of UK.' On occasion, it may be closed if there's a family wedding, christening or funeral under way.

Rice Bowl (mains from Rs70; ☺ 10am-3pm & 6-9pm) A simple, small place with an extensive Chinese menu, Rice Bowl offers tasty fuel for a day on the beaches of Cavelossim, with great chow mein and vegetable Peking rice.

Mike's Place (mains from Rs90) A popular place for evening meals and drinks, Mike's Place arranges live-music nights in its easy-going restaurant/bar and beach parties every Wednesday.

ENTERTAINMENT

Jazz Inn (☎ 9422437682; ☺ 11am-late) With a cosier, more-alternative vibe than Cavelossim's standard assortment of hotel bars and beach shacks, this wooden place, tucked off the main drag, serves up live music on Tuesday, Wednesday and Saturday evenings, blending classical, jazz fusion and other styles with great food and strong drinks.

Mobor

Little Mobor comprises the spit of land that licks down to the banks of the Sal River. Drive the road to its culmination and you'll pass the fancy entrances of the Holiday Inn and Leela on your right-hand side, and the picturesque fishing-boat lined Sal estuary on your left. Here you'll get a good glimpse of Goa's opposing faces: the gated decadence of the Leela – with its 12-hole golf course and gourmet Italian restaurant – and the poverty-stricken migrant fishermen who wake each morning at 3am to ply the seas and make ends meet.

Continue on almost to the end of the road, where piles of coconut husks are stacked, and follow the sign over the dunes to the Blue Whale beach shack. Here the sands quickly head towards idyllic. Wander to the tip of the peninsula, where the River Sal meets the sea, and you'll be guaranteed beachside bliss.

SLEEPING & EATING

ourpick **Blue Whale** (mains from Rs50) Stray beyond the Leela to the end of the Mobor peninsula, and you'll be rewarded with one of the most picture-perfect spots in the whole of Goa, at this simple beach shack with an extensive all-day menu, run by friendly local Roque Coutinho.

Leela Goa (☎ 2871234; www.theleela.com; d from Rs14,500; ✖ ☐ ☞) If you've the taste for luxury, the opulent Leela's the place to indulge it. Set amid 30 hectares of luxury, this enormous expanse of manicured Goan perfection has its own 12-hole golf course, and various rooms of varying degrees of decadence. Go for upmarket Indian and Goan cuisine at its signature Jamavar restaurant, or alfresco at Riverside, on the banks of the River Sal, which serves delicious Italian dishes along with a good dollop of *la dolce vita*.

GETTING THERE & AWAY

To the south of Mobor is the mouth of the Sal River. To continue down along the coast of South Goa you'll either need to backtrack and head north via Benaulim for the NH17 national highway or take the small road leading east from Cavelossim, cross by ferry to Assolna, and then continue down the coast road.

ASSOLNA TO AGONDA

One of the most beautiful roads in Goa is the coastal stretch between Assolna, on the south side of the Sal River, and the village of Agonda, some 20km south, and is perfect to explore if you've got your own transport. Hilly, winding and highly scenic, the road takes you into tiny villages, past *palácios* (palaces), through thick patches of coconut grove, and up to some stunning vistas out over the sea. Take a detour out to windswept Cabo da Rama fort along the way, of which little remains but the ghosts of conquerors past.

Assolna

If you get to Assolna by ferry from Cavelossim, turn left and follow the road to the T-junction, then right here, and you'll arrive at the village of Assolna, which has a lovely little collection of old-fashioned *palácios*. Though none are open for visiting, you won't miss the **Casa dos Costa Martins** a little further on, on the right-hand side of the road, an older home that was converted to Portuguese style during the 17th century. You'll still see a nod to its earlier Hindu incarnation in the oyster-shell peacock-tail motif (a typical Hindu symbol) above the front door.

Betul
☎ 0832

Continuing southwards from Assolna, opposite the narrow Mobor peninsula is the ramshackle fishing village of Betul. Few foreign tourists stay here and, apart from getting local boatmen to take you out on the river or watching the fishermen unload their catch at the harbour, there's not much to do, but it's a great place to wander along the tangle of fishing huts and boats of the bay and estuary. When the tide's in, you'll see seabirds diving for fish; when it's out, you'll see locals in the mud searching for crabs and other seafood. If you're feeling energetic, climb up to the cross-topped Baradi Hillock viewpoint at the south end of the village, especially nice at sunset, to see the glorious southern beach stretching off into the distance.

Cabo da Rama
The laterite spurs along the coastline of Goa, providing both high ground and ready-made supplies of building stone, were natural sites for fortresses, and there was thus a **fortress** at Cabo da Rama long before the Portuguese ever reached Goa.

Named after Rama of the Hindu Ramayana epic, who was said to have spent time in exile here with his wife Sita, the original fortress was held by various rulers for many years. It wasn't until 1763 that it was gained by the Portuguese from the Hindu Raja of Sonda and was subsequently rebuilt; what remains today, including the rusty cannons, is entirely Portuguese.

Although the fort saw no real action after the rebuild, it was briefly occupied by British troops between 1797 and 1802 and again between 1803 and 1813, when the threat of French invasion troubled the British enough to move in. Parts were used as a prison until 1955, before the whole thing was allowed to fall into ruin.

There is little to see of the old structure except for the front wall with its dry moat and unimposing main gate, and the small church that stands just inside the walls, but the views north and south are worth coming for. Services are still held in the chapel every Sunday morning.

To get to the fort from the coast road between Betul and Agonda, turn west at the red-and-green signposted turn-off about 10km south of Betul. The road dips into a lush valley then winds steeply up to a barren plateau punctuated by farmhouses and wandering stock. The fort is at the end of this road, about 3km from the turn-off.

There are local buses direct from Margao or Betul (Rs7, around 40 minutes) several times daily but since there's nothing to do once you've explored the fort, make sure you check on times for returning buses. There are a couple of simple cafes outside the fort entrance, serving snacks and ice-cold drinks to while away some time while waiting for a bus.

A return taxi to Cabo da Rama costs around Rs400 from Betul and Rs700 from Palolem, including waiting time.

Agonda
☎ 0832

Twelve kilometres south of the turn-off to Cabo da Rama (and 8km north of Palolem), the coast road passes the small village and spectacular beachfront of Agonda, a barely touched 2km of white sand and a favourite with visiting olive ridley marine turtles.

Over the last few years Agonda has experienced a rise in popularity, with ever more beachfront shack and hut operations lining its coconut groves behind the beach. But compared to Palolem further south, the pace remains slow and the wide beach relatively empty – partly because the surf here can be fierce and is rarely good for swimming.

Yet if you're looking for the ultimate laid-back experience, spending most of your time with a book and beach blanket, Agonda's an ideal place to be – and you might well find yourself staying on longer than you originally planned. Agonda has also become popular, of late, for its range of foreigner-run yoga, meditation and ayurveda set-ups, and you'll find no end of daily classes and courses on offer. Keep an eye out for signs detailing the season's latest set-ups posted around the Fatima Restaurant, and on lamp posts and telegraph poles the length of the beachside road.

To get to Agonda, coming from the north, look for the right-hand turn, signposted to the church and school, and with a handful of signs for beach-hut operations. Follow the winding road all the way down to the T-junction: beach huts range off the lane both to the left

GOA'S FORTS

It's well worth making time during your stay in Goa to head on up to one of its several surviving forts, which in their heyday topped windy bluffs all along the coast, and stood watch for several centuries over strategically important estuaries. Built by the Portuguese (but frequently on the sites of older defensive structures) soon after their 16th-century arrival into Goa, the forts were made of locally mined laterite, a red and porous stone, that proved, in most instances, a good match for the forces pitted against it.

Under the supervision of Italian architect Fillipo Terzi, the Portuguese developed their Goan bastions to be able to withstand the forces of gunpowder and cannonballs, their low walls thick and filled with earth 'cushions' to deflect cannon fire. Meanwhile, their bastions were built to be good swivelling spots for Portugal's own massive revolving cannons.

Inside the strong fort walls, the buildings were often carved directly out of the stone itself, with storerooms for supplies and weaponry connected by a maze of subterranean tunnels. Sometimes these tunnels led down as far as to the sea itself and hidden mooring points, which would prove vital to supply the forts during any lengthy times of siege.

Though the forts were made to withstand attacks from the sea by Portugal's main trade rivals, the Dutch and the British, they were never the sites of full-scale warfare, and as the threat of maritime invasion slowly faded during the 18th and 19th centuries, most forts fell into disrepair. Some, such as Cabo da Rama, Reis Magos and Fort Aguada, found favour as prisons, while others became army garrisons or plundering sites for building materials. Today, they're atmospheric relics of a bygone age, with the advantage of some picture-perfect views down over the coast they once guarded so closely.

and right, while to the right you'll find internet and travel agent facilities, a bookshop, as well as the odd small grocery shop and souvenir stand.

SLEEPING & EATING

These days you'll find a plethora of sleeping options in Agonda but, since most is of the beach-hut variety, the management, prices and quality can vary vastly from season to season. It pays to walk along the beach and see what takes your fancy, but listed here are some dependable, longer-standing options. Most beach huts have good restaurants, with parachute silk and floor cushions in abundance, and many are atmospherically candlelit come nightfall.

Fatima Restaurant (veg thali Rs50) Beloved by locals and visitors alike, teensy Fatima, with just four tables, set nearby the church, is an Agonda institution, with a long and tasty menu whipped up inside its improbably small kitchen. The vegetable thalis are very popular, and can easily become a habit.

La Dolce Vita (mains from Rs80; ☽ daily from 6.30pm) The best Italian food in the area is dished out daily at Dolce Vita, an Italian-run place with gingham tablecloths and a long, sprawling blackboard menu, to the south end of Agonda Beach. The pizzas are thin, the sal-

ads are crisp and the cake is, well, green: if, that is, you order the 'fresh cream cake', tinged a light emerald colour, but no less tasty for it.

Fatima Guesthouse (☎ 2647477; d from Rs600) An ever-popular guest house with clean rooms, a pool table and highly obliging staff, situated on the southern stretch of Agonda's beach road. Staff will oblige in booking day trips, and there's usually some yoga going on here too.

Abba's Gloryland (☎ 2647822; hut/r Rs600/800) On the opposite side of the road from the beach, this friendly, family-run place offers cool, tiled rooms with a lockable cupboard and attached bathroom, and nice, light huts with cool slate floors. And in case you need to brush up on your Ten Commandments, there's a framed poster to remind you.

Sandy Feet (☎ 9049114770; whatsup.sandyfeet4u@ gmail.com; huts from Rs1000) A popular beach hut operation situated towards the north end of Agonda, the huts here are comfy and close to the sands, but the best reason to come is for the fantastic Nepali food, especially the vegetable *momos* (Rs90) and lip-smackingly spicy peanut salad (Rs90). Laid-back staff, good music and strong cocktails make this a great place to unwind, while if you're part

---

A HIDDEN HOTEL

Tucked away in the jungle towards the south end of Agonda, and rising like Greystoke from the tree line, is the eerie concrete shell of the abandoned Seema Hotel. In the early 1980s, the story goes, a handful of absentee landlords sold the palm groves in the southern portion of the beach to a hotel, allegedly backed by the former PM Rajiv Gandhi, who was later assassinated in 1991.

Agonda's toddy tappers, however, angered by the destruction of their livelihood, refused to move as building work got under way for a luxury hotel, with helipad, golf course and luxuriant swimming pool. The toddy tappers remained adamant, threatening to use force if necessary, and painting a rock in the bay with the ominous slogan, 'Your tourists will never be safe here'.

For reasons still unclear, the project collapsed soon after. Some claim it was this local pressure that caused the building work to be abandoned, others that one of Gandhi's business partners was involved in some dodgy dealings and ran out of funds, others still that the partners quarrelled to the point of no return.

Today the huge site remains in the hands of receivers, and the hotel's shell is home to troupe upon troupe of screeching monkeys, as well as a small team of round-the-clock security guards. They won't mind you wandering through, if you can pick your way through the jungle thickets, to take a closer look at the resort that never was.

---

of a group (or just feeling thirsty) go for a Sandy Bowl (Rs500), your choice of cocktail in a portion big enough to serve four.

Chattai (☎ 9822481360; www.chattai.co.in; hut Rs1200) Towards the north end of the beach, Chattai offers lovely, airy huts on the sands, with a touch more muslin-draped sophistication than most.

Praia de Agonda (☎ 9763129429; praiadeagonda@ gmail.com; huts from Rs1200) A well-run and child-friendly set-up at the south end of Agonda's hosting frequent, entertaining open-mic nights when anyone with a few chords and the nerve can serenade the audience with their 'Lolas' and 'Laylas'.

Turtle Lounge (☎ 9421152150; nilespagui@yahoo .com; huts Rs6500) With just two swish, boutique-style huts, Turtle Lounge is the place to come for sleek sophistication close to the sands. Lovely rooms, attentive staff and your very own muslin-shrouded sun lounges (complete with ice bucket) make this a super choice for a spot of luxury.

GETTING THERE & AWAY
It's quite easy to hire a scooter or motorbike from private vendors along the beach road, if you're planning on doing a bit of travelling about. Otherwise, autorickshaws depart from the main T-junction near Agonda's church, and cost Rs200 to Palolem, and Rs250 to Patnem, and local buses run from Chaudi sporadically throughout the day (Rs7), also setting down at the T-junction.

CHAUDI
☎ 0832

Also known as Canacona, the bustling small town of Chaudi, with all its essential services ranged along its single main street (which is also the NH17 highway), is the place to come to get things done, if you're staying in Palolem, Agonda, Patnem or around.

Here you'll find several banks and ATM machines, pharmacies, doctors, a supermarket of sorts, a post office, and places to buy a local mobile phone, as well as a good fruit and vegetable market and bakeries for stocking up on self-catering essentials.

Travellers and locals alike love the grimy **Hotel Udupi** (veg thali Rs35; ☺ 7am-9pm), which dishes up south Indian favourites. Try the onion *rava dosa* (a crumpet-like rice-flour pancake with fried onions, stuffed with spicy potatoes) for Rs17, washed down with a hot cup of chai (Rs5).

Chaudi also has the south's biggest railway station (Canacona), about 1.5km northeast of town and the gateway, by rail, to Palolem.

PALOLEM
Palolem's stunning crescent beach was, as recently as 10 years ago, another of Goa's undiscovered gems, with few tourists and even fewer facilities to offer them. Nowadays, it's no longer quiet or hidden, but remains one of Goa's most beautiful spots, with a friendly, laid-back pace, and lots of budget accommodation ranged along the sands.

Some people are less fond of the recent developments in the area, dismissively labelling the Palolem of today 'Pálaga', making reference to a certain Spanish concrete-block holiday destination – and it's true that it's becoming increasingly rare to get an inch of sand to yourself. With the advent of cheap charter flights from Britain you might also see disturbing signs of the stag-weekend phenomenon: groups of lads, in football shirts and fairy wings, escorting a sozzled groom-to-be down Palolem's main strip.

With that caveat in mind, Palolem's still a wonderful place to be. The nightlife remains mostly sleepy – there are no real clubs or pubs and the place goes to sleep, aside from the occasional late-night beach bar and 'silent party' (see the box, p209), when the music stops at 10pm.

But if you're looking for a lovely place to lay up, rest a while, swim in calm seas and choose from an infinite range of yoga, massages and therapies on offer – without expecting a quiet, rustic beachside scene – Palolem may well be the ideal destination for you.

Around the headland from Palolem is a small, rocky bay named **Colomb**, where rustic restaurants and local homes shelter among a peaceful clump of coconut trees. The rocky bay here is probably better suited to paddling than swimming (but wear rubber shoes of some description to avoid laceration), but the short walk to Palolem to the north and Patnem to the south makes this a good low-key choice. It's a good place for long-stayers to seek out simple village homes, available for rent by the month or season.

Information

Palolem's beach road is lined with travel agencies, internet cafes and places to change money. There are no ATM machines near Palolem's beach, but one on the road to Chaudi and two in Chaudi itself. An autorickshaw from Palolem to Chaudi costs Rs100, or you can walk the flat 2km in a leisurely 45 minutes.

Butterfly Bookshop (☎ 9341738801; Palolem Beach Rd; ✆ 9am-late) The best of several good bookshops in town, this cute and cosy place (with resident cat) stocks best sellers, classics, and a good range of books on yoga, meditation and spirituality.

Activities

Palolem and Patnem are these days the places to be if you're keen to fill your days with yoga, belly dance, reiki, t'ai chi or tarot. There are courses and classes on offer all over town, with locations and teachers changing seasonally. Bhakti Kutir (p207) offers daily drop-in yoga classes, as well as longer residential courses, but it's just a single yogic drop in the area's ever-changing alternative therapy ocean.

Kayaks are available for hire on Palolem Beach; an hour's paddling (occasionally with a life jacket included) will cost Rs300. It's also very slowly becoming an adventure-sport base; local operators are starting to dabble in canyoning trips and trekking. Ask around and keep an eye peeled for signs. Meanwhile,

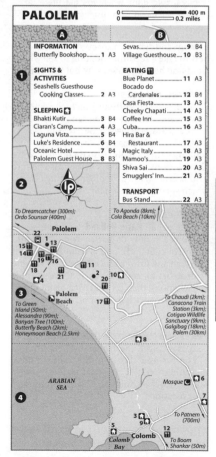

PALOLEM   0   400 m
                              0   0.2 miles

INFORMATION
Butterfly Bookshop......1 A3

SIGHTS & ACTIVITIES
Seashells Guesthouse
  Cooking Classes........2 A3

SLEEPING
Bhakti Kutir................3 B4
Ciaran's Camp.............4 A3
Laguna Vista...............5 B4
Luke's Residence.........6 B4
Oceanic Hotel.............7 B4
Palolem Guest House....8 B3

Sevas.........................9 B4
Village Guesthouse....10 B3

EATING
Blue Planet................11 A3
Bocado do
  Cardenales..............12 B4
Casa Fiesta................13 A3
Cheeky Chapati..........14 A3
Coffee Inn.................15 A3
Cuba.........................16 A3
Hira Bar &
  Restaurant..............17 A3
Magic Italy................18 A3
Mamoo's...................19 A3
Shiva Sai...................20 A3
Smugglers' Inn...........21 A3

TRANSPORT
Bus Stand..................22 A3

To Dreamcatcher (300m);
Ordo Sounsar (400m)

To Agonda (8km);
Cola Beach (10km)

Palolem

To Green
Island (50m);
Alessandra (90m);
Banyan Tree (100m);
Butterfly Beach (2km);
Honeymoon Beach (2.5km)

Palolem
Beach

To Chaudi (2km);
Canacona Train
Station (3km);
Cotigao Wildlife
Sanctuary (9km);
Galgibag (18km);
Polem (30km)

ARABIAN
SEA

Mosque

To Patnem
(700m)

Colomb
Bay

Colomb

To Boom
Shankar (50m)

THE SOUTH'S HIDDEN COVES

On the coastal strip around Palolem and Agonda, three tiny coves, accessible only by hiking there or taking a fishing boat, grace the lovely coastline. The most northerly is **Cola Beach**, accessible from the main coastal road a couple of kilometres north of Agonda; look out for the small signpost.

Further south, you'll find **Honeymoon Beach** and then **Butterfly Beach**, two lovely coves, the latter named for its lepidopterous inhabitants. If you're planning on walking to Butterfly Beach, it's a stiff one-hour jaunt with a steep ascent then descent to the beach, so allow plenty of time to get there and back. Bear in mind there's nowhere to buy a cold drink when you get there, so come equipped with sustenance.

---

massage and ayurveda are everywhere, and it's best to take a recommendation to see whose hands-on healing powers are hot this season.

COOKING CLASSES

Palolem is slowly cottoning on to the demand for cooking classes, and you can stir up a tasty masala at **Seashells Guesthouse** (☎ 9326113466; per person Rs200; ⏱ 11.30am), which runs hour-long cooking courses daily. Also on offer here are Hindi lessons for Rs200 per class. Also be sure to look around town for other cooking classes, which spring up seasonally.

DANCE CLASSES

British expat **Katie Holland** (www.katie-holland .net) runs a variety of classes, workshops and intensive courses in and around Palolem, in Egyptian and fusion dance. Check her website or drop her an email for current class details and locations, then get yourself a-shaking and a-shimmying with the best of 'em.

T'AI CHI

Glen Pelham-Master (☎ 9923944687), husband of belly-dancing Katie Holland, offers a range of courses and classes in the Palolem area, including t'ai chi, personal training and a host of other techniques. Call for details and class locations.

Tours

At the north end of Palolem Beach, you'll find no end of local fishermen willing to take you out on dolphin-spotting and fishing expeditions, or trips up to nearby Butterfly and Honeymoon Beaches.

Canopy Ecotours (☎ 9372109987; www.canopygoa .com; trips per person from Rs1000) If you're a fan of our feathered friends, venture out into the wilds to meet them with Canopy, an environmentally sensitive operation also offering unusual butterfly-spotting, dragonfly-spotting and wildlife photography trips. Its outings will take you to remote corners of the Western Ghats, and are highly recommended for an alternative – and ecologically minded – introduction to the Goan countryside.

Sleeping

Most of Palolem's accommodation is of the simple beach-hut variety, with little to distinguish where one outfit stops and next door's begins. Since the huts are dismantled and rebuilt with each passing season, standards can vary greatly from one year to the next. It's best to walk along the beach and the lane directly behind it and check out a few before making your decision; a simple hut without attached bathroom will usually cost upwards of Rs400, while something more sophisticated can run to Rs2000 and beyond. Colomb also has some good options, and you'll still be within walking distance to Palolem.

Palolem Guest House (☎ 2644879; www.palolem guesthouse.com; d Rs600-1200; ⌘) If you pale at the thought of another night in a basic beach hut, this splendid place offers lots of plain but comfortable rooms with solid brick walls ranged around a nice leafy garden. And all just a quick walk from the beach.

Laguna Vista (☎ 2644457; Colomb; huts from Rs600) A variety of decent huts are on offer at this secluded, relaxed place in Colomb; prices rise according to the size, view and facilities of the hut in question. Many people come here for the food, with great Tibetan *momos* (steamed dumplings) and Nepali thalis on offer, along with live music on weekend evenings. Its French co-owner also runs informal cooking courses in gourmet French cuisine. Ask staff for details.

Sevas (☎ 2639194; www.sevaspalolemgoa.com; huts from Rs800; ⌘) Next door to Bhakti Kutir, Sevas offers a comparably atmospheric experience for a far lower price. Huts and cottages are well maintained and set in pretty grounds; the family-sized cottage is a particular treat for folks travelling with children, with its wraparound corridor, perfect for those games of hide-and-seek. Staff are generally friendly, internet is on offer, and the simple menu is healthy and good.

Dreamcatcher (☎ 2644873; dreamcatcherjack@yahoo .com; hut from Rs1200) Eye-catching huts are on offer at Dreamcatcher, set just back from the beach and running alongside the small river at the north end of Palolem Beach. The beauty here is in the riverside restaurant, the attention to detail in the spacious huts (each of which is individually named), the bubbling central fountain, and the wide range of holistic treatments and massage on offer. Consult the noticeboard here for details of other spiritual goings-on.

Ordo Sounsar (☎ 9822488769; www.ordosounsar.com; huts with/without bathroom Rs2000/1500) Set almost as far north up Palolem Beach as it's possible to go, across a rickety bridge spanning a wide creek, this hidden haven makes a cool, quiet alternative to some of the elbow-to-elbow options further on down the sands.

Village Guesthouse (☎ 2645767; www.villageguest housegoa.com; d from Rs2000; ✖ ▯) Brand new on the Palolem scene and billing itself as 'Palolem's first boutique guest house', the Village's eight lovely doubles are a cut above the sometimes motley rest. Nicely furnished with sparkling new bathrooms, four-poster beds, and nice homely touches, it makes a terrific-value place to be based, despite being set back considerably from the beach.

Luke's Residence (☎ 2643003; www.lukesresidence .com; d Rs2500) Set in a quiet, green part of Palolem, about 10 minutes' walk from the beach, Luke's is praised by its oft-returning guests for its warm, helpful hospitality and great food. The beds are comfy; most rooms would easily fit three or four beach huts inside. Rates include a simple breakfast.

Bhakti Kutir (☎ 2643472; www.bhaktikutir.com; cottages from Rs2500; ▯) Ensconced in a thick wooded grove between Palolem and Patnem Beaches, Bhakti's well-equipped rustic cottages are a little on the pricey side these days, but still offer a unique jungly retreat. There are daily drop-in yoga classes, and the outdoor restaurant, beneath billowing parachute silks, turns out imaginative, healthful stuff.

Oceanic Hotel (☎ 2643059; www.hotel-oceanic.com; d from Rs2500; ✖ ▯ ▮) This nice white building, set a fair distance from the beach on the road between Palolem and Patnem, is an

ever-popular six-room place, made particularly appealing by its small swimming pool and patio restaurant perched alongside.

Ciaran's Camp (☎ 2643477; www.ciarans10.com; r Rs2500-3900; ✖ ▯) Some people love it, others aren't so taken, but Ciaran's has worked hard to keep its distinction over the years. Rooms are very pleasant, set around a pretty garden, and all with their own verandah area. There's also an inviting restaurant that churns out barbecued seafood at candlelit tables under white umbrellas. Ciaran's also has a lovely one-bedroom village house for rent in Chandor (p187). Contact the camp for more details.

Alessandra (www.alessandra-resort.com; huts from Rs3000) An ever-popular beachfront option, Alessandra has high-quality huts on offer, including one – with its own bath tub – right on the beach itself. Come here also to enjoy the good food on offer: the pad thai noodles and iced coffee are season-long hits.

Eating

Palolem's beach is lined with beach shacks, offering all-day dining and ultrafresh seafood as the catch comes in and the sun goes down. As with accommodation, places here change hands and quality seasonally, but we've listed a few well-established options. Colomb has some decent choices too.

Hira Bar & Restaurant (breakfast from Rs12; ✖ breakfast & lunch) The best place to start the morning in Palolem with a simple *bhaji-pau* and a glass of chai, along with locals on their way out to work.

Shiva Sai (veg thali Rs40; ✖ breakfast & lunch) A thoroughly local lunch joint, knocking out tasty thalis of the vegie, fish and Gujarati kinds, and a good line in breakfasts, such as banana pancakes (Rs40).

our pick **Mamoo's** (mains from Rs40) Don't be put off by the rather dark, cavernous interior: here's where you'll find Palolem's very best Indian food, in delicious and generous portions. For a taste sensation, explore the variety of vegetarian tandoori options; you'll likely be back the following night to continue trawling the extensive menu.

Boom Shankar (Colomb; mains Rs50-130) This place is as popular for its view over the bay as for its cuisine. The Indian, Goan, Chinese, Thai and Western food here is good value, but it's the sunset cocktails, and attendant happy hour, that draw long-staying visitors here day after week after month.

Casa Fiesta (mains Rs50-140) This garden-based casa has been knocking out tasty Mexican food for years, with the Latin tunes adding to the commendable attempt at making authentic Mexican burritos in a Goan beach town. Beware: don't come here if you're in a hurry. Service is notoriously slow, and you might find yourself knocking down one too many margaritas while waiting for anything edible to arrive.

Blue Planet (dishes from Rs60; [V]) Tasty vegan and organic treats served up with love by a local couple at this shady retreat from the hot Palolem day. Bring your water bottles here to be refilled with safe, filtered drinking water for just Rs3 per litre (free to restaurant patrons), to do your little bit towards reducing Palolem's plastic problem.

Coffee Inn (sandwiches from Rs70; [💻]) If you're craving a cappuccino, roam for foam no further than Coffee Inn, which grinds its own blend of beans to perfection. Its breakfasts are immense, as are its scrummy sandwiches: try the delicious smoked mozzarella kind, which arrives thick with roasted vegetables and pesto. There's also free wi-fi if you're here with a laptop.

Banyan Tree (mains from Rs80) One of the best beach bets for Thai specialities, the simple Banyan Tree cooks up tasty Thai curries of the green, red, yellow and potato-and-peanut-rich Massaman varieties, with regular live music and open-mic sessions several evenings each week.

Bocado do Cardenales (Colomb; mains from Rs80; [🕒] lunch & dinner) It's not often you see a Spanish restaurant in Goa, so make the most of a craving for tapas with a trip to this mellow little restaurant. Especially recommended is the cooling gazpacho soup, followed by a portion of locally made masala-chai flavoured ice cream.

Cheeky Chapati (mains from Rs100) The best time to visit this woodsy, British-run place is after 7pm on a Sunday, when old-fashioned roasts grace the menu, and plates arrive at tables piled high with potatoes, vegetables and all the trimmings. Go for the delicious vegetarian option, a tasty paneer (unfermented cheese) and tofu pie served with red onion gravy.

Cuba (mains from Rs100) For scrambled eggs, soups and sundowners alike, perennially popular Cuba, down on the beach and with a bar on the beach road, has it all. Its Indian food is tasty and filling, as are its Chinese spe-

cialities, and the Cuba experience is enhanced by a great music collection, and a laid-back, lazy vibe.

Smugglers' Inn (mains from Rs120) If you're craving full English breakfasts or Sunday dinner with all the trimmings, the Smugglers' Inn, with its football on TV and weekly quiz nights, provides that little bit of Britain in the midst of beachside India.

Magic Italy (mains Rs160-200; [🕒] 6.30-11pm) A place popular for its atmosphere and large portions of pizza and pasta. Its pizzas can be a bit hit-and-miss, sometimes appetising and at other times only average; perhaps it's trading on its long-established success just a little too much, but it remains a nice option for when the urge for Italian strikes.

Getting There & Away

There are hourly buses to Margao (Rs25, one hour) from the bus stop on the corner of the road down to the beach. There are also regular buses to nearby Chaudi (Rs5), the nearest town, from which you can get frequent buses to Margao and Panaji or south to Karwar and Mangalore. The closest train station is Canacona in Chaudi.

An autorickshaw from Palolem to Patnem costs Rs50; an autorickshaw from Palolem to Chaudi costs Rs100. A prepaid taxi from Dabolim Airport to Palolem costs Rs850.

SOUTH OF PALOLEM
Patnem
☎ 0832

Smaller and less crowded than Palolem to the north, pretty Patnem makes a quiet and friendly alternative. The surf here is lively, making it great for swimming some days, and impossible on others, when an equally lively undertow is present. Its main beach road hosts a string of stalls selling the usual variety of clothes, Kashmiri jewellery and trinkets, without the attendant hard-sell of Palolem, while its beach is backed by a line of huts and shacks, offering happy hours, all-day menus and a whole host of hut accommodation.

ACTIVITIES

Goa Sailing (☎ 9850458865; www.goasailing.com) Catamarans are the order of the day at highly professional Goa Sailing, which allows you to build your own itinerary to experience the thrill of sailing these 15ft beauties, with or

---

SILENCE – I'M DANCING!

Several years ago, new government regulations came into force which ordered that all loud music be switched off at 10pm sharp. Though in other parts of the state this signalled the death knell of the party scene, one enterprising group of individuals decided to do something inventive about it. To circumvent the ban, this international group, known as Silent Noise, recently brought to Goa several hundred sets of wireless headphones, to reinstate all-night partying – only this time without the noise.

The basic premise of a 'silent party' is to don your headphones, often with two channels of music on offer, and then party the night away to your choice of DJ, in inner bliss but outer silence, the only noise being an occasional whoop when a popular tune comes on. Silent parties are fast catching on, but Silent Noise's remain the original and best. Check their website for details, and be suspicious of impersonators: you have to cough up a hefty deposit to take a set of headphones for the evening, and we've had reports that one unscrupulous operator has a hard time parting with the capital at the end of the silent evening's partying.

Information on Palolem's original 'silent parties' can be found at Silent Noise's www.silentnoise.in

---

without an instructor. Take an hour's lesson or a whole-day trip down south, with lunch and impromptu dolphin-watching thrown in…so to speak.

Harmonic Healing Centre (☎ 2512814; www.harmonicingoa.com) Set high on a hill at the northern end of Patnem Beach and with regular classes, workshops and treatments – including reiki, yoga, massage, tarot readings and chiropractic treatments – Harmonic is a one-stop centre for all things calming and curative. Consult the website for up-to-date listings on how to get yourself harmonious.

Magic Cinema (meals Rs60; ☸ from 7pm) Set up in a coconut grove behind the beach, Magic Cinema screens both current and classic films (including the occasional kids' favourite) on a sizeable open-air screen every evening at 7pm and 9pm, with good Indian food (and perhaps a beer or two) served alongside, should you desire it.

SLEEPING & EATING

Long-stayers will revel in Patnem's choice of village homes and apartments available for rent. A very basic house can cost Rs10,000 per month while a fully equipped apartment will go for anything up to Rs40,000.

Goyam & Goyam (☎ 9822685138; www.goyam.net; huts from Rs2500) Comfortable, cute and well-equipped pastel-shaded huts are the trademark here, with plenty of character and lots of room between each one ensuring a bit of privacy.

Home (☎ 2643916; home.patnem@yahoo.com; mains from Rs80) This hip, relaxed restaurant, run by a lovely British couple, serves up unquestion-

ably the best food in Patnem. Fill up for breakfast with a thick, delicious rosti topped with fried eggs, cheese and tomatoes, or stop in for coffee and the best chocolate brownies in India. Home also rents out nicely decorated, light rooms (Rs1000 to Rs2500). Call to book or ask at the restaurant.

Micky Huts & Rooms (☎ 9850484884; huts Rs200) If you don't blanche at basic, this is the best bargain on the whole of Patnem Beach, run by the friendliest and most obliging local family you could imagine. There's no signpost: just head for the huge patch of bamboo beside the small stream towards the northern end of the beach, and enquire at Micky's small attached restaurant.

Papaya's (☎ 9923079447; www.papayasgoa.com; huts Rs1500) Lovely rustic huts head back into the palm grove from Papaya's popular restaurant. Each is lovingly tended to, with lots of wood and floating muslin, and the staff is incredibly keen to please.

GETTING THERE & AWAY

The main entrance to Patnem Beach is reached from the country lane running south from Palolem (past the Oceanic Hotel), then turning right at the rather misleadingly named Hotel Sea View. Alternatively, walk about 20 minutes along the path from Palolem via Colomb Bay, or catch a bus heading south (Rs4).

Rajbag
☎ 0832

Quiet little Rajbag is these days dominated by the presence of the grand luxury

---

DETOUR: NETRAVALI BUBBLE LAKE

If you're in the mood for some adventure, arm yourself with your own set of wheels and some serious determination, and set off into the South Goa countryside to track down the mysterious **Netravali 'bubble lake'**, actually the bathing tank of the small Hindu Gopinath temple.

It's known in Konkani as the *Budbudyanchi Talli*. Streams of bubbles constantly bob up to the lake's surface, the streams getting faster if you clap your hands close to the lake's surface, but no one knows quite why.

And if you manage to make it out here, reward yourself with a trip to the nearby **waterfall** at the village of Savare, a 45-minute walk through dense jungle, after which you can cool off with a refreshing dip in the waterfall's pool.

It's hard to give directions how to get to Netravali, since we're not quite sure how we managed it – through trial and error – ourselves. Suffice to say, the bubble mystery is real, and the journey through the countryside (including along some very steep roads through the wild Forestry Department–managed tract of forest known as the **Netravali Protected Area**) is stunning. Coming from Palolem or Chaudi on the NH17, turn off at the Forest Checkpoint on the left-hand side, and prepare for a true voyage of discovery.

Intercontinental Goa Lalit (☎ 2667777; www.ichotels group.com; d from US$160; ⊠ ☐ ☻), and most of its visitors are consequently hotel guests. It makes for a nice walk, however, from Patnem Beach to the north, clambering across the rocks along the way. Like many beaches in this area, beware of the treacherous undertow when swimming. There are a couple of villas with rooms for rent in Rajbag, but we've heard several reports of highly unscrupulous behaviour on the part of one manager; it's likely best to avoid the hassle and base yourself in Patnem instead.

If you're in the mood for a special day trip, consider chartering **Faraway Cruises** (☎ 9850649512, 9828829788; www.farawaycruisesgoa .com), to cruise the south Goan waters aboard the 18m wooden boat, *Isla*. It can take cruisers up as far as Cabo da Rama fort and back, with dolphin-watching, lunch and swimming stops along the way. Special itineraries can be arranged for creating that ultimate romantic moment.

One very good reason to venture to Rajbag is to seek out the stellar **Vernekar Restaurant** (mains from Rs20; ☿ dinner). A good bet is to ask local rickshaw drivers how to get to this little place down a lane back from the main road past the Intercontinental. It offers a mean tandoori chicken and the world's finest *aloo gobi* (potato and cauliflower in a spicy masala sauce) for less than the price of a Coke at the hotel itself. Eat along with locals at one of only four plastic tables. It might be simple, but it serves up some of the very best, super-spicy grub in South Goa.

Meanwhile, venture down to the end of the main Rajbag road, which ends abruptly at the banks of the Talpona River, to get your hole-in-the-wall *feni* fix from one of a range of pokily atmospheric **local bars**.

COTIGAO WILDLIFE SANCTUARY

About 9km east of Palolem, and a good day trip, is the beautiful, remote-feeling **Cotigao Wildlife Sanctuary** (☎ 2965601; admission/camera Rs5/25; ☿ 7am-5.30pm), Goa's second-largest sanctuary and easily its most accessible, if you've your own transport.

Don't expect to bump into its more exotic residents (including gaurs, sambars, leopards and spotted deer), but frogs, snakes, monkeys, insects and blazingly plumed birds are in no short supply. Marked trails are hikable; set off early morning for the best sighting prospects from one of the sanctuary's two forest watchtowers – though heed the park warden's recent warning: 'Don't climb too high, madam, for ladder is under repair.' The watchtowers are 6km and 9km from the park entrance, so to get there in time to see the creatures at their most active, get going from Palolem, Patnem or nearby at the crack of dawn.

GALGIBAG

Picture a postcard-perfect beach, back by gently swaying pine trees and flanked, in mirror-image, by two twinkling rivers. Add some sea eagles riding the currents high overhead, a beach shack or two at the northernmost reach, and the nesting places of the rare, long-lived olive ridley marine turtles, and you've got

Galgibag, around 16km from Chaudi and accessed by a lovely road that runs along the south shores of the Talpona River.

Don't come to Galgibag to swim – undertows and currents are strong – but it's unsurpassed for a quiet, nature-immersed walk. Stop off for sustenance at the family-run **Surya's Beach Café** (vegetable curry Rs50), nestled at its southern end in the trees, just before the river, specialising in seafood, mussels and oysters. Even top British celebrity chef Gordon Ramsay has allegedly dined at – and recommended – this place, as Surya's business card proudly notes.

POLEM

In the very far south of the state, just a hop, skip and a jump to Karnataka, lies Goa's southernmost beach, ranged around a beautiful small bay on the seafront of the small village of Polem. Though the village itself seems to have been lumbered with an unsavoury reputation – due to its secretive, lucrative line in interstate liquor smuggling – it's actually a fine, friendly spot for a sea-side stroll or a picnic on the deserted and pristine sands, with a beautiful view of a cluster of rocky islands out towards the horizon. Tourist development thankfully hasn't yet made it as far as Polem, and the beach retains a decidedly local feel, with a handful of fishermen bringing in their catch to the northern end and nothing much else to keep you company except scuttling crabs and circling seabirds.

For a fishy lunch so fresh it's still dithering, stop off at the **Kamaxi Hotel** (☎ 2640145; ☽ lunch & dinner) in among the palms, run by the eccentric local, Laxaman Raikar. He stocks Kingfisher, if you're in need of something cold and frothy, and also has three exceedingly basic, somewhat grim and grotty rooms for rent – in case you get seriously stranded – for Rs200 apiece.

To get to Polem, take a bus from Chaudi (Rs12, 50 minutes) and get off at the bus stop, around 3km after the petrol station. The stop is directly opposite the turn-off to the beach. Then it's a 1km walk to the village and beach.

Around Goa

It's easy to forget that Goa is part of a far, far bigger country, but there are several interesting and highly worthwhile excursions, no more than a day's journey across the border into Karnataka, one of India's most interesting states.

Gokarna is situated about 60km south of the Goan border in northern Karnataka. The village itself is one of the most holy Hindu sites in South India, but it's the beautiful beaches that have drawn travellers over the years – many of them ex-Goa hippies escaping the hype, or new adventurers who've heard the rumours.

About 50km southeast of Gokarna are Jog Falls, the highest in India. The flow of the falls is not as grand as it once was, but an exploration of the surrounding countryside still makes for a worthy excursion. The ultimate journey from Goa, however, is to Hampi, the magnificent ruined city of the Vijayanagar empire and a renowned travellers' centre. Its Virupaksha Temple stands proudly at almost 50m, and is one of the earliest structures in this evocatively historical area. Hampi's Vittala Temple, with its magnificent sculpture and alluring 'musical' pillars, is unlike anything you'll see in Goa, and will likely form one of your most distinct memories of a visit here, long after you've returned home.

HIGHLIGHTS

- Trek the spectacular countryside around India's highest waterfall, **Jog Falls** (p216)
- Mingle with pilgrims, escapists and other assorted arrivals among the temples and beaches of **Gokarna** (opposite)
- Chat with Lakshmi, the temple elephant, in the thick of **Hampi Bazaar** (p218)
- Explore the extraordinary World Heritage–rated remains at Hampi's **Vittala Temple** (p218)

Hampi ★

★Gokarna

★ Jog Falls

AROUND GOA

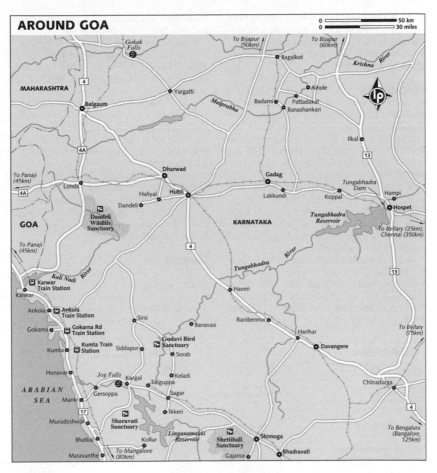

AROUND GOA

GOKARNA

☎ 08386

A quaint and low-key settlement on the Arabian Sea, Gokarna is where hordes of Hindu pilgrims gather throughout the year to pay their respects in the ancient temples. During major Hindu festivals (see p22) the village is at its dramatic best, and while the main village is definitely temple, rather than tanning, orientated, a few out-of-town beaches provide an ideal opportunity for some carefree beachside lazing.

Information

There are lots of places to access the internet, including many of the guest houses.

Pai STD Shop (Main St; ☾ 9am-9pm) Changes cash and travellers cheques and gives advances on Visa.

Shree Radhakrishna Bookstore (Car St; ☾ 10am-6pm) Good selection of new and secondhand books.

Sub post office (1st fl, cnr Car & Main Sts; ☾ 10am-4pm Mon-Sat)

Sights & Activities
TEMPLES

Non-Hindus are not allowed inside Gokarna's temples. However, there are plenty of colourful rituals to be witnessed around town. At the western end of Car St is the **Mahabaleshwara Temple**, home to a revered lingam (phallic representation of Shiva). Nearby is the **Ganapati Temple**, while at the other end of the street is the **Venkataraman Temple**. About 100m further south is **Koorti Teertha**, the large temple tank (reservoir) where locals, pilgrims and immaculately dressed Brahmins perform their ablutions next to washerwomen on the temple ghats (steps or landings).

BEACHES

Gokarna's 'town beach' is dirty, and not intended for casual bathing. The best sands are due south, and can be reached via a footpath that begins south of the Ganapati Temple and heads down the coast (if you reach the bathing tank – or find yourself clawing up rocks – you're on the wrong path).

A 20-minute hike on the path brings you to the top of a barren headland with expansive sea views. On the southern side is **Kudle** (kood-lay) **Beach**, the first of Gokarna's pristine beaches. Basic snacks, drinks and accommodation are available here.

South of Kudle Beach, a track climbs over the next headland, and a further 20-minute walk brings you to **Om Beach**, with a handful of chai shops and shacks. South of Om Beach lie the more isolated **Half-Moon Beach** and **Paradise Beach**, which come to life in season, between November and March. They are a 30-minute and one-hour walk, respectively.

Depending on demand, fishing boats can ferry you from Gokarna Beach to Kudle (Rs100) and Om (Rs200). An autorickshaw from town to Om Beach costs around Rs150.

Don't walk around after dark, or alone at any time – it's easy to slip on the paths or get lost, and muggings have occurred. For a small fee, most lodges in Gokarna will safely store valuables and baggage while you chill out in the beach huts.

AYURVEDA

Quality ayurvedic therapies and packages are available at specialist ayurvedic centres in SwaSwara (opposite) and Om Beach Resort (opposite).

Sleeping

With a few exceptions, the choice here is between rudimentary beach-hut accommodation, or a basic but more comfortable room in town. Some hotels in town cater to pilgrims, and may come with certain attendant rules and

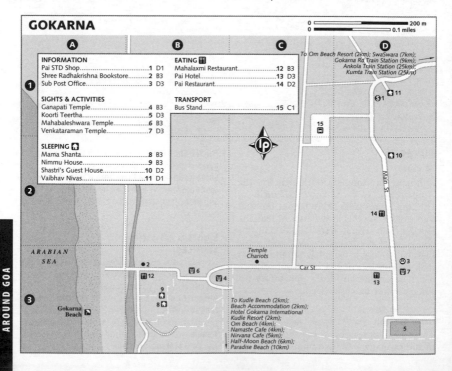

GOKARNA

0 _____ 200 m
0 _____ 0.1 miles

INFORMATION
Pai STD Shop.................................1 D1
Shree Radhakrishna Bookstore..........2 B3
Sub Post Office...............................3 D3

SIGHTS & ACTIVITIES
Ganapati Temple............................4 B3
Koorti Teertha...............................5 D3
Mahabaleshwara Temple.................6 B3
Venkataraman Temple.....................7 D3

SLEEPING
Mama Shanta.................................8 B3
Nimmu House................................9 B3
Shastri's Guest House....................10 D2
Vaibhav Nivas..............................11 D1

EATING
Mahalaxmi Restaurant...................12 B3
Pai Hotel.....................................13 D3
Pai Restaurant.............................14 D2

TRANSPORT
Bus Stand....................................15 C1

To Om Beach Resort (2km); SwaSwara (7km);
Gokarna Rd Train Station (9km);
Ankola Train Station (25km);
Kumta Train Station (25km)

Main St

ARABIAN SEA

Temple Chariots

Car St

Gokarna Beach

To Kudle Beach (2km);
Beach Accommodation (2km);
Hotel Gokarna International
Kudle Resort (2km);
Om Beach (4km);
Namaste Cafe (4km);
Nirvana Cafe (5km);
Half-Moon Beach (6km);
Paradise Beach (10km)

AROUND GOA

regulations. Prices quoted here may increase depending on local pilgrimage demand.

BEACHES

Both Kudle and Om Beaches have several shacks offering budget huts and rooms – shop around. Places also open up on Half-Moon and Paradise beaches from November to March. Most places provide at least a bed roll, but bring your own sheets or sleeping bag if you're fussy. Padlocks are provided and huts are secure. Communal washing and toilet facilities are simple.

Namaste Cafe (☎ 257141; Om Beach; s without bathroom Rs150, deluxe hut Rs600) In and out of season, Namaste is the place to hang. Its restaurant-bar cooks up great bites and is the premier Om chill-out spot. In season it also offers basic huts (Rs50) at Paradise Beach and cottages at Namaste Farm (from Rs400) on the headland.

Nirvana Cafe (☎ 329851; Om Beach; s without bathroom Rs250, cottage Rs600) Located on the southern end of Om Beach is this pleasant option, with a handful of cute and rustic cottages with little sit-outs, nestled amid shady palms and groves.

Hotel Gokarna International Kudle Resort (☎ 257843; Kudle Beach; d with/without AC Rs1500/1200; 🍴) Run by the same management that owns Hotel Gokarna International in town, this midrange option has smart rooms and a lovely garden out the front overlooking the sea. The waves wash up to its gates during high tide!

SwaSwara (☎ 257132, 04842668221; www.swaswara .com; Om Beach; d 7 nights Indian/foreigner Rs120,000/ US$2300; 🍴 💻 🏊) No short stays on offer here, but you can chill out at this elegant and superbly designed red laterite resort for a full week, and enjoy a holiday based around yoga and ayurvedic treatments. Rates include full board, transport, leisure activities and daily yoga sessions. Weeklong ayurvedic treatment packages kick off at around US$570.

GOKARNA

Vaibhav Nivas (☎ 256714; off Main St; d Rs200, s/d without bathroom Rs100/150; 💻) The cell-like rooms at this place tucked away from the main drag come with mosquito nets and hot water in the morning. There's also a rooftop restaurant.

Mama Shanta (☎ 256213; r with/without bathroom Rs150/120) Just past Nimmu House is this rather gloomy and basic homestay, but the kindly old lady of the house does her best to make you feel at home. It's right next to the beach.

Shastri's Guest House (☎ 256220; dr_murti@rediff mail.com; Main St; s/d Rs150/200) This place has a hostel-like feel to it. The singles are tiny; the doubles in the new block out the back are bright and airy, with squat loos. Some have balconies and palm-tree views.

Nimmu House (☎ 256730; nimmuhouse@yahoo .com; s/d old block Rs250/500, new block Rs300/1000; 💻) Just off the foot trail along the beach is this pleasant option run by a friendly family. The rooms in the new block are nice, with tiled floors and balconies.

our pick **Om Beach Resort** (☎ 257052; www.om beachresort.com; Bangle Gudde; d incl breakfast Indian/ foreigner Rs2100/US$80; 🍴 💻) This little jewel sits on a headland 2km out of Gokarna off the Om Beach road. Set amid lawns and shady trees, its red-brick cottages are excellently designed, and its restaurant serves some delectable seafood. There's a professional ayurvedic centre on site, offering short sessions (from Rs750) as well as longer treatment packages.

Eating

The chai shops on all Gokarna's beaches rustle up basic snacks and meals.

Pai Hotel (Car St; mains Rs20-35; 🕑 6am-9.30pm) A good place for veg food.

Pai Restaurant (Main St; mains Rs25-40; 🕑 6.30am-9.30pm) This place draws in visiting pilgrims with its vegetarian fare.

Mahalaxmi Restaurant (meals Rs30-70) This popular hang-out promises 'all types of world famous dishes' (eg banana pancakes and cornflakes!) in myriad ways. The ambience, however, is relaxing.

Namaste Cafe (meals Rs30-80; 🕑 7am-11pm) Om Beach's social centre serves decent Western standbys – pizzas and burgers – and some Israeli specials.

Getting There & Away

BUS

From Gokarna's rudimentary **bus stand**, rickety buses rumble north to Karwar (Rs29, 1½ hours), which has connections to Goa. Direct buses run northeast to Hubli (Rs92, four hours), where you can change for Hospet and Hampi. There are two direct evening buses to Bengaluru (semi-deluxe/ sleeper Rs256/456, 12 hours).

TRAIN

Only slow passenger trains stop at **Gokarna Rd train station** (☎ 279487), 9km from town. A 10.40am train heads daily to Margao in Goa (Rs21, three hours). To head further south to Mangalore (Rs42, five hours), a train departs daily at 4.20pm.

A better idea is to head out by local bus to **Kumta station** (☎ 223820) 25km away, to board one of the expresses which stop there. From Kumta, the 2.14am *Matsyagandha Express* goes to Mangalore (sleeper Rs168, four hours); the return train leaves Kumta at 6.38pm for Margao (sleeper Rs141, 3½ hours) in Goa. Many of the hotels and small travel agencies in Gokarna can book tickets. Ankola Station, 25km south of Gokarna, is also a convenient railhead.

Autorickshaws charge Rs100 to go to Gokarna Rd station. Buses go hourly (Rs7) and also meet arriving passenger trains. A bus to Kumta station is Rs12.

JOG FALLS

☎ 08186

Nominally the highest waterfalls in India, the Jog Falls only come to life during the monsoon. At other times, the Linganamakki Reservoir further up the Sharavati River limits the water flow. The tallest of the four falls is the Raja, which drops 293m.

To get a good view of the falls, bypass the scrappy area close to the bus stand and hike to the foot of the falls down a 1200-plus step path. It takes about an hour to get down and two to come up. Watch out for leeches in the wet season.

The **tourist office** (☎ 244732; ⏱ 10am-5pm Mon-Sat) is above the food stalls close to the bus stand. On site is the **KSTDC Hotel Mayura Gerusoppa** (☎ 244732; s/d Rs300/400), about 150m from the car park, with enormous, musty rooms.

Stalls near the bus stand serve omelettes, thalis, noodles and rice dishes, plus hot and cold drinks. KSTDC's mediocre **restaurant** (meals Rs30-50) is just next door.

Jog Falls has buses roughly every hour southeast to Shimoga (Rs45, three hours), and three daily to Karwar via Kumta (Rs43, three hours), where you can change for Gokarna (Rs12, one hour) and head north to Goa. For Mangalore, change at Shimoga.

HAMPI

☎ 08394

Unreal and bewitching, the forlorn ruins of Hampi lie scattered over a landscape that leaves you spellbound the moment you cast your eyes on it. Heaps of giant boulders perch precariously over miles of undulating terrain, their rusty hues offset by jade-green palm groves, banana plantations and paddy fields, while the azure sky painted with fluffy white cirrus adds to the magical atmosphere. A World Heritage Site, Hampi is a place where you can lose yourself among the ruins, or simply be mesmerised by the vagaries of nature, wondering how millions of years of volcanic activity and erosion could have resulted in a landscape so fascinating.

Hampi is a major pit stop on the traveller circuit, with the cooler months of November to March being the peak season. While it's possible to see the main sites in a day or two, this goes against Hampi's relaxed grain; plan on lingering for a while.

History

Hampi and its neighbouring areas find mention in the Hindu epic Ramayana as Kishkinda, the realm of the monkey gods. In 1336 Telugu prince Harihararaya chose Hampi as the site for his new capital, Vijayanagar which, over the next couple of centuries, grew into one of the largest Hindu empires in Indian history. By the 16th century it was a thriving metropolis of about 500,000 people, its busy bazaars dabbling in international commerce, brimming with precious stones and merchants from faraway lands. All this ended in a stroke in 1565, when a confederacy of Deccan sultanates razed Vijayanagar to the ground, striking it a death blow from which it never recovered.

A different battle rages in Hampi today, between conservationists bent on protecting Hampi's architectural heritage and the locals who have settled there. A master plan is being prepared to notify all of Hampi's ruins as protected monuments, while resettling villagers at a new commercial-cum-residential complex away from the architectural enclosures. However, implementation is bound to take time, given the resistance from the locals who fear their livelihoods might be affected by the relocation process. **Global Heritage Fund** (www.globalheritagefund.org) has more details about Hampi's endangered heritage.

Orientation

Hampi Bazaar and the southern village of Kamalapuram are the two main points of entry to the ruins. Kamalapuram has the KSTDC Hotel and the archaeological museum. But the main travellers' scene is Hampi Bazaar, a village crammed with budget lodges, shops and restaurants, all dominated by the majestic Virupaksha Temple. The ruins are divided into two main areas: the Sacred Centre, around Hampi Bazaar; and the Royal Centre, towards Kamalapuram. To the northeast across the Tungabhadra River is the village of Anegundi (see p221).

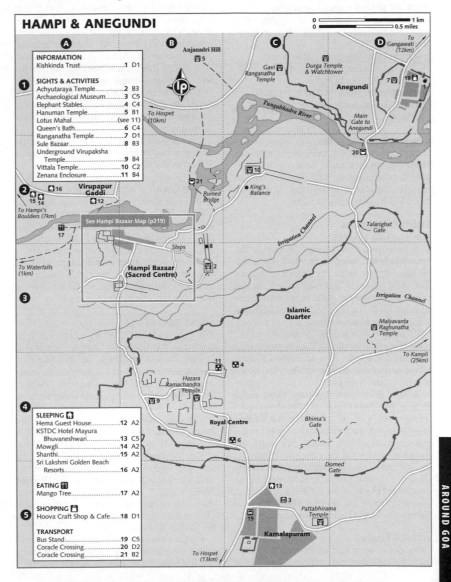

HAMPI & ANEGUNDI

INFORMATION
Kishkinda Trust.....................**1** D1

SIGHTS & ACTIVITIES
Achyutaraya Temple..............**2** B3
Archaeological Museum.........**3** C5
Elephant Stables....................**4** C4
Hanuman Temple...................**5** B1
Lotus Mahal.....................(see 11)
Queen's Bath.........................**6** C4
Ranganatha Temple................**7** D1
Sule Bazaar...........................**8** B3
Underground Virupaksha
    Temple............................**9** B4
Vittala Temple.......................**10** C2
Zenana Enclosure..................**11** B4

SLEEPING
Hema Guest House................**12** A2
KSTDC Hotel Mayura
    Bhuvaneshwari................**13** C5
Mowgli..................................**14** A2
Shanthi.................................**15** A2
Sri Lakshmi Golden Beach
    Resorts............................**16** A2

EATING
Mango Tree...........................**17** A2

SHOPPING
Hoova Craft Shop & Cafe......**18** D1

TRANSPORT
Bus Stand..............................**19** C5
Coracle Crossing...................**20** D2
Coracle Crossing...................**21** B2

Information

Andhra Bank (Map p219) Has an ATM off the entrance to Hampi Bazaar.

Aspiration Stores (Map p219; ☺ 10am-1pm & 4-8pm) For books on the area. Try *Hampi* by John M Fritz and George Michell, a good architectural study.

Canara Bank (Map p219; ☎ 241243; ☺ 11am-2pm Mon-Tue & Thu-Fri, 11am-12.30pm Sat) Changes travellers cheques and gives cash advances on credit cards.

Hampi Heritage Gallery (Map p219; ☺ 10am-1pm & 3-6pm) Sells books and offers half-day walking or cycling tours for Rs200.

Sree Rama Cyber Cafe (Map p219; per hr Rs30; ☺ 7am-11pm) The best of Hampi's internet cafes. It also burns CDs of digital snaps for Rs50.

Tourist Office (Map p219; ☎ 241339; ☺ 10am-5.30pm Sat-Thu) Can arrange guides for Rs300/500 for a half/full day.

Dangers & Annoyances

Hampi is generally a safe, peaceful place. However, don't wander around the ruins after dark or alone, as muggings are not unreported. Besides, it can be dangerous terrain to get lost in, especially at night.

Sights & Activities

VIRUPAKSHA TEMPLE

The focal point of Hampi Bazaar is the **Virupaksha Temple** (Map p219; ☎ 241241; admission Rs2; ☺ dawn-dusk), one of the city's oldest structures. The main *gopuram* (gateway tower), almost 50m high, was built in 1442, with a smaller one added in 1510. The main shrine is dedicated to Virupaksha, a form of Shiva.

If Lakshmi (the temple elephant) and her attendant are around, she'll bless you on the forehead for a coin. The adorable Lakshmi takes her morning bath at 8.30am, just down the way by the river ghats.

To the south, overlooking Virupaksha Temple, **Hemakuta Hill** (Map p219) has a scattering of early ruins, including monolithic sculptures of Narasimha (Vishnu in his manlion incarnation) and Ganesh. It's worth the short walk up for the view over the bazaar. At the east end of Hampi Bazaar is a **Nandi statue** (Map p219), around which stand some of the colonnaded blocks of the ancient marketplace. This is the main location for **Vijaya Utsav**, the Hampi arts festival held in November.

VITTALA TEMPLE

From the eastern end of Hampi Bazaar, a track, best covered on foot, leads left along the riverbank to the **Vittala Temple** (Map p217; Indian/foreigner Rs10/250; ☺ 8.30am-5.30pm), about 2km away. The undisputed highlight of the Hampi ruins, the 16th-century temple is in fairly good condition, though a few cement scaffolds have been erected to keep the main structure from collapsing.

Work possibly started on the temple during the reign of Krishnadevaraya (1509–29) but it was never finished or consecrated. Yet, the temple's incredible sculptural work remains the pinnacle of Vijayanagar art. The outer 'musical' pillars reverberate when tapped, but authorities have placed them out of tourists' bounds for fear of further damage, so no more do-re-mi. Don't miss the temple's showcase piece: the ornate stone chariot that stands in the temple courtyard, whose wheels were once capable of turning.

Retain your ticket for same-day admission into the Zenana Enclosure and Elephant Stables in the Royal Centre.

SULE BAZAAR & ACHYUTARAYA TEMPLE

Halfway along the path from Hampi Bazaar to the Vittala Temple, a track to the right leads over the rocks to deserted **Sule Bazaar** (Map p217), one of ancient Hampi's principal centres of commerce. At the southern end of this area is the **Achyutaraya Temple** (Map p217). Its isolated location at the foot of Matanga Hill makes it quietly atmospheric, doubly so since it is visited by few tourists.

ROYAL CENTRE

While it can be accessed by a 2km foot trail from the Achyutaraya Temple, the Royal Centre is best reached via the Hampi-Kamalapuram road. It's a flatter area compared to the rest of Hampi, where the boulders have been shaved off to create stone walls. A number of Hampi's major sites stand here, within the walled ladies' quarters called the **Zenana Enclosure** (Map p217; Indian/foreigner Rs10/250; ☺ 8.30am-5.30pm). There's the **Lotus Mahal** (Map p217), a delicately designed pavilion which was supposedly the queen's recreational mansion. The Lotus Mahal overlooks the **Elephant Stables** (Map p217), a grand building with domed chambers where state elephants once resided. Your ticket is valid for same-day admission to the Vittala Temple.

Further south, you'll find various temples and elaborate waterworks, including the **Underground Virupaksha Temple** (Map p217;

HAMPI BAZAAR

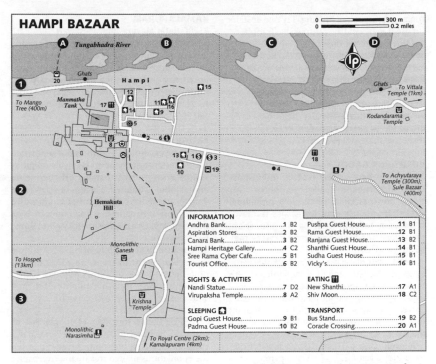

0 — 300 m
0 — 0.2 miles

INFORMATION	
Andhra Bank	1 B2
Aspiration Stores	2 B2
Canara Bank	3 B2
Hampi Heritage Gallery	4 C2
Sree Rama Cyber Cafe	5 B1
Tourist Office	6 B2

SIGHTS & ACTIVITIES	
Nandi Statue	7 D2
Virupaksha Temple	8 A2

SLEEPING	
Gopi Guest House	9 B1
Padma Guest House	10 B2

Pushpa Guest House	11 B1
Rama Guest House	12 B1
Ranjana Guest House	13 B2
Shanthi Guest House	14 B1
Sudha Guest House	15 B1
Vicky's	16 B1

EATING	
New Shanthi	17 A1
Shiv Moon	18 C2

TRANSPORT	
Bus Stand	19 B2
Coracle Crossing	20 A1

8.30am-5.30pm) and the **Queen's Bath** (Map p217; 8.30am-5.30pm), deceptively plain on the outside but amazing within.

ARCHAEOLOGICAL MUSEUM

The **archaeological museum** (Map p217; ☎ 241561; Kamalapuram; admission Rs5; 10am-5pm Sat-Thu) has well-displayed collections of sculptures from local ruins, Neolithic tools, 16th-century weaponry and a large floor model of the Vijayanagar ruins.

Sleeping

There's little to choose between many of the basic rooms in Hampi Bazaar and Virupapur Gaddi. If you need AC and cable TV, stay in Kamalapuram. Prices listed can shoot up by 50% or more during Christmas, and drop just as dramatically in the low season (April to September).

HAMPI BAZAAR

Shanthi Guest House (Map p219; ☎ 241568; s/d Rs250/300, without bathroom Rs150/250) An oldie but a goodie, Shanthi offers a peaceful courtyard with a swing chair, and has plastic creep-

ers and divine posters decorating its basic rooms. There's a small shop that operates on an honour system.

Gopi Guest House (Map p219; ☎ 241695; kiran gopi2002@yahoo.com; d Rs300;) The Gopi empire has expanded to a renovated block across the road, which contains four pleasant rooms with en suite. The rooftop room, equipped with a carom board and guitar, is a nice place to hang out. It also makes a mean cup of espresso (Rs30).

Vicky's (Map p219; ☎ 241694; vikkyhampi@yahoo.co.in; d Rs350;) One of the village's larger operations done up in pop purple and green, with 10 brightly painted and tiled rooms, internet access and the requisite rooftop cafe.

Pushpa Guest House (Map p219; ☎ 241440; d/tr Rs400/500) The fresh new rooms here have pink walls and brightly printed upholstery, with a cordial family playing host. The lovely sit-out on the 1st floor gives it an edge over its competitors.

Padma Guest House (Map p219; ☎ 241331; d Rs400-800) The astute Padma might have got her spellings wrong ('Recommendation by Lovely Plant', reads her business card!), but the tidy rooms are more than inviting. Try one upstairs for great views of the Virupaksha Temple.

Other good options:

Sudha Guest House (Map p219; ☎ 652752; d from Rs200) Has a good family vibe and a riverside location.

Rama Guest House (Map p219; ☎ 241962; s/d Rs300/400) Some rooms are a little low on light, but the cool rooftop cafe seals the deal.

Ranjana Guest House (Map p219; ☎ 241696; d Rs400-600) On par with Padma Guest House. The terrace rooms have great views and TV.

VIRUPAPUR GADDI

Many travellers prefer the tranquil atmosphere of Virupapur Gaddi, across the river to the north of Hampi Bazaar. A small boat (Rs10) frequently shuttles across the river from 7am to 6pm. During the monsoon, the river runs high and ferry services may be suspended.

Hema Guest House (Map p217; ☎ 9449103008; dm/bungalows Rs100/500) One of Virupapur Gaddi's most popular spots, this place has rows of cute and comfy cottages laid out in a shady grove, and scores with its informal restaurant in a beautiful wooden belvedere overlooking the river.

Mowgli (Map p217; ☎ 329844; hampimowgli@hotmail.com; d from Rs250; 🖳) With prime views across the rice fields, shady gardens sheltering hammocks, and thatched-roof bungalows, this is a top-class chill-out spot. The rooms with views are the most expensive, around Rs500.

Shanthi (Map p217; ☎ 325352; d without bathroom Rs300, cottages Rs600) Bungalows here have rice-paddy, river and sunset views, and porches with couch swings. The restaurant does good thalis (Rs45) and pizzas (Rs70 to Rs85).

Sri Lakshmi Golden Beach Resorts (Map p217; ☎ 08533287008, 9448436537; d incl breakfast from Rs2000; 🔀 🍴) A welcome change from Hampi's basic sleeping options, this resort-style place amid paddy fields has a range of cosy cottages. The pool, sadly, won't be in commission until early 2010.

Hampi's Boulders (off Map p217; ☎ 08539265939, 9448034202; Narayanpet; d incl full board with/without AC from Rs8000/6000; 🔀 🍴) The only luxury option in these parts, this 'eco-wilderness' resort sits amid leafy gardens in Narayanpet, 7km west of Virupapur Gaddi. Accommodation is in chic cottages designed like boulders, and the food is good. The downside: you're way removed from the buzz.

KAMALAPURAM

KSTDC Hotel Mayura Bhuvaneshwari (Map p217; ☎ 08394-241574; d/tr from Rs825/1125; 🔀) This tidy government place, about 3km south of the Royal Centre, has well-appointed rooms and creature comforts such as TV and AC. A huge plus is the bar – the only legal one close to Hampi – and ayurvedic sessions (from Rs1550) on request.

Eating

With one exception, Hampi is not renowned for its restaurants. Due to Hampi's religious significance, meat is usually off the menu, and alcohol is banned. Places are open from 7am to 10pm. Several of Hampi's lodges also sport rooftop restaurants; good ones include those at Gopi Guest House, Vicky's and Rama Guest House.

New Shanthi (Map p219; mains Rs30-50) A hippie vibe, complete with trance music and acid-blue lights, hangs over this popular option serving a good selection of juices and shakes. The bakery churns out passable cookies and crumbles.

ourpick Mango Tree (Map p217; mains Rs30-90) Creativity blends with culinary excellence at this rural-themed chill-out joint, spread out under the eponymous mango tree by the riverbanks. The walk out here is through a banana plantation, and the food is delicious – the restaurant does lip-smacking dosas for breakfast and dinner. The ambience is simply overwhelming, and the terraced seating perfect for whiling away a lazy afternoon, book in hand.

Shiv Moon (Map p219; mains Rs35-90) This friendly place with pleasant views sits by the river to the east of Hampi Bazaar. It gets good reviews for the quality of its food, though the owners often tend to get politely pushy.

Waterfalls (off Map p217; mains Rs40-60) About a 2km walk west of Hampi Bazaar is this appealing operation tucked away beside shady banana plantations en route to a group of small waterfalls. The tasty Indian fare justifies the walk out of town.

Getting There & Away

While some private buses from Goa and Bengaluru will drop you at the bus stand in Hampi Bazaar, you have to go to Hospet to catch most buses out. The first bus from Hospet (Rs10, 30 minutes, half-hourly) is at 6.30am; the last one back leaves Hampi Bazaar at 8.30pm. An autorickshaw costs around

---

THE KISHKINDA TRUST

Since 1995, the **Kishkinda Trust** (TKT; ☎ 08533267791, 9449284496; www.thekishkindatrust.org) has been actively involved in promoting rural tourism, sustainable development and women's empower-ment in Anegundi, alongside its work preserving the architectural and living heritage of the Hampi World Heritage Site. The first project in 1997 created a cottage industry of crafts using locally produced cloth, banana fibre and river grass. It now employs over 600 women, and the attractive crafts produced are marketed in ethnic product outlets across India, along with the village outlet at the **Hoova Craft Shop & Cafe** (p222).

The trust's other projects include holding cottage industry workshops and sensitising the village folk in regard to self-help and sustainable ecotourism. Its homestay program has met with enormous success, and the revenue generated through tourism now goes into community welfare, training and empowerment of village personnel as well as running interaction programs in village schools. An information and interpretation centre has also been set up, while more self-help projects have recently taken their positions at the starting line.

Rs100. See p222 for transport information for Hospet.

The overnight private sleeper bus to/from Goa (Rs550), which runs from November to March, is a popular option – but don't expect a deep sleep. If you're heading south, KSRTC has a daily Rajahamsa bus service between Hampi Bazaar and Bengaluru (Rs301, 8½ hours) leaving at 8.45pm. Numerous travel agents in Hampi Bazaar are eager to book onward bus, train and plane tickets, or arrange a car and driver.

Getting Around

Once you've seen the main sights in Hampi, exploring the rest of the ruins by bicycle is the thing to do. The key monuments are haphaz-ardly signposted all over the site; while they're not quite adequate, you shouldn't get lost. Bicycles cost about Rs30 per day in Hampi Bazaar; mopeds can be hired for around Rs200, plus petrol. You can take your bicycle or motorbike (extra Rs10) across the river on the boat.

Walking is the only way to see all the nooks and crannies, but expect to cover at least 7km just to see the major ruins. Autorickshaws and taxis are available for sightseeing, and will drop you as close to each of the major ruins as they can. A five-hour autorickshaw tour costs Rs300.

Organised tours depart from Hospet; see p222 for details.

AROUND HAMPI
Anegundi

Across the Tungabhadra River, about 5km northeast of Hampi Bazaar, sits Anegundi, an ancient fortified village that's part of the Hampi World Heritage Site but pre-dates Hampi by way of human habitation. Gifted with a landscape similar to Hampi, quainter Anegundi has been spared the blight of com-mercialisation, which is why it remains a chosen getaway for those who want to soak up the local atmosphere without having to put up with the touristy vibe.

SIGHTS & ACTIVITIES

Mythically referred to as Kishkinda, the king-dom of the monkey gods, Anegundi retains many of its historic monuments, such as sections of its defensive wall and gates, and the **Ranganatha Temple** (Map p217; ☉ dawn-dusk) devoted to Rama. The whitewashed **Hanuman Temple** (Map p217; ☉ dawn-dusk), accessible by a 570-step climb atop the Anjanadri Hill, has fine views of the rugged terrain around. Many believe this is the birthplace of Hanuman, the Hindu monkey god who was Rama's devo-tee and helped him in his mission against Ravana. The hike up is pleasant, though you'll be courted by impish monkeys, and within the temple you'll find a horde of chillum-puffing resident sadhus!

The **Kishkinda Trust** (TKT; Map p217; ☎ 08533267791, 9449284496; www.thekishkindatrust.org), a nonprofit organisation that manages tourism in Anegundi, has a slew of nature and adven-ture activities that you can indulge in. Options include rock climbing, camping, trekking, rappelling and zoomering. Equipment and trained instructors are provided. A string of cultural events, such as performing arts ses-sions and classical and folk-music concerts, are also conducted from time to time.

AROUND GOA

SLEEPING

Anegundi has several homestays, managed by the Kishkinda Trust. Contact the trust for bookings. Meals can also be provided by some of the guest houses upon prior notice.

Champa Guest House (d incl breakfast Rs600) Champa offers basic but pleasant accommodation in two rooms, and is looked after by an affable village family.

TEMA Guest House (d incl breakfast Rs600; 💻) For an alternative experience try the two rooms here, attached to the trust's information centre, where you can read up on local heritage and sit in during community interaction programs.

Naidile Guest House (r Rs1000) A charmingly rustic air hangs over this place, a renovated village home in the heart of Anegundi where you can savour all the sights and sounds of the ancient village. It can sleep up to five people.

SHOPPING

Hoova Craft Shop & Cafe (Map p217; 🕑 9.30am-5pm Mon-Sat, 9.30am-2pm Sun) Here you can also pick up sundry souvenirs made by women's self-help groups of the village. It's also a lovely place for a laid-back meal or snack (from Rs20).

GETTING THERE & AWAY

Anegundi can be reached by crossing the river on a coracle (Rs10) from the pier east of the Vittala Temple. If and when the new bridge is completed, you can simply cycle across.

Alternately, you can get to Anegundi by taking a bus (Rs20, one hour) from Hospet.

HOSPET

☎ 08394 / pop 164,200

This busy regional centre is the transport hub for Hampi. There's no reason to linger unless you desire an air-conditioned hotel room and cable TV.

Information

Internet joints are common, with connections costing Rs30 per hour. ATMs are common too. The bus-stand cloakroom holds bags for Rs10 per day.

KSTDC tourist office (☎ 228537, 221008; Shanbag Circle; 🕑 10am-5.30pm Mon-Sat) Offers a Hampi tour (Rs175), daily from 9.30am to 5.30pm. The quality of

guides varies. Call ahead as tours won't run with fewer than 10 people.

State Bank of India (☎ 228576; Station Rd; 🕑 10.30am-4pm Mon-Sat) Changes currency.

Sleeping & Eating

Hotel Priyadarshini (☎ 228838; www.priyainhampi .com; Station Rd; s/d from Rs1300/1500; 🏵 💻) Handily located between the bus and train stations, the fresh rooms here have balconies and TV. The outdoor nonveg restaurant-bar Manasa (mains Rs60 to Rs120) has a good menu.

Hotel Malligi (☎ 228101; www.malligihotels.com; Jabunatha Rd; d with/without AC from Rs1500/650; 🏵 💻 🏊) Only the more expensive rooms here, some with a vague contemporary look, are worth it. A couple of decent restaurants, a pool (Rs35 for nonguests and guests in the cheapest rooms) and a gym are on site.

Udupi Sri Krishna Bhavan (meals Rs15-45; 🕑 6am-11pm) Opposite the bus stand, this clean spot dishes out Indian vegie fare, including thalis for Rs27.

Getting There & Away

BUS

The **bus stand** (☎ 228802) has services to Hampi from Bay 10 every half-hour (Rs10, 30 minutes). Two overnight buses head to Panaji (Rs215, 11 hours) via Margao. Express buses run to Bengaluru (ordinary/deluxe Rs320/400, nine hours); two buses go to Badami (Rs130, six hours), or you can take a bus to Gadag (Rs52, 2½ hours) and transfer. There are frequent buses to Bijapur (Rs130, six hours) and Hyderabad (Rs340, 10 hours). For Gokarna, take a bus to Hubli (Rs82, 4½ hours) and change. For Mangalore, take a morning bus to Shimoga (Rs145, five hours) and change.

TRAIN

Hospet's **train station** (☎ 228360) is a Rs15 autorickshaw ride from town. Every Monday, Wednesday, Thursday and Saturday, a 6.30am express heads to Vasco da Gama (sleeper/ 2AC Rs178/643, 8½ hours). The daily *Hampi Express* heads to Hubli at 7.50am (2nd class Rs43, 3½ hours) and then to Bengaluru at 7.50pm (sleeper/2AC Rs193/738, 10 hours).

To get to Badami, catch a Hubli train to Gadag and change there.

Directory

CONTENTS

Accommodation	223
Business Hours	225
Children	225
Climate Charts	226
Customs	227
Dangers & Annoyances	227
Embassies & Consulates	228
Food	229
Gay & Lesbian Travellers	229
Holidays	229
Insurance	229
Internet Access	230
Legal Matters	230
Maps	231
Money	231
Photography	232
Post	232
Shopping	233
Solo Travellers	235
Telephone & Fax	235
Time	235
Tourist Information	235
Travellers with Disabilities	236
Visas	236
Volunteer Work	236
Women Travellers	236

ACCOMMODATION

Goa's accommodation can be split quite distinctly into budget, midrange and top-end categories. Budget accommodation comes in the form of basic, no-frills hotel rooms (especially in the larger towns) and bamboo beach huts clustered in the palm groves back from the beach, the latter definitely being the most appealing. Midrange accommodation is usually in simple, but comfortable, family-run guest houses, some equipped with more mod cons and atmosphere (and perhaps even a small swimming pool) than others. Top-end options are generally swish five-star resorts or beautiful boutique hotels, with the occasional luxury villa or carefully crafted luxury tent complex thrown in for good measure.

The price of most hotels, guest houses and beach huts is calculated on the basis of high, middle and low seasons. The high season cov-

ers the period from early November to late March (with the exception of the ultra-high or 'peak' period between 22 December and 5 January), the middle season includes October, April and May, and the low season is from June to September. Unless otherwise stated, prices in this book are for the high (but not peak) season, for rooms with attached bathroom. Rooms with air-conditioning are identified using the abbreviation 'AC'. Outside of the high season, count on discounts of 25% in the middle season and up to 60% or even more in the low season.

If you turn up at a popular beach, without a booking, during peak season, try to get there as early in the day as possible and check into whatever you can find available, at least for one night. This will give you time to trawl for your perfect accommodation option without hauling your luggage around in the blistering sun, and allow you to negotiate a better deal by not appearing too desperate. Meanwhile, if you're travelling in low season, check in advance to see that your accommodation of choice is actually open: most beach-hut operations and many hotels close down altogether from June to September, or even longer.

If you arrive early in the season, or are intending to stay for a few months, you'll find the widest range of available rooms, giving you scope to shop around and bargain. The rule of thumb is that the longer you stay, the cheaper it gets, and if you're staying for a while, it's well worth considering renting a house or apartment. You'll find handwritten signs for houses to rent in most village lanes, or ask at grocery shops and bakeries, whose staff usually know of a place or two.

Accommodation in this book is categorised as budget (under Rs1000), midrange (Rs1000 to Rs2500) and top end (over Rs2500), though the lines are sometimes blurred by places that offer the whole range. Very generally, the higher the price tag, the closer you'll get to Goa's golden sands. This rule particularly applies to budget beach huts.

Bear in mind there's a 'luxury' tax of 8% on rooms over Rs500, and up to 12% for those around Rs800 and above. For most budget places, the prices quoted include this tax, but at midrange and top-end hotels you can expect tax to be added to the bill. Many midrange and top-end hotels add a further, rather hefty 10% 'service tax'. When you're negotiating prices before you check in, clarify whether tax is included or not. Also beware of check-out times, which vary enormously throughout Goa: Panaji's often come in at a harsh 9am, or sometimes even earlier.

Beach Huts

The quintessential Goan accommodation experience is the bamboo beach hut, also sometimes known locally as 'coco-huts'. These were originally constructed on stilts, using surrounding coconut trees as support, but nowadays bamboo huts have moved far beyond their primitive genesis. It's not hard to tell a budget hut from a more expensive one; the better it looks, the more it costs. Palolem is a good example of the range of huts available; the beach is still predominantly lined with flimsy, coconut-matting versions, but sandwiched between them an increasing number of larger and infinitely more stylish options; some huts are even double-storey affairs with spacious hot-water bathrooms and four-poster beds. There are also more linear, but often roughly slapped together, wooden huts constructed of plywood, not quite as pretty as their original, ecofriendly neighbours.

The decor in these kit homes often accounts for price variations – a coat of paint and a few decorative cushions on a makeshift balcony can mean a difference of a few hundred rupees. Though absolutely atmospheric, a downside to the beach-hut experience can be one's proximity to the neighbours, whose nocturnal noises are often no more than a foot of air and flimsy sheet of bamboo away: if you're bothered by noise, don't forget to pack earplugs, or plump for a slightly wider-spaced option. Remember, too, that almost

---

BOOK YOUR STAY ONLINE

For more accommodation reviews and recommendations by Lonely Planet authors, check out the online booking service at www.lonelyplanet.com/hotels. You'll find the true, insider low-down on the best places to stay. Reviews are thorough and independent. Best of all, you can book online.

---

all beach huts are packed away for the season during April and May, to be reassembled around mid-October.

Camping

Given the range of budget accommodation, few people travel with their own tent, and there are no official campsites on which to pitch one. If you're up for a bit of tented luxury living, however, Goa's got quite a few upscale options: try Azuska Retreat (p139), on the edge of the Bhagwan Mahavir Wildlife Sanctuary, Yoga Magic (p167) near Anjuna, or Elsewhere's Otter Creek tents (p175) near Mandrem.

Guest Houses

The most common form of midrange accommodation is the guest house, for the most part friendly, well equipped and family run. Staying in such a place can be a wonderful way to get an insight into Goa, and can sometimes be more comfortable and economical than staying in a beach hut – or at least makes a nice change after a few weeks of sand between the sheets.

Hotels & Resorts

Goa excels at fancy five-star hotel resorts, run by slick international chains such as Intercontinental and Kempinski, where you'll find water sports, fine dining, comfortable AC rooms, spas, pools and sometimes even a golf course. More exciting than this for some travellers are the boutique hotels that are springing up across the state, many located in historic heritage homes. Check individual listings for details, and consider at least a night or two, if your budget runs to it, in one of these unique establishments.

Rental Accommodation

Renting houses by the month or longer is not uncommon in Goa, particularly given the increasing number of Westerners who live in Goa for six or so months of every year. Ask around, check out noticeboards at foreigner hot spots, or simply select the area in which you would like to live and take note of phone numbers on the many 'for rent' signs. The better the facilities, the more you'll pay. Prices go from Rs10,000 per month for a simple local-style village house, to Rs50,000 per month for a well-equipped apartment, with wi-fi, TV and a daily cleaning service.

PRACTICALITIES

- The electric current in Goa is 230V to 240V AC, 50 cycles. Sockets are of a three round-pin variety, similar (but not identical) to European sockets. There are two sizes; one large, one small (the latter is more common). European round-pin plugs will go into the smaller sockets, but the fit can be loose. Universal adaptors are widely available at electrical shops in Goa for around Rs20. Electricity in Goa can be unpredictable – save your work regularly if you're using a computer, and use a voltage regulator for sensitive electrical equipment.

- Although India officially uses the metric system, imperial weights and measures are still sometimes used. You may hear the term lakh (one lakh equals 100,000) and crore (one crore equals 10 million) referring to rupees, car costs or anything else.

- Goa has three English-language dailies: the *Herald,* the *Navhind Times* and the local version of the *Times of India*. Many foreign newspapers and magazines are available in bookshops and large hotels, though they're usually more expensive than back home.

- The government TV broadcaster is Doordarshan. Satellite TV, which has BBC World, CNN, Star World and Star Movies, MTV, VH1 and HBO, is more widely watched.

- All India Radio (AIR) transmits local and international news. There are plenty of private broadcasters in addition to this government-controlled station, many broadcasting in English.

BUSINESS HOURS

Though many local shops and offices stop for a daily siesta, shutting up shop from around 1pm to 3pm, others – especially in the most touristed areas – remain open from around 10am to 6pm daily. Government offices are generally open from 10am to 5pm Monday to Saturday, and are closed every second Saturday. Sunday is a day of rest, and places such as Panaji and Margao are likely calmer and quieter that you'll ever have witnessed in an Indian town. Restaurants are mostly open all day long, without an afternoon break in service. Those with opening hours outside the 8am to 10pm norm are specified in individual listings.

Banks are generally open from 10am to 2pm Monday to Friday, and 10am to noon on Saturday, though some stay open till 4pm daily, and many ATM machines are 24-hour. Tourist-oriented businesses such as travel agencies, internet cafes and souvenir shops stay open on Sundays too, and well into the evening.

CHILDREN

Goa is probably the most family-friendly state in India – almost everywhere you go you'll find enthusiastic babysitters and a whole community of travellers with children just itching to share their stories of life on the road. There are scores of parents with young children who are keen on broadening their children's horizons

from as early an age as possible, and you will find that your kids will benefit enormously from the range of activities and ideas on offer. Some destinations (particularly Palolem, Arambol, Calangute and Anjuna) have seasonally running schools and kindergartens for travellers' children, offering the kids a chance to swap their own stories of India, and have a nice half-day rest from their parents.

For more information on travelling with kids, pick up a copy of Lonely Planet's *Travel with Children*.

Practicalities

Items such as disposable nappies are available in almost every Goan town, but come at quite a premium (at least, for the half-decent variety) and with the additional dilemma of how to dispose of them. The enormous environmental damage caused by such waste leads some parents to do what the locals do: switch to the washable kind instead, and have them washed by a local laundry service. Wet wipes are also available, but are actually rather expensive: a small, simple pack can cost between Rs100 and Rs200, so bring as much of this crucial product as you can from home.

Formula milk is available in Goa, in both local and Nestlé brands (for various baby age-groups and including nondairy options), and is carried by most chemists and supermarkets, but if you're looking for a specific brand, bring along enough to supply you for the whole trip. Jars of baby food are few and far between outside the foreigner-slanted supermarkets in Anjuna (p164) and Candolim (p147). Many parents with small children have thrived without the need for a backpack-full of tiny jars, feeding babies on the traveller staples of rice and mild lentil dhal, bananas, yoghurt, porridge and well-mashed cooked vegetables. Even at the simplest of places, the chef will likely be thrilled to rustle up something to suit a baby's palate.

If you're in Goa with a smaller child, don't be concerned about breastfeeding in public; simply throw a light cotton shawl over yourself and baby to avoid any unwanted attention. Don't forget to bring a hat and plenty of sunscreen for tiny people, as well as a baby-friendly version of mosquito repellent. Heat rash is common – if not inevitable – in Goa's warmer months, while conjunctivitis spreads like wildfire in October, and impetigo is rather rampant in April. All you can do is treat these things topically, and pop to a local doctor if you're concerned.

For kids at toddler age and above, you'll find these days that most salads are washed in filtered or bottled water (even in many local, nontraveller restaurants), and that you'll have no difficulty in pandering to almost any small traveller's culinary whims. A plain dosa (rice-flour pancake) with a banana lassi (yoghurt shake) makes a reasonably nutritious and fail-safe breakfast standby for even the most choosy children, if you're caught in a town without the usual beach shack bonanza of options.

Sights & Activities

Goa is a beach baby's delight, and though you should be aware of the safety of the sea (some beaches have stronger waves, currents and undertows than others), you'll find there's no end of fun to be had in frolicking along the sands. Buckets, spades, arm bands and inflatables are usually available from a shop or two on the main road to most beaches, though it's a good idea, if you're travelling with small children, to bring a decent life vest or other swimming aid along from home.

For more specific suggestions, see p28.

CLIMATE CHARTS

The climate in Goa affects the character, customs and culture of the entire state. The main feature of note is its long-awaited monsoon, which douses Goa liberally between June and

the end of September, and altogether sees 250cm to 300cm of rain.

During the two months preceding the onset of the monsoon, the heat and humidity increases and normally clear skies become hazy, with high winds and lightning storms arriving just before the rains. Goans make many preparations before the onset of the monsoon, pickling, drying and otherwise preserving food, stocking up on dry firewood, securing fly-away structures and disassembling beach huts for the off-season. Fishing ceases almost entirely throughout this period due to the unpredictably stormy conditions.

Surprisingly, the temperature throughout the spectacular wet-weather conditions remains fairly constant, varying from a maximum of 28°C or 29°C in July to a maximum of 33°C in May, with minimums for the same months of 24°C and 26.5°C.

For more information, see p17.

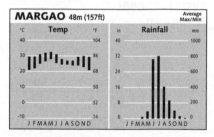

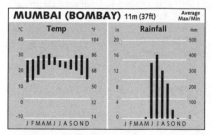

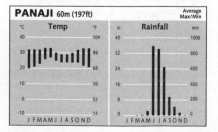

CUSTOMS

The usual duty-free regulations for India apply in Goa: 1L of spirits and 200 cigarettes (or 50 cigars, or 250g of tobacco) per person, though it's rare, if you're arriving direct into Goa by plane, that this is applied.

DANGERS & ANNOYANCES

Despite stories of violent crime, drug-related misdeeds and police corruption (some of them internationally high-profile and involving tourists) Goa remains essentially a safe destination for travellers. Goans feared the worst after the November 2008 Mumbai bombings, security was tightened in their aftermath and many visitors stayed away, but fortunately Goa hasn't been the target of terror-related attacks. So long as you check the news before you travel, and adhere to a few very basic and internationally applicable safety precautions, you should stay as safe and secure in Goa as you would anywhere else in the world.

Airport Taxis

To avoid paying an exorbitant amount for a taxi from Dabolim Airport to your chosen destination, make straight for the prepaid taxi counter just outside the airport doors. This will ensure you a fair, fixed price to any destination in Goa. When you arrive, it's fine to tip your taxi driver, but don't stand for any nonsense regarding 'additional charges'.

Muggings & Druggings

From time to time there are reports of 'date rape' or theft-related druggings, usually in busy, trendy tourist bars. Be wary, though not terrified, of accepting food or drinks from strangers or even new friends.

There have also been incidents of attacks on women (see p236). Goans are understandably concerned by these incidents and blame them on criminals from neighbouring states. Some measures have been introduced, such as limited street lighting and security patrols on some beaches, but it's still not a good idea for women – or men, for that matter – to wander alone in dark areas around beach shacks at night.

Scams

Incredibly, the age-old export scam is still doing the rounds in India. Even more incredibly, people are still falling for it. The scam basically involves being befriended and eventually offered the opportunity to export products (jewellery, precious stones or carpets are common) to sell elsewhere at enormous profit. Or, after you've been plied with meals and entertainment, you'll be given a sob story about your new friend's inability to obtain an export licence. Don't be fooled; these guys are smooth operators and even worldly travellers have been successfully buttered up by the initial hospitality and generosity.

Theft

In general, it's worth considering whether your passport and other valuables are safer at your hotel or on your person. If you're staying in a hotel, guest house, beach-hut operation or family home where there is a safe or similar lockable facility, it might be worthwhile leave them there, rather than in your room.

TIPS FOR SAFE TRAVEL

While the majority of travellers in Goa will have no serious or life-threatening problems, tourists have occasionally been the target of theft or assault. There are some common-sense steps you can take to minimise the risk:

■ Don't open the door to someone you don't know.

■ Leave windows and doors locked when you're sleeping and when you're out; things have been stolen using hooks through windows.

■ Avoid quiet, poorly lit streets or lanes – take the longer way if it's brighter and more populated, and walk with confidence and purpose.

■ If you are being sexually harassed or assaulted on public transport, embarrass the culprit by loudly complaining, and report them to the conductor or driver.

■ As tempting as it is to stare someone down, women should just ignore stares. Dark or reflective glasses can help.

DIRECTORY

There have been isolated reports, over the years, of violent robberies of tourists in Goa, so exercise the same sort of caution you would when at home and remember that, if you do have something stolen while in Goa, you must report it to the police if you want to make an insurance claim at home: being friendly, patient and persistent with the local police should get you your paperwork in the end. Many policemen are helpful, but if you continually have trouble reporting a crime, try enlisting the assistance of the Goa Tourism Development Corporation (GTDC) in Panaji.

Touts

When arriving by train or bus at a town or beach destination, visitors may be met by taxi drivers, autorickshaw drivers or other individuals who want to take you to a 'nice' hotel – usually the one that pays them a healthy commission. Touts do have a use, though – not all of their recommendations are bad ones, and they can be of definite use in finding you a place to stay during the sometimes jam-packed peak season.

EMBASSIES & CONSULATES

It's important to realise what your own embassy can and can't do to help you if you get into trouble. Generally it won't be much help if the trouble you're in is your own fault. Remember that you are bound by the laws of the country you are in; your embassy will not be sympathetic if you end up in jail after committing a crime locally, even if such actions are legal in your own country.

Most foreign diplomatic missions are in Delhi, but there are also a few consulates in the other major cities of Mumbai (Bombay), Kolkata (Calcutta) and Chennai (Madras).

Australia Chennai (☎ 044-28601160; 512 Raheja Towers, 177 Anna Salai, Anna Salai); Delhi (☎ 011-41399900; www.ausgovindia.com; 1/50G Shantipath, Chanakyapuri); Mumbai (Map pp78-9; ☎ 022-66692000; 36 Maker Chambers VI, 3rd fl, 220 Nariman Point)

Bangladesh Delhi (☎ 011-24121394; www.bhcdelhi.org; EP39 Dr Radakrishnan Marg, Chanakyapuri); Kolkata (☎ 033-22475208; 9 Circus Ave)

Bhutan (☎ 011-26889230; Chandragupta Marg, Chanakyapuri, Delhi)

Canada Chennai (☎ 044-28330888; 18 Khader Nawaz Khan Rd); Delhi (☎ 011-41782000; www.dfait-maeci.gc.ca/new-delhi; 7/8 Shantipath, Chanakyapuri); Mumbai (Map p84; ☎ 022-67494444; 6th fl, Fort House, 221 Dr DN Rd)

France Delhi (☎ 011-24196100; www.france-in-india.org; 2/50E Shantipath, Chanakyapuri); Mumbai (Map pp78-9; ☎ 022-66694000; 7th fl, Hoechst House, Nariman Point)

Germany Chennai (☎ 044-24301600; 9 Boat Club Rd, RA Puram); Delhi (☎ 011-26871837; www.new-delhi.diplo.de; 6/50G Shantipath, Chanakyapuri); Kolkata (☎ 033-24791141; 1 Hastings Park Rd, Alipore); Mumbai (Map pp78-9; ☎ 022-22832422; 10th fl, Hoechst House, Nariman Point)

Israel Delhi (☎ 011-30414500; http://delhi.mfa.gov.il; 3 Aurangzeb Rd); Mumbai (Map pp78-9; ☎ 022-22822822/22819993; Earnest House, 16th fl, NCPA Marg, Nariman Point)

Italy Delhi (☎ 011-26114355; www.ambnewdelhi.esteri.it; 50E Chandragupta Marg, Chanakyapuri); Mumbai (Map pp78-9; ☎ 022-23804071; Kanchanjunga, 1st fl, 72G Deshmukh Marg, Kemp's Corner)

Japan Chennai (☎ 044-24323860; 12/1, Cenetoph Rd 1st Street, Teynampet); Delhi (☎ 011-26876564; www.in.emb-japan.go.jp; 50G Shantipath, Chanakyapuri); Mumbai (Map pp78-9; ☎ 022-23517101; 1 ML Dahanukar Marg, Cumballa Hill)

Malaysia Chennai (☎ 044-28226888; 44 Tank Bund Rd, Nungambakkam); Delhi (☎ 011-26111291; www.kln.gov.my/perwakilan/newdelhi; 50M Satya Marg, Chanakyapuri); Mumbai (Map p94; ☎ 022-26455751/2; Notan Plaza, 4th fl, Turner Rd, Bandra West)

Maldives Chennai (☎ 044-24331696; Balaji Dental & Craniofacial Hospital, 30 KB Dasan Rd, Teynampet); Delhi (☎ 011-41435701; www.maldiveshighcom.in/; B2 Anand Niketan); Kolkata (☎ 033-22485400; Ground fl, Hastings Chambers, KS Roy Rd); Mumbai (Map p84; ☎ 022-22078041; 212A Maker Bhawan No 3, New Marine Lines, Churchgate); Trivandrum (☎ 0471-2558189; 13/1245 TC, Kumarapuram)

Myanmar Delhi (☎ 011-24678822; 3/50F Nyaya Marg);
Kolkata (☎ 033-24851658; 57K Ballygunge Circular Rd)
Nepal Delhi (☎ 011-23327361; Barakhamba Rd); Kolkata
☎ 033-24561224; 1 National Library Ave, Alipore)
Netherlands Chennai (☎ 044-43535381; 76 Venkatakri-
sha Rd, Mandaveli); Delhi (☎ 011-24197600; http://india
.nlembassy.org/; 6/50F Shantipath, Chanakyapuri); Mumbai
(Map p84; ☎ 022-22194200; Forbes Bldg, Home St, Fort)
New Zealand Chennai (☎ 044-28112472; Rane Engine
Valves Ltd, 132 Cathedral Rd); Delhi (☎ 011-26883170;
www.nzembassy.com; 50N Nyaya Marg, Chanakyapuri);
Mumbai (Map pp78-9; ☎ 022-23520022; Aashiana, 1st fl,
5 Altamount Rd, Breach Candy)
Pakistan (☎ 011-24676004; 2/50G Shantipath,
Chanakyapuri, Delhi)
Singapore Chennai (☎ 044-28158207; 17-A North Boag
Rd, T Nagar); Delhi (☎ 011-46000915; www.mfa.gov.sg
/newdelhi; E6 Chandragupta Marg); Mumbai (Map pp78-9;
☎ 022-22043205; Maker Chambers IV, 10th fl, 222
Jamnalal Bajaj Rd, Nariman Point)
South Africa Delhi (☎ 011-26149411; www.dha.gov
.za; B18 Vasant Marg, Vasant Vihar); Mumbai (Map pp78-9;
☎ 022-23513725; Gandhi Mansion, 20 Altamount Rd,
Cumballa Hill)
Sri Lanka Chennai (☎ 044-24987896; 196 TTK Rd,
Alwarpet); Delhi (☎ 011-23010201; www.newdelhi.mission
.gov.lk; 27 Kautilya Marg, Chanakyapuri); Mumbai (Map p84;
☎ 022-22045861; Mulla House, 34 Homi Modi St, Fort)
Switzerland Delhi (☎ 011-26878372; www.eda.admin.ch;
Nyaya Marg, Chanakyapuri); Mumbai (Map pp78-9; ☎ 022-
22884563-65; 102 Maker Chambers IV, 10th fl, 222 Jamnalal
Bajaj Marg, Nariman Point)
Thailand Chennai (☎ 044-42300730; 21/22 Arunacha-
lam Rd, Kotturpuram); Delhi (☎ 011-26118104; www
.thaiemb.org.in; 56N Nyaya Marg, Chanakyapuri); Kolkata
(☎ 033-24407836; 18B Mandeville Gardens, Gariahat);
Mumbai (Map pp78-9; ☎ 022-22823535; Dalamal House,
1st fl, Jamnalal Bajaj Marg, Nariman Point)
UK Chennai (☎ 044-42192151; 20 Anderson Rd); Delhi
(☎ 011-26872161; www.ukinindia.com; Shantipath,
Chanakyapuri); Kolkata (☎ 033-22885172; 1 Ho Chi Minh
Sarani); Mumbai (Map pp78-9; ☎ 022-66502222; Naman
Chambers, C/32 G Block Bandra Kurla Complex, Bandra East)
USA Chennai (☎ 044-28574242; Gemini Circle, 220 Anna
Salai); Delhi (☎ 011-24198000; http://newdelhi.usemb
assy.gov/; Shantipath, Chanakyapuri); Kolkata (☎ 033-
39842400; 5/1 Ho Chi Minh Sarani); Mumbai (Map pp78-9;
☎ 022-23633611; Lincoln House, 78 Bhulabhai Desai Rd,
Breach Candy)

FOOD

Food is a definite highlight of a trip to Goa.
A budget meal, with a soft drink, comes in at
under Rs200 for two courses, a midrange option will cost Rs200 to Rs500, and a top-end

option over Rs500. If you add alcohol, the
prices increase considerably (aside from those
ever-present beach-shack happy hour deals).

For more information about food in Goa,
see p52.

GAY & LESBIAN TRAVELLERS

While overt displays of affection between
members of the opposite sex, such as cud-
dling and hand holding, are frowned upon
in India, it is not unusual to see Indian men
holding hands with each other or engaged in
other close affectionate behaviour. This does
not mean they are gay.

Homosexual relations between men are illegal in India, although there is no legislation
forbidding lesbian relations. The gay movement is confined almost exclusively to larger
cities, and Mumbai is really the only place
where there's a real 'scene' to be found. Since
marriage is seen as important, being gay has
a particular stigma – most stay in the closet or
risk being disowned by their families.

However, Goa's liberal reputation draws a
lot of gay men, and there's a discreet scene,
mainly around the Calangute-Baga area. A
couple of the beach shacks are also becoming a bit braver with respect to gay events,
and you might find the occasional gay night
on offer. As with relations between hetero-
sexual Western couples travelling in India,
gay and lesbian travellers should exercise dis-
cretion and refrain from displaying affection
in public.

HOLIDAYS

The three official public holidays in India are
Republic Day (26 January), Independence Day
(15 August), and Mahatma Gandhi's Birthday
(2 October). In addition to these, holidays are
called during major festivals such as Diwali,
Dussehra and Holi, Nanak Jayanti, Buddha
Jayanti, and Easter and Christmas.

INSURANCE

A travel insurance policy to cover theft, loss
and medical problems is a wise idea, if only
because of the cosmic law that if you have it
you won't need it. There is a wide variety of
policies and your travel agent will have recommendations. Some policies specifically exclude
'dangerous activities', which can mean diving,
motorcycling and even trekking. This is especially relevant in Goa, where most people
hire a scooter or motorcycle at some time.

Other increasingly popular activities in Goa are scuba-diving and water sports such as waterskiing and paragliding, all of which may require special stipulations when you take out your travel insurance. For more information about health insurance see p246.

If your goods are stolen, you will also be required to file a police report (p227) to claim insurance.

Worldwide travel insurance is available at www.lonelyplanet.com/travel_services. You can buy, extend and claim online anytime – even if you're already on the road.

INTERNET ACCESS

Internet and email services in Goa are plentiful, reliable and relatively cheap. In all major towns, beach resorts and even some small villages, you'll easily find somewhere to check email. The most common places offering internet access are travel agencies and STD/ISD phone offices, but you'll also find many dedicated internet cafes. Many hotels and guest houses also offer internet access for guests, for an additional cost. Average charges are around Rs40 per hour (though some places charge up to Rs60), usually with a minimum of 15 minutes (Rs10 to Rs15).

If you're travelling with a laptop remember that you'll need a universal adaptor. These are readily available in Goa, though finding a surge protector is more difficult. If you want to ensure that your computer's innards stay intact through power surges, it's worth investing in one at home to bring with you.

In recent years, wireless internet has become more widely available. Some traveller-orientated cafes even offer it for free.

See p21 for some internet resources.

LEGAL MATTERS

Travellers should note that they can be prosecuted under the law of their home country regarding age of consent, even when abroad.

Drugs

For a long time Goa was a place where you could indulge in all sorts of illicit drugs with relative ease – they were cheap and readily available, and the risks were minimal. Ecstasy, LSD (acid) and ketamine are all still present, though since the virtual death of the trance-party scene, hashish (charas) – often brought down from Manali and the Kullu Valley in Himachal Pradesh, and peddled around the beach resorts – has reclaimed its place as the drug of choice.

Would-be users should not be lulled into a false sense of security in Goa. Think extremely carefully about the risks before partaking. In addition to the numerous overdoses that happen here, the drug laws in India are among the toughest in the world; possession of even a relatively small amount of hash (10g or so) can lead to 10 years in jail and a Rs100,000 fine. Fort Aguada jail houses a number of prisoners, including Westerners, who are serving drug-related sentences.

Police

There was a period when police often conducted 'raids' of foreigners in Goa. These would take place at roadblocks or even at private homes or hotel rooms. Usually searches yielded nothing, but there were occasions where hapless searchees were planted with drugs and ended up in prison. Raids have decreased in recent years, perhaps in part due to increased efforts by the government to crack down on corruption in the public service. However, the fact remains that both drugs and corruption are still a problem in Goa, with drug use among travellers giving some poorly paid policemen opportunities for extortion.

Probably the best way to deal with police extortion, should it happen to you, is through polite (and though it might pain you), respectful persuasion. If that fails, attempt to bargain down the 'fine' before paying up, and try to establish the identity (or at least a good mental image) of the policeman.

In practical terms, the most contact the average traveller is likely to have with the law will be on the street. You may be unlucky enough to be flagged down for not wearing a helmet on certain parts of the NH17, or checked for papers by an opportunistic police officer who is hoping to extract a 'fine'. If this happens, keep your cool and you may be able to negotiate the fine down to zero. For more information about such encounters, see p244.

Smoking & Spitting

On 1 January 2000, a law came into force in Goa banning smoking, spitting and the chewing of tobacco in all public places. It's a welcome move, but clearly impossible to enforce except in government buildings and places such as train stations where transgressors face a Rs1000 fine. Smoking is banned in many restaurants, while some others have nonsmoking areas.

Both laws are implemented in Goa in a typically *susegad* (relaxed or laid-back) style; ashtrays are often provided in restaurants that bear 'no smoking' signs and most bars and beach shacks have no problem whatsoever with smokers of cigarettes, or, in some cases, something stronger.

MAPS

There are plenty of maps available, but none are accurate enough to guide you around the back roads without having to stop and ask for directions. A map is available from the GTDC (Rs25), which is decent for general orientation. A good source of information on maps is www.indiamapstore.com.

MONEY

The rupee (Rs) is divided into 100 paise (p). There are coins of 5, 10, 20, 25 and 50 paise, and Rs 1, 2 and 5, as well as notes of Rs 10, 20, 50, 100, 500 and even 1000, which feel all the more valuable because they're so hard to come by.

ATMs are so widely available now that you can rely on them as your primary source of cash, though you could also carry a bit of hard currency (or travellers cheques) as backup. You need to show your passport when you are changing money or cashing travellers cheques.

See the inside front cover for exchange rates at the time of writing, and p18 for typical costs. Prices quoted in this book are in Indian rupees (Rs), unless otherwise stated.

ATMs

A number of banks have introduced 24-hour ATMs into Goa, and more are constantly opening. These take international cards using the Cirrus, Maestro, MasterCard and Visa networks. The main banks with ATMs are ICICI, Centurion, HDFC and UTI. Often ATMs are attached to the bank, but not inside it, installed in an air-conditioned cubicle (which you may need your card to access) and sometimes guarded by 24-hour armed security. At present, you can find ATMs in Panaji (Panjim), Margao (Madgaon), Mapusa, Calangute, Candolim, Vasco da Gama, Ponda, Colva, Palolem and Chaudi. Plan ahead when you're heading to the beaches away from these towns.

Cash

It pays to have some US dollars, pounds sterling or euros for times when you can't find an ATM, change travellers cheques or use a credit card. You won't have any problem changing money in all tourist areas. The best rates are usually at Thomas Cook and the State Bank of India, while next best are private moneychangers. Hotels offer the least attractive rates. When changing money, don't accept notes that are damaged because you might be hard-pressed to pass them on.

Credit Cards

Credit cards are accepted in most major tourist centres, but don't expect to be able to use a card in budget hotels or restaurants. Upmarket hotels accept them, as do most travel agencies and practically all department stores. MasterCard and Visa are the most widely accepted cards. Cash advances on credit cards can be made at branches of Thomas Cook and Bank of Baroda, as well as at most moneychangers (which are often travel agencies) at beach resorts.

Encashment Certificates

All money is meant to be changed at official banks or moneychangers, and you are supposed to be given an encashment certificate for each transaction. These can be useful if you want to change excess rupees back to hard currency, buy a tourist-quota train ticket or if you need to show a tax clearance certificate. ATM receipts serve the same purpose.

International Transfers

International money transfers can be arranged through Thomas Cook or Western Union; both have branches in Panaji and some of the larger towns in Goa, and Western Union transfers can frequently be made at post offices. Charges for this service are high – if you have a credit card it's cheaper to get someone to deposit money in your home account and draw a cash advance.

Moneychangers

Private moneychangers are everywhere in towns and beach resorts. They keep longer hours than banks, and are quick and efficient. Many travel agencies double as exchange offices and give cash advances on credit cards. Check rates at the banks first.

Tipping

There's no official policy on tipping in India, though it's always appreciated as a supplement to waiters' wages and 10% of a bill is absolutely acceptable. The exceptions to this rule are five-star international hotels, where tipping hotel porters is the norm, as elsewhere in the world. Taxi drivers don't need to be tipped, but if you've hired the driver for the day it's generally a good idea to add on a little extra for getting you safely home.

Travellers Cheques

All major brands of travellers cheques are accepted in India, with American Express (Amex) and Thomas Cook being the most widely traded. Pounds sterling, euros and US dollars are the safest bet. Charges for changing travellers cheques vary but hot competition among private moneychangers means you can usually change cheques without commission.

All travellers cheques are replaceable, but this does little good if you have to go home and apply for them at your bank. Keep an emergency stash of cash in a separate place from your cheques, along with a record of cheque serial numbers, proof of purchase slips and your passport number.

If your travellers cheques are lost or stolen, contact the following office in Panaji immediately:

Thomas Cook (☎ 0832-2221312; www.thomascook .co.in; 8 Alcon Chambers, Dayanand Bandodkar Marg; ☾ 9.30am-6pm Mon-Sat year round, 10am-5pm Sun Oct-Mar)

PHOTOGRAPHY

It's easy, in almost every tourist spot, to have photos downloaded from memory card to CD, and extra memory cards are also easy to obtain.

Goans are generally quite mellow about having their photograph taken; do ask before snapping shots of women, older people or any sort of religious official. An easy way to make friends is to take their address and offer to send or email a copy of the photo (as long as you do it, of course).

It can also be tempting to take photos of some of the colourful scenes at the Anjuna flea market and the other big markets, but some of the vendors (both Western and Indian) strongly object to being photographed.

In general don't take photos inside temples, and ask before you use a camera and flash in a church. For more on photography, pick up Lonely Planet's *Travel Photography: A Guide to Taking Better Pictures*.

POST

The Indian postal and old-fashioned poste restante services are generally good. Letters almost always reach you, and letters you send almost invariably reach their destination, although they can take up to three weeks.

It costs Rs8 to send a small postcard or aerogramme anywhere in the world from India, and Rs15 for a large postcard or a standard letter (up to 20g). Sending post via the electronic Speedpost system (either within India or to elsewhere in the world) is faster and far more reliable, but you'll pay about double for the privilege.

Receiving Mail

Have letters addressed to you with your surname in capitals and underlined, followed by poste restante, GPO and the city or town in question. Many 'lost' letters are simply misfiled under forenames, so always check under both your given and last name. Letters sent via poste restante are generally held for one month only, after which they might be returned to the sender or just left in a box under the counter until they disintegrate.

Sending Mail

Sending parcels from Goa requires a little more than arriving at the post office with your package, and it may take you a couple of trips before your parcel is on its merry way. First, take the parcel to a wrapping service (there's usually one very close to the post office – look for signs reading 'parcel post'), and get it stitched up. It can be quite an experience to watch your package being transformed with boxes, linen, calico and newspaper. You may even find that your possessions are sewn up with a needle and thread, and the stitching sealed with wax.

Book packages (up to 5kg) can be sent without a customs form and for considerably less money. They will need to be wrapped in a manner that allows the contents to be inspected on the way.

At the post office you'll get the necessary customs declaration forms, which will be attached to the parcel. To avoid excise duty at the delivery end, specify that the contents are a 'gift' with a value of less than Rs1000.

As with letters, Speedpost is available at major post offices (such as Panaji and Margao), and charges to various destinations are as follows:

Australia Rs700 for the first kilogram, plus Rs300 for each additional kilogram.

Europe (incl the UK) Rs950 for the first kilogram, plus Rs300 for each additional kilogram.

USA Rs775 for the first kilogram, plus Rs400 for each additional kilogram.

This is more expensive than ordinary post (which will cost Rs570/645/500 for 1kg respectively), but is faster and much more reliable.

Sending parcels in the other direction (to India) is akin to gambling. Don't count on anything bigger than a letter getting to you, and don't count on a letter getting to you if there's anything of value inside it.

SHOPPING

Although Goa is not renowned for its handicrafts, a vibrant market culture lures traders from all over India. While this means that you are unlikely to take home much that is genuinely Goan (apart from the odd decorative bottle of *feni* – palm liquor), it also means that you can find almost anything from Kashmiri carpets to fabrics from Rajasthan, carvings from Karnataka and paintings from Nepal.

The state's biggest market – and one of the key tourist attractions – is the Anjuna flea market held every Wednesday in season, while Mapusa's Friday market is a popular local affair. Panaji and Margao also have busy municipal markets, with plenty of colour

and a good line in spices if you're looking for a tasty masala or two.

In Panaji the main shopping street is 18th June Rd, a long thoroughfare lined with craft and clothing shops, emporiums and shops selling cashews and spices; MG Rd also has a collection of modern Western department stores. Perhaps the greatest concentration of department stores, boutiques, jewellery and craft shops, though, is in Calangute, on both the road that leads down to the main beach, and the Calangute–Candolim road. Prices are high here but so is the quality of the merchandise.

Be careful when buying items that include delivery to your home country. You may well be assured that the price includes home delivery and all customs and handling charges, but you may later find that you have to collect the item yourself from your country's main port or airport, and pay customs and handling charges.

Bargaining

While stores in the larger towns often have fixed prices, you are generally expected to bargain at markets, though some Western traders at Anjuna market have fairly fixed prices, and are inflexible when it comes to deviating from them. Mostly, however, bargaining is the name of the game; see above for some pointers.

What to Buy
ANTIQUES

Articles more than 100 years old are not permitted to be exported from India without an

---

THE ART OF HAGGLING

The friendly art of haggling is an absolute must in most parts of Goa, unless you don't mind paying above market value. Traders in towns and markets are accustomed to tourists who have lots of money and little time to spend it, meaning that a shopkeeper's 'very good price' might in fact be a rather bad one.

If you have absolutely no idea what something should really cost, a good rule of thumb is to bank on paying half of what you're originally quoted. The vendor will probably look aghast and tell you that this is impossible, as it's the very price they had to pay for the item themselves. This is when the battle for a bargain begins and it's up to you and the salesperson to negotiate a price. You'll find that many shopkeepers lower their so-called final price if you proceed to head out of the shop and tell them that you'll think about it.

Don't lose your sense of humour and sense of fairness while haggling – it's not a battle to squeeze every last rupee out of a poor trader, and not all vendors are out to make a fool of you. In essence, the haggle itself is often the very spirit, and the fun, of the Indian shopping experience.

export clearance certificate. If you have doubts about any item and think it could be defined as an antique, check with the **Archaeological Survey of India** (http://asi.nic.in/) at the Archaeological Museum in Old Goa.

BRONZE FIGURES & WOODCARVING

Delightful small images of gods are made by the age-old lost-wax process. In this process, a wax figure is made, a mould is formed around it, then wax is melted and poured out, leaving the hollow shell. Molten metal is poured in and once it's solidified the mould is broken open. Figures of Ganesh, and of Shiva in his incarnation as dancing Nataraja, are among the most popular.

In South India, images of the gods are also carved out of sandalwood. Rosewood is used to carve animals, elephants in particular. Carved wooden furniture and other household items, either in natural finish or lacquered, are also made in various locations.

CARPETS

It may not surprise you that India produces and exports more handcrafted carpets than Iran, but it probably is more of a surprise that some of them are of virtually equal quality. India's best carpets come from Kashmir, and these can be found in traders' shops in Goa.

Carpets are either made of pure wool, wool with a small percentage of silk to give it a sheen (known as 'silk touch'), or pure silk. The latter are more for decoration than hard wear. Expect to pay from Rs7000 for a good quality 1.2m by 1.8m carpet, but don't be surprised if the price is more than twice as high.

CLOTHING

Western-brand clothing stores are all the rage in Panaji and Calangute these days. Big names now make much of their produce in India, and these shops, which cater almost exclusively to tourists, sell their brand-name gear at prices lower than you'd find at home. Don't expect the cheap knock-offs you might pick up in Bangkok – here, Levi jeans go for around Rs2000 and Lacoste polo shirts retail at Rs1000.

JEWELLERY

The heavy folk-art jewellery of Rajasthan has particular appeal for Western tastes. Tibetan jewellery is even chunkier and more folklike than the Rajasthani variety. If you're looking for fine jewellery, as opposed to folk jewellery, you may well find that much of what is produced in India is way over the top for your taste.

LEATHERWORK

Indian leatherwork is not made from cowhide but from buffalo, camel, goat or some other form of animal. Chappals, the basic sandals found all over India, are the most popular buy.

MUSICAL INSTRUMENTS

Indian musical instruments are an interesting buy in India, and you'll see new and secondhand guitars, sitars and tablas at the Anjuna flea market. There are also instrument shops in Panaji and Margao. Easier to carry (and even easier to play) are CDs. You'll find Bollywood soundtracks, local legends, Goa Trance and mainstream Western music at shops and stalls all over Goa for between Rs100 and Rs600.

PAPIER-MÂCHÉ

This is probably the most characteristic Kashmiri craft. The basic papier-mâché article is made in a mould, then painted and polished in successive layers until the final intricate design is produced. Prices depend upon the complexity and quality of the painted design and the amount of gold leaf used. Items include bowls, cups, containers, jewellery boxes, letter holders, tables, lamps, coasters, trays and so on. A cheap bowl might cost only Rs50, while a large, well-made item might approach Rs1000.

SILKS & SARIS

Silk is cheap and the quality is often excellent. If you are buying a silk sari, it helps to know a bit about the silk and the sari. Saris are 5.5m long, unless they have fabric for a choli (sari blouse) attached, in which case they are 6m. Sari silk is graded and sold by weight (grams per metre).

TEXTILES

This is still India's major industry and 40% of the total production is at the village level, where it is known as *khadi* (homespun cloth). Bedspreads, tablecloths, cushion covers or fabric for clothing are popular *khadi* purchases. There is an amazing variety of cloth styles, types and techniques around the country. In Gujarat and Rajasthan heavy material is embroidered with tiny mirrors and beads to produce everything from dresses to stuffed toys to wall hangings. Tie-dye work is also popular in Rajasthan and Kerala. In Kashmir embroidered materials are made into shirts and dresses. Batik is a relatively recent technique introduced from Indonesia that has become widespread; *kalamkari* (textile art that is hand painted or block printed) cloth from Andhra Pradesh and Gujarat is a similar but older craft.

SOLO TRAVELLERS

The general consensus is that travelling in Goa is markedly easier than travelling in the rest of the country, and many solo travellers wander down this way for some relaxation and respite from the challenge of travelling in the rest of India. It's a sociable place, so you only have to be as solo as you want to be. While most visitors to the Calangute-Baga beach resort areas travel in couples or groups, there are many solo travellers further north in the Arambol-Anjuna-Vagator area and further south around Palolem. Meeting them at beach shacks, bars and parties is not difficult.

The downside to being a solo female is that often people will think that you obviously want company. Keep a book on hand to give off the appearance of busy contentedness so that unwanted company can be deterred. On the whole though, travelling as a solo female couldn't be easier. Attitudes to women are more liberal and accepting than in many other parts of India, and you can largely be yourself without running the risk of misinterpretation and mistreatment. Like anywhere, however, there are a few basic risks to be aware of (see p227 and p236).

TELEPHONE & FAX

Mobile phones are common throughout Goa, and your own mobile phone will likely work while in Goa, though call costs are unsurprisingly excessive. Though cheap international calls can still be made at the many internet cafes, which also have a STD/ISD phone booth or two (costing Rs25 to Rs40 per minute, depending on the country you're calling), many visitors opt to purchase a local SIM card, with prepaid credit.

You can do this from many internet cafes and mobile phone shops; it costs around Rs700, plus the cost of 'unlocking' your phone

if it's not already done. The most basic model of Nokia phone (usefully equipped with flashlight to see you through all those late-night power cuts) costs around Rs1000. Bring along two passport photos of yourself, and a copy of your passport and visa. Note that local SIM cards won't work outside Goa, except for receiving calls and sending text messages.

Many STD/ISD offices have fax facilities, but these don't generally come cheap. Sending a fax internationally can cost between Rs40 and Rs100 per page, while faxes sent within India should only cost around Rs10 per page. You can receive faxes for around Rs10 per page. Private internet cafes also often offer this service, and many hotels have fax facilities.

Phone Codes

The area code for everywhere within the state of Goa is ☎ 0832, which you only need to dial when calling from outside the state or from a mobile phone.

To make an international call, you need to dial ☎ 00 (international access code from India), plus the country code (of the country you are calling), the area code and local number.

To make a call to Goa from outside the country, dial the international access code of the country you are in plus ☎ 91 (international country code for India), then ☎ 832 (Goa's area code omitting the initial 0) and then the local number.

TIME

India is 5½ hours ahead of GMT/UTC, 4½ hours behind Australia (EST) and 10½ hours ahead of the USA (EST). It is officially known as IST – Indian Standard Time, although many Indians prefer to think it stands for Indian Stretchable Time. When it's noon in London, it's 5.30pm in Goa.

TOURIST INFORMATION

Within Goa you'll find representatives of the national **Government of India Tourist Office** (www.incredibleindia.org), and the state government's own tourism body, the **Goa Tourism Development Corporation** (GTDC; www.goa-tourism.com), both with head offices in Panaji (p112).

The GTDC is the most active of the two in Goa, running a number of decent (though not exciting) hotels and a range of whirlwind day trips. These are bookable at the Panaji office or at any GTDC hotel, and many depart daily.

If you're on a very tight time schedule, they can prove a good way of seeing a number of sights at a breakneck pace.

TRAVELLERS WITH DISABILITIES

There are few provisions for disabled travellers in Goa outside of the most top-end hotels, and thus the mobility-impaired traveller will face a number of challenges. Few older buildings have wheelchair access; toilets have certainly not been designed to accommodate wheelchairs; and footpaths are generally riddled with potholes and crevices, littered with obstacles and packed with throngs of people. Nevertheless, the difficulties are far from insurmountable and if you want to visit Goa, don't be put off. If your mobility is restricted you will need an able-bodied companion to accompany you, and you'd be well-advised to hire a private vehicle with a driver.

The **Royal Association for Disability and Rehabilitation** (RADAR; ☎ +44 (0)20-72503222; www .radar.org.uk; 12 City Forum, 250 City Rd, London EC1V 8AF, UK) may be able to offer further information on the logistics of travelling in India. Also check out **Mobility International USA** (MIUSA; ☎ 541-3431284; www.miusa.org; PO Box 10767, Eugene, OR 97440, USA).

For specific information about disability issues in Goa, contact **Disability Goa** (www.disability goa.com), or contact **Timeless Excursions** (www .timelessexcursions.com), which arranges Indian holidays and tours for travellers with disabilities.

VISAS

Everyone except for Bhutanese and Nepalese citizens needs to obtain a visa before entering India. This should be done well in advance of travel; check the website of your local Indian consulate or embassy for up-to-date details.

Tax Clearance Certificates

If you stay in India for more than 120 days, you officially need a 'tax clearance certificate' to leave the country, but we've never heard from anyone who has actually been asked for this document on departure. In Panaji, go to the foreign section of the **Income Tax Office** (Shanta Bldg, Emidio Gracia Rd) with your passport and a handful of bank exchange or ATM receipts (to show you have been changing foreign currency into rupees officially).

Visa Extensions

Officially, you can only get another six-month tourist visa by leaving the country and coming back in on a new visa, and many travellers head off on a quick 'visa run' to Sri Lanka, Nepal or home, to replenish their tourist visa. You may hear stories of people obtaining visa extensions through 'unofficial' channels; ask someone who's done this successfully, and expect to pay dearly for the rather shady service.

People travelling on tourist visas are not required to register with the Foreigners' Regional Registration Office (FRRO); the form that you fill out each time you check into a hotel, beach hut or guest house takes the place of this. Only foreigners with visas valid for longer than 180 days are required to register, as are nationals of Pakistan and Afghanistan. FRRO can be located in Mumbai as follows:

FRRO Mumbai (☎ 022-22620446; Annex Bldg No 2, CID, Badaruddin Tyabji Rd, near Special Branch)

VOLUNTEER WORK

A growing number of charity organisations have opportunities for volunteer work in Goa; see p72 and p67 for more information. If you're planning on working with children, try to file your application as early as possible, since you'll have to undergo background and criminal record checks to be accepted to most positions in children's homes.

WOMEN TRAVELLERS

Most solo female travellers to Goa, aside from the occasional lewd comment or beachside ogling, experience few problems during a stay in the state.

However, for some Indian men a perfect weekend away with their (male) friends is a boozy trip to Goa, and though it generally doesn't get beyond being extremely annoying, it can ruin an otherwise perfectly lovely day at the beach. It's not uncommon to see hapless women surrounded by groups of Indian men wearing matching 'I Heart Goa' singlets all insisting on 'one photo', which will later be presented at home as their reputation-enhancing 'holiday romance'. That said, those same men are also keen to take pictures of couples, Western children and even entire tourist families as evidence of their 'new friends', so it's not only women who are singled out for this irritating behaviour.

On the other hand, Goa is considered to be one of the most liberal states in the country, where women hold positions of high esteem and are not as guarded, in terms of their dress or behaviour, as elsewhere. Moreover, 40-or-so years of Western women swimming on Goan beaches has meant that locals are used to seeing foreigners cavorting in bikinis, though it pays, away from the beach, to cover up as usual (see p18 for more). If you do find yourself the target of unwanted attention or advances, raise your voice to embarrass the offender, preferably referring to him as 'brother'; this association, in general, is enough to rob the culprit of a substantial degree of his passion.

Nevertheless, the sad fact remains that foreign women have been raped, and worse, in Goa. It pays to keep your wits about you and avoid situations that make you more vulnerable, including walking alone at night along unlit stretches of road or beach. Diminished mental alertness, through use of drugs and alcohol, might also make you more of a target and less able to defend yourself, should the worst come to the worst. In all, it's best to stay vigilant, though not fearful, throughout your stay.

Transport

CONTENTS

Getting There & Away	**238**
Entering The Region	238
Air	238
Land	239
Getting Around	**241**
Bicycle	241
Boat	241
Bus	241
Car	241
Hitching	241
Local Transport	242
Motorcycle	242
Train	244

Tickets for flights, tours and rail journeys can be booked online at www.lonelyplanet.com /travel_services.

GETTING THERE & AWAY

ENTERING THE REGION
The standard Indian immigration and customs procedures apply when entering Goa internationally by air; for customs information, see p227. There are no formalities to deal with if you're entering Goa overland from elsewhere in India.

Passport
You must have a valid Indian visa to enter Goa on an international flight. You might sometimes (but not always) be asked to provide evidence of a return ticket, though in practice all international flights to Goa are package deals, and usually include a return portion (whether or not you intend to use it). Always keep a photocopy of your passport and visa somewhere safely stowed, just in case you lose them.

AIR
Airports & Airlines
INTERNATIONAL FLIGHTS
To get to Goa by air, you may be flying into **Mumbai Airport** (BOM; Chhatrapati Shivaji International Airport; ☎ domestic 02226264000, international 02226813000; www.csia.in) and taking an onward domestic connection. See p103 for details.

Otherwise, you will be flying into Goa's **Dabolim Airport** (GOI; Dabolim International Airport; ☎ 0832-540806).

Only a handful of charter companies operate international flights into Dabolim Airport, most from the UK, Germany and Russia. Be aware that in principle, at least, it's illegal to enter India on a scheduled flight and leave on a charter flight, or vice versa. Chances are, however, this won't be checked.

Reliable charter flight booking services in the UK or Germany:
Thomson Airlines (www. thomson.co.uk)
Monarch Airlines (holidays.monarch.co.uk)
Condor Airlines (www.condor.com)

DOMESTIC FLIGHTS
Numerous domestic airlines fly daily in and out of Goa, most flights taking off and landing throughout the morning and early afternoon, to a number of Indian destinations.

Of them, **Indigo** (☎ 1800 1803838 toll free; www.go indigo.in), **GoAir** (☎ 1800 222111 toll free; www.goair .in) and **Spicejet** (☎ 1800 1803333 toll free; www .spicejet.com) are the cheapest, and **Kingfisher** (☎ 1800 1800101 toll free; www.flyingfisher.com) and **Jet Airways** (☎ 1800 225522 toll free; www.jetairways .com) by far the most comfortable.

A return flight from Mumbai to Goa (the direct journey takes around 45 minutes) can cost around US$150, sometimes even less.

It's cheapest and easiest to book online as far in advance of your travel as possible, and any enquiries are best made to the airlines' toll-free numbers in India.

THINGS CHANGE...

The information in this chapter is particularly vulnerable to change. Check directly with the airline or a travel agent to make sure you understand how a fare (and ticket you may buy) works and be aware of the security requirements for international travel. Shop carefully. The details given in this chapter should be regarded as pointers and are not a substitute for your own careful, up-to-date research.

CLIMATE CHANGE & TRAVEL

Climate change is a serious threat to the ecosystems that humans rely upon, and air travel is the fastest-growing contributor to the problem. Lonely Planet regards travel, overall, as a global benefit, but believes we all have a responsibility to limit our personal impact on global warming.

Flying & Climate Change

Pretty much every form of motor travel generates CO_2 (the main cause of human-induced climate change) but planes are far and away the worst offenders, not just because of the sheer distances they allow us to travel, but because they release greenhouse gases high into the atmosphere. The statistics are frightening: two people taking a return flight between Europe and the US will contribute as much to climate change as an average household's gas and electricity consumption over a whole year.

Carbon Offset Schemes

Climatecare.org and other websites use 'carbon calculators' that allow jetsetters to offset the greenhouse gases they are responsible for with contributions to energy-saving projects and other climate-friendly initiatives in the developing world – including projects in India, Honduras, Kazakhstan and Uganda.

Lonely Planet, together with Rough Guides and other concerned partners in the travel industry, supports the carbon offset scheme run by climatecare.org. Lonely Planet offsets all of its staff and author travel.

For more information check out our website: lonelyplanet.com.

Dabolim Airport's arrivals hall is equipped with a money-exchange office, GTDC tourist office, Airtel office for purchasing mobile phone credit, and charter airline offices. There are two prepaid taxi booths (one in the arrivals hall and the other just outside), for heading by taxi elsewhere in the state.

LAND

Car & Motorcycle

Hiring a self-drive car in any of the main cities in India and driving to Goa is possible, but given the danger and expense is not recommended.

Hertz (www.hertz.com) will charge around Rs1700 per day for a basic car. You'll be required to leave an insurance deposit of around Rs20,000 and hold an international driving permit. There are also some private operators that can hire cars for less than Rs1000 per day.

The other option is to make your way to the nearest taxi rank and start bargaining. The 600km trip from Mumbai to Goa takes about 14 hours; many drivers will happily do this in one stretch. You'll have to pay for the taxi's return trip, so the cost will be at least Rs8000 – unless you're part of a group, it's likely to be cheaper to fly.

Motorcycles, on the other hand, are a particularly popular way to get around India. The **Royal Enfield** (www.royalenfield.com) is synonymous with motorcycle travel in India. Protective clothing and gear is best brought from home. For more information on motorcycle travel, see p242.

Bus

India has a comprehensive and extensive public bus system, but most state-run vehicles are decrepit and overcrowded. From neighbouring states you'll find frequent bus services into Goa – it's just a matter of turning up at the bus station and checking timetables or jumping on the next available bus.

There are also plenty of private bus companies running into Goa from Mumbai, Pune, Bengaluru (Bangalore), Mangalore and other interstate cities. These are more expensive, but faster and more comfortable, with reclining seats and options of AC or even 'sleeper' class. One of the most popular options for bus travel to and from Goa is **Paulo Travels** (www.paulotravels .com). Consult its website for the most up-to-date prices and route information.

MUMBAI

For details of bus services from Mumbai, see p104.

Buses for Mumbai depart from Panaji (p119) and Margao (p184) daily; see individual chapters for details and prices.

Train

The **Konkan Railway** (www.konkanrailway.com), the main train line running through Goa, connects Goa with Mumbai to the north, and with Mangalore to the south. Its main train station in Goa is Madgaon station in Margao (p184), from which there are several useful daily services to Mumbai. Note that services and prices change seasonally, and it's a good idea to have a thorough look at the Konkan Railway website for the most up-to-date information.

You can also book *Konkan Kanya Express* (Goa–Mumbai or Mumbai–Goa) tickets online from the Konkan Railway website, subject to a long list of conditions: you can only book between two and seven days in advance of travel, only in three-tier sleeper AC class for a cost of Rs1500 per ticket, and with no date changes permitted.

All other train bookings are best made at Margao's Madgaon station (p184), at the train reservation office at Panaji's Kadamba bus stand (p119) or at any travel agent selling train tickets (though you'll probably pay a small commission for the convenience). Make sure you book as far in advance as possible for sleepers, since they fill up quickly.

Other smaller, useful Goan railway stations include Pernem for Arambol, Thivim for Mapusa and the northern beaches, Karmali (Old Goa) for Panaji and Canacona for Palolem.

For more details about travelling by train from Mumbai, see p104.

MAIN TRAIN SERVICES BETWEEN GOA AND MUMBAI

Konkan Kanya Express (KKE; train number 0111; 1AC/2AC/3AC/2nd-class sleeper Rs1832/1092/796/293) departs Mumbai's Chhatrapati Shivaji Terminus (CST) at 11.05pm, arriving at Margao's Madgaon station the next morning at 10.45am. In the opposite direction, the *KKE* (train number 0112) departs Margao at 6pm daily, and arrives at Mumbai CST at 5.50am.

Mandovi Express (train number 0103; 1AC/2AC/3AC/2nd class Rs1832/1092/796/165) departs Mumbai CST at 6.55am and arrives at Margao at 6.45pm. In the opposite direction, the *Mandovi Express* (train number 0104) departs Margao at 9.40am and arrives at CST at 9.45pm.

Jan Shatabdi Express (train number 2051; AC seat/2nd class Rs680/197) departs Mumbai's CST at 5.10am and arrives in Margao at 2.10pm. In the opposite direction, the *Jan Shatabdi Express* (train number 2052) departs Margao at 2.30pm and arrives at Mumbai's CST at 11.20pm.

TRAIN TYPES & CLASS

Indian trains have a whole host of different categories and classes when it comes to calculating fares and comfort levels.

The most basic is **2nd-class seating** ('2nd class'), which has hard seats; five or six people will more than likely cram onto a bench made for three. A close second in terms of general discomfort is the **2nd-class sleeper** (or 'sleeper class'), which has open carriages with seats that fold down to form three tiers of beds.

Air-conditioned sleepers are a step up in comfort and security, since each carriage is divided into small compartments. Bedding and sometimes food is provided, and gets higher in quality as you go higher in price. The most common are **three-tier** (six beds in a compartment, '3AC') and **two-tier** (four beds in a compartment, '2AC'). Best is **1st class air-con** (two beds in a compartment; '1AC'). 2AC is about twice the price of 3AC; 1AC is about double that again. Sleeping berths are only available between 9pm and 6am.

Finally there's **chair car** ('AC Seat'), which is individual reclining seats on some air-conditioned trains (such as the *Jan Shatabdi Express*).

Fares are calculated by distance and class, and are mostly fixed regardless of which train you are on and where you are going. To learn more above travelling by train in India, **Train Travel in India** (www.seat61.com/India.htm) is an invaluable resource.

RESERVATIONS

There are reservation charges for sleeper class (Rs40) and anything above that, such as 3AC, 2AC and 1AC (Rs60). The easiest way to reserve a ticket is to head to the station itself.

At most major stations there's a separate section in the booking hall dealing with the tourist quota. Only foreigners and nonresident Indians are allowed to use this facility. You must pay in foreign currency (cash or travellers cheques in US dollars or pounds sterling) or with rupees backed up by exchange certificates or ATM receipts. Only a limited number of seats are allocated to tourists, so if you can't get on it's worth trying for a normal reservation. When booking any ticket at a train station, you must fill out a reservation form *before* queuing.

If the train you want is fully booked, it's often possible to get a Reservation Against Cancellation (RAC) ticket. This entitles you to board the train and at least get a simple seat. Once the train is moving, the Travelling Ticket Examiner (TTE) will find you a berth – which he usually, quite miraculously, does.

GETTING AROUND

BICYCLE

Goa offers plenty of variety for cycling, with relatively smooth-surfaced highways, rocky dirt tracks, coastal routes through coconut palms and winding country roads through spice plantations, rural villages and ancient temples. A bicycle can also simply be a convenient way of getting around beach towns.

If you want a quality machine for serious touring, it's worth bringing your own. The downside is that your bike is likely to be a curiosity and more vulnerable to theft. Bring spare tyres, tubes, patch kits, chassis, cables, freewheels, a pump with the necessary connection and spokes, tools and a repair manual.

Hire

Hiring a bicycle is not difficult in Goa, but hiring a *good* bicycle is not so easy. Every beach in Goa has a multitude of people who are prepared to rent out bicycles – just ask around and someone will rent you *their* bicycle, more often than not an Indian-made single-gear rattler. Away from the main tourist areas, you won't find bicycle-hire places.

Expect to pay around Rs5 an hour or Rs30 per day (less to hire for a week or more). If you just want to hire a bike for a day in the high season, you may have to pay up to Rs80.

Purchase

For a long stay of three months or more in Goa, it's worth considering buying a bicycle locally. Every town has at least a couple of shops selling various brands of basic Indian bikes including Hero, Atlas, BSA and Raleigh, almost always painted jet black. You should be able to pick up a secondhand bike for Rs1000 to Rs1500.

BOAT

One of the joys of travelling around Goa is joining locals on flat-bottomed passenger-vehicle ferries that cross the state's many rivers. Ferries have been commuting people across waters for decades, but services are gradually being put out of business by massive bridge-building projects.

See p200 for more details.

BUS

Goa boasts an extensive network of buses, shuttling to and from almost every tiny town and village. There are no timetables, bus numbers, or, it seems, fixed fares, though it would be hard to spend more than Rs20 on any one single journey (and fares are usually far less). Buses range from serviceable to spluttering, and most pack passengers to bursting point, but are a fun and colourful way to experience local life. Head to the nearest bus stand (often called the Kadamba bus stand, after the state's biggest bus company) and scan the signs posted on the buses' windscreens to find the service you're after, or ask a driver who'll point you in the right direction. Check individual destination listings for more detailed information on services.

CAR

It's easy, in most destinations, to organise a private car with a driver if you're planning on taking some long-distance day trips. Prices vary, but you should bank on paying around Rs1500 to Rs2000 for a full day out on the road.

It's also possible, if you've the nerves and the skills, to procure a self-drive car, giving you the (white-knuckle) freedom to explore Goa's highways and byways at your own pace. A small Chevrolet or Maruti will cost around Rs600 to Rs900 per day and a jeep around Rs1000, excluding petrol; there are few organised car-hire outlets, so ask around for a man with a car willing to rent it to you.

Note the slightly mystifying signposts posted on Goa's major NH17 national highway, which advise of different speed limits (on the largely single-carriageway road) for different types of vehicles.

HITCHING

Hitching is never entirely safe in any country in the world, and we don't recommend it. On the other hand, many travellers argue

TRANSPORT

ROAD DISTANCE CHART (km)

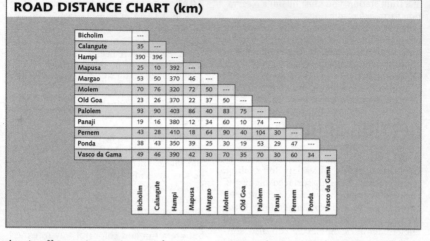

	Bicholim	Calangute	Hampi	Mapusa	Margao	Molem	Old Goa	Palolem	Panaji	Pernem	Ponda	Vasco da Gama
Bicholim	---											
Calangute	35	---										
Hampi	390	396	---									
Mapusa	25	10	392	---								
Margao	53	50	370	46	---							
Molem	70	76	320	72	50	---						
Old Goa	23	26	370	22	37	50	---					
Palolem	93	90	403	86	40	83	75	---				
Panaji	19	16	380	12	34	60	10	74	---			
Pernem	43	28	410	18	64	90	40	104	30	---		
Ponda	38	43	350	39	25	30	19	53	29	47	---	
Vasco da Gama	49	46	390	42	30	70	35	70	30	60	34	---

that it offers an interesting insight into a country. Ultimately it's up to you, but be mindful of the fact that people travelling in pairs will be safer than those going it alone. Solo women in particular are unwise to hitchhike.

The Goan caveat to the standard 'don't do it' is that sometimes (particularly at night when options are scarce) it may be practical to hail down a passing motorcycle. Assuming the person can drive, you're probably safer on the back of a stranger's motorcycle than you are in a car.

LOCAL TRANSPORT
Autorickshaw
An autorickshaw is a yellow-and-black three-wheeled contraption powered by a noisy two-stroke motorcycle engine. It has a canopy, a driver up front and seats for two (though we've managed two with four small children) passengers behind. This typically Indian mode of transport is cheaper than a taxi and generally a better option for short trips – count on Rs50 for a very short journey and Rs100 for a slightly longer one. Flag down an autorickshaw and negotiate the fare before you jump in (don't even try asking the driver to turn on the meter); if he's charging too much, let him go – there'll be another along soon.

Motorcycle Taxi
Goa is the only state in India where motorcycles are a licensed form of taxi. You can tell the

motorcycle taxis (or pilots as they are sometimes called) by the yellow front mudguard. They gather, along with taxis and autorickshaws, at strategic points in towns and beach resorts. They're fun and they're fast – no other form of transportation can efficiently navigate through traffic quite so quickly. The downside is that there's an increased element of danger – motorcycle pilots may be experienced riders but that doesn't stop them coming off or colliding with other vehicles and you've got little or no protection in the event of a crash. As with autorickshaws, negotiate a good rate before jumping on.

Taxi
Taxis, ranging from black and yellow Ford Ambassadors to white air-conditioned Maruti vans, are widely available for hopping town-to-town. A full day's sightseeing, depending on the distance, is likely to be around Rs1500 to Rs2000. You'll rarely find a taxi with a functioning meter, so agree on a price before you agree to be a passenger.

MOTORCYCLE
Getting around Goa by scooter or motorcycle is probably the most popular form of transport, both for locals and tourists. If you plan to spend most of your time lying on the beach you may have little use for a motorcycle, but if you've the urge to explore even slightly far afield, you'll soon find it's a hassle without your own transport. The freedom, therefore, that a motorcycle affords is hard to beat.

Driving Licence

An international driving permit is not technically mandatory, but it's wise to bring one. The first thing a policeman will want to see if he stops you is your licence, and an international permit is incontrovertible. Permits are available from your home automobile association.

Fuel & Spare Parts

Petrol is expensive compared to the cost of living in India. At the time of research it cost Rs56 per litre. However, distances are short and the small bikes (such as the Honda Kinetic or Activa) are very economical, so you won't spend a lot of money on fuel and certainly less than you'd spend if you were catching a taxi around. There are petrol stations in all the main towns such as Panaji, Margao, Mapusa, Ponda and Vasco da Gama, including a 24-hour service station in Margao and another on the highway near Cuncolim. There's also a very busy pump in Vagator. Where there are no petrol pumps, general stores sell petrol by the litre; they don't advertise the fact, so you'll have to ask around. Sometimes petrol in plastic bottles has been diluted, so it may be wise to buy it from the same people you hired the bike from, who cares about its condition more than a man in a village store. A litre of petrol from a plastic bottle costs around Rs55.

While it's usually possible to find someone selling petrol, if you're heading for a day ride inland or even along the coast, make sure you have adequate fuel to begin with; many rental motorcycles have broken gauges.

A Honda Kinetic holds 7L of fuel, and should go 40km on 1L. A 100cc Yamaha takes 10L to 11L and also does 40km per litre. Enfields hold about 18L; new models will do about 35km per litre, while older ones do considerably less.

Hire

Hiring a motorcycle in Goa is easy. Hirers will probably find you, and are more often than not decent guys who are just looking to make a bit of cash on the side. Private bike owners are not technically allowed to rent out a machine. This means that if you are stopped by the police for any reason, your hirer would prefer that you say you have borrowed it from a 'friend'. Laws on this sort of thing are almost universally ignored in North Goa where anything goes, but police can be more opportunistic in the south. It's a good idea to keep registration papers in the bike – it gives the police one less argument against you, and if you don't have a valid licence, or you're not wearing a helmet on NH17 (the national highway), you'll need all the help you can get.

If you leave the state, you may need to produce original documents for the vehicle you are driving or riding. If you want to go further afield from Goa, you need to hire from a licensed agency to stay within the law.

WHICH BIKE?

At the bottom end of the scale are the most popular rental bikes – gearless scooters such as the 100cc Honda Kinetics or Bajaj scooters. They have *no* street cred whatsoever, but are extremely practical and easy to ride, which makes them the obvious choice if you don't have a lot of motorcycle-riding experience. You only need a car driving licence to ride these bikes.

Next up the scale are the 100cc and 135cc bikes – Yamaha being the most common. Fuel economy is good, they go faster than a Kinetic, and they tend to be a bit more comfortable over a long distance. Although they're easy to ride, you'll need to have had some experience on a motorcycle.

Finally, at the top of the pile are the real bikes – classic Enfield Bullets. Made in India since the 1950s, this old British-designed machine is real currency for image and status; the thumping sound of the engine reverberates around the hills of Anjuna and Vagator in the high season. They are far less fuel-friendly, require more maintenance than the others, and take a little getting used to. Most of the Enfields available for hire are 350cc, but there are also some 500cc models around.

COSTS

Outside of the high season you can get a scooter for as little as Rs100 per day. During high season (December to February) the standard rate is Rs250 to Rs300. If you can get an old Kinetic down to Rs130 or so, you're doing very well. Expect to pay Rs400 for a 100cc bike and up to Rs600 for an Enfield. Obviously, the longer you hire a bike (and the older it is), the cheaper it becomes.

Make absolutely sure that you agree with the owner about the price. Clarify whether one day is 24 hours, and that you won't be asked to pay extra for keeping it overnight.

You may be asked to pay cash up front (which is fair, given that they're handing over their motorbike), but get a written receipt of some sort to that effect. Also try to take down the phone number of the owner, or his mechanic, in case something goes wrong with the bike.

WHAT TO LOOK FOR

It makes sense to check the bike over before you hire it and make a note of any damage or broken parts, so that you're not blamed for it later. Make sure brakes, lights and the all-essential horn are working. You can manage without a petrol gauge but it's nice when it works. Mirrors are useful, but many older rental bikes are missing them. Take a look at the condition of the tyres to make sure that there's at least a skerrick of tread on them.

On the Road
GETTING STOPPED BY THE POLICE

The travellers' grapevine is littered with tales of tourists being stopped by the police; 'no licence', 'no helmet' or 'dangerous driving' can all be reason enough for the police to demand on-the-spot payment of a 'fine' – a backhander, by any other name. Many people get away without any hassle, however, so there's no point in worrying too much about it. In recent years Goan police have been pulled into line and extortion of foreigners is on the decline.

THE HELMET ISSUE

Whether or not helmets should be obligatory for two-wheeler riders has been an issue for decades. After a long period of dilly-dallying, the government finally decided that helmets should indeed become mandatory as of 15 August 2004. And yet the issue rages on. The Motor-cycle Action Group (MAG) strongly opposes the law. It argues that casualties would be decreased through less reckless, negligent and drink driving, rather than through compulsory use of helmets (in addition to asserting that carrying a helmet is inconvenient, wearing one causes dandruff and hair loss, and may also cause women's hair to become dishevelled!).

In practical terms, be aware that accidents happen frequently on Goa's roads and the decision is yours. Use your head and protect it – or not – as you wish.

ROAD CONDITIONS & SAFETY

If you've never biked or scooted before, bear in mind that Goan roads are treacherous, filled with human, bovine, canine, feline, me-chanical and avian obstacles, as well as a good sprinkling of potholes and hairpin bends. Also be on the lookout for 'speed breakers'. Speed humps are stand-alone back breakers or come in triplets. The extra nasty ones are lined up in groups of fives, and none of them are particularly well signed.

In all, take it slowly, try not to drive at night (and if you do, watch out for sleeping black cows – a serious obstacle on an unlit road), don't attempt a north–south day trip on a 50cc bike, and the most cautious of riders might even consider donning a helmet or shoes. In addition, bear in mind that Goa's NH17 is a highway in name only: in no other way does it resemble the highways – or even byways – you'll be used to back home.

ROAD RULES

Road rules in India are applied mainly in theory. Driving is on the left, vehicles give way to the right and road signs are universal pictorial signs. At busy intersections, traffic police are often on hand to reduce the chaos. Otherwise, make good use of your horn. Also, never forget that the highway code in India can be reduced to one essential truth – 'Might is Right' – meaning the bigger the vehicle, the more priority you're accorded.

Organised Tours

Classic Bike Adventure (☎ 0832-2268467; www.classic -bike-india.com; Casa Tres Amigos, Socol Vado No 425, Assagao) is a long-established company that organises motorbike tours on Enfields through the Himalayas, Nepal, South India and Goa. The 1500km 'Goa and South India' tour costs €1350, including accommodation and meals, with full insurance and support. The group also organises other trips around the area; check out its website.

Purchase

Buying (and later selling) a motorcycle during a stay in Goa is not as practical or economical as it is in other parts of the country.

If you do plan to buy a bike, there are plenty of secondhand machines around – check advertisements in the daily papers or head to the Anjuna flea market on Wednesday.

TRAIN

Goa's rail services, though great for getting to and from the state itself, aren't actually very useful for getting around. You're far better off travelling by bus, taxi or under your own steam, since train services aren't particularly fast, frequent or reliable.

There are two railways in Goa. The first is the South Central Railway, which has its terminus in Mormugao (past Vasco da Gama) and runs east, through Margao and into Karnataka. This line is actually the most useful for getting around, since it's often used by tourists day-tripping to Dudhsagar Falls; see p139 for details.

The other railway is the main Konkan Railway train line, which runs from Mumbai (Bombay) to Mangalore (in Karnataka). Konkan Railway stations in Goa, from north to south, are: Pernem (for Arambol), Thivim (for Mapusa), Karmali (for Old Goa and Panaji), Verna, Margao (for Colva and Benaulim), Bali, Barcem and Canacona (for Palolem).

There are reliable travel agents all over Goa that can book train tickets for you, or you can go directly to the booking offices themselves; the main booking offices are at Panaji's Kadamba bus station, and at Margao's Madgaon train station. See p240.

TRANSPORT

Health

CONTENTS

Before You Go	**246**
Insurance	246
Vaccinations	246
Medical Checklist	247
Internet Resources	247
Further Reading	247
In Transit	**247**
Deep Vein Thrombosis (DVT)	247
Jet Lag & Motion Sickness	248
In Goa	**248**
Availability & Cost of Health Care	248
Infectious Diseases	248
Traveller's Diarrhoea	250
Environmental Hazards	250
Travelling with Children	251
Women's Health	251
Traditional Medicine	251

The potential dangers of going anywhere can seem frightening, but in reality few travellers to Goa will experience anything more than upset stomachs. These days many travellers to Goa also travel with their children – even tiny babies – and the overwhelming majority of small visitors contract nothing worse than an itchy dose of heat rash.

BEFORE YOU GO

Pack medications in their original containers. Also bring a letter from your physician describing your medical conditions and any medications or syringes you may need to carry. If you have a heart condition, bring a copy of your ECG. Bring extra medication in case of loss or theft; it can be difficult to find some newer drugs, particularly the latest antidepressants, blood-pressure medications and contraceptive pills.

INSURANCE

Don't travel without health insurance – accidents happen, especially, it seems, when you don't have insurance. Declare any existing medical conditions you have – you won't be covered for pre-existing problems that are undeclared.

Find out in advance if your insurance plan will make payments directly to providers or if it will reimburse you later for overseas health expenditures. (In many countries doctors expect payment in cash.) You may prefer a policy that pays doctors or hospitals directly. If you do have to claim later, make sure you keep all the relevant documentation.

Some policies ask that you telephone (reverse charges) to a centre in your home country, where an immediate assessment of your problem will be made.

VACCINATIONS

Specialised travel-medicine clinics are your best source of information. They stock all available vaccines and will be able to give specific recommendations for you and your trip.

Most vaccines don't give immunity until at least two weeks after they're taken, so visit a doctor four to eight weeks before departure. Ask your doctor for an International Certificate of Vaccination (otherwise known as the 'yellow booklet'), which will list all the vaccinations you've received.

Recommended Vaccinations

The World Health Organization (WHO) recommends these vaccinations for travellers to India (as well as being up to date with measles, mumps and rubella vaccinations):

Adult diphtheria and tetanus Single booster recommended if none in the previous 10 years. Side effects include sore arm and fever.

Hepatitis A Provides almost 100% protection for up to a year; a booster after 12 months provides another 20 years' protection. Mild side effects such as headache and sore arm occur in 5% to 10% of people.

Hepatitis B Considered routine for most travellers. Given as three shots over six months. A rapid schedule is also available, as is a combined vaccination with hepatitis A. In 95% of people lifetime protection results. Side effects are mild, usually headache and sore arm.

Polio Polio is still present in India. Only one booster is required as an adult for lifetime protection. Inactivated polio vaccine is safe during pregnancy.

Typhoid Recommended for all travellers to India, even if you only visit urban areas. The vaccine offers around 70% protection, lasts for two to three years and

comes as a single shot. Tablets are also available but the injection has fewer side effects. Sore arm and fever may occur.
Varicella If you haven't had chickenpox, discuss this vaccination with your doctor.

These immunisations are recommended for long-term travellers (more than one month) or those at special risk:
Japanese B encephalitis Three injections in all. Booster recommended after two years. Sore arm and headache are the most common side effects. On rare occasions, an allergic reaction of hives and swelling can occur up to 10 days after the doses.
Meningitis Single injection. There are two types of vaccination: quadrivalent vaccine gives two to three years' protection; meningitis group C vaccine gives around 10 years' protection. Recommended for long-term backpackers aged under 25.
Rabies Three injections in all. A booster after one year will then provide 10 years' protection. Side effects are rare – occasionally headache and sore arm.
Tuberculosis (TB) This is a complex issue. Adult long-term travellers are usually recommended to have a TB skin test before and after travel, rather than vaccination. Only one vaccine given in a lifetime.

Required Vaccinations
Proof of yellow-fever vaccination is only required if you have visited a country in the yellow-fever zone within six days prior to entering India. If you are travelling to India from Africa or South America, check to see if you require proof of vaccination.

MEDICAL CHECKLIST
Recommended items for a personal medical kit:
- antifungal cream, eg Clotrimazole
- antibacterial cream, eg Muciprocin
- antibiotic for skin infections, eg Amoxicillin/Clavulanate or Cephalexin
- antihistamine – there are many options, eg Cetrizine for daytime and Promethazine for night-time
- antiseptic, eg Betadine
- antispasmodic for stomach cramps, eg Buscopan
- contraception
- decongestant, eg Pseudoephedrine
- DEET-based insect repellent
- diarrhoea medication – consider an oral rehydration solution (eg Gastrolyte), diarrhoea 'stopper' (eg Loperamide) and anti-nausea medication (eg Prochlorperazine)

- antibiotics for diarrhoea include Norfloxacin or Ciprofloxacin; for bacterial diarrhoea Azithromycin; for Giardia or amoebic dysentery Tinidazole
- first-aid items such as Elastoplast, scissors, bandages, gauze, thermometer (but not mercury), sterile needles and syringes, safety pins and tweezers
- ibuprofen or another anti-inflammatory
- indigestion tablets, eg Quick-Eze
- iodine tablets (unless you are pregnant or have a thyroid problem) to purify water
- laxatives, eg Coloxyl
- paracetamol
- pyrethrin to impregnate clothing and mosquito nets
- steroid cream for allergic/itchy rashes, eg 1% to 2% hydrocortisone
- sunscreen and hat
- thrush (vaginal yeast infection) treatment, eg Clotrimazole pessaries or Diflucan tablet
- Ural or equivalent if prone to urine infections

INTERNET RESOURCES
There is a wealth of travel health advice on the internet. Some good resources:
Centers for Disease Control and Prevention (CDC; www.cdc.gov) Good general information.
MD Travel Health (www.mdtravelhealth.com) Complete travel health recommendations for every country, updated daily.
World Health Organization (WHO; www.who.int/ith /en/) Superb, annually revised book *International Travel & Health* is available online.

FURTHER READING
Lonely Planet's pocket-sized *Healthy Travel – Asia & India* is packed with information including pretrip planning, first aid, immunisation, diseases and what to do if you get sick on the road.

IN TRANSIT

DEEP VEIN THROMBOSIS (DVT)
Deep vein thrombosis (DVT) occurs when blood clots form in the legs, chiefly because of prolonged immobility. The longer the flight, the greater the risk. The chief symptom is swelling or pain of the foot, ankle or calf. If a blood clot travels to the lungs, it may cause chest pain and difficulty in

breathing. Travellers with these symptoms should seek medical attention.

To prevent DVT on long flights, walk about the cabin, contract leg muscles while sitting, drink plenty of fluids, and avoid alcohol and tobacco.

JET LAG & MOTION SICKNESS
Jet lag is common when crossing more than five time zones; it results in insomnia, fatigue, malaise or nausea. To avoid jet lag drink plenty of nonalcoholic fluids and eat light meals. Upon arrival, seek exposure to natural sunlight and readjust your schedule (for meals, sleep etc) as soon as possible.

Antihistamines such as dimenhydrinate (Dramamine), promethazine (Phenergan) and meclizine (Antivert, Bonine) are the first choice for motion sickness. Their main side effect is drowsiness. Ginger works like a charm for some people.

IN GOA

AVAILABILITY & COST OF HEALTH CARE
Although there are reasonable facilities in Panaji (Panjim), Margao (Madgaon) and Vasco da Gama, Goa does not have the quality of medical care available in the West. The best facilities in Goa are at the **Goa Medical College Hospital** (☎ 0832-2458700) at Bambolim, 9km south of Panaji on the NH17 national highway. In the event of a serious accident this is the best place to go; it has a brain scanner and most other facilities.

In North Goa you'll also find **Mapusa Clinic** (☎ 0832-2263343; Mapusa Clinic Rd, Mapusa; ☒ consultations 10am to noon & 4-6pm), and in Margao, the **main hospital** (☎ 0832-2705664; Padre Miranda Rd).

Goa's **ambulance service** (☎ 108) isn't always the quickest to respond; it may be quicker, in an emergency, to jump in a taxi.

For more minor ailments and complaints, Goa has lots of GPs (general practitioners) and family doctors: just ask at your hotel or guest house, or check with locals for a good recommendation. Upmarket hotels also often have a reliable doctor on call.

Often, you just need to drop in to a GP's office during consultation hours (without an appointment) and a consultation costs in the region of Rs100. Prescriptions rarely cost more than Rs50 when filled at pharmacies.

There are well-stocked pharmacies in all Goan towns selling drugs manufactured under licence to Western companies. You can buy far more over the counter here than you can in the West, often without prescription.

INFECTIOUS DISEASES
Dengue Fever
This mosquito-borne disease is becoming increasingly problematic. As there is no vaccine available, it can only be prevented by avoiding mosquito bites. The mosquito that carries dengue bites day and night.

Symptoms include high fever, severe headache and body ache (dengue was previously known as 'breakbone fever'). Some people develop a rash and experience diarrhoea. There is no specific treatment – just rest and paracetamol. Don't take aspirin; it increases the likelihood of haemorrhaging.

See a doctor so you can be diagnosed and monitored.

Hepatitis A
This food- and water-borne virus infects the liver, causing jaundice (yellow skin and eyes), nausea and lethargy. There is no specific treatment for hepatitis A, other than time for the liver to heal. All travellers to India should be vaccinated.

Hepatitis B
The only sexually transmitted disease that can be prevented by vaccination, hepatitis B is spread by body fluids. Long-term consequences can include liver cancer.

Hepatitis E
Transmitted through contaminated food and water, hepatitis E has similar symptoms to hepatitis A, but is less common. It is a severe problem in pregnant women and can result in the death of both mother and baby. There is no vaccine; prevention is by following safe eating and drinking guidelines.

HIV
India has one of the highest growth rates of HIV in the world. HIV is spread via contaminated body fluids. Avoid unsafe sex, unsterile needles (including in medical facilities) and procedures such as tattoos.

Japanese B Encephalitis

This mosquito-transmitted viral disease is rare in travellers. Vaccination is recommended for travellers spending more than one month in rural areas. There is no treatment; one third of infected people die while another third suffer brain damage.

Malaria

Malaria is caused by a parasite transmitted by the bite of an infected mosquito. The most important symptom of malaria is fever, but general symptoms such as headache, diarrhoea, cough or chills may also occur. Blood samples are used to diagnose.

Antimalaria medications should be combined with the following mosquito bite prevention steps:

- Use an insect repellent containing DEET. Natural repellents such as citronella must be applied more frequently.
- Sleep under a mosquito net impregnated with pyrethrin.
- Choose accommodation with screens and fans (if not air-conditioned).
- Impregnate clothing with pyrethrin in high-risk areas.
- Wear long sleeves and light-coloured trousers.
- Use mosquito coils.
- Spray your room with insect repellent before going out for your evening meal.

Many medications must be taken for four weeks after leaving the risk area. There are various options on the market.

- Combination of Chloroquine and Paludrine – limited effectiveness in parts of South Asia. Common side effects include nausea (40% of people) and mouth ulcers.
- Doxycycline – broad-spectrum antibiotic taken daily. Potential side effects include photosensitivity (a tendency to sunburn), thrush (in women), indigestion, heartburn, nausea and interference with the contraceptive pill. More serious side effects include ulceration of the oesophagus. Must be taken for four weeks after leaving the risk area.
- Lariam (Mefloquine) – weekly tablet. Rare but serious side effects include depression, anxiety, psychosis and fits. Should not be taken by those with a history of depression, anxiety, other psychological disorder or epilepsy.

- Malarone (combination of Atovaquone and Proguanil) – side effects are mild and uncommon, usually nausea and headache. Best choice for scuba-divers and those on short trips to high-risk areas. Must be taken for one week after leaving the risk area.

Rabies

Around 30,000 people die annually in India from rabies. This fatal disease is spread by the bite or lick of an infected animal – most commonly a dog or monkey. Seek medical advice immediately after any animal bite and commence postexposure treatment. Pre-travel vaccination means postbite treatment is greatly simplified.

If you are bitten, gently wash the wound with soap and water, and apply iodine-based antiseptic. If you are not vaccinated you need to receive rabies immunoglobulin as soon as possible, and this is almost impossible to obtain in much of India.

STDs

Sexually transmitted diseases most common in India include herpes, warts, syphilis, gonorrhoea and chlamydia. People carrying these often have no signs of infection.

Condoms prevent gonorrhoea and chlamydia but not warts or herpes. If after a sexual encounter you develop any rash, lumps, discharge or pain when passing urine, seek immediate medical attention.

If you have been sexually active during your travels, have an STD check on your return home.

Tuberculosis

While TB is rare in travellers, those who have significant contact with the local population (such as medical and aid workers and long-term travellers) should take precautions.

Vaccination is usually only given to children under five, but adults at risk are recommended to have pre- and post-travel TB testing. The main symptoms are fever, cough, weight loss, night sweats and tiredness.

Typhoid

Spread via food and water, this bacterial infection gives a high and slowly progressive fever, headache and maybe a dry cough and stomach pain. It is treated with antibiotics.

HEALTH

Vaccination is recommended for travellers spending more than a week in India. Vaccination is not 100% effective; still be careful with what you eat and drink.

TRAVELLER'S DIARRHOEA

Traveller's diarrhoea is defined as the passage of more than three watery bowel actions within 24 hours, plus at least one other symptom such as fever, cramps, nausea, vomiting or feeling generally unwell.

This is by far the most common problem affecting travellers – between 30% and 70% of people suffer from it within two weeks of starting their trip. In over 80% of cases it is caused by bacteria, and therefore responds promptly to antibiotics.

Treatment consists of staying well hydrated; rehydration solutions like Gastrolyte are best. Antibiotics such as Norfloxacin, Ciprofloxacin or Azithromycin kill the bacteria quickly.

Loperamide is a 'stopper' and doesn't address the problem. It can be helpful for long bus rides, though. Don't take Loperamide if you have a fever or blood in your stools.

Seek medical attention if you do not respond to antibiotics.

Amoebic Dysentery

Amoebic dysentery is rare in travellers but is often misdiagnosed. Symptoms are similar to bacterial diarrhoea: fever, bloody diarrhoea and generally feeling unwell. Always seek reliable medical care if you have blood in your diarrhoea.

Treatment involves Tinidazole or Metronidazole to kill the parasite and a second drug to kill the cysts. If left untreated, complications such as liver or gut abscesses can result.

Giardiasis

Giardia is a relatively common parasite in travellers. Symptoms include nausea, bloating, excess gas, fatigue and intermittent diarrhoea. The parasite eventually goes away if left untreated, but can take months. The treatment of choice is Tinidazole with Metronidazole.

ENVIRONMENTAL HAZARDS
Diving & Surfing

Divers and surfers should seek specialised advice before they travel to ensure their medical kit contains treatment for coral cuts and tropical ear infections. Divers should also get specialised dive insurance through an organisation such as **Divers Alert Network** (DAN; www.danseap.org) and have a dive medical before they travel.

Heat

For most people it takes at least two weeks to adapt to the hot climate. Swelling of feet and ankles is common, as are muscle cramps caused by excessive sweating. Prevent these by keeping well hydrated, and taking it easy when you first arrive. Rehydration solution and salty food help. Treat cramps with rest and rehydration with double-strength rehydration solution.

Dehydration is the main contributor to heat exhaustion. Symptoms include: weakness, headache, irritability, nausea, sweaty skin, a fast, weak pulse, and a normal or slightly elevated body temperature.

Treatment involves getting out of the heat, fanning the sufferer and applying cool wet cloths to the skin, laying the sufferer flat with their legs raised and rehydrating them with water and salt (¼ teaspoon per litre).

Heatstroke is a serious medical emergency. Symptoms come on suddenly and include weakness, nausea, a hot dry body with a body temperature of over 41°C, dizziness, confusion, loss of coordination, fits and eventually collapse and loss of consciousness. Seek medical help and get the person out of the heat, removing their clothes, fanning them and applying cool wet cloths or ice to their body, especially the groin and armpits.

Prickly heat is a common rash in the tropical regions, caused by sweat trapped under the skin. The result is an itchy rash of tiny lumps. Treat prickly heat by moving out of the heat and into an air-conditioned area for a few hours. Cool showers also help in treating the rash. Creams and ointments clog the skin and should be avoided. Locally purchased prickly heat powder can be helpful.

Tropical fatigue is common in long-term expatriates based in the tropics. It's rarely due to disease and is caused by climate, excessive alcohol intake and the daily demands of a different culture.

Insect Bites & Stings

Bedbugs don't carry disease but their bites are itchy. You can treat the itch with an antihistamine. Lice inhabit various parts of your body but most commonly your head and pubic area. Transmission is via close contact with an infested person. They can be difficult to treat and you may need numerous applications of an anti-lice shampoo with pyrethrin. Pubic lice are usually contracted from sexual contact.

Ticks are contracted after walking in rural areas. Ticks are commonly found behind the ears, on the belly and in armpits. See a doctor if you get a rash at the site of the bite or elsewhere, fever or muscle aches. The antibiotic Doxycycline prevents tick-borne diseases.

Bee and wasp stings mainly cause problems for people who are allergic to them; adrenalin injections (eg Epipen) should be carried for emergencies.

Skin Problems

There are two common fungal rashes that affect travellers in humid climates. The first occurs in moist areas such as the groin, armpits and between toes. It starts as a red patch that slowly spreads and is usually itchy. Treatment involves keeping the skin dry, avoiding chafing and using antifungal cream such as Clotrimazole or Lamisil. Tinea versicolour is also common – this fungus causes small, light-coloured patches, mostly on the back, chest and shoulders. Consult a doctor.

Cuts and scratches become easily infected in humid climates. Wash wounds in clean water and apply antiseptic. Be particularly careful with coral cuts, which become easily infected. If you develop signs of infection (increasing pain and redness) see a doctor.

Sunburn

Even on a cloudy day sunburn can occur rapidly. Use strong sunscreen (at least SPF30), making sure to reapply after swimming, and wear a wide-brimmed hat and sunglasses. Avoid lying in the sun during the hottest part of the day (10am to 2pm). If you become sunburnt, apply cool compresses and take painkillers. One percent hydrocortisone cream applied twice daily is also helpful.

TRAVELLING WITH CHILDREN

See p225 for more information on travelling with children.

WOMEN'S HEALTH

In most places in Goa, sanitary products (pads, rarely tampons) are readily available. Birth control options may be limited, so bring adequate supplies of your own form of contraception.

Heat, humidity and antibiotics can contribute to thrush. Treatment is with antifungal creams and pessaries such as Clotrimazole. A practical alternative is a single tablet of Fluconazole (Diflucan). Urinary tract infections can be precipitated by dehydration or long bus journeys without toilet stops; bring suitable antibiotics.

Pregnant Women

Pregnant women should receive specialised advice before travelling. The ideal time to travel is in the second trimester (between 16 and 28 weeks), when the risk of pregnancy-related problems is at its lowest.

Ensure that your travel insurance policy covers all pregnancy-related possibilities, including premature labour.

Malaria is a high-risk disease for pregnant women, and WHO recommends they do *not* travel to areas with Chloroquine-resistant malaria. None of the more effective anti-malaria drugs are completely safe in pregnancy. Traveller's diarrhoea can quickly lead to dehydration and result in inadequate blood flow to the placenta. Many drugs used to treat various diarrhoea bugs are not recommended in pregnancy. Azithromycin is considered safe.

TRADITIONAL MEDICINE

You've come to the right place if you're interested in traditional medicine. There is a strong culture of holistic healing in Goa, from ayurveda to reflexology to reiki. As with all medicine, some practitioners are better than others. Ask around and do your research before you commit to anything – be wary of people who offer treatments but have no experience or qualifications whatsoever.

HEALTH

Language

CONTENTS

Hindi	**252**
Conversation & Essentials	252
Numbers	253
Konkani	**253**
Conversation & Essentials	253
Numbers	254
Marathi	**254**
Conversation & Essentials	254
Numbers	255

As a legacy of its unusual colonial history, Goa has inherited a mixture of languages. Portuguese is still spoken as a second language by a few Goans, although it is gradually dying out. Children in Goa are obliged to learn Hindi in school and Konkani is the official language of the state. As well as being the main language of Mumbai, Marathi is also taught as a standard subject in Goa. English is widely spoken in tourist areas in Goa and Mumbai.

The primary language used in many schools is actually English, also an official language of India. Arguments about continuing or abandoning this policy rage on. How can Indians get away from their colonial past, many ask, if they are still forced to use the language of the colonisers? Others feel that English gives a distinct advantage to their children, who will need it if they are to find good jobs. Meanwhile, children in Goa are taught three or four languages as a standard part of the school syllabus.

For a more comprehensive guide to the languages of India, get a copy of Lonely Planet's *India Phrasebook*.

HINDI

Hindi is an official language of India, along with English. Major efforts have been made to promote Hindi as the national language of India and to gradually phase out English, but a stumbling block to this plan is that Hindi, the predominant language in the north, bears little relation to the Dravidian languages of the south.

Hindi is written from left to right in Devanagari script. While the script may be unfamiliar, English speakers will recognise many of Hindi's grammatical features. English speakers will also find most Hindi sounds are similar to their English counterparts, but there are a few tricky ones. It's important to pay attention to the pronunciation of vowels and especially to their length, eg **a** compared to **aa**. The combination **ng** after a vowel indicates that it is nasalised (ie pronounced with air flowing through the nose).

For a far more comprehensive guide to Hindi, get a copy of Lonely Planet's *Hindi, Urdu & Bengali* phrasebook.

CONVERSATION & ESSENTIALS

Beware of the Hindi *achaa*, an all-purpose word for 'OK'. This can also mean 'OK, I understand what you're saying, but I'm not necessarily agreeing' (such as when negotiating a price with a taxi driver).

Hello.	*namaste*
Goodbye.	*namaste*
Excuse me.	*kshamaa keejiye*
Please.	*meharbani seh*
Yes.	*jee haang*
No.	*jee naheeng*
Thank you.	*danyavaad*

How are you?
  aap (kaise/kaisee) haing (m/f)
Very well, thank you.
  bahut achaa, shukriaya
What's your name?
  aapka shubh naam kya hai

Do you speak English?
  kya aap angrezi samajhte hain
I don't understand.
  meri samajh men nahin aaya

Where is a hotel?
  hotal kahan hai
How far is ...?
  ... kitni duur hai

How do I get to ...?
... kaiseh jaateh hai

How much?
kitneh paiseh/kitneh hai
This is expensive.
yeh bahut mehnga hai
What's the time?
kitneh bajeh hain

big	*bhada*
small	*chhota*
today	*aaj*
day	*din*
night	*raat*
week	*haftah*
month	*mahina*
year	*saal*
medicine	*dava-ee*

NUMBERS

Rather than counting in tens, hundreds, thousands, millions and billions, the Indian numbering system goes tens, hundreds, thousands, hundred thousands, ten millions. A hundred thousand is a lakh, and 10 million is a crore. These two words are almost always used in place of their English equivalent. Thus you'll see 10 lakh rather than one million and one crore rather than 10 million. Furthermore, the numerals are generally written that way too – thus three hundred thousand appears as 3,00,000 not 300,000 and ten million five hundred thousand would appear numerically as 1,05,00,000 (one crore, five lakh) not 10,500,000. If you say something costs five crore or is worth 10 lakh, it always means 'of rupees'.

When counting from 10 to 100 in Hindi, there's no standard formula for compiling numbers – they are all different. In the list below we've just given you enough to go on with.

1	*ek*
2	*do*
3	*tin*
4	*char*
5	*panch*
6	*chhe*
7	*saat*
8	*aath*
9	*nau*
10	*das*

20	*bis*
21	*ikkis*
30	*tis*
40	*chalis*
50	*panchas*
60	*saath*
70	*sattar*
80	*assi*
90	*nabbe*
100	*so*
1000	*ek hazaar*
100,000	*ek laak* (written 1,00,000)
10,000,000	*ek krore* (written 1,00,00,000)

KONKANI

After a long and hard-fought battle Konkani was recognised in 1987 as the official language of Goa, becoming a national language in 1992. Before then, argument had raged that Konkani was actually no more than a dialect of Marathi, the official language of the much larger Maharashtra.

An Indo-Aryan language related to Gujarati and Marathi, Konkani has also been influenced by Sanskrit, Portuguese, Perso-Arabic and Kannada. The Devanagari script (used to write Hindi and Marathi) is now the official writing system for Konkani in Goa.

There are many different ways of writing Konkani in the Roman alphabet, and the Konkani words included in this chapter are only approximate transliterations.

CONVERSATION & ESSENTIALS

Hello.	*paypadta*
Goodbye.	*mioshay*
Excuse me.	*upkar korxi*
Please.	*upkar kor*
Yes.	*oi*
No.	*naah*
Thank you.	*dev borem korum*

How are you?
(kosso/kossem) assa (m/f)
Very well, thank you.
bhore jaung
What's your name?
tuje naav kide

Do you speak English?
to English hulonk jhana
I don't understand.
mhaka kay samzona na

Where is a hotel?
hotel khoy aasa
How far is ...?
anig kitya phoode ...
How do I get to ...?
maka kashe ... meltole

How much?
kitke poishe laqthele
This is expensive.
chod marog
What's the time?
vurra kitki jali

big	*hodlo*
small	*dhakto*
today	*aaj*
day	*dees*
night	*racho*
week	*athovda*
month	*mohino*
year	*voros*
medicine	*vokot*

NUMBERS

There are two different counting systems in Konkani. Hindu Goans use the system shown in the list below, but for Catholic Goans there are differences: *vis-ani-ek* rather than *ekvis* for 21, for example.

1	*ek*
2	*don*
3	*tin*
4	*char*
5	*panch*
6	*sou*
7	*saat*
8	*aat*
9	*nov*
10	*dha*
20	*vis*
21	*ekvis*
30	*tis*
40	*chalis*
50	*ponnas*
60	*saatt*
70	*sottor*
80	*oichim*
90	*novodh*
100	*chembor*
1000	*ek hazaar*
100,000	*laak* (written 1,00,000)
10,000,000	*krore* (written 1,00,00,000)

MARATHI

Marathi is the official language of the state of Maharashtra and is widely spoken in Mumbai.

One of India's national languages, Marathi belongs to the Indo-Aryan language family and has been influenced by neighbouring languages including Telugu and Kannada. As a result of this you may notice considerable dialectal variation in Marathi as you move around the region.

In Mumbai you may also encounter 'Mumbai slang', which mixes Marathi with Hindi, Gujarati, Konkani and English, and can often be heard in Bollywood movies.

CONVERSATION & ESSENTIALS

Hello.	*namaskar*
Goodbye.	*namaskar*
Excuse me.	*maaf kara*
Please.	*krupaya*
Yes.	*ho*
No.	*nahi*
Thank you.	*dhanyawad*

How are you?
tumhi kase aahat
Very well, thank you.
mee thik aahe, dhanyawad
What's your name?
aapla nav kai aahe

Do you speak English?
tumhala english yeta ka
I don't understand.
mala samjat nahi

Where is a hotel?
hotel kuthe aahe
How do I get to ...?
... kasa jaycha mhanje sapdel

How much?
kevdhyala/kai kimmat
This is expensive.
khup mahag aahe
What's the time?
kiti vajle

big	*motha/mothi* (m/f)
small	*lahan*
today	*aaj*
day	*divas*

night	ratra
week	aathavda
month	mahina
year	varsha
medicine	aushadh

NUMBERS

1	ek
2	don
3	tin
4	char
5	pach
6	saha
7	sat
8	aath
9	nou
10	daha
20	vees
30	tees
40	chaalees
50	pannaas
60	saat
70	sattar
80	ainshee
90	navvaa
100	shambhar
1000	ek hazar
100,000	ek laak (written 1,00,000)
10,000,000	daha koti (written 1,00,00,000)

Glossary

The following are terms you may come across during your Goan travels. For definitions of Goan and Indian food and drink, see p60.

auto-da-fé – trial of faith
autorickshaw – small, noisy, three-wheeled, motorised contraption used for transporting passengers short distances
avatar – incarnation of a deity, usually of *Vishnu*
ayurveda – ancient study of healing arts and herbal medicine

baksheesh – tip, bribe or donation
balcão – shady porch at front of traditional Goan house, usually with benches built into the walls
betel – nut of the areca palm; the nut is mildly intoxicating and is chewed with *paan* as a stimulant and digestive
Bhagavad Gita – Hindu song of the Divine One; *Krishna*'s lessons to Arjuna, emphasising the philosophy of bhakti (faith); part of the *Mahabharata*
Brahma – source of all existence and also worshipped as the creator in the Hindu Trimurti (triple form) of Vishnu, Brahma and Shiva; depicted as having four heads (a fifth was burnt by *Shiva*'s 'central eye' when Brahma spoke disrespectfully)
Brahmin – member of the priest *caste,* the highest Hindu *caste*
bund – embankment or dyke, used in Goa to protect *khazans*

caste – four classes into which Hindu society is divided; one's hereditary station in life
chandra – moon, or the moon as a god, worshipped particularly in Goa at the Chandreshwar (Bhutnath) Temple, on Chandranath Hill
charas – resin of the cannabis plant; also referred to as hashish
chillum – pipe of a hookah; used to describe the small clay pipes for smoking marijuana
crore – 10 million

Dalit – preferred term for India's casteless class; see *Untouchable*
dekhni – traditional Goan dance
deepastambha – lamp tower; a prominent and distinctive feature of many temples
dhaba – basic restaurant or snack bar
Dhangars – tribe of Goa's indigenous people

dharma – Hindu and Buddhist moral code of behaviour; natural law
Dravidian – general term for the cultures and languages of the south of India, including Tamil, Malayalam, Telugu and Kannada
dulpod – traditional Goan dance
Durga – the Inaccessible; a form of *Shiva's* wife Devi; a beautiful but fierce woman riding a tiger; major goddess of the Sakti cult

fado – melancholy song of longing, popular in Portuguese colonial era

Ganesh – Hindu god of good fortune; elephant-headed son of *Shiva* and *Parvati;* also known as Ganpati
garbhagriha – inner sanctum of a Hindu temple
ghat – steps or landing on a river; range of hills, or road up hills; the Western Ghats are the range of mountains that run along India's west coast, effectively forming the eastern border of Goa
GTDC – Goa Tourism Development Corporation

Hanuman – Hindu monkey god and follower of Rama; prominent in the *Ramayana*
Harijan – name given by Gandhi to India's *Untouchables;* the term is no longer considered acceptable; see also *Dalit* and *Untouchable*

Jainism – religion and philosophy founded by Mahavira in the 6th century BC in India; its fundamental tenet is nonviolence

karma – principle of retributive justice for past deeds
khadi – homespun cloth
khazans – low-lying areas alongside Goa's rivers, reclaimed by building *bunds;* the flow of salt and fresh water is regulated to allow the land to be used for a variety of purposes
khell tiatr – form of *tiatr*
Krishna – *Vishnu's* eighth incarnation, often coloured blue; he revealed the *Bhagavad Gita* to Anjuna
Kshatriya – Hindu *caste* of warriors and administrators
KTC – Kadamba Transport Corporation; Goa's state bus company
Kunbis – Descendants of Goa's first inhabitants; among the state's poorest groups
kusada – sea snake

lakh – 100,000
lingam – phallic symbol representing the god *Shiva*

Mahabharata – Great Vedic (see *Vedas*) epic poem of the Bharata dynasty

Mahadeva – Great God; *Shiva*

Mahadevi – Great Goddess; Devi

mahatma – literally 'great soul'

maidan – open grassed area in a city

mandapa – pillared pavilion of a temple

mando – famous song and dance form, introduced originally by the Goan Catholic community

Manguesh – an incarnation of *Shiva*, worshipped particularly in Goa

Manueline – style of architecture typical of that built by the Portuguese during the reign of Manuel I (r 1495–1521)

Maratha – warlike central Indian people who controlled much of India at various times; fought the *Mughals*

marg – major road

masjid – mosque

moksha – liberation from the cycle of rebirth

monsoon – rainy season between June and October

Mughal – Muslim dynasty of Indian emperors from Babur to Aurangzeb, which lasted from 1526 to 1707

Nandi – bull, vehicle of *Shiva;* his images are usually found at *Shiva* temples

Nataraja – *Shiva* in his incarnation as the cosmic dancer

paan – mixture of betel nut and various spices, chewed for its mildly intoxicating effect, and as a digestive after meals

panchayat – local government; a panchayat area typically consists of two to three villages, from which volunteers are elected to represent the interests of the local people (the elected representative is called the panch; the elected leader is the sarpanch)

Parasurama – sixth incarnation of *Vishnu*, and the 'founder' of Goa

Parvati – the Mountaineer; a form of Devi

pousada – Portuguese for hostel

prasad – food offering

puja – offerings or prayers; literally 'respect'

raj – rule or sovereignty

raja, rana – king

Ramayana – story of Rama and *Sita;* one of India's most well-known legends, retold in various forms throughout almost all of Southeast Asia

ramponkar – traditional Goan fisherman; fishes the coastal waters from a wooden boat, using a hand-hauled net (rampon)

reredos – ornamental screen behind the altar in Goan churches

saquão – central courtyard in traditional Goan houses

Sati – wife of *Shiva;* became a *sati* (honourable woman) by immolating herself; although banned more than a century ago, the act of *sati* is occasionally performed, though not in Goa

satyagraha – literally 'insistence on truth'; nonviolent protest involving a fast, popularised by Gandhi; protesters are *satyagrahis*

Scheduled Castes – official term for *Dalits* or *Untouchables*

Shiva – the Hindu Destroyer god; also the Creator, in which form he is worshipped as a *lingam;* also spelt Siva

shri – honorific; these days the Indian equivalent of Mr or Mrs; also spelt sri, sree, shree

Sita – the goddess of agriculture in the *Vedas;* commonly associated with the *Ramayana*, in which she is abducted by Ravana and carted off to Lanka

sitar – Indian stringed instrument

sossegado – see *susegad*

Sudra – caste of labourers

susegad – Goan expression meaning relaxed or laid-back

tabla – pair of drums

taluka – administrative district or region

tank – reservoir

tiatr – locally written and produced drama in the Konkani language

tikka – mark devout Hindus put on their foreheads with *tikka* powder

toddy tapper – one who extracts toddy (palm sap) from palm trees

Untouchable – lowest *caste* or 'casteless' for whom the most menial tasks are reserved; name derives from the belief that higher castes risk defilement if they touch one (formerly known as *Harijan*, now *Dalit* or *Scheduled Castes*)

Upanishads – esoteric doctrine; ancient texts forming part of the *Vedas* (although of a later date)

varna – concept of *caste*

veda – knowledge

Vedas – Hindu sacred books; a collection of hymns composed in preclassical Sanskrit during the second millennium BC and divided into four books: *Rig-Veda, Yajur-Veda, Sama-Veda* and *Atharva-Veda*

Velips – traditional forest-dwelling people

Vishnu – the Preserver and Restorer; part of the Trimurti (triple form) with *Brahma* and *Shiva*

waddo – section or ward of a village; also known as a vaddo

wallah – man or person; can be added onto almost anything to denote an occupation, thus dhobi-wallah, taxi-wallah, chai-wallah

The Authors

AMELIA THOMAS
Coordinating Author, Central Goa, North Goa, South Goa, Around Goa

Amelia Thomas is a writer and journalist working throughout India and the Middle East. She has worked on numerous Lonely Planet titles, and her book *The Zoo on the Road to Nablus*, telling the true story of the last Palestinian zoo, was published in 2008. Her four small children, aged between 10 months and five years, enjoy accompanying her on assignments – particularly the Goan kind, which sees them conducting their own research into sandcastles, rock pools and Indian ice cream. Her forthcoming book, *'Hypnosis!'*, tells the incredible, colourful tale of Abbé Faria, Goan priest and hypnotist extraordinaire.

AMY KARAFIN
Mumbai (Bombay)

Indian in several former lives, Amy Karafin headed straight to India after university for an extended trip that would turn out to be karmically ordained. She spent the next few years alternating between New York and faraway lands until, fed up with the irony of being a travel editor in a Manhattan cubicle, she relinquished her MetroCard and her black skirts to make a living on the road. She's been freelancing seminomadically ever since, spending big chunks of time in Senegal, Guinea and India. She lives mostly in Brooklyn now, but also sometimes in Mumbai and Dakar.

CONTRIBUTING AUTHOR

Dr Trish Batchelor wrote the health chapter. Trish is a general practitioner and travel medicine specialist who works at the CIWEC Clinic in Kathmandu, Nepal, as well as being a Medical Advisor to the Travel Doctor New Zealand clinics. Trish teaches travel medicine through the University of Otago, and is interested in underwater and high-altitude medicine, and in the impact of tourism on host countries. She has travelled extensively through Southeast and East Asia and particularly loves high-altitude trekking in the Himalayas.

LONELY PLANET AUTHORS

Why is our travel information the best in the world? It's simple: our authors are passionate, dedicated travellers. They don't take freebies in exchange for positive coverage so you can be sure the advice you're given is impartial. They travel widely to all the popular spots, and off the beaten track. They don't research using just the internet or phone. They discover new places not included in any other guidebook. They personally visit thousands of hotels, restaurants, palaces, trails, galleries, temples and more. They speak with dozens of locals every day to make sure you get the kind of insider knowledge only a local could tell you. They take pride in getting all the details right, and in telling it how it is. Think you can do it? Find out how at **lonelyplanet.com**.

Behind the Scenes

THIS BOOK

This 5th edition of *Goa & Mumbai* was written by Amelia Thomas (coordinating author and Goa) and Amy Karafin (Mumbai). The Health chapter was written by Dr Trish Batchelor. Marika McAdam wrote the previous edition. Paul Harding updated the 3rd edition with assistance from Lucas Vidgen and Susan Derby. This guidebook was commissioned in Lonely Planet's Melbourne office, and produced by the following:

Commissioning Editors Jennifer Garrett, Will Gourlay, Shawn Low, Suzannah Shwer, Sam Trafford
Coordinating Editor Martine Power
Coordinating Cartographer Anthony Phelan
Coordinating Layout Designer Indra Kilfoyle
Managing Editors Brigitte Ellemor, Annelies Mertens
Managing Cartographer Alison Lyall
Managing Layout Designer Sally Darmody
Assisting Editor Janice Bird
Project Manager Chris Girdler
Cover Image research provided by lonelyplanetimages.com

Thanks to Lucy Birchley, Laura Crawford, Hunor Csutoros, Eoin Dunlevy, Quentin Frayne, Corey Hutchison, Adrian Persoglia, Alison Ridgway, Amanda Sierp, Geoff Stringer, Juan Winata

THANKS
AMELIA THOMAS

Many thanks, first, to Pinky and her fabulous family, without whom everyday life would have been impossible. Thanks, too, to Shilpa, for the soft landing, and to Tanya, Shubangi and the second Pinky, who do such wonderful work with our tinies. Thanks to Sarina, Sam, Will, Alison, the other authors, and the team at LP for being great to work with, as always, to Nich and Cheryl for the morning *bhaji-paus* and evening G&Ts, and to Cassidy, Tyger, Cairo, Gal and Zeyah for forsaking the Middle East to set up camp, instead, on the shores of the Arabian Sea.

AMY KARAFIN

My sincere thanks go to the people of Mumbai for putting up with my questions and for having created such a fascinating place. I'm also deeply grateful to Akash Bhartiya, assistant researcher, Hindi tutor and loyal kulfi partner; Mom and Dad; Manik and Surekha Bhartiya; Sarina Singh, Sam Trafford and Will Gourlay; Malini and Hari Hariharan; Jayasree Anand and Sandhya Kanneganti; Raghu Raman; Sunjoy Monga; the original members of the Barry Karafin International Executive Club; Hervé, Charlie and Hernan; and SN Goenka

---

THE LONELY PLANET STORY

Fresh from an epic journey across Europe, Asia and Australia in 1972, Tony and Maureen Wheeler sat at their kitchen table stapling together notes. The first Lonely Planet guidebook, *Across Asia on the Cheap,* was born.

Travellers snapped up the guides. Inspired by their success, the Wheelers began publishing books to Southeast Asia, India and beyond. Demand was prodigious, and the Wheelers expanded the business rapidly to keep up. Over the years, Lonely Planet extended its coverage to every country and into the virtual world via lonelyplanet.com and the Thorn Tree message board.

As Lonely Planet became a globally loved brand, Tony and Maureen received several offers for the company. But it wasn't until 2007 that they found a partner whom they trusted to remain true to the company's principles of travelling widely, treading lightly and giving sustainably. In October of that year, BBC Worldwide acquired a 75% share in the company, pledging to uphold Lonely Planet's commitment to independent travel, trustworthy advice and editorial independence.

Today, Lonely Planet has offices in Melbourne, London and Oakland, with over 500 staff members and 300 authors. Tony and Maureen are still actively involved with Lonely Planet. They're travelling more often than ever, and they're devoting their spare time to charitable projects. And the company is still driven by the philosophy of *Across Asia on the Cheap*: 'All you've got to do is decide to go and the hardest part is over. So go!'

and everyone at Dhamma Pattan, Dhamma Na-
gajjuna, Dhamma Vijaya, and Dhamma Khetta.
Bhavatu sabba mangalam.

OUR READERS
**Many thanks to the travellers who used the last
edition and wrote to us with helpful hints, useful
advice and interesting anecdotes:**

Holten Askepovey, Ollie Blake, Brian Conway-Smith, Xavier
Corte, Yvonne Cunningham, Greg Elms, Melwin Falcao, Jerry
Fernandes, Lucie Fox, Denis Harman, Hun Hinseh, Arthur Ituassu,
Matt Jones, Vlastimil Koncel, Teija Makinen, Iain Mcintyre, Steve
Meldrum, Pradad Naik, Leigh Parsons, Patrrick Patrrick, Leyu Qiu,
Leila Qizilbash, Martin R, M Reilly, Inigo Schmitt-Reinholtz, David
Siddall, S J Srinivas, Diane Strong

ACKNOWLEDGMENTS
**Many thanks to the following for the use of their
content:**
Globe on title page ©Mountain High Maps 1993
Digital Wisdom, Inc.

SEND US YOUR FEEDBACK
We love to hear from travellers – your comments keep us on our toes and help make
our books better. Our well-travelled team
reads every word on what you loved or
loathed about this book. Although we can-
not reply individually to postal submissions,
we always guarantee that your feedback
goes straight to the appropriate authors, in
time for the next edition. Each person who
sends us information is thanked in the next
edition – and the most useful submissions
are rewarded with a free book.

To send us your updates – and find out
about Lonely Planet events, newsletters
and travel news – visit our award-winning
website: **lonelyplanet.com/contact**.

Note: we may edit, reproduce and incorp-
orate your comments in Lonely Planet products such as guidebooks, websites and digital
products, so let us know if you don't want
your comments reproduced or your name
acknowledged. For a copy of our privacy
policy visit lonelyplanet.com/privacy.

BEHIND THE SCENES

Index

A

accommodation 223-4
activities 70-4, *see also individual activities*
Afonso de Albuquerque 32-3, 109
Agonda 202-4
air travel
    air fares 238
    airports 238-9
    charter flights 238
    to/from Goa 238
    to/from Mumbai 103-4
Aldona 144-5
Anegundi 221-2, **217**
animals 63-4, *see also individual animals*
Anjuna 164-8, **165**, 7, 11
antiques 233-4
Arambol (Harmal) 175-8, **176**, 9
architecture 49-51, 82, 136
    books 49
    Old Goa 126
area codes, *see inside front cover*
Arossim 192
art galleries, *see* museums & galleries
arts 47-51, *see also* books, dance, music
Assolna 201-2
Aswem 174
ATMs 231
autorickshaws 242
ayurveda 74
    Agonda 202
    Anjuna 165-6
    Baga 156-7
    Calangute 156-7
    Gokarna 214
    Majorda 193
    Mandrem 174-5

B

Baga 154-61, **155**
bargaining 233
beach parties, *see* trance parties
beaches 20, 150-1, 186-7
    Agonda 202-4
    Anjuna 164-8, **165**, 11

000 Map pages
000 Photograph pages

Arambol (Harmal) 175-8, **176**, 9
Arossim 192
Aswem 174
Baga 154-61, **155**
Benaulim 197-8, **195**
Betalbatim 194
Bogmalo 191-2
Butterfly Beach 206
Calangute 154-61, **155**
Candolim 147-54, **148**
Cavelossim 199-201
Chowpatty Beach 86, **78-9**
Cola Beach 206
Colomb 205-8
Colva 194-7, **195**, 10
Galgibag 210
Half-Moon Beach 214
Honeymoon Beach 206
Kudle Beach 214
Majorda 193
Mandrem 174-5
Miramar Beach 120
Mobor 201
Morjim 174
Nerul (Coco) Beach 147
Om Beach 214
Palolem 204-8, **205**, 5
Paradise Beach 214
Patnem 208-9
Polem 211
Querim 178
Rajbag 209
Sinquerim 147-54, **148**
Utorda 192
Vagator 168-72, **169**
Varca 198-9
Velsao 192
Benaulim 197-8, **195**
Betalbatim 194
Betim 145
Betul 202
Bhagwan Mahavir Wildlife
    Sanctuary 138
bhaji-pau 54, 9
bicycle travel, *see* cycling
birds 65-6
birdwatching
    books 66
    Cavelossim 200
    Dr Salim Ali Bird Sanctuary 122

Mumbai 88-9
    Sanjay Gandhi National Park 106
boat travel 241, *see also* ferries, sailing
boat trips
    Baga 157
    Bogmalo 191
    Candolim 150
    Cavelossim 200
Bogmalo 191-2
Bollywood 50, 86, 8
Bombay, *see* Mumbai
Bondla Wildlife Sanctuary 137
books 20-1
    animals 65
    architecture 49
    birdwatching 66
    culture 43
    environment 62
    food 52, 59
    Mumbai 80
    social issues 21
    yoga 74
Britona 145
buildings & structures
    Chhatrapati Shivaji Terminus
        (Victoria Terminus) 85
    Gateway of India 81
    High Court 84
    Panaji Central Library 114
    Professed House of the Jesuits 127
    Secretariat Building 113
    Taj Mahal Palace & Tower 81
    University of Mumbai 84
    Viceroy's Arch 129-30
bus travel
    to/from Goa 239-40
    to/from Mumbai 104
    travel within Goa 241
    travel within Mumbai 105
business hours 225

C

Calangute 154-61, **155**
Camões, Luís Vaz de 114
Candolim 147-54, **148**
car travel
    hire 241
    road distance chart **242**
    road rules 244
    safety 244

to/from Goa 239
travel within Goa 241
carpets 234
caste 45
cathedrals, *see* churches & cathedrals
Cavelossim 199-201
caves
  Elephanta Island 106
  Kanheri Caves 106
  Rivona Buddhist Caves 188-9
cell phones 235
cemeteries
  British cemetery 121
  Divar Island 131
Chandor 187-8
Chapora 168-72, **169**
Chaudi 204
Chhatrapati Shivaji Terminus
  (Victoria Terminus) 85
children, travel with 170, 225-6
  Anjuna 166
  itineraries 28
Chorao Island 122
Christianity 46-7
churches & cathedrals, *see also*
  mosques, synagogues, temples
  Basilica of Bom Jesus 127
  Chapel of St Anthony 129
  Chapel of St Catherine 126-7
  Chapel of St Sebastian 112-13
  Church & Convent of St Cajetan
    128
  Church & Convent of St Monica
    128
  Church of Nossa Senhora Mae de
    Deus (Pomburpa) 145
  Church of Nossa Senhora Mae de
    Deus (Saligao) 157
  Church of Our Lady of
    Compassion 131
  Church of Our Lady of Miracles 162
  Church of Our Lady of Pilar 133
  Church of Our Lady of the
    Immaculate Conception 113-14
  Church of Our Lady of the Mount
    130
  Church of Our Lady of the Rosary
    129
  Church of St Alex 188
  Church of St Andrew 132
  Church of St Anne 132
  Church of St Augustine 128
  Church of St Francis of Assisi 125-6
  Church of St Lawrence
    (Agassaim) 132

Church of St Lawrence
  (Fort Aguada) 149
Church of St Thomas 144-5
Church of the Holy Spirit 183
Mount Church 183
Nossa Senhora de Penha de
  Franca 145
Our Lady of Mercy Church 196
Reis Magos Church 145-7
Sé Cathedral 125
St Alex's Church 156
St Thomas' Cathedral 84
cinema 50
climate 17-18, 226
coconut 53
Colomb 205-8
Colva 194-7, **195**, 10
Colvale 163
conservation 67-8
consulates 228-9
Corjuem Island 144
costs 18, *see also inside front cover*
Cotigao Wildlife Sanctuary 210
courses
  cooking 59-60, 115, 206
  crafts 90
  dance 206
  language 90
  t'ai chi 206
  yoga 90
credit cards 231
cricket 51, 101
culture 42-51
Curtorim 188
customs regulations 227
cycling 241, 10

D
dance 47-8
dangers 227, *see also* safe travel
deforestation 68-9
dengue fever 248
Dhangars, the 139
Dharavi 91
disabilities, travellers with 236
Divar Island 130-1
diving 70-1
  Baga 156
  Bogmalo 191
  Calangute 156
  safety 71
dolphin-watching
  Benaulim 197
  Candolim 150
  Cavelossim 200

Colva 194
Panaji 115
Utorda 193
Dona Paula 120-1
Dr Salim Ali Bird Sanctuary 122
drinks 55-6
  feni 53, 57
driving, *see* car travel
driving licence 243
drugs 230
Dudhsagar Falls 139

E
economy 44
Edgar, Anita 164
electricity 225
Elephanta Island 106
embassies 228-9
emergencies 112
environmental issues 67-9
events calendar 22-4
exchange rates, *see inside front cover*

F
fado 48
Faria, Abbé 113
fax services 235
feni 53, 57
Fernandes, Remo 48
ferries 104, 200
festivals 22-4
  Carnival 22, 118
  Fama de Menino Jesus Festival
    196
  Feast of St Francis Xavier 24, 127
  Festa das Bandeiras 130
  Ganesh Chaturthi 23
  Hanuman Festival 22
  Mumbai Festival 22
  Reis Magos Festival 22
  Shantadurga 22
  Siolim Zagor 24, 173
film 50
fishing 193
flea markets, *see* markets
food 52-5, 229
  bhaji-pau 54, 9
  books 52, 59
  coconut 53
  courses 59-60, 115
  customs 59
  etiquette 59
  festivals 56-7
  religion 59
  restaurants 57-8

food *continued*
 street food 58
 vegetarian travellers 58-9
 websites 54, 56, 57
football 51, 101
forts 203
 Cabo da Rama 202
 Cabo Raj Bhavan 121
 Chapora Fort 170, 11
 Corjuem Fort 144
 Fort Aguada 148-9, **148**
 Reis Magos Fort 145-7
 Terekhol Fort 178

G
Galgibag 210-11
galleries, *see* museums & galleries
gardens, *see* parks & gardens
Gaspar Dias 120
Gateway of India 81
gay travellers 229
geography 62-3
ghats
 Mahalaxmi Dhobi Ghat 87
Goa Trance 48, *see also*
 trance parties
Goa Velha 131-2
Gokarna 213-16, **214**

H
haggling 233
Hampi 216-21, **217**, **219**
Harmal, *see* Arambol
health 246-51
 insurance 246
 internet resources 247
 traditional medicine 251
 vaccinations 246-7
hepatitis 248
Hindi 252-3
Hinduism 30, 46
historic buildings, *see* houses &
 mansions
history 29-41
 Arrival of Albuquerque 32-3
 End of an Empire 38-9
 'Goa Dourada' 35
 Hampi 216-17
 Independence 39-40
 Inquisition, the 34-5, 47
 Kadamba period 30-1

000 Map pages
000 Photograph pages

Maratha dynasty 35-7
Mauryan period 29-30
Mumbai 76-7
Muslim Bahmani period 31-2
Old Goa 123-5
Panaji 109
Portuguese Conquest 33-4
Portuguese Rule 37-8
Post-Independence 40-1
prehistoric period 29
hitching 241-2
HIV 248
holidays 17-18, 229
horse riding
 Majorda 193
 Mumbai 89
Hospet 222
houses & mansions
 Braganza House 188
 Calizz 149
 Casa Araujo Alvares 186
 Casa dos Costa-Frias 149
 Casa dos Monteiros 149
 Casa dos Proença 156
 Fernandes House 187
 Sat Burnzam Ghor 183

I
immigration 238
Inquisition, the 34-5, 47
insurance 229-30
 health 246
internet access 230
internet resources 21
 air tickets 238
 culture 48, 51
 food & drink 54, 56, 57
 health 247
 music 48, 49
Islam 47
itineraries 25-8
 Along the Mandovi River 143
 Driving Route 185
 Goa with Children 28
 Goa's Markets 28
 Inland Adventure 27
 Mumbai 82
 North Goa 25
 South Goa 26

J
Japanese B Encephalitis 249
jet lag 248
jewellery 234
Jog Falls 216

K
Kadambas, the 30-1, 131, 138
Khan, Shamim 161
Khandepar 138
Konkani 40, 42, 253-4

L
language 60-1, 252-5
 courses 90
legal matters 230-1
leopards 106
lesbian travellers 229
lions 106
literature 49, *see also* books
Loutolim 185-6

M
Madgaon, *see* Margao
magazines 225
Majorda 193-4
malaria 249
mando 48
Mandrem 174-5
mansions, *see* houses & mansions
maps 231
Mapusa 161-4, **162**, 9
Marathi 254-5
Margao 181-4, **182**
markets
 Anjuna 168, 7
 Baga 160
 Calangute 160
 itinerary 28
 Mapusa 162-3, 9
 Margao 183
 Mumbai 103
 night markets 160
 Panaji 119
massage 74
 Agonda 202
 Anjuna 165-6
 Baga 156-7
 Calangute 156-7
 Gokarna 214
 Majorda 193
 Mandrem 174-5
 Patnem 209
Mayem Lake 144
measures 225, *see also* inside front
 cover
medical services 248, *see also*
 health
meditation 74, 177, 202
metric conversions, *see* inside front
 cover

Miramar 120
mobile phones 235
Mobor 201
Molem 138-9
money 18, 231-2, *see also inside front cover*
Monga, Sunjoy 88-9
Morjim 174
mosques, *see also* churches & cathedrals, synagogues, temples
Haji Ali's Mosque 87-8
Jama Masjid 114
Safa Shahouri Masjid 133
motorcycle travel 242-4
driving licence 243
hire 243-4
road rules 244
to/from Goa 239
tours 244
Mumbai (Bombay) 75-106, **78-9**, **6, 8**
accommodation 92-6
activities 88-9
attractions 81-8
Central Suburbs 95, 98, 100, **94**
children 91
Churchgate 94, 98, **84**
Colaba 92, 93-4, 96-7, **83**
courses 90
drinking 99-100
entertainment 100-1
food 96-9
Fort Area 82-5, 92-3, 97-8, **84**
history 76-7
internet access 77
itineraries 82
medical services 77
money 80
shopping 101-3
tourist information 80
tours 91
travel to/from 103-4
travel within 104-6
walking tour 89-90, **90**
museums & galleries
Archaeological Museum (Hampi) 219
Archaeological Museum (Old Goa) 126
Chhatrapati Shivaji Maharaj Vastu Sangrahalaya (Prince of Wales Museum) 82
Goa State Museum 114-15
Houses of Goa Museum 145

Kerkar Art Complex 157
Kristu Kala Mandir Art Gallery 126
Mani Bhavan 86
Menezes Braganza Institute 114
Museum of Christian Art 129
National Gallery of Modern Art 82
Naval Aviation Museum 191
Pilar Seminary Museum 133
music 47-8
musical instruments 234

N
Naroa 143
national parks, *see* sanctuaries & protected areas
Nehru, Jawaharlal 39
Netravali Bubble Lake 210
newspapers 225

O
O'Coqueiro 146
observatories & planetariums
Nehru Centre 88
Public Observatory 115
Old Goa 122-30, **123**, **10**
architecture 126
attractions 125-30
history 123-5
olive ridley marine turtles 65, 174, 202

P
palaces
Bishop's Palace 115
Casa Braganza 156
Palácio do Deão 188
Taj Mahal Palace & Tower 81
Palolem 204-8, **205**, **5**
Panaji 109-20, **110**, **6**
accommodation 116-17
attractions 112-15
drinking 118
emergency services 112
entertainment 118-19
festivals 118
food 117-18
history 109
internet access 112
medical services 112
shopping 119
tourist information 112
tours 115, 115-16

travel to/from 119-20
travel within 120
Panjim, *see* Panaji
papier-mâché 234
parks & gardens, *see also* sanctuaries & protected areas
Azad Maidan 114
Campal Gardens 115
Municipal Gardens 114
Parsi community 87
parties 171, 209
passports 238
Patnem 208-9
photography 232
Pilar Seminary 132-3
Pinto Revolt 147
Piró, Caterina a 129
planetariums, *see* observatories & planetariums
planning 17-21
plants 67
Polem 211
Pomburpa 145
Ponda 133-4, **8**
Ponda taluka (district) 134-7, **133**
postal services 232-3

Q
Quepem 188
Querim 178

R
rabies 249
radio 225
Rajbag 209-10
ramponkars 68
reiki 74
Palolem 205-6
Patnem 209
Reis Magos 145-7
Remo Fernandes 48
responsible travel 18-20
Ribandar 122
Rivona Buddhist Caves 188-9
road distance chart **242**

S
Sá, Garcia de 129
safe travel 227
diving 71
driving 244
hitching 241-2
sailing 208-9
Sancoale 190

sanctuaries & protected areas
   Bhagwan Mahavir Wildlife
      Sanctuary 138
   Bondla Wildlife Sanctuary 137
   Cotigao Wildlife Sanctuary 210
   Dr Salim Ali Bird Sanctuary 122
   Sanjay Gandhi National Park 106
Sao Antonio Islet 190
Sao Jacinto 190
saris 234
Sarosh-Rebelo, Nazneen 153
scams 227
shopping 233-5, see also markets
   Anjuna 168
   Baga 160-1
   Calangute 160-1
   itinerary 28
   night markets 160
silent parties 209
silks 234
Singh, Prime Minister Manmohan
   41
Sinquerim 147-54, **148**
Siolim 173-4
snakes 64-5
Sobhraj, Charles 146
solo travellers 235
sossegado, see susegad
spice farms 134, **8**
sports 51
St Francis Xavier 36-7, 127
susegad 42
synagogues, see also churches &
   cathedrals, mosques, temples
   Keneseth Eliyahoo Synagogue 82

T
t'ai chi 74, 205, 206
Talaulim 132
Tambdi Surla 139-40
taxi travel 242
telephone services 235
temples 136, see also churches &
   cathedrals, mosques, synagogues
   Achyutaraya Temple 218
   Elephanta Island 106
   Ganapati Temple 213-14
   Hanuman Temple 221
   Mahabaleshwara Temple
      213-14
   Mahalaxmi Temple 87, 115

   Maruti Temple 115, 162
   Ranganatha Temple 221
   Shri Chandreshwar (Bhutnath)
      Temple 189
   Shri Damodar Temple 188
   Shri Laxmi Narasimha Temple
      136
   Shri Mahalaxmi Temple 137
   Shri Mahalsa Temple 135, 135-6
   Shri Manguesh Temple 135
   Shri Naguesh Temple 136-7
   Shri Ramnath Temple 137
   Shri Saptakoteshwara Temple
      143
   Shri Shantadurga Temple 137
   Shri Tambdi Surla Mahadeva
      Temple 139-40
   Underground Virupaksha Temple
      218-19
   Venkataraman Temple 213-14
   Virupaksha Temple 218
   Vittala Temple 218
textiles 234-7
theatre 51
theft 227-8
tiatr 51
tiffins 97
tigers 106
time 235
Torda 145
tourist information 80, 235-6
tours 72
   Calangute 157
   motorcycle travel 244
   Mumbai 91
   Palolem 206
traditional medicine 251
train travel 7
   to/from Goa 240-1
   to/from Mumbai 104
   within Goa 244-5
   within Mumbai 105-6
trance parties 171, 209, **11**
travel to/from Goa 238-41
travel to/from Mumbai 103-4
travel within Goa 241-5
travel within Mumbai 104-6
tuberculosis 249
turtles 65, 174, 202
TV 225
typhoid 249-50

U
Usgalimal Rock Carvings 189
Utorda 192-3

V
vacations 17-18, 229
Vagator 168-72, **169**
Varca 198-9
Vasco da Gama 189-90
vegetarian travellers 58-9
Velsao 192
Vipassana meditation 177
visas 236, see also passports
volunteering 72-3, 199, 236

W
water sports 71
   Baga 156
   Benaulim 197
   Calangute 156
   Candolim 150
   Colva 194
   Mumbai 89
   Palolem 205-6
   Patnem 208-9
weather 17-18, 226
websites, see internet resources
weights 225, see also inside
   front cover
wildlife 63-7, see also animals,
   plants
wildlife watching 20, 67, 71-2
   Bhagwan Mahavir Wildlife
      Sanctuary 138
   Bondla Wildlife Sanctuary 137
   Cotigao Wildlife Sanctuary 210
   Sanjay Gandhi National Park
      106
women in Goa 44
women travellers 235, 236-7
   safe travel 227
women's health 251
woodcarving 234

Y
yoga 74
   Agonda 202
   Anjuna 165-6
   Baga 156-7
   Calangute 156-7
   Mandrem 174-5
   Morjim 174
   Mumbai 90
   Palolem 205-6
   Patnem 209
Yusuf Adil Shah 32, 109

Z
Zoroastrians 87

000 Map pages
000 Photograph pages